THE RECORD PRODUCERS FILE

A Directory of Rock Album
Producers 1962–1984

This book is dedicated to Rod Coxon, my father-in-law. It is also for Doreen, Laura and James ("It's finished at last!")

THE
RECORD PRODUCERS
FILE

A Directory of Rock Album
Producers 1962–1984

Bert Muirhead

BLANDFORD PRESS
POOLE · DORSET

First published in the U.K. 1984 by Blandford Press
Link House, West Street, Poole, Dorset, BH15 1LL

Distributed in the United States by
Sterling Publishing Co., Inc.,
2 Park Avenue, New York, N.Y. 10016

British Library Cataloguing in Publication Data

Muirhead, Bert
  The record producers file.
    1. Rock music—History and criticism
    2. Sound recording producers—Directories
    I. Title ·
  784.5'4'0025   ML3534

ISBN 0 7137 1429 8 (Hardback)
    0 7137 1430 1 (Paperback)

Project editor: Bert Muirhead
Senior research assistants: Richie Roberts and Eric Carrol
Research assistants: David Greig and Alan Gavin
Typing and transcription services: Jeanne Finnie

Stored, updated, written and supplied as keystroked
information on a Tandy (Radio Shack) TRS-80 Model II
microcomputer using a 'Scripsit' program.
Phototypeset by Saxon Printing Ltd., Derby.
Printed in Great Britain by Pitman Press Ltd., Bath.

Contents

Acknowledgements   6

Introduction   7

Abbreviations of Record Company Names   9

Directory of Producers   11

League Tables of Producers' Chart Successes   248

Index of Groups, Artists and Soundtracks   225

Acknowledgements

Thanks to all at Tandy (UK), Edinburgh Branch, with special thanks above and beyond the call of duty to managers past (Donny Morrison) and present (Ronnie Fullarton). (Tandy are known in the USA as Radio Shack.)

Special thanks to Radio Forth (194m Medium Wave) for their help and a big thank you to Jan Henderson and Susan Tait at the Radio Forth record library.

Thanks to John Tobler, Terry Hounsome, Eric Carroll, *Billboard, Music Week* and all the other weekly pop papers, Robert Christgau and Pete Frame

Hello to: Cynthia Rose, Andy Childs, Nigel Cross, Peter O'Brien, Brian Finnie, Norbert Obermanns, Jake, Nick & Elvis - the holy trinity, John Koenig, Richard Groothuizen, John Wagstaff, James Quinn Devlin, Jamie Spencer, Stuart Bell, Nigel Dick, Giovanni Dadomo, Al Clark, Eugene Manzi, Mike Heneghan, Gareth Davies, Eugene Beer, Mike Davies, Eddie Blower and Mungo, Ted Carroll, Mark Hagen, Ronnie Gurr, John Poole, Sandy and his merry man at Fast Product, Lindsay Hutton, Taras Ostashewsky, Kenny MacDonald, Dave Belcher, Johnny Rogan, Tony Fletcher, Trevor Dann, Paul Charles, Stuart Grundy, John Peel, Ira Robbins, Christopher and Zoe, Madge and George and everybody at the Green Tree Tavern, High Street, Burntisland, Fife, Scotland (a pub in the finest rock 'n' roll tradition; it rarely closes!)

A final thank you to Hugh Mackay, WS - my legal adviser and a worthy succesor to J.Cheaver Loophole, Legal Eagle.

Introduction

By way of introducing the book I have explained its background and also how you go about using it.

Compiling this volume involved the following primary research; firstly I physically checked out the credits on every album in my own collection, some 15,000. This was followed by checking out Radio Forth's record library of some 20,000 albums. Two other major collections were consulted - John Tobler's (15,000 plus) and Eric Carroll's (3,000 plus). In addition, my former business venture (Ezy Ryder Records) had some 12,000 titles in stock and my current venture, Hot Wacks Records, about half that total. In all, during 1983, I must have perused at least 75,000 album sleeves. Allowing for some duplication, this was quite a mammoth task, to put it mildly.

I also spoke to and interviewed some 40 or so record producers mentioned herein to confirm several titles. Lastly, I checked out several reliable guides; *Billboard's* new releases page and Rolling Stone's and Robert Christgau's record guides being particularly helpful.

It is probably quicker to tell you what you will NOT find in this volume. I have left out all compilation and "Best Of's" as they are essentially duplications of existing material. There are very few live albums included as, by their very nature, they do not require to be "produced", merely recorded for posterity (and possibly studio enhanced at a later date).

I have not included albums that were self-produced by the groups or individuals involved. I am fairly confident of having logged the bulk of the major rock albums of the last twenty years and barring any glaring omissions, it is safe to assume that any major rock album not included here was produced solely by the group or individual in question.

The scope of the book is restricted to those producers who have broached either the British or American album charts (or bubbled under). I apologise in advance for the lack of information regarding Canadian, continental European or Australian producers and groups. I have, however, included those few producers who regularly chart in the UK or the US (Conny Plank, Dieter Dierks, Vanda and Young, Bruce Fairbairn *et al*). Similarly reggae, blues, jazz and mainstream C&W and Soul producers (eg Freddie Perren, Bruce Iglauer, Nick Perls, Narada Michael Walden, George Duke, Michael Zager, Cerrone, Buddy Killen, Jerry Crutchfield, Fred Foster, Owen Bradley, Manfred Eicher, Orrin Keepnews, Norman Granz, Norman Whitfield, Thom Bell, Gamble and Huff etc.) will have to wait until future volumes.

The only concession to self-production I have made is in the case of recording artists whose outside productions are at least equal or greater in quantity than that artist's own recorded output. This willingness to help others, for whatever reason (patronage, profit or the chance to experiment with somebody else's reputation rather than one's own), is only to be encouraged. To that end I have included the records of David Bowie, John Cale, Brian Eno, Robert Fripp, Todd Rundgren and Frank Zappa along with a few others, I have also included the self-produced records by the former Beatles as well as Brian Wilson's contribution to the Beach Boys. Without whom I'm not sure where pop would be today, but would probably still be performed by ageing matinee idols in evening jackets.

The information is arranged as follows:

A001 Alan V. Abrahams (1)

w.Bones Howe (2)   Juice Newton (3)   *After The Dust Settled* (4)   RCA (5)   1977

(1) This is the record producer, the code letters preceding his name are applied to the Index of Artists at the end of this listing

(2) If any album was co-produced by another producer or had more than one producer involved it will be mentioned in this column. The major producers are cross-referenced.

(3) The group or individual involved

(4) The album title.

(5) The record label and year of release. If two labels are listed the first named is the UK label and the second is the US label. If only one label is named then that is the label that issued the record on both sides of the Atlantic or, the album in question may only have been issued in one territory. With regard to year of release, I have generally quoted that as quoted on the album sleeve. In some cases however I have mentioned the year the album entered the charts (usually in the case of December release records charting in January.)

I am aware that there are bound to be omissions. These will be corrected as and when I unearth the relevant discs. In the meantime I will gladly correspond with anyone wanting to help out in any way. Please contact me at:
Hot Wacks
16 Almondbank Terrace
Edinburgh EH11 1SS,
Scotland, UK

The following volumes may be of some interest:
New Rock Record (2nd Edition) by Terry Hounsome (Blandford Press)

A companion volume to this book, Rock Record lists, more fully, details of 6,000 groups, 40,000 albums and over 35,000 musicians and session men. In short, fuller details on most of the albums mentioned herein can be gleaned from New Rock Record.

To find out more about the technical side of record producing, as well as the personalities behind it, The Record Producers (BBC Publications) by John Tobler and Stuart Grundy comprises of twelve long interviews with major producers (Lieber & Stoller, Mickie Most, Tom Dowd, Glyn Johns, Todd Rundgren, Mike Chapman, Phil Spector, Tony Visconti and Richard Perry amongst others.)

Lastly, as a reader service, Hot Wacks record-finding service can supply the bulk of the records mentioned here via their mail order outlet. For details write to:

Hot Wacks Records
16 South Saint Andrew Street
Edinburgh EH2 2AZ, Scotland

One last thought, no doubt many readers will ask why singles have not been included. The answer is simply due to lack of space. A similar volume devoted to singles would be at least 3 or 4 times the size of this volume (1000 pages!). This is no great drawback as far as the computer is concerned and I have the information near at hand anyway.

BERT MUIRHEAD, July 1984

Abbreviations of
Record Company Names

Where it has not been possible to list record label names in full the following abbreviations have been used.

A
Abcko (Abk)
Ace Of Clubs (AOC)
Albion (Alb)
Allegiance (Alleg)
Alligator (Allig)
Antilles (Ant)
Aquarius (Aqu)
Ariola (Ari)
Ariola-America (Ariola-Am)
Armageddon (Arm)
Asylum (Asy)
Atlantic (Atl)
Automatic (Auto)
Avatar (Avat)

B
Backstreet (Backstr)
Barking Pumpkin (B.Pumpkin)
Beggars Banquet (B.Banquet/B.Banq)
Bemisbrain (Bemis)
Big Top (B.Top)
Blue Horizon (B.Horizon)
Blueprint (Bluep)
Boardwalk (Board)
Boulevard (Boul)
Bronze (Bron)
Brown Bag (B.Bag)
Buddah (Bud)
Burning Rome (B.Rome)

C
Cameo-Parkway (Cameo P)
Capitol (Cap)
Carrere (Car)
Casablanca (Casab)
Charisma (Char)
Cherry Lane (C.Lane)
Cherry Red (Cherry)
Chipping Norton (C.Norton)
Chrysalis (Chrys)
Cleveland International (Cleve Int)
Coast To Coast (CTC)
Colgems (Colg)
Columbia (UK) (Col)
Cottillion (Cott)
Countryside (Country)

Crazy Cajun (C.Cajun)
Criminal (Crim)
Crystal Clear (Crystal)

D
Dandelion (Dand)
Dark Horse (D.Horse)
Decca (Dec)
Don't Fall Off The Mountain (DFOTM)
Dunhill (Dunh)

E
Elektra (Elek)
Elektra/Asylum (E/A)
Emerald City (Emerald)
EMI-America (EMI-Amer)
Enterprise (Enterp)

F
First American (First Am)
Flying Fish (F.Fish)
Fontana (Font)
Free Flight (F.Flight)
Full Moon (F.Moon)

G
Gaff Masters (GM)
Geffen (Geff)
Genetic (Gen)
Golden Disc (G.Disc)
Goughsound (Gough)
Graduate (Grad)

H
Happy Hermit (H.Hermit)
Happy Tiger (Happy T.)
Harvest (Harv)
Hologram (Holog)

I
Impression (Imp)
Impulse (Imp)
Infinity (Infin)
Inner City (I.City)
Instant (inst)
International Artists (IA)
Island (Isl)

J
Janus (Jan)
John Hammond Records (JHR)
Just Sunshine (Just Sun)

K
Kama Sutra (KS)
Kicking Mule (K.Mule)
Kirshner (Kir)
Korova (Kor)

L
Lamborghini (Lamborg)
Lee Hazelwood International (LHI)
Liberty (Lib)
Lifesong (Lifes)
Little Ricky (L.Ricky)
London (Lon)
Lorimar (Lori)

M
Magnet (Mag/Ma)
Marc On Wax (Marc On)
Max's Kansas City (MKC)
Midsong (Mid)
Mirage (Mir)
Mooncrest (Mooncr)
Muscle Shoals Sound (MSS)

N
National Lampoon (N.Lamp)
Natural Resources (Nat Res)
Nemperor (Nemp)
Network (Netw)

O
Original Sound (Orig Sound)
Oyster (Oys)

P
Pacific Arts (P.A.)
Paramount (Para)
Parlophone (Parl)
Parrot (Parr)
Passport (Passp)
Peach River (P.River)
Penny Farthing (P.Farthing)
Philadelphia International (Phil Int)
Philips (Phil)
Phil Spector International (PSI)
Phonogram (Phonog)
Polydor (Poly)
Portrait (Port)
Power Exchange (P.Exchange)
Private Stock (P.Stock)

R
Radar (Rad)
Radial Choice (Radial)
Rare Earth (Rare/RE)
Reaction (Reac)
Red Lightnin' (Red L)
Regal Zonophone (Regal Z)
Ridge Runner (R.Runner)
Ripple (Rip)
Rocket (Rock)
Rolling Stones Records (RSR)
Rollin' Rock (Rollin')
Rounder (Roun)

S
San Francisco (San Fran)
Scotti Brothers (Scotti)
Screen Gems Corporation (SGC)
Shelter (Shelt)
Side Effects (Side Eff)
Sidewalk (Side)
Singlebrook (Single)
Situation 2 (Sit 2)
Some Bizarre (SB)
Sounds Of The South (SOTS)
South Coast (S.Coast)
Spindizzy (Spin)
Spring (Spr)
Stateside (Sta)
Step Forward (Step For)
Straight (Str)
Strugglebaby (Struggle)
Sugar Maple (S.Maple)

T
Takoma (Tak)
Tappan Zee (TZ)
Total Sound (T.Sound)
Transatlantic (Tra)
Tumbleweed (Tumble)
20th Century (20th Cent)

V
Vertigo (Vert)
Virgin (Virg)
Vocallion (Voc)

W
Westbound (West)
White Whale (W.Whale)
Wild Bunch (W.Bunch)
Windfall (Windf)
Wooden Nickel (W.Nickel)
World Pacific (World Pac)
World Wide Artists (WWA)

Directory of Producers

A001 Alan Abrahams

	Memphis Horns	*Get Up And Dance*	RCA	1977
w. Bones Howe	Juice Newton	*After The Dust Settles*	RCA	1976
	Pure Prairie League	*Dance*	RCA	1976
	Pure Prairie League	*Live – Takin The Stage*	RCA	1977
	Pure Prairie League	*Just Fly*	RCA	1978
	Wha–Koo	*Fragile Line*	CBS	1979

A002 Mark Abramson

	Randy Burns	*Still On Our Feet*	Polydor	1973
w. P. Rothchild	Paul Butterfield	*Butterfield Blues Band*	Elektra	1966
w. P. Rothchild	Paul Butterfield	*East West*	Elektra	1967
	Judy Collins	*A Maid of Constant Sorrow*	Elektra	1964
w. J.Holzman	Judy Collins	*Judy Collins Concert*	Elektra	1964
w. J.Holzman	Judy Collins	*#3*	Elektra	1965
	Judy Collins	*Fifth Album*	Elektra	1965
	Judy Collins	*In My Life*	Elektra	1967
	Judy Collins	*Whales & Nightingales*	Elektra	1971
	Judy Collins	*Living*	Elektra	1971
	Judy Collins	*True stories*	Elektra	1973
	David Frye	*I Am The President*	Elektra	1969
w. J.Holzman	Love	*Love*	Elektra	1966
w. J.Holzman	Phil Ochs	*In Concert*	Elektra	1966
	Tom Rush	*Take A Little Walk With Me*	Elektra	1966
	The Wackers	*Shredder*	Elektra	1972

A003 John Acock

	Steve Hackett	*Voyage Of The Acolyte*	Char/Chry	1975
	Steve Hackett	*Please Don't Touch*	Char/Chry	1978
	Steve Hackett	*Spectral Morning*	Char/Chry	1979
	Steve Hackett	*Defector*	Char/Chry	1980
	Steve Hackett	*Cured*	Char/Epic	1981
	Steve Hackett	*Highly Strung*	Char/Epic	1983
	Steve Hackett	*Bay Of Kings*	Lamborg.	1983

A004 Lou Adler

	Cheech and Chong	*Cheech and Chong*	Odc	1971
	Cheech and Chong	*Big Bambu*	Ode	1972
	Cheech and Chong	*Los Cochinos*	Ode	1973
	Cheech and Chong	*Wedding Album*	Ode	1974
	Cheech and Chong	*Sleeping Beauty*	Ode	1976
	Cheech and Chong	*Up In Smoke*	WB	1978
	Merry Clayton	*Gimme Shelter*	Ode	1970
	The City	*Now That Everything's Been Said*	Ode	1968
w. John Phillips	Jimi Hendrix	*Monterey Pop Festival*	Reprise	1970
	Carole King	*Music*	Ode	1971
	Carole King	*Tapestry*	Ode	1972
	Carole King	*Rhymes and Reasons*	Ode	1972
	Carole King	*Fantasy*	Ode	1973
	Carole King	*Wrap Around Joy*	Ode	1974
	Carole King	*Thoroughbred*	Ode	1975
	Carole King	*Speeding Time*	Atlantic	1983
	L.A. Gospel Choir	*The Gospel According To Bob Dylan*	Ode	1971

	The Mamas and Papas	*If You Can Believe Your Eyes And Ears*	Dunhill	1966
	The Mamas And Papas	*The Mamas & The Papas*	Dunhill	1966
	The Mamas And Papas	*Deliver*	Dunhill	1967
	The Mamas And Papas	*The Papas & The Mamas*	Dunhill	1968
w. John Phillips	The Mamas And Papas	*Monterey Pop Festival*	Dunhill	1971
	Barry McGuire	*Eve Of Destruction*	ABC	1965
	Scott McKenzie	*The Voice Of*	CBS	1967
	John Phillips	*John Phillips*	Dunhill	1970
	Johnny Rivers	*At The Whiskey A GoGo*	Imperial	1964
	Johnny Rivers	*Here We A GoGo Again*	Imperial	1964
	Johnny Rivers	*In Action*	Imperial	1965
	Johnny Rivers	*Rocks The Folk*	Imperial	1965
	Johnny Rivers	*Meanwhile Back At The Whiskey A GoGo*	Imperial	1965
	Johnny Rivers	*And I Know You Wanna Dance*	Imperial	1966
	Johnny Rivers	*Changes*	Imperial	1966
	Johnny Rivers	*Slim Slo Slider*	Imperial	1970
	soundtrack	*The Rocky Horror Picture Show*	Ode	1974
	Spirit	*Spirit*	Ode	1968
	Spirit	*The Family That Plays Together Stays Together*	Ode	1968
	Spirit	*Clear*	Ode	1969
	Tufano—Giammarese	*Tufano—Giammarese*	Ode	1973

A005 Brian Ahern

w. Bernie Leadon	David Bromberg	*Midnight On The Water*	CBS	1975
	Dianne Brooks	*Backstairs Of My Life*	WB	1976
	Johnny Cash	*Silver*	CBS	1979
	Johnny Cash	*Johnny 99*	CBS	1983
	Rodney Crowell	*Ain't Livin' Long Like This*	WB	1977
	Jonathan Edwards	*Rockin' Chair*	WB	1976
	Jonathan Edwards	*Sailboat*	WB	1977
	Emmylou Harris	*Pieces Of The Sky*	WB	1975
	Emmylou Harris	*Elite Hotel*	WB	1976
	Emmylou Harris	*Luxury Liner*	WB	1977
	Emmylou Harris	*Quarter Moon In A Ten Cent Town*	WB	1978
	Emmylou Harris	*Blue Kentucky Girl*	WB	1979
	Emmylou Harris	*Light Of The Stable*	WB	1979
	Emmylou Harris	*Roses In The Snow*	WB	1980
	Emmylou Harris	*Evangeline*	WB	1981
	Emmylou Harris	*Cimarron*	WB	1981
	Emmylou Harris	*Last Date*	WB	1982
	Emmylou Harris	*White Shoes*	WB	1983
	Emmylou Harris		WB	1984
	Albert Lee	*Hiding*	A&M	1979
	Anne Murray	*Snowbird*	Capitol	1970
	Anne Murray	*Danny's Song*	Capitol	1973
	Anne Murray	*Love Song*	Capitol	1974
	Anne Murray	*Highly Prized Possession*	Capitol	1974

	Anne Murray & Glen Campbell	Anne Murray & Glen Campbell	Capitol	1972
	Mary Kay Place	Tonite! At The Capri Lounge	CBS	1976
	Mary Kay Place	Aimin' To Please	CBS	1977
	Peter Pringle	Peter Pringle	WB	1976
	Billy Joe Shaver	When I Get My Wings	Capricorn	1977
	Jesse Winchester	Nothin' But A Breeze	Bearsville	1977

A006 Ron and Howie Albert

	The Boyzz	Too Wild To Tame	Epic	1978
	Harry Chapin	Sequel	Boardwalk	1981
	John Cougar	John Cougar	Riva	1979
	Crosby,Stills & Nash	Crosby,Stills & Nash	Atlantic	1977
	Crosby,Stills & Nash	Allies (2 tracks only)	Atlantic	1983
	Curved Air	Midnight Wire	BTM	1975
w. D.Randell	Terri De Sario	Pleasure Train	Casablanca	1978
w. Tom Dowd	Firefall	Elan	Atlantic	1978
w. K.Lehning	Firefall	Undertow	Atlantic	1979
	Firefall	Break Of Dawn	Atlantic	1982
w. E.Kramer	Fotomaker	Fotomaker	Atlantic	1978
	Gang Of 4	Hard	EMI	1983
	Chris Hillman	Slippin' Away	Asylum	1976
	McGuinn Clark and Hillman	McGuinn Clark and Hillman	Capitol	1979
	McGuinn Clark and Hillman	City	Capitol	1080
	Mink De Ville	Where Angels Fear To Tread	Atlantic	1983
	Henry Paul Band	Grey Ghost	Atlantic.	1979
	Pierce Arrow	Pity The Rich (2 tracks)	CBS	1978
	Procol Harum	Something Magic	Chrysalis	1977
	Pure Prairie League	Can't Hold Back	RCA	1979
	Michael Quatro	Bottom Line	Spector	1981
	Rhodes,Chalmers, Rhodes	Scandal	Radio	1980
w. B.Halverson	Stephen Stills	Stills	CBS	1975
w. S. Stills	Stephen Stills	Thoroughfare Gap	CBS	1978
	Sutherland Brothers	Reach For The Sky	CBS	1975
	Sutherland Brothers	Slipstream	CBS	1976
	Joe Vitale	Roller Coaster Weekend	Atlantic	1974
	White Witch	Spiritual Greeting	Capricorn	1974
	Tony Wilson	Catch One	Bearsville	1978
	Betty Wright	Live	TK/Alston	1978

A007 Richie Albright

	Jessi Colter	That's The Way A Cowboy Rocks	Capitol	1978
	Waylon Jennings	What Goes Around Comes Around	RCA	1979
	Waylon Jennings	Music Man	RCA	1980
	Waylon and Jessi	Leather and Lace	RCA	1981
	Johnny Rodriguez	Foolin' With Fire	Epic	1984
	Billy Joe Shaver	Billy Joe Shaver	CBS	1982
	Hank Williams,Jnr	The New South	WB–Curb	1977

A008 John Alcock

	Bandit	*Bandit*	Arista	1976
	Commander Cody	*Rock 'n' Roll Again*	Arista	1977
	John Entwistle	*Whistle Rhymes*	Track	1972
	John Entwistle's Ox	*Mad Dog*	Decca/MCA	1975
	Flash Fearless	*Flash Fearless Versus the Zorg Women*	Chrysalis	1975
	Liar	*Set The World On Fire*	Bearsville	1978
	Mandalaband	*Mandalaband*	Chrysalis	1975
	Ro Ro	*Meet At The Water*	EMI	1972
	The Runaways	*And Now The Runaways*	Mercury	1978
w. Andy Johns	Danny Spanos	*Danny Spanos*	Windsong	1980
	Thin Lizzy	*Jailbreak*	Vert/Mer	1976
	Thin Lizzy	*Johnny The Fox*	Vert/Mer	1977

A009 Morry Alexander

Barry Goldberg	*Barry Goldberg And Friends*	Record Man	1976
Harvey Mandel	*Blues from Chicago*	Cherry Red	1976

A010 Tom Allom

Andy Bown	*Come Back Romance All Is Forgiven*	EMI	1977
Michael Chapman	*Life On The Ceiling*	Crim/P.A.	1979
Dave Cousins	*Two Weeks Last Summer*	A&M	1972
Decameron	*Third Light*	Tra.	1975
Doc Holliday	*Doc Holliday*	A&M	1971
George Hatcher Band	*Dry Run*	UA	1976
George Hatcher Band	*Talkin' Turkey*	UA	1977
Hudson Ford	*Free Spirit*	A&M	1974
Hudson Ford	*Nickelodeon*	ÄM	1974
Hudson Ford	*Worlds Collide*	A&M	1975
Jack The Lad	*Jackpot*	UA	1976
Judas Priest	*Unleashed In The East*	CBS	1979
Judas Priest	*British Steel*	CBS	1980
Judas Priest	*Point Of Entry*	CBS	1981
Judas Priest	*Screaming For Vengeance*	CBS	1982
Judas Priest	*Defenders Of The Faith*	CBS	1984
Kix	*Kix*	Atlantic	1981
Krokus	*Headhunter*	Arista	1983
Siren	*Siren*	Dand/Elek	1969
Strawbs	*Hero and Heroine*	A&M	1974
Strawbs	*Ghosts*	A&M	1974
Strawbs	*Nomadness*	A&M	1975
Tourists	*Reality Effect*	Logo/Epic	1979
Tourists	*Luminous Basement*	RCA	1980
Pat Travers	*Go For What You Know*	Polydor	1979
Whitford/St. Nicholas	*Whitford/St.Nicholas*	CBS	1981
(ex-Aerosmith and Ted Nugent band members)			
Wishbone Ash	*New England*	MCA/Atl	1976
Wishbone Ash	*Front Page News*	MCA	1977

A011 Tommy Allsup

Asleep At The Wheel	*Comin' Right At Ya*	UA	1973
Asleep At The Wheel	*Texas Gold*	Capitol	1975
Asleep At The Wheel	*Wheelin' and Dealin'*	Capitol	1976

	Asleep At The Wheel	*The Wheel*	Capitol	1977
	Alvin Crow	*High Riding*	Polydor	1977

A012 Ron Altbach

	Celebration	*Almost Summer*	MCA	1978
	Celebration	*Celebration*	PA Stern	1979
	(group featured Mike Love of the Beach Boys)			

A013 Don Altfeld

	Albert Hammond	*It Never Rains In Southern California*	Mums	1972
	P F Sloan	*Raised On Records*	Mums	1972

A014 Billy Altman

	Joe King Carasco	*Joe King Carasco and The Crowns*	Stiff/Ant	1980
	(Altman was formerly reviews editor Creem magazine)			

A015 David Anderle

w. Russ Miller	David Ackles	*David Ackles*	Elektra	1970
	(later reissued as *The Road To Cairo*)			
	Marc Benno	*Marc Benno*	A&M	1970
	Marc Benno	*Minnows*	A&M	1971
	Marc Benno	*Ambush*	A&M	1972
	Bonnie Bramlett	*Sweet Bonnie Bramlett*	CBS	1973
	Circle Jerks	*Wild In The Streets*	Step For.	1981
	Judy Collins	*Who Knows Where The Time Goes*	Elektra	1968
	Color Me Gone	*Color Me Gone*	A&M	1984
	Rita Coolidge	*Rita Coolidge*	A&M	1971
	Rita Coolidge	*Nice Feeling*	A&M	1971
	Rita Coolidge	*Anytime Anywhere*	A&M	1972
	Rita Coolidge	*The Lady's Not For Sale*	A&M	1972
	Rita Coolidge	*Fall Into Spring*	A&M	1974
	Rita Coolidge	*It's Only Love*	A&M	1975
w. Booker T.	Rita Coolidge	*Love Me again*	A&M	1978
w. Booker T.	Rita Coolidge	*Satisfied*	A&M	1979
w. B.Worrell	Rita Coolidge	*Never Let You Go*	A&M	1983
	Rita Coolidge and Kris Kristofferson	*Full Moon*	A&M	1973
	Rita Coolidge and Kris Kristofferson	*Natural Act*	A&M	1978
	Chris De Burgh	*Eastern Wind*	A&M	1980
	Doc Holliday	*Rides Again*	A&M	1981
w. Russ Miller	Diane Hildebrand	*Early Morning Blues And Greens*	Elektra	1965
	Booker T. Jones	*Try And Love Again*	A&M	1978
	Kris Kristofferson	*Who's To Bless And Who's To Blame*	Monument	1975
	Kris Kristofferson	*Surreal Thing*	Monument	1976
	Kris Kristofferson	*Easter Island*	Monument	1978
	Kris Kristofferson	*Shake Hands With The Devil*	Monument	1979
w. W.Brill	Annabel Lamb	*The Flame*	A&M	1984
w. Glyn Johns	Lambert & Nuttycombe	*At Home*	A&M	197
	Mother Hen	*Mother Hen*	RCA	1971

17

	Scott McKenzie	*Stained Glass Morning*	A&M	1970
w. Glyn Johns	The Ozark Mountain Daredevils	*The Ozark Mountain Daredevils*	A&M	1974
	The Ozark Mountain Daredevils	*It'll Shine When It Shines*	A&M	1975
	The Ozark Mountain Daredevils	*The Car Over The Lake Album*	A&M	1975
	The Ozark Mountain Daredevils	*Men From Earth*	A&M	1976
	Willie Phoenix	*Willie Phoenix*	A&M	1982
	Rhinoceros	*Satin Chickens*	Elektra	1969
	Rick Roberts	*Windmills*	A&M	1972
	Cory Wells	*Touch Me*	A&M	1978

A016 Tom Anderson

	Commander Cody	*We Got A Live One Here*	WB	1976

A017 Craig Anderton

	Linda Cohen	*Leda*	Poppy	1972
	Linda Cohen	*Angel Alley*	Tomato	1974

A018 Bob Andrews

w. B.Schwarz	Carlene Carter	*Carlene Carter*	WB	1978
	Dance Band	*Fancy Footwork*	Double D	1980
	Dugites	*Dugites*	Deluxe	1980
	The Equators	*Hot*	Stiff	1981
	Johnny G	*Water Into Wine*	B.Banq	1982
	Jona Lewie	*Heart Skips Beat*	Stiff	1982
	London Cast	*Oklahoma! Live At The Palace*	Stiff	1980
	Shakin' Pyramids	*Celts and Cobras*	Virgin	1982
w. A.Winstanley	Tenpole Tudor	*Eddie, Old Bob, Dick and Gary*	Stiff	1981

A019 John Anthony

	Ace	*Five-A-Side*	Anchor	1974
	Ace	*Time For Another*	Anchor	1975
	Genesis	*Trespass*	Char/ABC	1970
	Genesis	*Nursery Cryme*	Char/Bud	1971
	Gypsy	*Brenda and The Rattle-snake*	UA	1972
	Halfbreed	*Halfbreed*	UA	1975
	Peter Hammill	*Fools Mate*	Charisma	1971
	Peter Hammill	*Chameleon In The Shadow Of Night*	Charisma	1973
	Headstone	*Bad Habits*	EMI	1974
	David Kent	*David Kent*	Epic	1982
	(keyboard player with the Hall & Oates band)			
	Lindisfarne	*Nicely Out Of Tune*	Char/Elek	1970
	Nutz	*Nutz*	A&M	1974
	Nutz	*Nutz Too*	A&M	1975
	Al Stewart	*Orange*	CBS	1972
	Malcolm Tomlinson	*Rock 'n' Roll Heart*	A&M	1979
	Tubes	*Now*	A&M	1977
	Van Der Graaf Generator	*The Least We Can Do Is Wave To Each Other*	Char/Dunh	1969

Van Der Graaf Generator	*H To He Who Am The Only One*	Charisma	1970
Van Der Graaf Generator	*Pawn Hearts*	Charisma	1971
Eugene Wallace	*Book Of Fool*	EMI	1974
Wondergap	*Wondergap*	A&M	1978

(Featuring Jim Ryan, formerly of The Critters)

A020 Mike Appel

	Jeff Conaway	*Jeff Conaway*	CBS	1979

(Conaway was one of the co-stars of Grease)

	Arlyn Gayle	*Back To The Midwest Night*	ABC	1978
w. J.Cretecos	Bruce Springsteen	*Greetings From Asbury Park*	CBS	1973
w. J.Cretecos	Bruce Springsteen	*The Wild, The Innocent & The E. Street Shuffle*	CBS	1973
w. Jon Landau	Bruce Springsteen	*Born To Run*	CBS	1975

A021 Robert Appere

	Brian Cadd	*White On White*	Capitol	1976
	Yvonne Elliman	*Night Flight*	RSO	1978
	Yvonne Elliman	*Yvonne*	RSO	1979
	Matthew Moore	*Winged Horses*	Caribou	1978
	Nigel Olsson	*Nigel Olsson*	Rocket	1975
w. J.Weston	Shawn Phillips	*Bright White*	A&M	1974
	Randy Richards	*Randy Richards*	A&M	1978
	Brian and Brenda Russell	*Word Called Love*	Rocket	1976
	The Section	*Forward Motion*	WB	1973
	Neil Sedaka	*Laughter In The Rain*	Polydor	1974
	Neil Sedaka	*Steppin' Out*	Polydor	1976
	Neil Sedaka	*In The Pocket*	Elektra	1980
w. C.Rainbow	John Townley	*Townley*	Harvest	1979
	Kenny Young	*Clever Dogs Chase The Sun*	WB	1972
	Kenny Young	*Last Stage To Silverwood*	WB	1973

A022 Rod Argent

w. Chris White	Colin Blunstone	*One Year*	Epic	1971
w. Chris White	Colin Blunstone	*Ennismore*	Epic	1972

(Argent and White produced all of Argent's studio albums)

A023 Roger Armstrong

	The Damned	*Machine Gun Etiquette*	Chiswick	1979
	Johnny Moped	*Cycle-delic*	Chiswick	1978
	The 101'ers	*Elgin Avenue Breakdown* (2 tracks only)	Chiswick	1981
	The Radiators	*TV Tube Heart*	Chiswick	1977
	Skrewdriver	*All Screwed Up*	Chiswick	1977

A024 Brooks Arthur

	Peter Allen	*Taught By Experts*	A&M	1976
	soundtrack	*All The Right Moves*	Casablanca	1983
	Debby Boone	*Debby Boone*	WB	1979
	Keith Carradine	*Lost And Found*	Asylum	1978

	Phil Cody	*Phil Cody*	Reprise	1976
	(Cody is Neil Sedaka's long time songwriting partner)			
	Crystal Mansion	*Crystal Mansion*	20th Cent	1979
	Janis Ian	*Stars*	CBS	1974
	Janis Ian	*Aftertones*	CBS	1975
	Janis Ian	*Between The Lines*	CBS	1975
	Barry Mann	*Barry Mann*	Casab	1980
	Bette Midler	*Broken Blossom*	Atlantic	1977
	Bernadette Peters	*Now Playing*	MCA	1981
	Carole Bayer Sager	*Carole Bayer Sager*	Elektra	1977
	Carole Bayer Sager	*Too*	Elektra	1978
w. B.Bacharach	Carole Bayer Sager	*Sometimes Late At Night*	*Boardwalk*	1981
w. Neil Bogart	Robin Williams	*Reality,What A Concept*	Casab	1979
	Junko Yagami	*I Wanna Make A Hit Wit-Choo*	Vanguard	1984

A025 Andy Arthurs

	Advertising	*Advertising Jingles*	EMI	1978
	(group included Tot Taylor, later famous with Mari Wilson)			
w. S.Stevenson	A.Raincoat	*Digalongamax*	EMI	1975
	Chords	*So Far Away*	Polydor	1980
	Little Bo Bitch	*Little Bo Bitch*	Cobra	1979
	(Released in the USA under the name of The Lonely Boys, on Harvest)			
	999	*999*	UA	1978

A026 Robert Ash

	Albania	*Are You All Mine*	Chiswick	1981
w. C.Blackwell	B-52's	*Party Mix*	Island	1981

A027 Peter Asher

	Broadway Cast	*The Pirates Of Penzance*	Elektra	1981
	Andrew Gold	*What's Wrong With This Picture ?*	Asylum	1976
	Jo Mama	*Jo Mama*	Atlantic	1970
	(Featured Carole King and Danny Kootch)			
	Tony Kosinec	*Bad Girl Songs*	CBS	1971
	Bonnie Raitt	*The Glow*	WB	1979
	Ronin	*Ronin*	Mercury	1980
	(Featured Waddy Wachtel and Dan Dugmore of the Ronstadt band)			
	Linda Ronstadt	*Heart Like A Wheel*	Asylum	1975
	Linda Ronstadt	*Prisoner In Disguise*	Asylum	1975
	Linda Ronstadt	*Hasten Down The Wind*	Asylum	1976
	Linda Ronstadt	*Simple Dream*	Asylum	1977
	Linda Ronstadt	*Living In The USA*	Asylum	1978
	Linda Ronstadt	*Mad Love*	Asylum	1980
	Linda Ronstadt	*Get Closer*	Asylum	1982
	Linda Ronstadt	*What's New*	Asylum	1983
	John David Souther	*Black Rose*	Asylum	1976
	John Stewart	*Willard*	Capitol	1970
	James Taylor	*James Taylor*	Apple	1968
	James Taylor	*Sweet Baby James*	WB	1970
	James Taylor	*Mud Slide Slim and the Blue Horizon*	WB	1971
	James Taylor	*One Man Dog*	WB	1972
	James Taylor	*JT*	CBS	1977
	James Taylor	*Flag*	CBS	1979

| | James Taylor | *Dad Loves His Work* | CBS | 1981 |
| | Tony Joe White | *Tony Joe White* | WB | 1971 |

A028 Jack Ashkinazy

| | The Cates Gang | *Come Back Home* | Metromedia | 1970 |
| | (group was an forerunner of The Cate Brothers Band) | | | |

A029 Tony Ashton

	Tony Ashton & Jon Lord	*Tony Ashton & Jon Lord*	Purple	1974
	Chas and Dave	*Chas and Dave*	EMI	1977
	Chas and Dave	*Don't Give A Monkeys*	EMI	1979
	Chas and Dave	*Live At Abbey Road*	EMI	1981
	Kilburn and The High Roads	*Wotabunch*	WB	1978
	McGuinness Flint	*Rainbow*	Bronze	1973
	Medicine Head	*One and One is One*	Polydor	1973
	Medicine Head	*Thru' A Five*	Polydor	1975
	Medicine Head	*Two Man Band (4 tracks)*	Barn	1976
	Stackridge	*Extravaganza*	Rocket	1974

A030 Jon Astley

w. Phil Chapman	Bethnal	*Crash Landing*	Vertigo	1979
	Eric Clapton	*Just One Night*	RSO	1980
w. Phil Chapman	Distractions	*Nobody's Perfect*	Island	1980
w. Doug Bennett	Bryn Haworth	*Keep The Ball Rolling*	A&M	1979
w. Phil Chapman	Carolyn Mas	*Modern Dreamer*	Mercury	1981
w. Phil Chapman	Sandy McLelland and the Back Line	*Sandy McLelland and the Back Line*	Mercury	1979
w. Phil Chapman	Pretty Things	*Cross Talk*	WB	1980
w. Glyn Johns	The Who	*Who Are You*	Polydor	1978

A031 Audie Ashworth

	J J Cale	*Naturally*	Shelter	1971
	J J Cale	*Really*	Shelter	1972
	J J Cale	*Okie*	Shelter	1974
	J J Cale	*Troubador*	Shelter	1976
	J J Cale	*5*	Shelter	1979
	J J Cale	*Shades*	Shelter	1980
	J J Cale	*Grasshopper*	Shelter	1982
	J J Cale	*#8*	Shelter	1983
	Dianne Davidson	*Baby*	Janus	1971
	Dianne Davidson	*Backwoods Woman*	Janus	1972
	Charlie Dore	*Where To Now ? (3 tr.)*	Island	1979
	Bryn Haworth	*Grand Arrival*	A&M	1980
w. J J Cale	Gordon Payne	*Gordon Payne*	A&M	1978
	Leon Russell	*Hank Wilson's Back*	Shelter	1973
w. H McCracken	Don Schlitz	*Dreamer's Matinee*	Capitol	1980
w. L.George	John Starling	*Long Time Gone*	S.Hill	1980

A032 Mark Avnet

w. Lou Natkin	The Honeys	*Ecstasy*	Rhino	1983

A033 David Axelrod

	Merl Saunders	*Merl Saunders*	Fantasy	1974
	Nancy Wilson	*At My Best*	ASI	1981
	Jimmy Witherspoon	*Evening Blues*	Stateside	1964
	(David Axelrod is an accomplished recording artist, having recorded at least nine albums since 1969)			

21

A034 Hoyt Axton

Commander Cody	*Tales from The Ozone*	WB	1975

B001 Rodger Bain

Alquin	*Nobody Can Wait Forever*	Polydor	1975
Barclay James Harvest	*Everyone Is Everybody Else*	Polydor	1974
Barclay James Harvest	*Live*	Polydor	1974
Black Sabbath	*Black Sabbath*	Vert/WB	1970
Black Sabbath	*Paranoid*	Vert/WB	1971
Black Sabbath	*Master Of Reality*	Vert/WB	1971
Arthur Brown	*Dance*	Gull	1974
Budgie	*Budgie*	MCA	1971
Dirty Tricks	*Dirty Tricks*	Polydor	1974
Freedom	*Through The Years*	Vert/Cott	1971
Judas Priest	*Rocka Rolla*	Gull/Visa	1974
Wild Turkey	*Battle Hymn*	Chrysalis	1971

B002 Glenn A. Baker

The Beatles	*The Beatles Talk Down Under*	Gough	1982

(Glenn A. Baker is a noted writer, journalist, broadcaster and album compiler)

B003 Roy Thomas Baker

Be Bop Deluxe	*Futurama*	Harvest	1975
Robert Calvert	*Captain Lockheed and The Starfighters*	UA/Passp	1974
The Cars	*The Cars*	Elektra	1978
The Cars	*Candy-O*	Elektra	1979
The Cars	*Panorama*	Elektra	1980
The Cars	*Shake It Up*	Elektra	1981
Cheap Trick	*One On One*	Epic	1982
Alice Cooper 80	*Flush The Fashion*	WB	1980
Devo	*On No It's Devo*	Virgin/WB	1982
Espionage	*Espionage*	A&M	1983
Foreigner	*Head Games*	Atlantic	1979
Lewis Furey	*The Humours Of Lewis Furey*	A&M	1976
Gasolin'	*#3*	CBS	1973
Gasolin'	*Stakkels Jim*	CBS	1974
Gasolin'	*Gasolin'*	CBS	1975
Gasolin'	*What A Lemon*	CBS	1976
Ian Hunter	*Overnight Angels*	CBS	1977
Hustler	*Play Loud*	A&M	1975
Jet	*Jet*	CBS	1975
Journey	*Infinity*	CBS	1978
Journey	*Evolution*	CBS	1979
Reggie Knighton Band	*Reggie Knighton Band*	CBS	1978
Lindisfarne	*Live*	Charisma	1972
Lindisfarne	*Roll On Ruby*	Char/Elek	1973
Lone Star	*Lone Star*	Epic	1976
Hilly Michaels	*Calling All Girls*	WB	1980
Nazareth	*Exercises*	Moon/WB	1972
Pilot	*Morin Heights*	EMI	1976

	Man	*Winos,Rhinos and*		
		Lunatics	UA	1972
	Richard Myhill	*The Richard Myhill Album*	EMI	1973
	Richard Myhill	*21 Days In Soho*	EMI	1974
	Queen	*Queen*	EMI/Elek	1973
	Queen	*Queen 2*	EMI/Elek	1974
	Queen	*Sheer Heart Attack*	EMI/Elek	1974
	Queen	*A Night At The Opera*	EMI/Elek	1975
	Queen	*Jazz*	EMI/Elek	1978
	(Queen 2 to Jazz inclusive were co-produced by the group)			
	Dusty Springfield	*It Begins Again*	Mercury	1978
	Starcastle	*Fountains Of Light*	Epic	1976
	Starcastle	*Citadel*	Epic	1977
w. F.Mercury	Peter Straker	*This One's On Me*	EMI	1977
	Ron Wood	*Gimme Some Neck*	CBS	1979
	The World	*Break The Silence*	WB	1983
	(Listed as "executive producer" on The World album)			

B004 Marty Balin

	Jesse Barrish	*Jesse Barrish*	RCA	1978
w. John Hug	Jese Barrish	*Mercury Shoes*	RCA	1978
	(Balin is former member of Jefferson Airplane and Starship, Barrish was a songwriter for the Starship)			

B005 Harry Balk

	Del Shannon	*Runaway*	Lon/B Top	1961
	Del Shannon	*Little Town Flirt*	Lon/B Top	1962
	Del Shannon	*Hats Off To Larry*	London	1963
	Del Shannon	*Handy Man*	Sta/Amy	1964
	Del Shannon	*1661 Seconds With*	Sta/Amy	1964
	Del Shannon	*Sings Hank Williams*	Sta/Amy	1964

B006 Russ Ballard

	America	*Your Move*	Capitol	1983
	Roger Daltrey	*Ride A Rock Horse*	Polydor	1975
w. D.Courtney	Leo Sayer	*Another Year*	Chry/WB	1975

B007 Adrian Barber

	Aerosmith	*Aerosmith*	CBS	1973
	Allman Brothers Band	*Allman Brothers Band*	Capricorn	1969

B008 Stephen Barncard

	Chilliwack	*Chilliwack*	AM	1981
w. Stuart A.Love	Jiva	*Still Life*	Polydor	1978
	New Riders of the Purple Sage	*Powerglide*	CBS	1972
	New Riders of the Purple Sage	*Gypsy Cowboy*	CBS	1972

B009 Steve Barri

	Bobby Bland	*California Album*	ABC/Dunh	1974
	Bobby Bland	*Dreamer*	ABC/Dunh	1974
	Bobby Bland	*Reflections in Blue*	ABC	1977
	Mel Brooks	*History Of The World*		
		Part 1	WB	1982

	Cashman and West	*A Song Or Two*	ABC	1972
	Cashman and West	*Moondog Serenade*	ABC	1973
	Cashman and West	*Lifesong*	ABC	1974
w. M.Omartian	Kerry Chater ____	*Part Time Love*	WB	1978
	Kerry Chater	*Love On A Shoestring*	WB	1978
	Cher	*I'd Rather Believe In You*	WB	1976
	Cherokee	*Cherokee*	ABC	1971
	Jerry Corbetta	*Jerry Corbetta*	WB	1978
	Bill Cosby	*Himself*	Motown	1982
	Couchois	*Couchois*	WB	1979
	Couchois	*Nasty Hardware*	WB	1980
	Dion	*Streetheart*	WB	1976
	Bo Donaldson & the Heywoods	*Bo Donaldson and the Heywoods*	ABC	1974
	Yvonne Elliman	*Yvonne (2 tracks only)*	RSO	1979
	Mama Cass Elliott	*Mama Cass*	Stateside	1969
	Kinky Friedman	*Kinky Friedman*	ABC	1974
	Four Tops	*Mainstreet People*	ABC	1973
	Four Tops	*Night Lights In Harmony*	ABC	1974
w P.F.Sloan	Grassroots	*Let's live For Today*	Dunhill	1967
	Grassroots	*Feelings*	Dunhill	1968
	Grassroots	*Lovin' Things*	Dunhill	1969
	Grassroots	*Leaving It All Behind*	Dunhill	1969
	Grassroots	*Move Along*	Dunhill	1972
	Grassroots	*A Lotta Mileage*	Dunhill	1973
	Hamilton,Joe Frank and Reynolds	*Hamilton,Joe Frank and Reynolds*	Probe	1971
	Hamilton,Joe Frank and Reynolds	*Hallway Symphony*	Probe	1972
w. Tony Peluso	Kidd Glove	*Kidd Glove*	Morocco	1984
	BB King and Bobby Bland	*Together For The First Time Live*	ABC	1974
	Bobby King	*Bobby King*	WB	1981
w. B.Potter	Bobby King	*Love In The Fire*	Motown	1984
	John Henry Kurtz	*Reunion*	ABC	1972
	Dennis Lambert	*Bags and Things*	ABC	1972
	Michael Lovesmith	*I Can Make It Happen*	Motown	1984
	Alan O'Day	*Appetizers*	Pacific	1977
	Alan O'Day	*Oh Johnny*	Pacific	1979
w. M.Omartian	Pratt & McClain	*Pratt & McClain*	ABC	1974
	Pratt & McClain	*Happy Days*	Reprise	1976
	Rejoice	*Rejoice*	Dunhill	1969
	Tommy Roe	*We Can Make Music*	ABC	1974
	Tommy Roe	*Dizzy*	ABC	1969
	John Sebastian	*Welcome Back*	Reprise	1976
	Shango	*Trampin'*	Dunhill	1970
w. D.Lambert & B.Potter	Dusty Springfield	*Cameo*	Phil/ABC	1973
	Temptations	*Surface Thrills*	Gordy	1983
w. Cass Elliott	Three's A Crowd	*Christopher's Movie Matinee*	Dunhill	1967
	Patty Weaver	*Patty Weaver*	WB	1982

B010 Jeff Barry

	Archies	*Sugar Sugar*	RCA	1969
	Chopper	*Chopper*	Ariola	1979
	Paul Davis	*A Little Bit Of Paul Davis*	Bang	1973
w. E.Greenwich	Neil Diamond	*The Feel Of ...*	Bang	1966
w. E.Greenwich	Neil Diamond	*Just For You*	Bang	1967
	soundtrack	*The Idolmaker*	A&M	1980
	Tommy James	*Midnight Rider*	Fantasy	1976
	Jay & The Americans	*Try Some Of This*	UA	1967
	Andy Kim	*Greatest Hits*	Capitol	1974
	King Harvest	*King Harvest*	A&M	1975
	Monkees	*More Of The Monkees*	RCA/Colg	1967
	Sha Na Na	*The Night Is Still Young*	KamaSutra	1972
	John Travolta	*Whenever I'm Away From You*	Midsong	1977

B011 Paul Bass (a.k.a Bassman)

	Clive Langer	*Splash*	F-Beat	1980
	Lew Lewis	*Save The Wail*	Stiff	1979
w. Will Birch	Howard Werth	*Six Of One and Half A Dozen of the other*	Metabop	1982

B012 David Batchelor

	Alex Harvey	*Presents The Loch Ness Monster*	K Tel	1977
	Sensational Alex Harvey Band	*Tomorrow Belongs To Me*	Vertigo	1975
	Sensational Alex Harvey Band	*The Penthouse Tapes*	Vertigo	1976
	Sensational Alex Harvey Band	*S.A.H.B. Stories*	Mountain	1976
	Sensational Alex Harvey Band	*Rock Drill*	Mountain	1978
	Skids	*Scared To Dance*	Virgin	1979
	Solid Senders	*Solid Senders*	Virgin	1978
	(Wilko Johnson's first post-Dr. Feelgood recordings)			
	Starjets	*Starjets*	Epic	1979
	Wales O'Regan	*Ready To Run*	Mountain	1977

B013 Mike Batt

	Autopilot	*Rapid Eye Movement*	Chrysalis	1981
	Mike Batt	*Schizophonia*	Epic	1977
	Mike Batt	*Tarot Suite*	Epic	1977
	Mike Batt	*Waves*	Epic	1980
	Mike Batt	*6 Days In Berlin*	Epic	1980
	Mike Batt	*Zero Zero*	Epic	1982
	soundtrack	*Caravans*	CBS	1978
w. Chris Neil	David Essex	*Imperial Wizard*	Mercury	1979
	David Essex	*The Whisper*	Mercury	1984
	Hapshash and the Coloured Coat	*Western Flyer*	Liberty	1969
	Kursaal Flyers	*The Golden Mile*	CBS	1976
	Linda Lewis	*Hacienda View*	Arista	1979
	Steeleye Span	*All Around My Hat*	Chrysalis	1975

	Steeleye Span	*Rocket Cottage*	Chrysalis	1976
	The Wombles	*Wombling Songs*	CBS	1973
	The Wombles	*Remember You're A Womble*	CBS	1974
	The Wombles	*Keep On Wombling*	CBS	1974
	The Wombles	*Superwombling*	CBS	1975

B014 Harold Battiste

	Dr.John	*Gris Gris*	Atlantic	1968
	Dr.John	*Babylon*	Atlantic	1968
w. J.Wexler	Dr.John	*Gumbo*	Atlantic	1972

B015 Jeffrey Baxter (also known as Jeff "Skunk" Baxter)

	Billy and the Beaters	*Billy and the Beaters*	Alfa	1981
	Bliss Band	*Dinner With Raoul*	CBS	1978
	Nils Lofgren	*Night Fades Away*	Backstreet	1981
	Nazareth	*Malice In Wonderland*	Mount/A&M	1980
	Nazareth	*The Fool Circle*	NEMS	1980
	Sneaker	*Sneaker*	Handshake	1981
	Sneaker	*Loose In The World*	Handshake	1982
w. John Boylan	Livingston Taylor	*Man's Best Friend*	Epic	1980
	Bob Welch	*Eye Contact*	RCA	1983
	Carl Wilson	*Youngblood*	Caribou	1983

B016 Bazza (Barry Farmer)

	Any Trouble	*Live At The Venue*	Stiff	1980
	Mike Berry	*Memories*	Polydor	1981
	Chicken Shack	*Roadies Concerto*	RCA	1981
	Klondike Pete	*Some Of The Fellers*	Big Beat	1980
	Kirsty MacColl	*Desperate Character*	Polydor	1981
	Wreckless Eric	*Big Smash*	Stiff/Epic	1980

B017 Kevin Beamish

	Stan Bush	*Stan Bush*	CBS	1983
	Charlie	*Charlie*	Mirage	1983
	Jefferson Starship	*Winds Of Change*	Grunt	1982
	Henry Paul Band	*Anytime*	Atlantic	1981
	Saxon	*Crusade*	Carrere	1984

B018 Curt Becher (formerly known as Curt Boettcher)

	Gordon Alexander	*Gordon's Buster (1 tr)*	CBS	1968
	Association	*And Then ....Along Comes The Association*	Valiant	1967
	Curt Boettcher	*There's An Innocent Face*	Elektra	1973
	Jameson	*Color Him In*	MGM	1967
	Mike Love	*Looking Back With Love*	CBS/Board	1981
w. Keith Olsen	Millenium	*Begin*	CBS	1970
w. B. Johnston	Sailor	*Checkpoint*	Epic	1977
	Sagittarius	*Present Tense*	CBS	1968
	Sagittarius	*The Blue Marble*	Together	1968
w. Keith Olsen	Song	*Album*	MGM	1967
	(group featured Mickey Rooney, Jnr)			
	Geno Washington	*That's Why Hollywood Loves Me*	DJM	1979

B019 Roger A. Bechirian

	Artist	Title	Label	Year
	Attractions	Mad About The Wrong Boy	F-Beat	1980
	Roger Bechirian	The Art Of Roger Bechirian Volume One	RivGlob	1982
	(sampler of the producer's works, released by Jake Riviera's Riviera Global company)			
	Blues Band	Itchy Feet	Arista	1981
	Blanket Of Secrecy	Ears Have Walls	WB	1982
	Carlene Carter	C'est Bon	Epic	1983
w. Nick Lowe	Elvis Costello	Trust	F-Beat/CBS	1981
w. C. Jordan	Flamin' Groovies	Jumpin' In The Night	Sire	1979
	Huang Chung	Huang Chung (3 tracks)	Arista	1982
	(Name later changed to Wang Chung for easier pronunciation)			
	Tony Koklin	Time Chaser	Chiswick	1981
	Lene Lovich	Flex	Stiff/Epic	1979
	Nick Lowe	The Abominable Showman	F-Beat/CBS	1983
w. Paul Cobbold	Robert Ellis Orrall	Contain Yourself	RCA	1984
	Photos	The Photos	Epic	1980
	The Rumour	Frogs, Sprouts, Clogs and Krauts	Stiff	1978
	Shakin' Pyramids	Celts and Cobras	Virgin	1982
w. A.McKenzie	Shakin' Pyramids	Rock 'n' Roll Records	Epic(USA)	1982
w. E.Costello	Squeeze	East Side Story	A&M	1980
	Undertones	Undertones	Sire	1979
	Undertones	Hypnotised	Sire	1980
	Undertones	Positive Touch	Ardeck	1981
	Undertones	The Sin Of Pride	Ardeck	1983

B020 Jeff Beck

Artist	Title	Label	Year
Upp	Upp	Epic	1975
Upp	This Way Up	Epic	1976
(Proteges of Beck, sometimes toured with him.)			

B021 Walter Becker and Donald Fagen (of Steely Dan)

Artist	Title	Label	Year
Pete Christlieb and Warne Marsh	Quintet	WB	1978

B022 Barry Beckett

	Artist	Title	Label	Year
	Greg Adams	Runaway Dreams	Attic	1979
	Joan Baez	Honest Lullaby	Portrait	1979
w. J.Wexler	Steve Bassett	Steve Bassett	CBS	1984
w. J.Johnson	Blackfoot	Flyin'	Atco	1975
w. B.Seidel	Billy Burnette	Gimme You	CBS	1981
w. R.Hawkins	Canned Heat	One More River To Cross	Atlantic	1974
w. J.Wexler	Kim Carnes	Sailin'	A&M	1976
	Beth Nielsen Chapman	Hearing It First	Capitol	1980
	Bob Crewe	Motivation	Elektra	1977
w. J.Wexler	Dire Straits	Communique	Vert/WB	1979
w. J.Wexler	Bob Dylan	Slow Train Coming	CBS	1979
w. J.Wexler	Bob Dylan	Saved	CBS	1980
w. P.Yarrow	Edwards and Ralph	Edwards and Ralph	Ariola	1978
w. J.Wexler	Jose Feliciano	Sweet Soul Music	P.Stock	1976
w. J.Johnson	Levon Helm	Levon Helm	Capitol	1982
	Eddie Hinton	Very Extremely Dangerous	Capricorn	1978

	Lenny Le Blanc	*Breakthrough*	Capitol	1981
w. R.Hawkins	Buzzy Linhart	*Pussycats Can Go Far*	Atco	1974
w. P.Yarrow	Mary McGregor	*Torn Between Two Lovers*	Ariola	1978
	Delbert McClinton	*The Jealous Kind*	Capitol	1980
	Delbert McClinton	*Plain From The Heart*	Capitol	1981
w. J.Wexler	McGuinn Hillman	*McGuinn Hillman*	Capitol	1980
	Frankie Miller	*Standing On The Edge*	Capitol	1982
	Muscle Shoals Horns	*Born To Get Down*	Bang	1976
	Muscle Shoals Horns	*Doin' It To The Bone*	Ariola-Am	1977
w. J.Wexler	Tony Orlando	*Tony Orlando*	Elektra	1978
w. R.Hawkins	Orleans	*Orleans*	ABC	1973
	John Prine	*Storm Windows*	Asylum	1980
w. J.Wexler	Sandford Townsend Band	*The Sandford Townsend Band*	WB	1976
w. J.Wexler	Santana	*Havana Moon*	CBS	1983
w. J.Johnson	Russell Smith	*Russell Smith*	Capitol	1982
w. Phil Ramone	Phoebe Snow	*Against The Grain*	CBS	1978
	Southside Johnny	*The Jukes*	Mercury	1979
w. J.Wexler	Mavis Staples	*Oh, What A Feeling*	WB	1979
w. J.Wexler	Staples Singers	*Unlock Your Mind*	WB	1978
	Starland Vocal Band	*4 x 4*	Windsong	1980
	Kate Taylor	*It's In There*	CBS	1979
	Jerry Jeff Walker	*Reunion*	S.Coast	1981

(As part of the Muscle Shoals Rhythm Section - Barry Beckett, Pete Carr, Jimmie Johnson, David Hood and Roger Hawkins — I include the following albums.)

	Bob Seger	*Night Moves (4 tracks)*	Capitol	1976
	Bob Seger	*Stranger In Town (5 tracks only)*	Capitol	1978
	Bob Seger	*Against The Wind*	Capitol	1980
	Paul Simon	*There Goes Rhymin' Simon (5 tracks)*	CBS	1973
	Bobby Womack	*Communication*	UA	1971
	Bobby Womack	*Understanding (6 tracks)*	UA	1972
	Bobby Womack	*Looking For A Love*	UA	1974

B023 Adrian Belew

	The Raisins	*The Raisins*	Struggle	1983

B024 Pete Bellotte

	Joy Fleming	*The Final Thing*	Atlantic	1979
	Giorgio and Chris	*Love's In You Love's In Me*	GTO	1978
	Gonzalez	*Move It To The Music*	Side/Cap	1979
	Elton John	*Victim Of Love*	Rock/MCA	1979
	Roberta Kelly	*Trouble Maker*	Oasis	1974
	Roberta Kelly	*Zodiac Lady*	Oas/Casab	1977
	Roberta Kelly	*Gettin' The Spirit*	Casab	1978
	Melba Moore	*Burn*	Epic	1979
	Donna Summer	*Love To Love You Baby*	GTO/Oasis	1975
w. G.Moroder	Donna Summer	*A Love Trilogy*	GTO/Oasis	1975
w. G.Moroder	Donna Summer	*Four Seasons Of Love*	GTO/Casab	1976
w. G.Moroder	Donna Summer	*I Remember Yesterday*	GTO/Casab	1977
w. G.Moroder	Donna Summer	*Once Upon A Time*	Casab	1977
w. G.Moroder	Donna Summer	*Live And More*	Casab	1978

w. G.Moroder	Donna Summer	*Bad Girls*	Casab	1979
w. G.Moroder	Donna Summer	*The Wanderer*	Geffen	1980

B025 Bill Belmont

	Country Joe McDonald	*Hold On It's Coming*	Vanguard	1971
	Country Joe McDonald	*Goodbye Blues*	Fantasy	1977
	Country Joe McDonald	*Leisure Sweet*	Fantasy	1979
w. S.Lawrence	Country Joe McDonald	*Child's Play*	Rag Baby	1983

B026 Doug Bennett

	Hawkwind	*Hall Of The Mountain Grill*	UA	1974
	Man	*All's Well That Ends Well*	MCA	1977
	Stiff Little Fingers	*Nobody's Heroes*	Chrysalis	1980
	Stiff Little Fingers	*Hankx!*	Chrysalis	1980
	Stiff Little Fingers	*Go For It*	Chrysalis	1981

B027 Paddy Bergin

	Depressions	*The Depressions*	Barn	1978

B028 Byron Berline

	Stone Mountain Boys	*Stone Mounbtain Boys*	Briar	1974

B029 Bert Berns

	Solomon Burke	*Greatest Hits*	Atlantic	1962
w. Jerry Wexler	Drifters	*Take You Where The Music's Playing*	Atlantic	1965
	Van Morrison	*T.B. Sheets*	Bang	1973
	Freddie Scott	*Are You Lonely For Me*	Joy/Bang	1967

B030 Peter Bernstein

	Cretones	*The Red Line*	Planet	1980
	Cretones	*Snap Snap*	Planet	1981

B031 Alan Betrock

	Richard Hell	*Destiny Street*	ID	1983
	Sneakers	*In The Red*	Car	1978
	Smithereens	*Beauty and Sadness*	L.Ricky	1983

(Alan Betrock is the publisher of New York Rocker which followed on from his TRM magazine. He is also the author of Girl Groups: The Story Of A Sound.)

B032 Martin Birch

	Black Sabbath	*Heaven and Hell*	Vert/WB	1980
	Black Sabbath	*Mob Rules*	Vert/WB	1981
	Blue Oyster Cult	*Cultosaurus Erectus*	CBS	1980
	Blue Oyster Cult	*Fire Of Unknown Origin*	CBS	1981
	Cortinas	*True Romances*	CBS	1978
	Wayne County	*Storm The Gates Of Heaven*	Safari	1978
	Deep Purple	*Stormbringer*	Purple/WB	1974
	Deep Purple	*Come Taste The Band*	Purple/WB	1975
	Deep Purple	*Made In Europe*	Purple/WB	1976
	Electric Chairs (with Wayne County)	*Electric Chairs*	Safari	1978

	Fleetwood Mac	*Mystery To Me*	Reprise	1973
	Fleetwood Mac	*Penguin*	Reprise	1973
	Roger Glover	*Elements*	Polydor	1978
	Iron Maiden	*Killers*	EMI/Harv	1981
	Iron Maiden	*Number Of The Beast*	EMI/Harv	1982
	Iron Maiden	*Piece Of Mind*	EMI/Harv	1983
	Jon Lord	*Sarabande*	Purple	1976
	Mainland	*Exposure*	Christy	1978
	Bernie Marsden	*And About Time Too*	EMI	1979
	Cozy Powell	*Over The Top*	Ari/Poly	1979
	Rainbow	*Rainbow*	Oys/Poly	1975
	Rainbow	*Rising*	Polydor	1976
	Rainbow	*On Stage*	Polydor	1977
	Rainbow	*Long Live Rock And Roll*	Polydor	1978
	Michael Schenker Group	*Assault Attack*	Chrysalis	1982
	Stray	*Saturday Morning Pictures*	Tra/Mer	1971
	Whitesnake	*Snakebite*	UA	1978
	Whitesnake	*Trouble*	UA	1978
	Whitesnake	*Love Hunter*	UA	1979
	Whitesnake	*Ready and Willing*	UA/Mirage	1980
	Whitesnake	*Come And Get It*	UA/Mirage	1981
	Whitesnake	*Live ... In The Heart Of The City*	UA/Mirage	1980
	Whitesnake	*Saints And Sinners*	Liberty	1982
	Whitesnake	*Slide It In*	Lib/Geff	1984

B033 Will Birch

w. John Wood	Any Trouble	*Wrong End Of The Race*	EMI-Amer	1984
	Billy Bremner	*Bash !*	Arista	1984
w. Paul Bass	Howard Werth	*Six Of One and Half A Dozen Of The Other*	Metabop	1982

B034 Chris Blackwell

	B-52's	*B-52's*	Island	1979
	B-52's	*Party Mix*	Island	1981
	Jim Capaldi	*Oh How We Danced*	Island	1972
	Jim Capaldi	*Short Cut Draw Blood*	Island	1975
w. Alex Sadkin	Joe Cocker	*Sheffield Steel*	Island	1982
	soundtrack	*Countryman*	Island	1982
	Derek And Clive	*Derek And Clive Live*	Island	1976
	Free	*Free*	Island	1977
	Claire Hammill	*One House Left Standing*	Island	1971
	Mike Harrison	*Smokestack Lightning*	Island	1972
w. Alex Sadkin	Grace Jones	*Warm Leatherette*	Island	1972
w. Alex Sadkin	Grace Jones	*Nightclubbing*	Island	1981
w. Alex Sadkin	Grace Jones	*Living My Life*	Island	1983
	Bob Marley and The Wailers	*Natty Dread*	Island	1974
w. Steve Smith	Bob Marley and The Wailers	*Live*	Island	1975
w. Jack Nuber	Bob Marley and The Wailers	*Babylon By Bus*	Island	1978
	Nirvana	*The Story Of Simon Simopath*	Island	1967

w. Alex Sadkin	Plastics	*Come Back*	Initiation	1981
	John Martyn	*One World*	Island	1978
	Reebop Kwaku Baah	*Reebop*	Island	1972
w. A.Toussaint	Jess Roden	*Jess Roden*	Island	1974
	Spencer Davis Group	*1st Album*	Fontana	1965
	Spencer Davis Group	*2nd Album*	Fontana	1966
	Spencer Davis Group	*Autumn '66*	Fontana	1966
w. C.Stainton	Spooky Tooth	*The Last Puff*	Island	1970
	soundtrack	*They Called It An Accident*	Island	1983
w. A.Sadkin	Third World	*Journey To Addis*	Island	1978
w. A.Sadkin	Third World	*Prisoner In The Street*	Island	1980
	Toots and The Maytals	*Just Like That*	Island	1980
w. S.Winwood	Traffic	*John Barleycorn Must Die*	Island	1970
	Traffic	*When The Eagle Flies*	Isl/Asy	1974
w. Bob Marley	Wailers	*Catch A Fire*	Island	1973
w. Bob Marley	Wailers	*Burnin'*	Island	1973
w. Mark M.Mundy	Steve Winwood	*Steve Winwood*	Island	1977

B035 Nick Blagona

	April Wine	*Harder Faster*	Capitol	1979
	Teaze	*Body Shots*	Aquarius	1980
	Nanette Workman	*Nanette Workman*	Atlantic	1974

B036 John Blair

	Jon & The Niteriders	*Surf Beat '80*	Bomp	1980

(Blair is a noted surf writer and publisher of the definitive discography on the subject.)

B037 Robert Blamire

	Scars	*Author, Author*	Pre	1981

B038 Bob Blank

	Aural Exciters	*Spooks In Space*	Ze	1979
	Eight Eyed Spy	*Eight Eyed Spy*	Fetish	1981
	Lydia Lunch	*Queen Of Siam*	Ze	1980
	Necessaries	*Big Sky*	Sire	1981
	Necessaries	*Event Horizon*	Sire	1982
	T. Ski Valley	*In The 80's*	Capo	1981

B039 Allan Blazek

w. Bill Szymczyk	Elvin Bishop	*Struttin' My Stuff*	Capricorn	1975
	Elvin Bishop Band	*Hometown Boy Makes Good*	Capricorn	1976
	Elvin Bishop	*Live-Raisin' Hell*	Capricorn	1977
	Martin Briley	*Fear Of The Unknown*	Mercury	1981
	Fandango	*One Night Stand*	RCA	1979
w.Jim Ed Norman	Glenn Frey	*No Fun Aloud*	Asylum	1982
w. Bill Szymczyk	J.Geils Band	*Hotline*	Atlantic	1974
	J.Geils Band	*Blow Your Face Out*	Atlantic	1976
w. Glenn Frey	Jack Mack and The Heart Attack	*Cardiac Party*	Full Moon	1982
	Outlaws	*Bring It Back Alive*	Arista	1978
	REO Speedwagon	*This Time We Mean It*	Epic	1975
	Snail	*Flow*	Cream	1979

w. Bill Szymczyk and Ed Mashal	Michael Stanley Band	*Stagepass*	Epic	1977
	Mickey Thomas	*As Long As You Love Me*	MCA	1977
w. Bill Szymczyk	Mickey Thomas	*Alive Alone*	Elektra	1981

B040 Ron Bledsoe

	David Allan Coe	*Once Upon A Rhyme*	CBS	1974
	David Allan Coe	*Long Haired Redneck*	CBS	1976
	David Allan Coe	*Tattoo*	CBS	1977
w. Troy Seals	Turley Richards	*West Virginia Superstar*	CBS	1976
	Earl Scruggs	*Duelling Banjos*	CBS	1973
	Earl Scruggs Revue	*Live At Kansas State*	CBS	1972
	Earl Scruggs Revue	*The Earl Scruggs Revue*	CBS	1973.
	Earl Scruggs Revue	*Where The Lilies Bloom (soundtrack album)*	CBS	1974
	Earl Scruggs Revue	*Rockin' Cross The Country*	CBS	1974
	Earl Scruggs Revue	*Volume 2*	CBS	1976
	Earl Scruggs Revue	*Family Portrait*	CBS	1976
	Earl Scruggs Revue	*Strike Anywhere*	CBS	1977
	Earl Scruggs Revue	*Super Jammin'*	CBS	1984

B041 Mike Bloomfield

w. N.Dayron	Barry Melton	*Melton,Levy and The Day Brothers*	CBS	1972
N.Gravenites	various artists	*Mill Valley Jam Session*	Polydor	1972

B042 Dave Bloxham

	Ducks De Luxe	*Ducks De Luxe*	RCA	1974
	G.T. Moore and The Reggae Guitars	*G.T. Moore and The Reggae Guitars*	Charisma	1974

B043 Barry Blue

w. Swain & Jolley	Bananarama	*Deep Sea Skiving*	Lon/Poly	1983
	Dana	*The Girl Is Back*	GTO/Epic	1979
	Dead End Kids	*Breakout*	CBS	1977
	Dooleys	*Secrets*	GTO	1981
	Heatwave	*Central Heating*	GTO/Epic	1978
	Heatwave	*Current*	Epic	1982
	Javaroo	*Out*	Capitol	1980
	Cheryl Lynn	*In Love*	CBS	1979
	Moon	*Turning The Tide*	Epic	1977

B044 Richard Bock

	Laurindo Almeida	*Brazilliance*	Pausa	1982
	Chet Baker	*Trumpet Artistry*	World Pac	1958
	Lord Buckley	*Far Out Humour*	World Pac	1959
	Kentucky Colonels	*Appalachian Swing*	World Pac	1960
	Gerry Mulligan	*The Genius Of Gerry Mulligan*	World Pac	1960
	Joe Pass	*Catch Me*	World Pac	1963
	Ravi Shankar	*In Concert*	World Pac	1962
	Gerald Wilson's Orchestra	*The Golden Sword*	World Pac	1984

B045 Neil Bogart

? and The Mysterians	*96 Tears*		Cameo-P	1966

B046 Ed Bogas

Clover	*Clover*	UA	1969
Clover	*Fourty-Niner*	UA	1970

(Has recently moved into soundtrack work. Notables include "Race For Your Life, Charlie Brown" and "Flashbeagle", of interest to all Snoopy fans.)

B047 John C.Bohannon

Flying Burritos	*Flying High*	JB	1978

B048 C. Bonafede

w. D.Bello	Buckinghams	*Kind Of A Drag*	USA	1967

B049 Christopher Bond

Daryl Hall and John Oates	*Daryl Hall and John Oates*	RCA	1975
Daryl Hall And John Oates	*Bigger Than Both Of Us*	RCA	1976
Daryl Hall and John Oates	*Beauty On A Back Street*	RCA	1977
Richie Havens	*Mirage*	A&M	1977
Richard Kerr	*Welcome To The Club*	A&M	1978
Klaatu	*Endangered Species*	Capitol	1980
Maria Muldaur	*Southern Winds*	WB	1978
Sons Of Champlin	*Loving Is Why*	Ariola-Am	1977
The States	*The States*	Chrysalis	1979
Gregg Sutton	*Soft As A Sidewalk*	CBS	1979

(Formerly a member of The Pets and KGB.)

B050 Tony Bongiovi

w. Jack Douglas	Aerosmith	*Rock In A Hard Place*	CBS	1982
	Balance	*Breaking Away*	CBS	1981
w. Lance Quinn	Bon Jovi	*Bon Jovi*	Mercury	1984
w. Lance Quinn	Cindy Bullens	*Desire Wire*	UA	1978
w. Lance Quinn	Carlene Carter	*Two Sides To Every Woman*	WB	1979
	DCA Experience	*Bicentennial Gold*	P.Stock	1976
w. Lance Quinn	Electrics	*State Of Shock*	Capitol	1981
w. Lance Quinn	Johnny's Dance Band	*Love Wounds Flesh Wounds*	Windsong	1978
w.Meco Monardo and Jay Ellis	Gloria Gaynor	Never Can Say Goodbye	MGM	1975
w. Alan Douglas	Jimi Hendrix	*Crash Landing*	Poly/Rep	1975
w. Alan Douglas	Jimi Hendrix	*Midnight Lightning*	Poly/Rep	1976
w. Meco and Harold Wheeler	Trini Lopez	*Transformed By Time*	Pye	1978
w. Harold Wheeler	Meco	*Star Wars and Other Galactic Funk*	RCA	1977
w. Harold Wheeler	Meco	*Adventures Of Every Kind*	RCA	1978
	Meco	*The Wizard Of Oz Kind*	RCA	1978
			RCA	1978
w. Harold Wheeler	Meco	*Superman and Other Galactic Heroes*	RCA/Casab	1979

33

w. Lance Quinn	Meco	Music From The Empire Strikes Back	RSO	1980
w. Lance Quinn	Meco	Star Wars Christmas Album	RSO	1980
w. D. Levine	Meco	Swingtime's Greatest Hits	Arista	1982
w. Lance Quinn	Meco	Pop Goes The Movies	Arista	1982
w. Lance Quinn	Orphan	Lonely At Night	Portrait	1983
w. Tony Erdelyi	Ramones	The Ramones Leave Home	Sire	1977
	Ramones	Rocket To Russia	Sire	1977
w. Bob Clearmountain	Rezillos	Can't Stand The Rezillos	Sire	1978
w. Meco Monardo	Samantha Sang	Samantha Sang	UA	1979
w. Lance Quinn & B. Clearmountain	Jorge Santana	Jorge Santana	Tomato	1978
w. Meco Monardo	Marlena Shaw	Take A Bite	CBS	1979
w. Lance Quinn	Sylvain Sylvain	Sylvain Sylvain	RCA	1980
w. Lance Quinn	Talking Heads	77	Sire	1977
w. Lance Quinn & B. Clearmountain	Tuff Darts	Tuff Darts	Sire	1978

B051 Simon Boswell

	Mark Andrews and The Gents	Big Boy	A&M	1980
	Crooks	Just Released	Blueprint	1980
	Live Wire	No Fright	A&M	1980
	Live Wire	Changes Made	A&M	1981
	Nine Below Zero	Third Degree	A&M	1982

B052 Bruce Botnick

	Butts Band	The Butts Band	Blue Thumb	1974
	soundtrack	Caddyshack	CBS	1980
	Paul Collins Beat	Paul Collins Beat	CBS	1979
w. Jack Nitzsche	Crazy Horse	Crazy Horse	Reprise	1971
	Doors	L.A. Woman	Elektra	1971
	Doors	Other Voices	Elektra	1971
	Les Dudek	Say No More	CBS	1977
	soundtrack	E.T.	MCA	1982
	Laughing Dogs	Laughing Dogs	CBS	1979
	Kenny Loggins	Alive	CBS	1980
	Kenny Loggins	High Adventure	CBS	1982
w. Arthur Lee	Love	Forever Changes	Elektra	1967
	Ray Manzarek	The Golden Scarab	Mercury	1974
	Dave Mason	Split Coconut	CBS	1975
	Eddie Money	Eddie Money	CBS	1978
	Eddie Money	Life For The Taking	CBS	1978
	MC5	Kick Out The Jams	Elektra	1969
	Joe Perry Project	I've Got The Rock And Rolls Again	CBS	1982
	Ross	The Pit And The Pendulum	RSO	1974
	Janne Schaffer	Earmeal	CBS	1979
	Ben Sidran	Feel Your Groove	Capitol	1971
	Ben Sidran	I Lead A Life	BlueThumb	1972
	Ben Sidran	Puttin' In Time On Planet Earth	BlueThumb	1973

Ben Sidran	*Don't Let Go*	BlueThumb	1974
Starwood	*Starwood*	CBS	1977
soundtrack	*Twilight Zone*	WB	1983
soundtrack	*Under Fire*	WB	1983
various artists	*California Jam 2*	CBS	1978
Tony Williams and Lifetime	*Believe It*	CBS	1976
Tony Williams and Lifetime	*Million Dollar Legs*	CBS	1976

B053 Dennis Bovell (a.k.a. Bluebeard)

Linton Kwesi Johnson	*Making History*	Island	1984
w. Martin Hayles Orange Juice	*Texas Fever*	Polydor	1984
The Pop Group	*Y*	Radar	1979
Slits	*Cut*	Isl/Ant	1979
Slits	*Return Of The Giant Slits*	CBS	1981
Thompson Twins	*In The Name Of Love (one track only)*	Hansa	1981

(Dennis Bovell is also a respected recording artist in his own right. His reggae productions are numerous and cannot be listed at this time.)

B054 Jimmy Bowen

Bellamy Brothers	*Strong Weakness*	Elek-Curb	1982
Delaney Bramlett and Blue Diamond	*Giving Birth To A Song*	MGM	1975
w. R.Ruff Delaney Bramlett	*Class Reunion*	Prodigal	1977
Tom Bresh	*Portrait*	ABC	1978
Glen Campbell	*Glen Travis Campbell*	Capitol	1973
Glen Campbell	*I Knew Jesus Before He Was A Star*	Capitol	1973
Glen Campbell	*Reunion*	Capitol	1975

(The reunion referred to was between Campbell and his long-time songwriter Jimmy Webb)

Lee Dresser	*El Camino Real*	Amos	1968
Evergreen Blueshoes	*The Ballad Of Evergreen Blueshoes*	Amos/Lon	1969

(Group featured a pre-Byrds and NRPS Skip Battin)

Crystal Gayle	*Cage The Songbird*	WB	1983
Tompal and The Glaser Brothers	*Loving Her Was Easier*	Elektra	1981
Tompal Glaser	*The Wonder Of It All*	ABC	1978
Merle Haggard	*Now Serving 190 Proof*	MCA	1979
Merle Haggard	*Back To The Barrooms*	MCA	1980
Roy Head	*Tonight's The Night*	ABC	1978
Roy Head	*In Our Room*	Elektra	1979
Johnny Lee	*Hey Bartender*	Full Moon	1983
Johnny Lee	*'Til The Bars Burn Down*	Full Moon	1984
Dean Martin	*The Nashville Sessions*	WB	1983
Tracy Nelson	*Time Is On My Side*	MCA	1976
Jack Nitzsche	*The Lonely Surfer*	Reprise	1967
Eddy Raven	*Desperate Dreams*	Elektra	1981
Mel Tillis	*Are You Sincere*	MCA	1979
Mel Tillis	*Mr. Entertainer*	MCA	1979

	Mel Tillis	*M-M-M-Mel Live*	MCA	1979
	Mel Tillis	*Me And Pepper*	Elektra	1979
	Mel Tillis	*Southern Rain*	Elektra	1980
	West Coast Pop Art Experimental Band	*Volume 3*	Reprise	1976
	Hank Williams,Jnr	*Family Tradition (3 tr)*	Elektra	1979
	Hank Williams,Jnr	*Whiskey Bent And Hell Bound*	Elektra	1979
	Hank Williams,Jnr	*Habits Old and New*	Elektra	1980
	Hank Williams,Jnr	*Rowdy*	Elektra	1981
	Hank Williams,Jnr	*The Pressure Is On*	Elektra	1981
	Hank Williams,Jnr	*High Notes*	Elektra	1982
	Hank Williams,Jnr	*Strong Stuff*	Elektra	1983
	Hank Williams,Jnr	*Man Of Steel*	WB	1983
	Hank Williams,Jnr	*Major Moves*	WB-Curb	1984
w. S.Whipple	Dennis William Wilson	*One Of Those People*	Elektra	1979

(Not to be confused, as one record importer was, with the late Dennis Wilson of the Beach Boys.)

B055 David Bowie

	Carmen	*Fandangos In Space*	R.Z/Dunh	1973
w. Mick Ronson	Dana Gillespie	*Weren't Born A Man (2 tracks only)*	RCA	1973
	Mott The Hoople	*All The Young Dudes*	CBS	1972
	Iggy Pop	*Raw Power*	CBS	1972
	Iggy Pop	*The Idiot*	RCA	1977
	Iggy Pop	*Lust For Life*	RCA	1977
	Iggy Pop	*T.V. Eye-Live*	RCA	1978
w. Mick Ronson	Lou Reed	*Transformer*	RCA	1972

(In addition to these outside productions Bowie has also co-produced the following of his own albums)

w. Ken Scott	David Bowie	*Ziggy Stardust and The Spiders From Mars*	RCA	1972
w. Ken Scott	David Bowie	*Pinups*	RCA	1973
w. Tony Visconti	David Bowie	*Diamond Dogs*	RCA	1974
w. Harry Maslin	David Bowie	*Young Americans*	RCA	1975
w. Harry Maslin	David Bowie	*Station To Station*	RCA	1976
w. Tony Visconti	David Bowie	*Heroes*	RCA	1977
w. Tony Visconti	David Bowie	*Low*	RCA	1977
w. Tony Visconti	David Bowie	*Stage*	RCA	1978
w. Tony Visconti	David Bowie	*Lodger*	RCA	1979
w. Tony Visconti	David Bowie	*Scary Monsters and Super Creeps*	RCA	1980
w. Nile Rodgers	David Bowie	*Let's Dance*	EMI-Amer	1983

B056 Tommy Boyce and Bobby Hart

	Dolenz, Jones, Boyce and Hart	*Dolenz, Jones, Boyce and Hart*	Capitol	1975
	Monkees	*The Monkees*	RCA/Colg	1967
	Louie Shelton	*Touch Me*	WB	1969

(Boyce and Hart recorded four albums together on A&M in their pre-Monkees involvement days.)

B057 Tommy Boyce

w. R.Hartley	Darts	*The Darts*	Magnet	1977

w. R.Hartley	Darts	*Everyone Plays Darts*	Magnet	1978
w. R.Hartley	Late Show	*Snap*	Decca	1979
	Iggy Pop	*Party*	Arista	1981

B058 Franklin Boyd

	Richie Bull	*The World Of Country Music Volume 4*	Decca	1973

B059 Joe Boyd

w. John Wood	The Act	*Too Late At 20*	Hannibal	1981
	Albion Band	*Rise Up Like The Lark*	Harvest	1978
w. John Wood	James Booker	*Junco Partner*	Island	1976
	Vashti Bunyan	*Just Another Diamond Day*	Philips	1968
w. John Wood	Julie Covington	*Julie Covington*	Virgin	1978
	Defunkt	*Thermonuclear Sweat*	Hannibal	1982
	Nick Drake	*Five Leaves Left*	Island	1969
	Nick Drake	*Bryter Later*	Island	1970
	Nick Drake	*Pink Moon*	Island	1972
w. Tod Lloyd	Fairport Convention	*Fairport Convention*	Polydor	1968
	Fairport Convention	*What We Did On Our Holidays*	Island	1969
	Fairport Convention	*Unhalfbricking*	Island	1969
	Fairport Convention	*Liege and Lief*	Island	1969
	Fairport Convention	*Full House*	Island	1970
	Fairport Convention	*Live at the L.A. Troubador*	Island	1976
	Fotheringay	*Fotheringay*	Island	1970
	soundtrack	*Jimi Hendrix*	WB	1973
	Mike Heron	*Smiling Men With Bad Reputations*	Island	1971
	Incredible String Band	*Incredible String Band*	Elektra	1966
	Incredible String Band	*The 5000 Spirits or The Layers Of The Onion*	Elektra	1967
	Incredible String Band	*The Hangman's Beautiful Daughter*	Elektra	1968
	Incredible String Band	*Big Tam and The Wee Huge*	Elektra	1968
	Incredible String Band	*I Looked Up*	Elektra	1970
	Incredible String Band	*Be Glad For The Song Has No Ending*	Island	1970
w. G.Prestopino	Kate and Anna McGarrigle	*Kate and Anna McGarrigle*	WB	1975
	Kate and Anna McGarrigle	*Dancer With Bruised Knees*	WB	1977
	John and Beverley Martin	*Stormbringer*	Island	1970
	John and Beverley Martin	*The Road To Ruin*	Island	1970
	Geoff and Maria Muldaur	*Pottery Pie*	Reprise	1970
	Geoff Muldaur	*Geoff Muldaur Is Having A Wonderful Time*	Reprise	1975
w. L.Waronker	Maria Muldaur	*Maria Muldaur*	Reprise	1974

w. L.Waronker	Maria Muldaur	*Waitress In A Donut Shop*	Reprise	1974
w. L.Waronker	Maria Muldaur	*Sweet Harmony*	Reprise	1976
w. R.Greene	Muleskinner	*Muleskinner*	WB	1974
	Poppie Nonenga	*Poppie Nonenga*	Hannibal	1984
	Richard and Linda Thompson	*Shoot Out The Lights*	Hannibal	1982
	Richard Thompson	*Hand Of Kindness*	Hannibal	1983
w. W.Lynn	Toots and The Maytals	*Reggae Got Soul*	Island	1976

B060 John Boylan

	Association	*The Association*	WB	1969
	Association	*Goodbye Columbus*	WB	1969
	Bear	*Greetings Children Of Paradise*	MGM	1968
	Brewer and Shipley	*ST-11261*	Capitol	1974
w. Tom Scholz	Boston	*Boston*	Epic	1976
	Jeffrey Comanor	*A Rumour In His Own Time*	Epic	1976
	Commander Cody	*Commander Cody and His Lost Planet Airmen*	WB	1975
	Charlie Daniels Band	*Million Mile Reflections*	Epic	1979
	Charlie Daniels Band	*Volunteer Jam V1*	Epic	1980
	Charlie Daniels Band	*Full Moon*	Epic	1980
	Charlie Daniels Band	*Windows*	Epic	1982
	Dillards	*Copperfields*	Elektra	1976
	Michael Dinner	*The Great Pretender*	Fantasy	1974
w. T.Boylan	Dane Donohue	*Dane Donohue*	CBS	1978
	Russ Giguere	*Hexagram 16*	WB	1971
	(Giguere was formerly in The Association)			
	Barry Goudreau	*Barry Goudreau*	CBS	1980
	(Goudreau was the other guitarist in Boston)			
	Great Buildings	*Great Buildings*	CBS	1981
	Dan Hill	*Partial Surrender*	Epic	1981
	Little River Band	*Diamantina Cocktail (4 tracks only)*	EMI/Cap	1977
	Little River Band	*Sleeper Catcher*	EMI/Cap	1978
	Little River Band	*First Under The Wire*	Capitol	1979
w. Frank Rand	Marcy Levy	*Marcella*	Epic	1982
	(Marcy Levy was previously a singer with Eric Clapton)			
	Roger McGuinn & Band	*Roger McGuinn and Band*	CBS	1975
	Michael Murphey	*Lonewolf*	Epic	1978
	Michael Murphey	*Peaks, Valleys, Honky Tonks and Alleys*	Epic	1979
	Danny O'Keefe	*So Long Harry Truman*	Atlantic	1975
	Sharon O'Neill	*Foreign Affairs*	CBS	1983
	Ozark Mountain Daredevils	*Ozark Mountain Daredevils*	CBS	1980
	Pure Prairie League	*If The Shoe Fits*	RCA	1975
	Pure Prairie League	*Two Lane Highway*	RCA	1975
	Quarterflash	*Quarterflash*	Geffen	1981
	Quarterflash	*Take Another Picture*	Geffen	1983
	R.E.O. Speedwagon	*You Can Tune A Piano But You Can't Tuna Fish*	Epic	1978
	(Credited as "executive producer")			

	Linda Ronstadt	*Linda Ronstadt*	Capitol	1972
w. J.D.Souther	Linda Ronstadt	*Don't Cry Now*	Asylum	1973
	Glenn Shorrock	*Victim Of The Peace*	Capitol	1983
	(Singer with the Little River Band)			
w. Jeff Baxter	Livingston Taylor	*Man's Best Friend*	Epic	1980
	Trillion	*Clear Approach*	Epic	1980
	Uncle Jim's Music	*Uncle Jim's Music*	Kapp	1971

B061 Terence Boylan

	Boylan	*Alias Boona*	MGM	1969
	(an early appearance by Walter Becker and Donald Fagen)			
w. John Boylan	Dane Donohue	*Dane Donohue*	CBS	1978
	(Terence Boylan recorded two excellent albums for Asylum in the late 1970s.)			

B062 Alan Brackett

	Randy Meisner	*Randy Meisner*	Asylum	1978
	(Alan Brackett is possibly a pseudonym for another producer with the same initials.)			

B063 Delaney Bramlett

	Elvin Bishop Band	*Rock My Soul*	CBS	1972
	Delaney Bramlett	*Something's Coming*	CBS	1972
	Delaney Bramlett	*Mobius Strip*	CBS	1973
	Eric Clapton	*Eric Clapton*	Poly/Atco	1970
	Delaney and Bonnie	*The Original Delaney and Bonnie*	Elektra	1969
w. J.Miller	Delaney and Bonnie	*On Tour*	Atco	1970
w. Tom Dowd and Jerry Wexler	Delaney and Bonnie	*To Bonnie From Delaney*	Atco	1970
	Delaney and Bonnie	*Motel Shot*	Atco	1971
	Delaney and Bonnie	*Delaney and Bonnie Together*	CBS	1972
	John Paul Hammond	*I'm Satisfied*	CBS	1972
	King Curtis	*Get Ready*	Atlantic	1971
	Bobby Whitlock	*Raw Velvet (1 track)*	CBS	1972

B064 John And Shann Bramley

	Marc Bolan	*Billy Super Duper*	Marc On	1982
	(The producers are also the authors of *Marc Bolan: Illustrated Disgography.*)			

B065 John Brand

	Gene Loves Jezebel	*Promises*	Sit 2	1983
	Magazine	*Play*	Virgin	1980
	Ruts D.C.	*Animal Now*	Virgin	1981

B066 Don Brewer

	Godz	*The Godz*	RCA	1978
	(Brewer sang and played drums with Grand Funk Railroad)			

B067 David Briggs

	Alice Cooper	*Easy Action*	WB	1970
	Grin	*Grin*	Epic/Spin	1971
	Grin	*1 + 1*	Epic/Spin	1972

	Grin	*All Out*	Epic	1972
	Grin	*Gone Crazy*	A&M	1973
	Nicky Hopkins	*The Tin Man Was A Dreamer*	CBS	1973
	Nils Lofgren	*Nils Lofgren*	A&M	1975
	Nils Lofgren	*Cry Tough*	A&M	1976
	Nils Lofgren	*Night After Night*	A&M	1977
	Kathi McDonald	*Insane Asylum*	Capitol	1974
w. Arif Mardin	Willie Nelson	*Shotgun Willie*	Atlantic	1973
	Elvis Presley	*The Elvis Medley*	RCA	1982
w. N.Venet	Murray Roman	*Busted*	UA	1972
	Murray Roman	*Theme For A Blind Man's Movie*	Tetra	1969
	Tom Rush	*Wrong End Of The Rainbow*	CBS	1970
	Bob Ruzicka	*Soft Rocker*	MCA	1973
	Bob Ruzicka	*Cold Hands Warm Heart*	MCA	1973
	Troy Seals	*Now Presenting*	Atlantic	1973
	Spirit	*The 12 Dreams of Dr. Sardonicus*	Epic	1970
	Spirit	*Feedback*	Epic	1971
	Simon Stokes	*Simon Stokes and the Black Whip Thrill Band*	Spin	1973
	soundtrack	*Where The Buffalo Roam*	Backstreet	1980
	Jerry Williams	*Jerry Williams*	Spin	1972

(A Nils Lofgren protege, features Grin as backing group.)

	Neil Young	*Everybody Know This Is Nowhere*	Reprise	1969
	Neil Young	*After The Gold Rush*	Reprise	1970
	Neil Young	*On The Beach (2 tr.)*	Reprise	1974
	Neil Young	*Tonight's The Night*	Reprise	1975
w. Tim Mulligan	Neil Young	*Zuma*	Reprise	1975
w. Tim Mulligan	Neil Young	*American Stars 'n' Bars*	Reprise	1977
w. Tim Mulligan	Neil Young	*Rust Never Sleeps*	Reprise	1979
w. Tim Mulligan and Ben Keith	Neil Young	*Comes A Time*	Reprise	1979
w. Tim Mulligan	Neil Young	*Live Rust*	Reprise	1979
w. Tim Mulligan	Neil Young	*Hawks And Doves*	Reprise	1980
w. Tim Mulligan	Neil Young	*Re-Ac-Tor*	Reprise	1981
w. Tim Mulligan	Neil Young	*Trans*	Geffen	1982

(All the Neil Young albums were also co-produced by Neil Young)

B068 Vic Briggs

	Sean Bonniwell	*T.S. Boniwell*	Capitol	1969

(This is the same T S Bonniwell of Music Machine and "Talk Talk".)

	Danny McCulloch	*Wings Of A Man*	Capitol	1969
	Hilton Valentine	*All In Your Head*	Capitol	1969

(Vic Briggs was a member of the Animals circa 1968)

B069 Wally Brill

	Henry Badowski	*Life Is A Grand*	A&M	1970
	Annabel Lamb	*Once Bitten*	A&M	1983
w. D.Anderle	Annabel Lamb	*The Flame*	A&M	1984

B070 Johnny Bristol

Boz Scaggs	*Slow Dancer*	CBS	1974

(Johnny Bristol is a highly regarded soul producer and also a fine
singer)

B071 Terry Britten

Cliff Richard	*Rock 'n' Roll Juvenile*	EMI	1979

(Released in the USA in 1980 with the title *We Don't Talk Anymore.*)

B A Robertson	*Initial Success*	Asylum	1980
B A Robertson	*Bully For You*	Asylum	1981

B072 David Bromberg

John Hartford	*Aereo-Plain*	WB	1971

(Bromberg is an accomplished recording artist with at least a dozen
albums to his credit, over half of them self-produced)

B073 Gerry Bron

	Bonzo Dog Band	*Gorilla*	Liberty	1967
w. Gus Dudgeon	Bonzo Dog Band	*The Doughnut In Granny's Greenhouse*	Liberty	1968
w. Tony Reeves	Colosseum	*Valentyne Suite*	Vertigo	1969
	Juicy Lucy	*Lie Back And Enjoy It*	Vertigo	1970
	Osibisa	*Welcome Home*	Bronze	1975
	Osibisa	*Ojah Awake*	Bronze	1976
	Osibisa	*Live At The Royal Festival Hall*	Bronze	1977
	Gene Pitney	*Pitney '75 (8 tracks)*	Bronze	1975
	U-Boat	*U-Boat*	Bronze	1977

(U-Boat was formed by Woody Woodmansey, who was Bowie's
drummer during the heady days of 1970-73.)

Uriah Heep	*Salisbury*	Vert/Mer	1970
Uriah Heep	*Very 'Eavy Very 'Umble*	Vert/Mer	1970
Uriah Heep	*Look At Yourself*	Bron/Mer	1971
Uriah Heep	*Demons and Wizards*	Bron/Mer	1972
Uriah Heep	*The Magician's Birthday*	Bron/Mer	1972
Uriah Heep	*Sweet Freedom*	Bron/WB	1973
Uriah Heep	*Live*	Bron/Mer	1973
Uriah Heep	*Wonderworld*	Bron/WB	1974
Uriah Heep	*Return To Fantasy*	Bron/WB	1975
Uriah Heep	*Firefly*	Bron/WB	1977
Uriah Heep	*Innocent Victim*	Bron/WB	1978
Uriah Heep	*Fallen Angel*	Bron/Chry	1978

B074 Harold Bronson

	Acid Casualties	*Panic Stations*	Rhino	1982
w.Richard Foos	Dr. Demento	*Dr. Demento's Dementia Royale*	Rhino	1980
w. Richard Foos	JC & The Brown Bag Blues Band	*JC & The Brown Bag Blues Band*	Rhino	1979
	Wild Man Fischer	*Wildmania*	Rhino	1977
w. Richard Foos	Kazoos Brothers	*Platefull Of Kazoos*	Rhino	1980
	Low Numbers	*Twist Again With The Low Numbers*	Rhino	1970
w. Richard Foos	various artists	*The International Elvis Impersonators Convention*	Rhino	1979

B075 Gary Brooker (of Procol Harum)

	Mickey Jupp	*Juppanese (side 2)*	Stiff	1979

B076 Harvey Brooks

w. John Simon	Electric Flag	*American Music Band*	CBS	1969
	Karen Dalton	*In My Own Time*	Just Sun	1969
	John Hall	*Action*	CBS	1973
w. N. Gravenites	Quicksilver Messenger Service	*Quicksilver Messenger Service*	Capitol	1968

B077 Ian Broudie

	Echo & The Bunnymen	*Crocodiles*	Kor/Sire	1980
	Echo & The Bunnymen	*Porcupine*	Kor/Sire	1983
	TV 21	*A Thin Red Line*	Decca	1981

B078 Michael Brovsky

	Joe Ely	*Live Shots*	MCA	1980
	Joe Ely	*Must Notta Gotta Lotta*	MCA	1981
	Joe Ely	*Hi-Res*	MCA/South	1984
	Ray Wyllie Hubbard & The Cowboy Twinkies	*Ray Wyllie Hubbard & The Cowboy Twinkies*	WB	1975
	Lost Gonzo Band	*Lost Gonzo Band*	MCA	1975
	Lost Gonzo Band	*Thrills*	MCA	1976
	Lost Gonzo Band	*Signs Of Life*	Capitol	1978
	Dave Van Ronk	*Songs For Ageing Children*	Cadet	1973
	James Talley	*Ain't It Somethin'*	Capitol	1977
	Jerry Jeff Walker	*Jerry Jeff Walker*	MCA	1972
	Jerry Jeff Walker	*Viva Terlingua*	MCA	1973
	Jerry Jeff Walker	*Ridin' High*	MCA	1975
	Jerry Jeff Walker	*Walker's Collectibles*	MCA	1975
	Jerry Jeff Walker	*A Good Night For Singing*	MCA	1976
	Jerry Jeff Walker	*A Man Must Carry On*	MCA	1977
	Jerry Jeff Walker	*Contrary To Ordinary*	MCA	1978
	Jerry Jeff Walker	*Jerry Jeff*	Elektra	1978

B079 Stoney Browder, Jnr

	Dr.Buzzard	*Meets King Penett*	RCA	1978
w. Gary Klein	Dr.Buzzard	*Dr. Buzzard Goes To Washington*	Elektra	1979

(Stony Browder, Jnr is the brother of August Darnell of Kid Creole & The Coconuts who evolved from Dr.Buzzard)

B080 David Brown

	Copperhead	*Copperhead*	CBS	1973

B081 John Brown (and Bernie Clarke)

	Aztec Camera	*High Land, Hard Rain*	RT/Sire	1983

B082 Malcolm Brown

	Vivian Stanshall	*Teddy Boys Don't Knit*	Charisma	1971

B083 Steve Brown

	Randy Edelman	*On Time*	Rocket	1982
w. P.Caplin	Haysi Fantayzee	*Battle Hymns For Children*	Regard	1983

	Elton John	*Empty Sky*	DJM	1969

B084 Terry Brown

	Edward Bear	*Edward Bear*	Capitol	1969
	Edward Bear	*Bearings*	Capitol	1970
	Drivers	*Short Cuts*	GRC	1983
	B B Gabor	*B B Gabor*	Bluep	1980
	Rush	*Rush*	Mercury	1974
	Rush	*Fly By Night*	Mercury	1975
	Rush	*2112*	Mercury	1976
	Rush	*Caress Of Steel*	Mercury	1976
	Rush	*All The World's A Stage*	Mercury	1977
	Rush	*Farewell To Kings*	Mercury	1977
	Rush	*Hemispheres*	Mercury	1978
	Rush	*Permanent Waves*	Mercury	1980
	Rush	*Moving Pictures*	Mercury	1981
	Rush	*Exit Stage Right*	Mercury	1981
	Rush	*Signals*	Mercury	1982
	(Mostly co-produced with Rush)			
w. Ken Morris	Surrender	*Surrender*	Capitol	1979
	Toronto	*Head On*	A&M	1981
	Domenic Troiano	*The Joke's On Me*	Capitol	1978
	Max Webster	*Mutiny Up My Sleeve*	Capitol	1978
	Max Webster	*Live Magnetic Air*	Capitol	1980

B085 Jackson Browne

	Jackson Browne	*For Everyman*	Asylum	1973
w. Al Schmitt	Jackson Browne	*Late For The Sky*	Asylum	1974
	Jackson Browne	*Running On Empty*	Asylum	1977
w. Greg Ladanyi	Jackson Browne	*Hold Out*	Asylum	1980
w. Greg Ladanyi	Jackson Browne	*Lawyers In Love*	Asylum	1983
	Greg Copeland	*Revenge Will Come*	Geffen	1982
w. Greg Ladanyi	David Lindley	*El Rayo-X*	Asylum	1981
w. John Hall, Graham Nash and Bonnie Raitt	various artists	*No Nukes*	Asylum	1979
	Warren Zevon	*Warren Zevon*	Asylum	1976
w. Waddy Wachtel	Warren Zevon	*Excitable Boy*	Asylum	1978

B086 Denny Bruce

	Marcia Ball	*Soulfull Dress*	Rounder	1984
	Chris Darrow	*Artist Proof*	Fantasy	1972
	Fabulous Thunderbirds	*Fabulous Thunderbirds*	Chry/Tak	1979
	Fabulous Thunderbirds	*What's The Word*	Chrysalis	1980
	Fabulous Thunderbirds	*Butt Rockin'*	Chrysalis	1981
	John Fahey	*Of Rivers And Religion*	Reprise	1972
	John Fahey	*After The Ball*	Reprise	1973
	Michael Fennelly	*Stranger's Bed*	Mercury	1975
	John Hiatt	*Slug Line*	MCA	1980
	John Hiatt	*Two Bit Monsters*	MCA	1981
w. John Fahey	Leo Kottke	*Mudlark*	Capitol	1971
	Leo Kottke	*Greenhouse*	Capitol	1972
	Leo Kottke	*My Feet Are Smiling*	Capitol	1973
	Leo Kottke	*Dreams, And All That Stuff*	Capitol	1974

	Leo Kottke	*Ice Water*	Capitol	1974
	Leo Kottke	*Chewing Pine*	Capitol	1975
	Leo Kottke	*Leo Kottke*	Chrysalis	1977
	Leo Kottke	*Burnt Lips*	Chrysalis	1978
w. Bart Bishop	Roulettes	*Roulettes*	Takoma	1981
	Colin Winski	*Rock Therapy*	Chrysalis	1980

B087 Lindsey Buckingham

w. Duanne Scott	Walter Egan	*Fundamental Roll*	UA/CBS	1977
w. R.Dashut	Walter Egan	*Not Shy*	Poly/CBS	1978

(All of Walter Egan's albums are of interest to anyone impressed by
Fleetwood Mac records from *Rumours* onwards.)

B088 Buddy Buie

	Atlanta Rhythm Section	*Atlanta Rhythm Section*	MCA	1972
	Atlanta Rhythm Section	*Back Up Against The Wall*	MCA	1972
	Atlanta Rhythm Section	*3rd Annual Pipe Dream*	Polydor	1974
	Atlanta Rhythm Section	*Dog Days*	Polydor	1975
	Atlanta Rhythm Section	*A Rock 'n' Roll Alternative*	Polydor	1976
	Atlanta Rhythm Section	*Red Tape*	Polydor	1976
	Atlanta Rhythm Section	*Underdog*	Polydor	1979
	Atlanta Rhythm Section	*Champagne Jam*	Polydor	1979
	Atlanta Rhythm Section	*Are You Ready*	Polydor	1979
	Atlanta Rhythm Section	*The Boys From Doraville*	Polydor	1980
	Atlanta Rhythm Section	*Quinella*	CBS	1981
	Classics IV	*Spooky*	Imperial	1968
	Classics IV	*Mamas and Papas/Soul Train*	Imperial	1968
	Classics IV	*Traces*	Imperial	1969
	Classics IV	*Song*	Imperial	1970
	Classics IV (with Dennis Yost)	*Classics IV (with Dennis Yost)*	MGM	1973
	Friends and Lovers	*Reach Out Of The Darkness*	MGM	1969
	Billy Joe Royal	*Cherry Hill Park*	CBS	1974
	Stillwater	*Stillwater*	Capricorn	1977
	Stillwater	*I Reserve The Right*	Capricorn	1978
	Swallow	*Swallow*	WB	1973

B089 Peter Bunetta and Rick Chudacoff

	Robbie Dupree	*Robbie Dupree*	Elektra	1980
	Robbie Dupree	*Street Corner Heroes*	Elektra	1981
	Steve Goodman	*High and Outside*	Asylum	1979
	Steve Goodman	*Hot Spot*	Asylum	1980
	Matthew Wilder	*I Don't Speak The Language*	Private	1984
	Lauren Wood	*Cat Trick*	WB	1981

B090 John Burgess

	Roger Cook	*Meanwhile*	Regal Z	1972
	Adam Faith	*Adam*	Parl	1960
	Adam Faith	*Beat Girl*	Columbia	1961
	Adam Faith	*Adam Faith*	Parl	1962
	Adam Faith	*From Adam With Love*	Parl	1963

Adam Faith	For You	Parl	1963
Adam Faith	On The Move	Parl	1964
Adam Faith	Faith Alive	Parl	1965
Freddie and The Dreamers	Freddie and The Dreamers	Columbia	1963
Freddie and The Dreamers	You Were Made For Me	Columbia	1964
Freddie and The Dreamers	Sing Along	Columbia	1965
Freddie and The Dreamers	In Disneyland	Columbia	1966
Freddie and The Dreamers	King Freddy and The Dreaming Knights	Columbia	1967
Philip Goodhand-Tait	Oceans Away	Chrysalis	1976
Manfred Mann	The Five Faces Of Manfred Mann	HMV/Ascot	1964
Manfred Mann	Mann Made	HMV/Ascot	1964
Manfred Mann	Soul Of Mann	HMV/Cap	1967
Peter And Gordon	Peter And Gordon	Columbia	1964
Peter And Gordon	In Touch	Columbia	1964
Peter And Gordon	Peter And Gordon	Columbia	1966
Peter And Gordon	Hurtin' 'n' Lovin'	Columbia	1965
Peter And Gordon	Somewhere	Columbia	1966

B091 Richard James Burgess

Adam Ant	Strip	CBS	1983
Spandau Ballet	Journeys To Glory	Chrysalis	1981
Spandau Ballet	Diamond	Chrysalis	1982

B092 Steve Burgh

David Bromberg	How Late'll Ya Play 'Til	Fantasy	1978
Suzanne Fellini	Heaven	Casab	1980
Steve Forbert	Alive On Arrival	Epic/Nemp	1978
Steve Forbert	Steve Forbert	Epic/Nemp	1982
Steve Goodman	Words We Can Dance To	Asylum	1976
Carolyn Mas	Carolyn Mas	Mercury	1979
Carolyn Mas	Hold On	Mercury	1980

B093 Jean-Jacques Burnel

Taxi Girl	Seppuku	Virgin	1981

B094 T-Bone Burnett

Leo Kottke	Time Step	Chrysalis	1983
Los Lobos	And Time To Dance	RT/Slash	1983

B095 John Burns

Genesis	Live	Charisma	1973
Genesis	Selling England By The Pound	Char/Atco	1973
Genesis	The Lamb Lies Down On Broadway	Char/Atco	1973
Keef Hartley	Lancashire Hustler	Deram	1973
Refugee	Refugee	Charisma	1974
Tyla Gang	Yachtless	Beserkley	1977

B096 Mike Butcher

Black Sabbath	*Sabbath Bloody Sabbath*	Vert/WB	1973
Black Sabbath	*Sabotage*	Vert/WB	1975

B097 Artie Butler

Neil Sedaka	*All You Need Is The Music*	Poly/Elek	1978
Stephen Sinclair	*Sad And Lonely Saturday Night*	MCA	1976

B098 Chris Butler

Waitresses	*Wasn't Tomorrow Wonderful*	Ze	1982

B099 Larry Butler

Calico	*Volume 2*	UA	1976
Roy Clark	*My Music*	MCA	1979
Mac Davis	*It's Hard To Be Humble*	Casab	1980
Raymond Froggatt	*Southern Fried Frog*	Jet	1978
Don McLean	*Chain Lightning*	EMI	1978
Don McLean	*Believers*	EMI	1981
Don McLean	*I Believe In You*	RCA	1982
Tom Rapp	*Sunforest*	B.Thumb	1973
Charlie Rich	*Nobody But You*	UA	1979
Kenny Rogers	*The Gambler*	UA	1979
Kenny Rogers	*Gideon*	UA	1980
Kenny Rogers and Dottie West	*Classics*	UA	1979
Jerry Jeff Walker	*Cow Jazz*	S.Coast	1982

B100 Kenneth Buttrey
w. Elliot Mazer

Area Code 615	*Area Code 615*	Polydor	1969
Leo Kottke	*Balance*	Chrysalis	1979

B101 David Byrne

B-52's	*Mesopotamia*	Island	1982
David Byrne	*The Catherine Wheel*	Sire	1981
Brian Eno/David Byrne	*My Life In The Bush Of Ghosts*	EG	1981
Fun Boy Three	*Waiting*	Chrysalis	1983

B102 Ossie Byrne
w. R.Stigwood

Bee Gees	*1st*	Polydor	1967

B103 Barrie Barlow

Richard Digance	*Commercial Road*	Chrysalis	1979

C001 Robin Geoffrey Cable

Chris De Burgh	*Far Beyond These Castle Walls*	A&M	1975

	Chris De Burgh	Spanish Train and Other Stories	A&M	1976
	Dickies	Dawn Of The Dickies	A&M	1979
	Esperanto	Last Tango	A&M	1975
	Stanley Frank	Play 'Til It Hurts	A&M	1981
	Dana Gillespie	Weren't Born A Man	RCA	1973
	Philip Goodhand-Tait	Philip Goodhand-Tait	DJM	1973
	Hudson Ford	Daylight	CBS	1977
	Krazy Kat	Troubled Air	Phonogram	1978
	William Lyall	Solo Casting	EMI	1976
	Elliot Murphy	Just A Story From America	CBS	1977
	Nilsson	Knillssonn	RCA	1977
	Private Lightning	Private Lightning	A&M	1980
	Sheena And The Rockets	Sheena And The Rockets	A&M	1981
	David Townsend	Making Up The Numbers	Mercury	1978
	Bonnie Tyler	Diamond Cut	RCA	1979
	Eugene Wallace	Dangerous	EMI	1975
	Jimmy Webb	Land's End	Asylum	1974

C002 Ken Caillatt

	Big Wha-Koo	Berkshire	ABC	1978
w. Richard Dashut	Fleetwood Mac	Rumours	WB	1977
w. Richard Dashut	Fleetwood Mac	Tusk	WB	1979
w. Richard Dashut	Fleetwood Mac	Live	WB	1980
w. Richard Dashut	Fleetwood Mac	Mirage	WB	1982

C003 Tony Calder

	Marianne Faithfull	Come My Way	Decca	1965
	Marianne Faithfull	Marianne Faithfull	Decca	1965

C004 John Cale

w. L.Merenstein	John Cale	Vintage Violence	CBS	1971
w. John McClure	John Cale and Terry Riley	Church Of Anthrax	CBS	1971
	John Cale	The Academy In Peril	Reprise	1972
	John Cale	Fear	Island	1974
	John Cale	Slow Dazzle	Island	1975
	John Cale	Helen Of Troy	Island	1972
	John Cale	Sabotage-Live	IRS	1979
	John Cale	Music For A New Society	Ze	1982
	John Cale	Caribbean Sunset	Ze	1984
	Dave Kubinec	Some Things Never Change	A&M	1978
	Nico	Desertshore	Reprise	1971
	Nico	The End	Island	1974
	Patti Smith	Horses	Arista	1975
	Squeeze	Squeeze	A&M	1978
	Stooges	The Stooges	Elektra	1969
	Jennifer Warren	Jennifer	Reprise	1972
	(later to become Jennifer Warnes)			

C005 J J Cale

	Jimmy Rogers	*Gold Tailed Bird*	Shelter	1973
w.Audie Ashworth	Leon Russell	*Hank Wilson's Back*	Shelter	1975

C006 Charles Calello

	American Standard Band	*American Standard Band*	Island	1979
	Shirley Ellis	*The Name Game*	Congress	1966
w. Bob Gaudio	Four Seasons	*Live*	WB	1981
	Richie Havens	*Connections*	Elektra	1980
	Janis Ian	*Who Really Cares*	MGM	1969
	Laura Nyro	*Eli And The Thirteenth Confession*	CBS	1968
w. Sandy Linzer	Odyssey	*Hollywood Party Tonight*	RCA	1978
w.Steve Lawrence	Rex Smith	*Sooner Or Later*	CBS	1979
	Rex Smith	*Forever*	CBS	1979
	Roger Voudouris	*On The Heels Of Love*	Boardwalk	1981

C007 Junior Campbell

	Barbara Dickson	*Answer Me*	RSO	1976

C008 Ron Capone

w. Jim Stewart	Black Oak Arkansas	*Early Times*	Stax	1974
w. Rick Taylor	Blue Steel	*Nothing But Time*	Asylum	1981
w. Butch Stone	Ruby Starr and Grey Ghost	*Ruby Starr and Grey Ghost*	Capitol	1976
w. Butch Stone	Ruby Starr	*Scene Stealer*	Capitol	1976

C009 Larry Carlton

	Larry Carlton	*Singing/Playing*	B.Thumb	1973
	Larry Carlton	*Larry Carlton*	WB	1978
	Larry Carlton	*Live In Japan*	WB	1979
	Larry Carlton	*Strikes Twice*	WB	1980
	Larry Carlton	*Sleepwalk*	WB	1982
	Larry Carlton	*Friends*	WB	1983
	Robert Kraft	*Retro Active*	WB	1980
	Gap Mangione	*Suite Lady*	A&M	1978
	Gap Magione	*Dancin' Is Makin' Love*	A&M	1979
	Vapour Trails	*Vapour Trails*	WB	1979

C010 Pete Carr

	Pete Carr	*Not A Word On It*	Big Tree	1976
	Pete Carr	*Multiple Flash*	Big Tree	1978
	Lenny Le Blanc	*Hound Dog Man*	Big Tree	1976
	Le Blanc and Carr	*Midnight Light*	Big Tree	1978
	Courtland Pickett	*Fancy Dancer*	Elektra	1973
	Sailcat	*Motorcycle Mama*	Elektra	1972

Jack Tempchin	*Jack Tempchin*	Arista	1978
(see also under Muscle Shoals Rhythm Section entry for
Barry Beckett B022)

C011 Fred Carter, Jnr.

Levon Helm	*American Son*	MCA	1980
John Stewart	*Cannons In The Rain*	RCA	1973

C012 J. Carter (works professionally as Carter)

w. R.Landis	Crimson Tide	*Crimson Tide*	Capitol	1978
	Deserters	*Siberian Nightlife*	Capitol	1983
	Sammy Hagar	*9 On A 10 Scale*	Capitol	1976
	Sammy Hagar	*Red*	Capitol	1977
	Sammy Hagar	*Musical Chairs*	Capitol	1978
	Sammy Hagar	*All Night Long*	Capitol	1978
	Sammy Hagar	*Loud And Clear*	Capitol	1980

(*Loud And Clear* is exactly the same album as *All Night Long*, with one extra track added.)

	Motels	*The Motels*	Capitol	1979
	Motels	*Careful*	Capitol	1980
	Prism	*Small Change*	Capitol	1981
	Prism	*Beat Street*	Capitol	1983
	Tonio K.	*La Bomba*	Capitol	1982
	Richard Torrance	*Double Take*	Capitol	1978
	Bob Welch	*French Kiss*	Capitol	1977
	Bob Welch	*Three Hearts*	Capitol	1979
	Bob Welch	*The Other One*	Capitol	1979
	Bob Welch	*Man Overboard*	Capitol	1980

C013 Jack Casady

Jorma Kaukonen	*Quah*	Grunt	1974

C014 Terry Cashman and Tommy West (see also Tommy West)

w. Steve Barri	Cashman and West	*Lifesong*	ABC	1974
	Jim Croce	*You Don't Mess Around With Jim*	Vert/ABC	1971
	Jim Croce	*Life And Times*	Vert/ABC	1972
	Jim Croce	*I Got A Name*	Vert/ABC	1974
	Jim Croce	*Photographs and Memories*	Lifes/ABC	1975
	Jim Croce	*The Faces I've Been*	Lifesong	1975
	Dion	*Born To Be With You*	PSI	1975
	Dion	*Return Of The Wanderer*	Lifesong	1978
	Henry Gross	*Henry Gross*	A&M	1974
	Henry Gross	*Plug Me Into Something*	A&M	1975
	Henry Gross	*Release*	Lifesong	1976
	Henry Gross	*Show Me To The Stage*	Lifesong	1977
	Henry Gross	*Love Is The Stuff*	Lifesong	1978
	William St.James	*A Song For Every Mood*	Probe	1973
	Tommy West	*Hometown Frolics*	Lifesong	1976

C016 Buzz Cason

Buzz Cason	*Buzz Cason*	DJM	1977
Crickets	*Rock Reflections*	UA	1971
Foxx	*The Revolt Of Emily Young*	Decca	1970
Mac Gayden	*Hymn To The Seeker*	ABC	1978
Mac Gayden	*Skyboat*	ABC	1978
Steve Gibb	*Let My Song*	Clouds	1979
Freddy Weller	*Go For The Night*	CBS	1980

C017 Peter Casperson

Jonathan Edwards	*Jonathan Edwards*	Atlantic	1971
Jonathan Edwards	*Honky Tonk Stardust Cowboy*	Atlantic	1972
Jonathan Edwards	*Have A Good Time For Me*	Atlantic	1973
Jonathan Edwards	*Lucky Day*	Atlantic	1974

C018 Tom Catalano

Neil Diamond	*Gold*	Uni	1971
Neil Diamond	*Stones*	MCA	1971
Neil Diamond	*Moods*	Uni	1972
Neil Diamond	*Hot August Night*	MCA	1972
Mary McGregor	*In Your Eyes*	EMI/Ari	1978
Anne Murray	*Keeping In Touch*	Capitol	1976
Helen Reddy	*Love Song For Jeffrey*	Capitol	1974

C019 Fred Catero

Crazy Horse	*Loose*	Reprise	1972
Lamb	*Lamb*	WB	1971
Santana	*Abraxas*	CBS	1970
John David Souther	*John David Souther*	Asylum	1972

C020 Andy Cavaliere

Grand Funk	*Grand Funk Lives*	Full Moon	1981

C021 Felix Cavaliere
w. Arif Mardin

Laura Nyro	*Christmas And The Beads Of Sweat*	CBS	1970
Jimmy Spheeris	*The Original Tap-Dancing Kid*	CBS	1973
Treasure	*Treasure*	Epic	1977

C022 Malcolm Cecil

Steve Hillage	Motivation Radio	Virgin	1977
Billy Preston	*It's My Pleasure*	A&M	1975
Christopher Rainbow	Home Of The Brave	Polydor	1975
Gil Scott-Heron	*Reflections*	Arista	1981
Gil Scott-Heron	*Moving Target*	Arista	1982

C023 Chas Chandler

The Animals	*Before We Were So Rudely Interrupted*	Barn/Jet	1977
Eric Burdon	*Survivor*	Polydor	1977
Buzzards	*Jellied Eels To Record Deals*	Chrysalis	1979

Jimi Hendrix Experience	*Are You Experienced*	Track/Rep	1967
Jimi Hendrix Experience	*Axis Bold As Love*	Track/Rep	1967
Slade	*Play It Loud*	Poly/Cot	1970
Slade	*Slayed*	Polydor	1972
Slade	*Flame (soundtrack)*	Poly/WB	1974
Slade	*Nobody's Fools*	Poly/WB	1976
Slade	*Whatever Happened To Slade?*	Barn	1977
Slade	*Alive Volume 2*	Barn	1978
Top Secret	*Another Crazy Day*	RCA	1981

C024 Mike Chapman

	Altered Images	*Bite*	Epic	1983
	Australian Crawl	*Sons Of Beaches*	EMI-Amer	1982
	Pat Benatar	*In The Heat Of The Night*	Chrysalis	1979
	Blondie	*Parallel Lines*	Chrysalis	1978
	Blondie	*Eat To The Beat*	Chrysalis	1979
	Blondie	*Autoamerican*	Chrysalis	1980
	Blondie	*The Hunter*	Chrysalis	1982
	Blue Rondo A La Turk	*Chewing The Fat*	Virgin	1982
	Danceclass	*Danceclass*	A&M	1982
	Michael Des Barres	*I'm Only Human*	Dreamland	1980
	Rick Derringer	*If I Weren't So Romantic, I'd Shoot You*	Blue Sky	1978
	Exile	*Mixed Emotions*	Rak/WB	1978
	Exile	*All There Is*	Rak/WB	1979
	Agnetha Faltskog	*Wrap Your Arms Around Me*	CBS	1983
	Nick Gilder	*City Nights*	Chrysalis	1978
	Knack	*Get The Knack*	Capitol	1979
	Knack	*...But The Little Girls Understand*	Capitol	1980
	Nervus Rex	*Nervus Rex*	Dreamland	1980
w. P.Coleman	Holly Penfield	*Full Grown Child*	Dreamland	1982
	Suzi Quatro	*If You Knew Suzi*	Rak/RSO	1978
	Suzi Quatro	*Suzi And Other Four Letter Words*	Rak	1979
	Suzi Quatro	*Rock Hard*	Dreamland	1980
	Shandi	*Shandi*	Dreamland	1980
	Smokie	*Midnight Cafe*	Rak/RSO	1976
	Smokie	*Bright Lights and Back Alleys*	Rak/RSO	1977
	Smokie	*The Montreux Album*	Rak/RSO	1978
w. P.Coleman	Spider	*Between The Lines*	Dreamland	1981
	Tanya Tucker	*Tear Me Apart*	MCA	1979

(See entry C026 for albums co-produced with Nicky Chinn.)

C025 Alex Chilton

The Cramps	*Songs The Lord Taught Us*	Illegal	1980

51

C026 Nicky Chinn and Mike Chapman

Mud	*Mud Rock*	Rak	1974
Mud	*Mud Rock 2*	Rak	1975
Suzi Quatro	*Suzi Quatro*	Rak/Bell	1973
Suzi Quatro	*Quatro*	Rak/Bell	1974
Suzi Quatro	*Your Mamma Won't Like Me*	Rak	1975
Smokie	*Pass It Around*	Rak	1975
Smokie	*Chaning All The Time*	Rak	1975
Sweet	*Funny How Sweet CoCo Can Be*	RCA	1971
Sweet	*Desolation Boulevard*	RCA	1974
Sweet	*Strung Up*	RCA	1975

C027 Phil Chapman

w. Jon Astley	Bethnal	*Crash Landing*	Vertigo	1979
w. Jon Astley	Distractions	*Nobody's Perfect*	Island	1980
w. Jon Astley	Carolyn Mas	*Modern Dreams*	Mercury	1981
w. Jon Astley	Sandy McLelland and The Black Line	*Sandy McLelland and The Back Line*	Mercury	1979
	Sandy McLelland	*McLelland*	Action	1981
w. Jon Astley	Pretty Things	*Cross Talk*	WB	1980

C028 Dave Charles

Andy Fairweather-Low	*Mega-Shebang*	WB	1980
Help Yourself	*The Return Of Ken Whaley*	UA	1973
Deke Leonard	*Kamikaze*	UA	1974
Barry Melton	*The Fish*	UA	1976
Neutrons	*Tales From The Blue Cocoons*	UA	1975
Kieran White	*Open Door*	Gull	1975

C029 Sam Charters

Country Joe and The Fish	*Electric Music For The Mind And Body*	Vanguard	1967
Country Joe and The Fish	*Feel Like I'm Fixin' To Die*	Vanguard	1967
Country Joe and The Fish	*Together*	Vanguard	1968
Country Joe and The Fish	*Here We Are Again*	Vanguard	1969
Country Joe McDonald	*Tonight I'm Singing Just For You*	Vanguard	1970
John Fahey	*Requia*	Vanguard	1967
The Frost	*Frost Music*	Vanguard	1969
The Frost	*Early Frost*	Vanguard	1978
Barry Melton	*Bright Sun Is Shining*	Vanguard	1970
Tina and David Meltzer	*Poet Song*	Vanguard	1970
Notes From The Underground	*Notes From The Underground*	Vanguard	1968
Tom Rush	*Blues,Songs,Ballads*	Prestige	1967
Otis Spann	*Cryin' Time*	Vanguard	1968
Eric Von Schmidt	*Eric Sings Von Schmidt*	Tra/Pres	1965

C030 Rick Chertoff

	The A's	The A's	Arista	1977
w. Nick Garvey	The A's	Woman's Got The Power	Arista	1981
	Baby Grand	Baby Grand	Arista	1978
	Baby Grand	Ancient Medicine	Arista	1978
	Breakwater	Splashdown	Arista	1980
	General Johnson	General Johnson	Arista	1976
	Cyndi Lauper	She's So Unusual	Portrait	1983
	Rex Smith	Everlasting Love	CBS	1981

C031 George Chkiantz

	B.B.Blunder	Worker's Playtime	UA	1971
	Hawkwind	In Search Of Space	Liberty	1971
w. G.Gomelsky	Julie Tippetts	Sunset Glow	Utopia	1975

C032 Steve Churchyard

	Cockney Rejects	Power And The Glory	EMI	1981
	Dave Davies	Chosen People	WB	1983
	PM	1 PM	Ariola	1980
	Stranglers	Feline	CBS/Epic	1982

C033 Roy Cicala

	Garland Jeffreys	American Boy And Girl	A&M	1979
	Orleans	Forever	Infinity	1979

C034 Steve Clark

	Tommy Roe	Sweet Pea	ABC	1976
	Tommy Roe	It's Now Winters Day	ABC	1967
	Tommy Roe	Phantasy	ABC	1968

C035 Eddie Clark (of Fastway)

	Tank	Filth Hound Of Hades	Kamaflage	1982

C036 Stanley Clarke

	Roy Buchanan	Loading Zone	Polydor	1977
	Rodney Franklin	Marathon	CBS	1984
	Kent Jordan	No Question About It	CBS	1984

C037 Tony Clarke

	Blue Jays	Blue Jays	Threshold	1975
	Clannad	Legend (Music from Robin Of Sherwood)	RCA	1984
	Four Tops	Nature Planned It	Motown	1972
	Justin Hayward	Songwriter	Decca/Lon	1977
	John Lodge	Natural Avenue	Decca	1977
	Moody Blues	In Search Of The Lost Chord	Deram/Lon	1968
	Moody Blues	On The Threshold Of A Dream	Deram/Lon	1969
	Moody Blues	To Our Children's Children's Children	Threshold	1969
	Moody Blues	A Question Of Balance	Threshold	1970
	Moody Blues	Every Good Boy Deserves Favour	Threshold	1971
	Moody Blues	Seventh Sojourn	Threshold	1972

	Moody Blues	*Octave*	Decca/Lon	1978

(Not to be confused with Tony Clark, Sky's producer.)

C038 Bob Clearmountain

	Bryan Adams	*You Want It You Got It*	A&M	1980
	Bryan Adams	*Cuts Like A Knife*	A&M	1983
w. Chris Gilbey	The Church	*The Church*	Carrere	1981
	The Church	*The Blurred Crusade*	Carrere	1982
	Hall & Oates	*Rock 'n Soul Part 1*	RCA	1983

(This album is a "Best Of" with the addition of two new tracks which Bob Clearmountain produced. He also mixed the sound for Hall & Oates "Rock 'n Soul Live" video release on RCA in 1984)

w. Chris Gilbey	Joey Harris	*Joey Harris and The Speedsters*	MCA	1983
	Garland Jeffreys	*Escape Artist*	Epic	1981
	Garland Jeffreys	*Rock & Roll Adult*	Epic	1981
	Garland Jeffreys	*Guts For Love*	Epic	1982
w. Tony Bongiovi	Rezillos	*Can't Stand The Rezillos*	Sire	1978
w. Tony Bongiovi and Lance Quinn	Jorge Santana	*Jorge Santana*	Tomato	1978
	Silencers	*Rock 'n' Roll Enforcers*	CBS	1980
	G. E. Smith	*In The World*	Mirage	1981
	Michael Stanley Band	*You Can't Fight Fashion*	EMI-Amer	1983
	Narada Michael Walden	*The Dance Of Life*	Atlantic	1979
	Narada Michael Walden	*Victory*	Atlantic	1980
	David Werner	*David Werner*	Epic	1979
	David Werner	*David Werner Live*	Epic	1979

C039 Jack Clement

	Waylon Jennings	*Dreaming My Dreams*	RCA	1975
w. Kevin Eggers	Townes Van Zandt	*Our Mother The Mountain*	Poppy	1969
w. Kevin Eggers	Townes Van Zandt	*Townes Van Zandt*	Tomato	1978
	Doc Watson	*Elementary*	Poppy	1972
	Doc and Merle Watson	*Two Days In November*	Poppy	1972

C040 Doug 'Cosmo' Clifford

	Doug Sahm	*Groovers Paradise*	Atlantic	1974
	Mark Spoelstra	*This House*	Fantasy	1972

C041 George Clinton

w. W.Collins	Bootsy's Rubber Band	*Stretchin' Out*	WB	1976
w. W.Collins	Bootsy's Rubber Band	*Ahh,..The Name Is Bootsy Baby*	WB	1978
w. W.Collins	Bootsy's Rubber Band	*Player Of The Year*	WB	1978
w. W.Collins	Bootsy's Rubber Band	*This Boot Is Made For Fonkin'*	WB	1979
w. W.Collins	Bootsy's Rubber Band	*Ultra Wave*	WB	1980
	The Brides Of Funkenstein	*Funk Or Walk*	Atlantic	1978
	The Brides Of Funkenstein	*Never Buy Texas From A Cowboy*	Atlantic	1979

	George Clinton	*Computer Games*	Capitol	1982
	George Clinton	*You Shouldn't 'Nuff Bit Fish*	Capitol	1984
	Dells	*New Beginnings*	ABC	1978
	Funkadelic	*Funkadelic*	Pye/West	1970
	Funkadelic	*Free Your Mind And Your Ass Will Follow*	Pye/West	1971
	Funkadelic	*Maggot Brain*	Westbound	1971
	Funkadelic	*Cosmic Slop*	Westbound	1973
	Funkadelic	*America Eats Its Young*	Westbound	1973
	Funkadelic	*Standing On The Verge Of Getting It On*	Westbound	1974
	Funkadelic	*Let's Take It To The Stage*	20th/West	1975
	Funkadelic	*Tales Of Kidd Funkadelic*	Westbound	1976
	Funkadelic	*Hardcore Jollies*	WB	1978
	Funkadelic	*One Nation Under A Groove*	WB	1978
	Funkadelic	*Uncle Jam Wants You*	WB	1979
	Funkadelic	*The Electric Spanking*		
w. W.Collins	Godmoma	*Godmoma Here*	Elektra	1981
		Of War Babies	WB	1981
	Eddie Hazel	*Games,Dames And Guitar Thangs*	WB	1977
	Parlet	*The Pleasure Principle*	Casab	1978
w. Ron Dunbar	Parlet	*Invasion Of The Body Snatchers*	Casab	1979
	Parlet	*Play Me Or Trade Me*	Casab	1980
	Parliament	*Osmium*	Invictus	1970
	Parliament	*Up For The Down Stroke*	Casab	1974
	Parliament	*Chocolate City*	Casab	1975
	Parliament	*Mothership Connection*	Casab	1975
	Parliament	*The Clones Of Doctor Funkenstein*	Casab	1976
	Parliament	*Funkentelechy*	Casab	1977
	Parliament	*P.Funk Earth Tour*	Casab	1977
	Parliament	*Motor Booty Affair*	Casab	1978
	Parliament	*Gloryhallastoopid*	Casab	1979
	Parliament	*Trombipulation*	Casab	1980
w. W.Collins	Fred Wesley	*A Blow For You A Toot For Me*	Atlantic	1977
w. W.Collins	Fred Wesley	*Say Blow By Blow Backwards*	Atlantic	1979
	Bernie Worrell	*All The Woo In The World*	Arista	1979
w. Ron Dunbar	Philippe Wynne	*Wynne Jamming*	Uncle Jam	1980
w. W.Collins	Sweat Band	*The Sweat Band*	Uncle Jam	1980

C042 Ed Cobb

	Chocolate Watch Band	*No Way Out*	Tower	1967
	Chocolate Watch Band	*The Inner Mystique*	Tower	1967
	Chocolate Watch Band	*One Step Beyond*	Tower	1967
	Cogic's	*Cogic's*	Nashboro	1984
	Lettermen	*Spin Away*	Capitol	1972
	Liberace	*Mr.Showmanship*	AVI	1978

	100% Whole Wheat	*Ice Fire And Desire*	AVI	1978
	Passion	*Featuring Au Luce*	AVI	1979
	Standells	*Dirty Water*	Tower	1966
	Standells	*Sometimes Good Guys Don't Wear White*	Tower	1966
	Standells	*The Hot Ones*	Tower	1967
w. Gloria Jones	La Verne Ware Singers	*Will You Be Ready*	Nashboro	1983

C043 Chuck Cochran

w. Merle Watson	Doc Watson	*Memories*	UA	1975
w. Garth Fundis	Doc Watson	*Doc And The Boys*	UA	1976

C044 Tommy Cogbill

	Arthur Alexander	*Arthur Alexander*	WB	1972
w. Chips Moman	Box Tops	*Dimensions*	Bell	1969
w. Tom Dowd	Wilson Pickett	*I'm In Love*	Atlantic	1967

C045 Bob Cohen

	Commander Cody and His Lost Planet Airmen	*Commander Cody and His Lost Planet Airmen*	Paramount	1970

C046 Jeffrey Cohen

	Rocky Sullivan	*Illegal Entry*	Rag Baby	1981

C047 Peter Coleman

	Pat Benatar	*Heat Of The Night*	Chrysalis	1979
w. N. Geraldo	Pat Benatar	*Get Nervous*	Chrysalis	1982
	Martin Briley	*One Night With A Stranger*	Mercury	1983
	Nick Gilder	*City Nights*	Chrysalis	1978
	Nick Gilder	*Frequency*	Chrysalis	1979
	Robbie Patton	*Message From Headquarters*	Atlantic	1982
w. Mike Chapman	Holly Penfield	*Full Grown Child*	Dreamland	1980
	Spider	*Spider*	Dreamland	1981
w. Mike Chapman	Spider	*Between The Lines*	Dreamland	1981
	Ravyns	*The Ravyns*	RDM-MCA	1984
	Paul Warren and Explorer	*One Of The Kids*	RSO	1980

C048 Mike Collier

	Downliner Sect	*The Sect*	Columbia	1964
	Downliner Sect	*The Country Sect*	Columbia	1965
	Downliner Sect	*The Rock sect's In*	Columbia	1966

C049 Pat Collier

	Robyn Hitchcock	*Black Snake Diamond Role*	Arm.	1980
	Soft Boys	*Underwater Moonlight*	Arm.	1980
	The Sound	*Shock Of Daylight*	Statik	1984
	Vibrators	*Guilty*	Anagram	1983

C050 Mel Collins

	Alan Bown	*Stretchin' Out*	Island	1971

C051 Peter Collins

	Belle Stars	*The Belle Stars*	Stiff/WB	1982
	Farmers Boys	*Get Out And Walk (2 tracks only)*	EMI	1983
	Nik Kershaw	*Human Racing*	MCA	1984
	Lambrettas	*Beat Boys In The Jet Age*	Rocket	1980
	Matchbox	*Matchbox*	Magnet	1979
	Matchbox	*Midnite Dynamos*	Magnet	1980
	Matchbox	*Rockabilly Rebels*	Mag/Sire	1980
	Matchbox	*Flying Colours*	Magnet	1981
	Musical Youth	*The Youth Of Today*	MCA	1982
	Musical Youth	*Different Style*	MCA	1983
	Piranhas	*The Pirhanas*	Sire	1980
	Roman Holliday	*Cookin' On The Roof*	Jive	1983
	Tygers Of Pan Tang	*The Cage*	MCA	1982
	Tracey Ullman	*You Broke My Heart In Seventeen Places*	Stiff/MCA	1983

C052 Phil Collins

w.Hugh Padgham	Phil Collins	*Face Value*	Virgin/Atl	1981
	Phil Collins	*Hello I Must Be Going*	Virgin/Atl	1982
	Frida (of Abba)	*Something's Going On*	Epic	1982
	John Martyn	*Glorious Fool*	WEA/Duke	1981

C053 William "Bootsy" Collins

	Godmoma	*Godmoma Here*	Elektra	1981
	Sweat Band	*The Sweat Band*	Uncle Jam	1980
	Fred Wesley	*A Blow For You A Toot For Me*	Atlantic	1977
	Fred Wesley	*Say Blow By Blow Backwards*	Atlantic	1979

(All co-produced with George Clinton)

C054 Stuart Colman

	Phil Everly	*Phil Everly*	Capitol	1982
	Billy Fury	*The One And Only*	Polydor	1983
	The Inmates	*Heatwave In Alaska*	WEA	1981
	Jets	*100% Cotton*	EMI	1982
	Pete Sayers	*Cyclone*	C.Roads	1981
	Shakin' Stevens	*Hot Dog*	Epic	1974
	Shakin' Stevens	*This Ole House*	Epic	1980
	Shakin' Stevens	*Shaky*	Epic	1981
	Shakin' Stevens	*Give Me Your Heart Tonight*	Epic	1982

C055 Bobby Colomby

w. Roy Halee	Blood Sweat & Tears	*3*	CBS	1970
	Blood Sweat & Tears	*New Blood*	CBS	1972
w. Roy Halee	Blood Sweat & Tears	*Brand New Day*	ABC	1977
w. Ed Mashal	Henry Gross	*What's In A Name*	Capitol	1980
	Mothers Finest	*Live*	Epic	1979
	Pages	*Future Strut*	Epic	1979
	Tavares	*Supercharged*	Capitol	1980
	T-Connection	*The Game Of Life*	Capitol	1983

C056 Tony Colton

	Artist	Title	Label	Year
	Phil Everly	*Sunset Towers*	Ode	1974
	Yes	*Time And A Word*	Atlantic	1970

C057 Roger Cook

	Artist	Title	Label	Year
	Brown's Home Brew	*Brown's Home Brew*	Bell	1972
	Brown's Home Brew	*Together*	Vertigo	1974
	Chanter Sisters	*Ready For Love*	Safari	1977
	Terry Stamp	*Fatsticks*	A&M	1975

C058 Stu Cook

	Artist	Title	Label	Year
	Roky Erikson and The Aliens	*Roky Erikson and The Aliens*	CBS	1980
	Roky Erickson and The Aliens	*The Evil One*	415	1981
	Explosives	*Restless Natives*	Ready-Go	1983

C059 Alice Cooper

	Artist	Title	Label	Year
w. Dick Wagner	Gentlemen Afterdark	*Gentlemen Afterdark*	G.A.D.	1983

C060 Miles Copeland

	Artist	Title	Label	Year
	Barry Diamond	*Fighter Pilot*	IRS	1983
	Renaissance	*Prologue*	EMI	1972

C061 Jerry Corbitt

	Artist	Title	Label	Year
	Charlie Daniels	*Charlie Daniels*	Capitol	1970
	Don McLean	*Tapestry*	UA	1971

C062 Denny Cordell

	Artist	Title	Label	Year
	Joe Cocker	*With A Little Help From My Friends*	Regal Z/A&M	1969
w. Leon Russell	Joe Cocker	*Joe Cocker*	Regal Z/A&M	1969
w. Leon Russell	Joe Cocker	*Mad Dogs and Englishmen*	A&M	1970
w. Nigel Thomas	Joe Cocker	*Something To Say*	Cube/A&M	1972
	Alan Gerber	*The Alan Gerber Album*	Shelter	1972
	Jim Horn	*Through The Eyes Of A Horn*	Shelter	1972
w. Leon Russell	Freddie King	*Texas Cannonball*	Shelter	1972
	Jesse,Wolf & Whings	*Jesse,Wolf and Whings*	Shelter	1972
w. Leon Russell	Mary McCreary	*Jezebel*	Shelter	1974
	Moody Blues	*The Magnificent Moodies*	Decca	1965
	Move	*The Move*	Regal Zono	1966
	Tom Petty and the Heartbreakers	*Tom Petty and the Heartbreakers*	Shelter	1976
w. Noah Shark	Tom Petty and the Heartbreakers	*You're Gonna Get It*	Shelter	1978
	Procol Harum	*A Whiter Shade Of Pale*	RZ/Deram	1967
	Procol Harum	*Shine On Brightly*	RZ/A&M	1969
	Willis Alan Ramsey	*Willis Alan Ramsey*	Shelter	1972
	Leon Russell	*Leon Russell*	Shelter	1970
	Leon Russell	*Leon Russell and The Shelter People*	Shelter	1971
	Leon Russell	*Carney*	Shelter	1972
	Leon Russell	*Hank Wilson's Back*	Shelter	1973

	Leon Russell	*Leon Live*	Shelter	1973
	Leon Russell	*Stop All That Jazz*	Shelter	1974
	Leon Russell	*Will O' The Wisp*	Shelter	1975
	(All the Leon Russell albums were co-produced by Leon Russell)			
	Ian Whitcomb	*You Turn Me On*	Ember	1973

C063 Ritchie Cordell

w. Glen Kolotkin	Doug and The Slugs	*Music For The Hard Of Thinking*	RCA	1983
w. Kenny Laguna	Tommy James and The Shondells	*Getting Together*	Roulette	1967
w. Kenny Laguna	Tommy James	*In Touch*	Fantasy	1976
w. Kenny Laguna	Joan Jett	*Joan Jett*	Ariola	1980
w. Kenny Laguna	Joan Jett	*Bad Reputation*	Epic/Board	1981
w. Kenny Laguna	Joan Jett	*I Love Rock 'n' Roll*	Epic/Board	1982
w. Kenny Laguna	Joan Jett	*Album*	Epic/MCA	1983
w. Glen Kolotkin	Ramones	*Subterannean Jungle*	Sire	1983
w. Glen Kolotkin	Shrapnel	*Shrapnel*	Elektra	1984
w. Glen Kolotkin	Stompers	*The Stompers*	Boardwalk	1983

C064 Henry Cosby

	Blood Sweat & Tears	*Mirror Image*	CBS	1974

C065 Elvis Costello

	Clive Langer	*Splash (1 track)*	F-Beat	1980
	Mental As Anything	*If You Leave Me Can I Come Too (1 track)*	A&M	1982
	Specials	*The Specials*	Two Tone	1980

C066 John Court

	Paul Butterfield Blues Band	*The Resurrection Of Pigboy Crabshaw*	Elektra	1967
	Paul Butterfield Blues Band	*In My Own Dream*	Elektra	1968
	Electric Flag	*A Long Time Comin'*	CBS	1968
	Electric Flag	*The Trip (soundtrack)*	Sidewalk	1968
	Richie Havens	*Something Else Again*	MGM	1967
	Richie Havens	*Mixed Bag*	MGM	1968
	Ian and Sylvia	*Lovin' Sound*	MGM	1972
	Jim Kweskin Jug Band	*Garden Of Joy*	Reprise	1967
	Gordon Lightfoot	*The Way I Feel*	UA	1967
	Gordon Lighfoot	*Sunday Concert*	UA	1969
w. John Simon	Gordon Lightfoot	*Did She Mention My Name*	UA	1968
	Danny O' Keefe	*American Roulette*	WB	1977
w. A.Grossman	Peter Paul & Mary	*In Concert Volume 1*	WB	1964
w. A.Grossman	Peter Paul & Mary	*In Concert Volume 2*	WB	1964
	David Sanborn	*Taking Off*	WB	1975

C067 David Courtney

	Roger Chapman	*Chappo*	Arista	1979
w. Adam Faith	Roger Daltrey	*Roger Daltrey*	Track/MCA	1973
w. Tony Meehan	Roger Daltrey	*One Of The Boys*	Poly/MCA	1977
	Joe Egan	*Out Of Nowhere*	Ariola	1979
	Joe Egan	*Map*	Ariola	1981
	Adam Faith	*I Survive*	WB	1974

w. Adam Faith	Leo Sayer	*Silverbird*	Chry/WB	1974
w. Adam Faith	Leo Sayer	*Just A Boy*	Chry/WB	1974
w. Russ Ballard	Leo Sayer	*Another Year*	Chry/WB	1975
	Leo Sayer	*Here*	Chry/WB	1979
	Waldorf and Travers	*Night Blindness*	UA	1979

C068 Larry Cox

	Jefferson Starship	*Dragonfly*	Grunt	1974
	Jefferson Starship	*Red Octopus*	Grunt	1975
	Jefferson Starship	*Spitfire*	Grunt	1978

C069 Bob Crewe

	Four Seasons	*Story*	P.Stock	1975
	Mitch Ryder	*Take A Ride*	Bell	1966
	Mitch Ryder	*Sock It To Me*	New Voice	1967
	Mitch Ryder	*Sings The Hits*	New Voice	1967
	Frankie Valli	*Close Up (4 tracks)*	P.Stock	1975
w. Bob Gaudio	Frankie Valli	*Heaven Above Me*	MCA	1980

C070 Steve Cropper

	Ambergris	*Ambergris*	Paramount	1970
	Jeff Beck Group	*The Jeff Beck Group*	Epic	1972
	Cate Brothers	*The Cate Brothers*	Asylum	1975
	Cate Brothers	*In One Eye And Out The Other*	Asylum	1976
	John Cougar	*Nothing Matters And What If It Did*	Riva	1980
w. Duck Dunn	Crimson Tide	*Reckless Love*	Capitol	1979
	Steve Cropper	*With A Little Help From My Friends*	Stax	1971
	Steve Cropper	*Playing My Thing*	MCA	1980
w. Bruce Robb	Steve Cropper	*Night After Night*	MCA	1982
	Ned Doheny	*Hard Candy*	CBS	1976
	Ned Doheny	*Prone*	CBS/Sony	1979
	Yvonne Elliman	*Rising Sun*	RSO	1975
	Jose Feliciano	*Memphis Menu*	RCA	1972
	Jose Feliciano	*Compartments*	RCA	1973
	Jose Feliciano	*For My Love ... And Other Music*	RCA	1974
	Robben Ford	*The Inside Story*	Elektra	1979
	Iron City Houseshakers	*Blood On The Bricks*	MCA	1981
w. M.Masser	Marilyn McCoo and Billy Davis	*Marilyn and Billy*	CBS	1978
	Harry Nilsson	*Flash Harry*	Mercury	1980
	Poco	*From The Inside*	Epic	1971
	John Prine	*Common Sense*	Atlantic	1975
	Otis Redding	*Dock Of The Bay*	Atlantic	1968
	Otis Redding	*The Immortal Otis Redding*	Atlantic	1972
	Mitch Ryder	*The Detroit-Memphis Experiment*	Dot	1970
	Skyking	*Secret Sauce*	CBS	1975
	(featuring the sons of Dave Brubeck)			
	Stuff	*Stuff It*	WB	1979
	Tower Of Power	*We Came To Play*	CBS	1978

C071 David Crosby

Byrds	The Byrds (the famous reunion album.)	Asylum	1973
David Crosby	If I Could Only Remember My Name	Atlantic	1971
Joni Mitchell	Joni Mitchell	Reprise	1968

C072 Christopher Cross
w. Michael Ostin

Alessi	Long Time Friends	Qwest	1982

C073 Rodney Crowell

	Bobby Bare	As Is	CBS	1981
	Roseanne Cash	Right Or Wrong	Ariola	1980
	Roseanne Cash	Seven Year Ache	Ari/CBS	1981
	Roseanne Cash	Somewhere In The Stars	Ariola	1982
	Guy Clark	South Coast Of Texas	WB	1981
	Guy Clark	Better Days	WB	1983
w. Lou Rubin	Johnny Cash, Jerry Lee Lewis, Marty Robbins	Survivors	CBS	1982
w. Craig Leon	Rodney Crowell	But What Will The Neighbours Think	WB	1980
	Rodney Crowell	Rodney Crowell	WB	1981
	Albert Lee	Albert Lee	Polydor	1982
	Sissy Spasek	Hangin' Up My Heart	WB	1983
	Larry Willoughby	Building Bridges	Atlantic	1983

C074 Peter Crowley

Heartbreakers	Live At Max's Kansas City	B.Banq/MKC	1979
The Troggs	Live At Max's Kansas City	MKC	1980
The Victims	Real Wild Child	G.Disc	1979

C075 David Cunningham

Wayne County	Things Your Mother Never Told You	Safari	1979
Flying Lizards	The Flying Lizards	Virgin	1980
Flying Lizards	The Fourth Wall	Virgin	1981

C076 Michael Cuscuna

	Ran Blake	Film Noir	Arista	1980
w. Bob Thiele	John Coltrane	To The Beat Of A. Different Drum	Impulse	1981
	Larry Coryell and Eleventh House	At Montreux	Vanguard	1978
	Cornell Dupree	Teasin'	Atlantic	1979
	Eddie 'Lockjaw' Davis	The Heavy Hitter	Muse	1979
	Dexter Gordon	Homecoming	CBS	1977
	Dexter Gordon	Manhattan Symphonie	CBS	1978
	Dexter Gordon	Great Encounters	CBS	1979
w. Jim Fishel	Dexter Gordon	Gotham City	CBS	1981
	Eddie Jefferson	The Live-liest	Muse	1979
	Garland Jeffreys	Garland Jeffreys	Atlantic	1973
	Eric Justin Kaz	If You're Lonely	Atlantic	1972
	Eric Kaz	Cul-De-Sac	Atlantic	1974
	Steve Lacy	Raps	Adelphi	1975

	Bonnie Raitt	*Give It Up*	WB	1972
w. Bob Thiele	Sonny Rollins	*There Will Never Be Another You*	Impulse	1978
w. Allan Landon	Chris Rush	*The Cosmic Comedy Of Chris Rush*	Atlantic	1973
	Pharoah Sanders and Norman Connors	*Beyond A Dream*	Novus	1981
	Woody Shaw	*Little Red's Fantasy*	Muse	1978
	Woody Shaw	*Stepping Stones*	CBS	1978
	Woody Shaw	*Woody 3*	CBS	1979
	Woody Shaw	*For Sure*	Columbia	1980
	Eric Von Scmidt	*2nd Right, 3rd Row*	Poppy	1972
	Horace Silver	*Sterling Silver*	UA	1979
	Chris Smither	*Don't It Drag On*	Poppy	1972
w. Ron Frangipane	Chris Smither	*I'm A Stranger Too*	Poppy	1973
	Henry Threadgill	*X-75 Volume 1*	Novus	1979

C077 Dick Cuthell

	Rico	*That man is Forward*	Two Tone	1981
	Rico	*Jama Rico*	Two Tone	1982

D001 George Daly

	Boulder	*Boulder*	Asylum	1979
	Pamela Polland	*Pamela Polland*	CBS	1972

D002 Charlie Daniels

	Jerry Corbitt	*Jerry Corbitt*	Capitol	1968
	Jerry Corbitt	*Corbitt*	Polydor	1979
w. N. Wilburn	Ramblin' Jack Elliott	*Bull Durham Sacks and Railroad Tracks*	Reprise	1970
	Youngbloods	*Ride The Wind*	WB	1971
	Youngbloods	*Elephant Mountain*	RCA	1972

D003 Rick Danko

	Bobby Charles	*Bobby Charles*	Bearsville	1972
w. Rob Fraboni	Rick Danko	*Rick Danko*	Arista	1978

D004 August Darnell

	Coconuts	*Don't Take My Coconuts*	EMI-Amer	1983
	Cristina	*Cristina*	Ze	1980
	Elbow Bones and The Racketeers	*New York At Dawn*	EMI-Amer	1984
	Funkapolitan	*Funkapolitan*	Decca	1982
	Gichy Dan	*Beechwood # 9*	RCA	1979
	Kid Creole & The Coconuts	*Off The Coast Of Me*	Ze/Ant	1980
	Kid Creole & The Coconuts	*Fresh Fruit In Foreign Places*	Ze/Sire	1981
	Kid Creole & The Coconuts	*Tropical Gangsters*	Ze	1982
	Kid Creole & The Coconuts	*Doppelganger*	Ze/Sire	1983
	Machine	*Machine*	RCA	1979

D005 Chris Darrow

w. Denny Bruce	Max Buda and Chris Darrow	*Eye Of The Storm*	Takoma	1981
	Guy Carawan	*The Telling Takes Me Home*	Curnon	1972
w.Denny Bruce and Michael O'Connor	Chris Darrow	*Artist Proof*	UA	1970
w. M.O'Connor	Chris Darrow	*Chris Darrow*	UA	1973
w. M.O'Connor	Chris Darrow	*Under My Own Disguise*	UA	1974
	Chris Darrow	*Fretless*	P.Arts	1979
	Chris Darrow	*A Southern California Drive*	W.Bunch	1981
	Toulouse Engelhardt	*Toullusions*	Briar	1975
w. Chester Crill	Kaleidoscope	*Kaleidoscope*	P.Arts	1976
	Maxfield Parrish	*It's A Cinch To Give Legs To Hard Boiled Eggs*	Curnon	1972
w. Chester Crill	Rank Strangers	*The Rank Strangers*	P.Arts	1977

D006 Richard Dashut

	Lindsey Buckingham	*Law And Order*	Mer/Asy	1981
w. L.Buckingham	Walter Egan	*Not Shy*	Poly/Col	1978
	Mick Fleetwood	*The Visitor*	RCA	1981
	Mick Fleetwood's Zoo	*I'm Not Me*	RCA	1983
	Shoes	*Tongue Twister*	Elektra	1981

D007 Ray Davies

	Cafe Society	*Cafe Society*	Konk	1975
	Turtles	*Turtle Soup*	W.Whale	1969

(Ray Davies has produced every Kinks album since Shel Talmy's involvement with the group ended in the sixties.)

D008 Dave Davies

w. John Gosling	Andy Desmond	*Living On A Shoestring*	Konk	1975

D009 Rhett Davies

w. Muff Winwood	After The Fire	*Laser Love*	CBS	1979
	B-52's	*Wild Planet*	Island	1980
w. Muff Winwood	Russ Ballard	*Winning*	Epic	1976
	Camel	*Moon Madness*	Decca	1976
	Camel	*A Live Record*	Decca	1978
	Eno	*Another Green World*	EG	1975
	Eno	*Before And After Science*	EG/Isl	1977
	Eno	*Music For Films*	EG	1978
	Grand Hotel	*Do Not Disturb*	CBS	1979
	Hitmen	*Torn Together*	CBS	1981
	Huang Chung	*Huang Chung*	Arista	1982
	King Crimson	*Discipline*	EG/WB	1981
	King Crimson	*Beat*	EG	1982
	OMD	*Dazzle Ships*	Virgin	1983
	Roxy Music	*Flesh And Blood*	EG/Atco	1980
	Roxy Music	*Avalon*	EG/Atco	1982
	Roxy Music	*The High Road*	EG/WB	1983
	Starjets	*Starjets*	Epic	1979

D010 Clifford Davis

Cliff Bennett	*Cliff Bennett's Rebellion*	CBS	1971
Noel Janus	*Heroes Of The World*	DJM	1977
Danny Kirwan	*Hello There Big Boy*	DJM	1979
Skid Row	*Skid*	CBS	1970

D011 Don Davis

Dells	*The Mighty Mighty Dells*	Chess	1974
Dramatics	*Do What You Wanna Do*	ABC	1976
Dramatics	*Joy Ride*	ABC	1976
Dramatics	*Shake It Well*	ABC	1977
Dramatics	*Watcha See Is Watcha Get*	Stax	1978
Dramatics	*Any Time, Any Place*	MCA	1979
David Ruffin	*So Soon We Change*	WB	1979
David Ruffin	*Gentleman Ruffin*	WB	1980
Skyliners	*The Skyliners*	Tortoise	1978
Johnnie Taylor	*Eargasm*	CBS	1976
Johnnie Taylor	*Rated Extraordinaire*	CBS	1977
Johnnie Taylor	*Ever Ready*	CBS	1978
Johnnie Taylor	*She's Killing Me*	CBS	1979
Johnnie Taylor	*A New Day*	CBS	1980
Robin Trower	*In City Dreams*	Chrysalis	1977
Robin Trower	*Caravan To Midnight*	Chrysalis	1978
Bobby Womack	*Pieces*	CBS	1978

D012 Jesse "Ed" Davis

	Gene Clark	*White Light*	A&M	1972
	Jesse "Ed" Davis	*Jesse Davis !*	Atco	1971
w. A.Galuten	Jesse "Ed" Davis	*Ululu*	Atco	1972
	Jesse "Ed" Davis	*Keep Me Comin'*	Epic	1973
	Jim Pulte	*Out The Window*	UA	1972
	Roger Tillison	*Roger Tillison's Album*	Atco	1971

D013 Paul Davis

James Anderson	*Strangest Feeling*	CBS	1982
Nigel Olsson	*Nigel*	Bang	1979

D014 Spencer Davis

Paul Korda	*Dancing In The Isles*	Janus	1978

D015 Bob Dawson

Artful Dodger	*Rave On*	Ariola	1980
Rosslyn Mountain Boys	*The Rosslyn Mountain Boys*	Adelphi	1976

D016 Norman Dayron

Mike Bloomfield	*Analine*	Takoma	1977
Mike Bloomfield	*Count Talent and The Originals*	TK	1978
Mike Bloomfield	*Between The Hard Place And The Ground*	Takoma	1979
Mike Bloomfield	*Living In The Fast Lane*	Waterhouse	1980

Mike Bloomfield	*Cruising For A Bruising*	*Takoma*	1981
Mike Bloomfield and	*Mike Bloomfield and*		
Woody Harris	*Woody Harris*	K.Mule	1979
Howlin' Wolf	*London Session*	RSR	1972
Barry Melton	*Melton,Levy and The*		
	Day Brothers	CBS	1972
Robert Nighthawk	*Live On Maxwell Street*	Rounder	1980
various artists	*Chicago Breakdown*	Takoma	1980
Zeet Band	*Moogie Woogie*	Chess	1970

D017 Richard De Bois

Jan Akkerman	*Jan Akkerman*	Atlantic	1978
Jan Akkerman	*Live*	Atlantic	1978
Jan Akkerman	*3*	Atlantic	1979
Jan Akkerman and	*Jan Akkerman and*		
Kaz Lux	*Kaz Lux*	Atlantic	1977

D018 Nick De Caro

Roberto Carlos	*Roberto Carlos*	CBS	1981
Mac Davis	*Fantasy*	CBS	1978
Helen Reddy	*We'll Sing In The*		
	Sunshine	Cap	1978
Samantha Sang	*Emotion*	P.Stock	1978
Livingston Taylor	*Three-Way Mirror*	Epic	1978

D019 Doug Decker

John Fahey	*Old Fashioned Love*	Takoma	1975
Bola Sete	*Ocean Lost Lake Arts*	Takoma	1972

D020 Bert De Coteaux

Bert De Coteaux	*Bert De Coteaux Plays A*		
	Stevie Wonder Songbook	RCA	1976
Dr.Feelgood	*Sneakin' Suspicion*	UA	1977
Gary Glitter	*G.G.*	Bell	1975
Albert King	*Truckload Of Lovin'*	RCA	1976
Ben E. King	*I Had A Love (side 2)*	Atlantic	1976
Ben E. King	*Supernatural*	Atlantic	1975
Linda Lewis	*A Tear And A Smile*	Epic	1983
Ramsey Lewis	*Tequila Mockingbird*	CBS	1977
Ramsey Lewis	*Love Notes*	CBS	1977
Les McCann	*Hustle To Survive*	Atlantic	1975
Manhattans	*Love Talk*	CBS	1979
w. Tony Sylvester Sister Sledge	*Circle Of Love*	Atlantic	1975
Lonnie Liston Smith	*Loveland*	CBS	1978
Lonnie Liston Smith	*Exotic Mysteries*	CBS	1978
Lonnie Liston Smith	*A Song For Children*	CBS	1979

D021 Dave Dee

Fats Domino	*Hello Josephine*	Atlantic	1974
Heavy Metal Kids	*Heavy Metal Kids*	Atlantic	1974

D022 Sean Delaney

Kiss	*Double Platinum*	Casab	1978
Gene Simmons	*Gene Simmons*	Casab	1978
Toby Beau	*Toby Beau*	RCA	1978

D023 John Delgatto

	Kentucky Colonels	*Livin' In The Past*	Tak-Briar	1975
w. Gene Parsons	Nashville West	*Nashville West*	Sierra	1975
w. Marley Brant	Gram Parsons and The Fallen Angels	*Live 1973*	Sierra	1982
	Wayne Stewart	*Aspen Skyline*	Briar	1979
	Scotty Stoneman	*Live In L.A. - 1965*	Sierra	1978
	various artists	*Flat Picking Guitar Festival*	K.Mule	1976

D024 Richard Delvy

A.B. Skhy	*A.B.Skhy*	MGM	1969
Challengers	*The Challengers Go Sidewalk Surfing*	Triumph	1966
Challengers	*Wipe Out*	Voc/GNP	1967
Challengers	*Vanilla Funk*	GNP	1970
Colours	*Colours*	Dot	1969
Good Guys	*Sidewalk Surfing*	GNP	1966
Hamilton Streetcar	*Hamilton Streetcar*	Dot	1970
Dick Monda	*Truth, Lies, Magic and Faith*	MGM	1970

D025 Greg Dempsey

Kathy Dalton	*Amazin'*	DiscReet	1973

D026 Jerry Dennon

Kingsmen	*Louie Louie*	Wand	1964
Kingsmen	*Volume 2*	Wand	1964
Kingsmen	*Volume 3*	Wand	1965
Kingsmen	*On Campus*	Wand	1965
Danny O'Keefe	*Seattle Tapes 1966*	First Am	1977
Sonics	*Original Northwest Punk*	First Am	1977
Ian Whitcomb	*You Turn Me On*	Ember	1973

D027 Ed Denson

Duck Baker	*When You Wore A Tulip*	K.Mule	1977
Robbie Basho	*Seal Of The Blue Lotus*	Takoma	1965
John Fahey	*Guitar Volume 4*	Takoma	1966
Nick Katzman	*Panic When The Sun Goes Down*	K.Mule	1977
Dale Miller	*Guitarists Choice*	K.Mule	1977
Chief O'Neal	*Chief O'Neals Favourite Melodies*	K.Mule	1977
Fred Sokolow	*Bluegrass Banjo Inventions*	K.Mule	1977
various artists	*A Tribute To John Fahey*	K.Mule	1977
various artists	*Flat Picking Guitar Festival*	K.Mule	1976

D028 Rick Derringer

Weird Al Jankovic	*In 3-D*	Scotti	1984

D029 Jimmy Destri

Joey Wilson	*Going Up*	Modern	1980
various artists	*Marty Thau Presents 2 x 5*	Jem	1980

D030 Don De Vito

Bob Dylan	*Desire*	CBS	1975`
Bob Dylan	*Hard Rain*	CBS	1976
Bob Dylan	*Street Legal*	CBS	1978
Bob Dylan	*At Budokan*	CBS	1978
Roger McGuinn	*Thunderbyrd*	CBS	1977
Topaz	*Topaz*	CBS	1977

(Topaz featured Rob Stoner and other Dylan honchos.)

D031 Jeff Dexter

w.Ian Samwell	America	*America*	WB	1971
w.Ian Samwell	Isaac Guillory	*Isaac Guillory*	Atlantic	1974
w. Ray Singer	Peter Sarstedt	*Tall Tree*	WB	1975

D032 Rob Dickins

Deaf School	*Don't Stop The World*	WB	1976
Deaf School	*2nd Honeymoon*	WB	1976
Shanghai	*Shanghai*	WB	1974

D033 Jim Dickinson

	Big Star	*Third Album*	Aura	1978
	Alex Chilton	*Like Flies On Sherbet*	Aura	1980
w. L.Waronker	Ry Cooder	*Into The Purple Valley*	Reprise	1972
w. L.Waronker	Ry Cooder	*Boomer's Story*	Reprise	1972
w. Tom Dowd	James Luther Dickinson	*Dixie Fried*	Atlantic	1972

D034 Jim Dickson

	The Byrds	*Preflyte*	Together	1963
	Hamilton Camp	*Paths Of Glory*	Elektra	1967
	Country Gazette	*A Traitor In Our Midst*	UA	1972
	Country Gazette	*Don't Give Up Your Day Job*	UA	1973
	Country Gazette	*Live*	Tra	1975
	Country Gazette	*Out To Lunch*	F.Fish	1976
	Country Gazette	*Sunny Side Of The Mountain*	Tra	1976
	Doug Dillard	*The Banjo Album*	Together	1969
	Dillards	*Back Porch Bluegrass*	Elektra	1963
	Dillards	*Live Almost*	Elektra	1964
	Dillards	*Pickin' and Fiddlin'*	Elektra	1965
w. Henry Lewy	Flying Burritos	*Burrito De Luxe*	A&M	1970
w. B.Hughes	Flying Burrito Brothers	*Flying Burrito Brothers*	A&M	1971
	Flying Burrito Brothers	*The Last Of The Red Hot Burritos*	A&M	1972
	Flying Burrito Brothers	*Honky Tonk Heaven*	A&M	1972
	Chris Hillman	*Morning Sky*	Sugar Hill	1983
	Hillmen	*The Hillmen*	Together	1964

D035 Dieter Dierks

Bullet	*No Mercy*	HMW/Arista	1984
Dokken	*Breaking The Chains*	Carrere	1982
Scorpions	*Lonesome Crow*	Brain/RCA	1972
Scorpions	*Fly To The Rainbow*	RCA	1974
Scorpions	*In Trance*	RCA	1976

Scorpions	Virgin Killer	RCA	1976
Scorpions	Taken By Force	RCA	1977
Scorpions	Lovedrive	Harv/Mer	1979
Scorpions	Animal Magnetism	Harv/Mer	1980
Scorpions	Blackout	Harv/Mer	1982
Scorpions	Love At First Sting	Harv/Mer	1984
Vic Vergat	Down To The Bone	Harvest	1981

D036 Richard Digby-Smith

Boxer	Below The Belt	Virgin	1975
Bronco	Ace Of Sunlight	Island	1971
Difference	Sign Of The Times	S.Maple	1983
Bryn Haworth	Let The Days Go By	A&M	1974
Bryn Haworth	Sunny Side Of The Street	Island	1975

D037 Andy Di Martino

Buckwheat	Buckwheat	London	1972
Buckwheat	Charade	London	1972
Buckwheat	Hot Tracks	London	1973
Captain Beefheart	Unconditionally Guaranteed	Virgin	1974
Captain Beefheart	Bluejeans and Moonbeams	Virgin	1974
Kent Morrill	The Dream Maker	Cream	1981
Wailers	Walk Thru' The People	Bell	1967

(Not the Bob Marley Wailers, but the North Western ones.)

D038 Richard Dodd

Blues Band	Brand Loyalty	Arista	1982

D039 Tom Donahue

w. Bob Mitchell	Beau Brummels	66	WB	1966
	Beau Brummels	Volume 44	Vault	1968
	Stoneground	Family Album	WB	1971
	Stoneground	Stoneground	WB	1971

D040 Bob D'Orleans

Leslie West	The Great Fatsby	Phantom	1975
West, Bruce and Laing	Live 'n' Kickin'	RSO	1974

D041 Joel Dorn (The Masked Announcer)

	David Allen	Continental American	A&M	1974
	Mose Allison	Western Man	Atlantic	1971
	Asleep At The Wheel	Collision Course	Capitol	1978
	Kenny Barron	Innocence	Wolf	1978
	King Curtis and Champion Jack Dupree	Blues At Montreux	Atlantic	1971
	Tommy Dorsey Band	Featuring Buddy Morrow	MCA	1981
	Edison Electric Band	Bless You Dr. Woodward	Cott	1970
	Roberta Flack	First Take	Atlantic	1969
	Roberta Flack	Quiet Fire	Atlantic	1971
	Roberta Flack	Killing Me Softly	Atlantic	1973
w. Arif Mardin	Roberta Flack and Donny Hathaway	Roberta Flack and Donny Hathaway	Atlantic	1972
	David Forman	David Forman	Arista	1976
	Steve Goodman	Say It In Private	Asylum	1977

Roland Kirk	*The Inflated Tear*	Atlantic	1968
Roland Kirk	*Prepare Thyself To Deal With A Miracle*	Atlantic	1973
Roland Kirk	*Boogie Woogie String Along*	WB	1978
Roland Kirk	*The Vibration Continues*	Atlantic	1978
Bonnie Koloc	*Wild And Recluse*	Epic	1978
Yusef Lateef	*10 Years Hence*	Atlantic	1975
Les McCann	*Much Les*	Atlantic	1969
Les McCann	*Talk To The People*	Atlantic	1972
Eugene McDaniels	*Outlaw*	Atlantic	1971
Don McLean	*Homeless Brother*	UA	1974
Neville Brothers	*Fiyo On The Bayou*	A&M	1981
Franklin Micare	*Franklin Micare*	P.Stock	1978
Bette Midler	*The Divine Miss M*	Atlantic	1972
Charles Mingus	*At Carnegie Hall*	Atlantic	1974
Dory Previn	*We're The Children Of Coincidence and Harpo Marx*	WB	1976
Lou Rawls	*Shades Of Blue*	Phil Int	1981
Leon Redbone	*On The Track*	WB	1975
Leon Redbone	*Double Time*	WB	1977
Leon Redbone	*Champagne Charlie*	WB	1978
Jess Roden	*The Player Not The Game*	Island	1977
Jess Roden	*Stonechaser*	Island	1980
Janis Siegel	*Experiment In White*	Atlantic	1982
Lucy Simon	*Lucy Simon*	RCA	1975
Vance 32	*Vance 32*	Atlantic	1975

D042 Alan Douglas

Lenny Bruce	*The Story Of Lenny*	Casablanca	1975
Jerry Garcia and Howard Wales	*Hooteroll*	Douglas	1972
Jimi Hendrix	*Crash Landing*	Poly/Rep	1975
Jimi Hendrix	*Midnight Lightning*	Poly/Rep	1976
Jimi Hendrix	*9 To The Universe*	Poly/Rep	1980
Jimi Hendrix	*The Jimi Hendrix Concerts*	CBS	1982
Lightnin' Rod	*Hustlers Convention*	UA	1973
New York City Band	*Sunnyside*	AI	1979

D043 Chip Douglas

Monkees	*Pisces, Aquarius, Capricorn and Jones*	RCA/Colg	1967
Linda Ronstadt	*Hand Sown, Home Grown*	Capitol	1969
Turtles	*Battle Of The Bands*	Lon/WW	1968

D044 Jack Douglas

w. Ray Colcord	Aerosmith	*Get Your Wings*	CBS	1974
	Aerosmith	*Toys In The Attic*	CBS	1975
	Aerosmith	*Rocks*	CBS	1976
	Aerosmith	*Draw The Line*	CBS	1977
	Aerosmith	*Live Bootleg*	CBS	1978
	Aerosmith	*Rock In A Hard Place*	CBS	1982
w. E.Leonetti	Artful Dodger	*Honor Among Thieves*	CBS	1976

w. E.Leonetti	Artful Dodger	*Babes On Broadway*	CBS	1977
	Cheap Trick	*Cheap Trick*	Epic	1977
	Cheap Trick	*At The Budokan*	Epic	1978
	(Credited as "mixing supervisor".)			
w. J.Richardson	Alice Cooper	*Muscle Of Love*	WB	1973
	Crowbar	*Crowbar*	Epic	1973
	Rick Duffy	*Tender Loving Abuse*	Polydor	1980
	Harlequin	*Love Crimes*	CBS	1981
	Knack	*Round Trip*	Capitol	1981
	Karen Lawrence	*Girls Night Out*	RCA	1981
w. John Lennon and Yoko Ono	John Lennon/Yoko Ono	*Double Fantasy*	Geffen	1980
	Frankie Miller	*Double Trouble*	Chrysalis	1976
	Montrose	*Jump On It*	WB	1976
	1994	*1994*	A&M	1978
	Graham Parker	*Another Grey Area*	RCA	1982
	Joe Perry	*Let The Music Do The Talking*	CBS	1980
	Rockets	*Back Talk*	Elektra	1981
	Sha Na Na	*Hot Sox*	K.Sutra	1974
	Patti Smith	*Radio Ethiopia*	Arista	1976
	Starz	*Starz*	Capitol	1976
	Starz	*Violation*	Capitol	1977
	Zebra	*Zebra*	Atlantic	1983

D045 Steve Douglas

	Collage	*The Collage*	Mercury	1967
	Mink De Ville	*Le Chat Bleu*	Capitol	1980
	Thorinshield	*Thorinshield*	Philips	1968

D046 Tom Dowd

	Allman Brothers	*Idlewild South*	Capricorn	1969
	Allman Brothers	*At Fillmore East*	Capricorn	1971
	Allman Brothers	*Eat A Peach*	Capricorn	1972
	Allman Brothers	*Enlightened Rogues*	Capricorn	1979
	Blackjack	*Blackjack*	Polydor	1979
	Black Oak Arkansas	*If An Angel Came To See You Would You Make Her Feel At Home*	Atco	1972
	Black Oak Arkansas	*Raunch 'n' Roll Live*	Atco	1973
	Black Oak Arkansas	*High On The Hog*	Atco	1973
	Black Oak Arkansas	*Street Party*	Atco	1974
	Cate Brothers	*Fire On The Tracks*	Atlantic	1979
w.Arif Mardin & Jerry Wexler	Cher	*3614 Jackson Highway*	Atlantic	1969
	Chicago	*X1V*	CBS	1980
	Eric Clapton	*461 Ocean Boulevard*	RSO	1974
	Eric Clapton	*One In Every Crwod*	RSO	1975
	Eric Clapton	*E.C. Was Here*	RSO	1975
	Eric Clapton	*Another Ticket*	RSO	1981
	Eric Clapton	*Money and Cigarettes*	Duck	1983
w. Arif Mardin & Jerry Wexler	Delaney and Bonnie	*To Delaney From Bonnie*	Atco	1970
	Derek and The Dominoes	*Layla*	Poly/Atl	1970

	Artist	Title	Label	Year
	Jackie De Shannon	Jackie	Atlantic	1972
	Jim Dickinson	Dixie Fried	Atlantic	1972
	Dr. John	Remedies	Atco	1970
	Firefall	Elan	Atlantic	1978
	Aretha Franklin	I Never Loved A Man Like You	Atlantic	1967
	Aretha Franklin	Aretha Arrives	Atlantic	1967
	Aretha Franklin	Aretha Now	Atlantic	1968
	Aretha Franklin	This Girl's In Love With You	Atlantic	1969
w. Jerry Wexler	Aretha Franklin	Soul '69	Atlantic	1969
w. Arif Mardin & Jerry Wexler	Aretha Franklin	Young, Gifted and Black	Atlantic	1972
w. Arif Mardin & Jerry Wexler	Aretha Franklin	With Everything I Feel In Me	Atlantic	1974
	Buddy Guy and Junior Wells	Play The Blues	Atlantic	1972
	Ronnie Hawkins	Ronnie Hawkins	Atlantic	1970
w. Jerry Wexler	Ronnie Hawkins	The Hawk	Atlantic	1971
	James Gang	Newborn	Atlantic	1975
	Jo Mama	J Is For Jump	Atlantic	1971
	King Curtis	Live At Small's Paradise	Atlantic	1966
	Kenny Loggins	Keep The Fire	CBS	1979
	Lulu	Melody Fair	Atco	1970
	Lynyrd Skynyrd	Gimme Back My Bullets	MCA	1976
	Lynyrd Skynyrd	One More From The Road	MCA	1976
	Lynyrd Skynyrd	Street Survivors	MCA	1977
	Herbie Mann	Memphis Underground	Atlantic	1969
w. Arif Mardin	Arif Mardin	Glass Onion	Atlantic	1969
	Marshall Tucker Band	Dedicated	WB	1981
	Meatloaf	Midnight At The Lost And Found	Epic	1983
	Eddie Money	No Control	CBS	1982
	Eddie Money	Where's The Party	CBS	1983
w. A. Galuten	James Montgomery Band	High Roller	Capricorn	1974
	Pablo Cruise	Reflector	A&M	1971
w. T. Cogbill	Wilson Pickett	I'm In Love	Atlantic	1967
	Ramatam	Ramatam	Atlantic	1972
	Terry Reid	River	Atlantic	1973
	Bruce Roberts	Bruce Roberts	Elektra	1978
	Sam (The Sham) Samudio	Hard And Heavy	Atlantic	1971
	Souther Hillman Furay Band	Trouble In Paradise	Asylum	1975
	P F Sloan	Measure Of Pleasure	Atco	1968
w. Arif Mardin & Jerry Wexler	Dusty Springfield	Dusty In Memphis	Atlantic	1968
	Rod Stewart	Atlantic Crossing	Riva/WB	1975
	Rod Stewart	A Night On The Town	Riva/WB	1975
	Rod Stewart	Footloose And Fancy Free	Riva/WB	1977
	Rod Stewart	Blondes Have More Fun	Riva/WB	1978

	Rod Stewart	Foolish Behaviour (1 track only)	Riva/WB	1980
	Rod Stewart	Body Wishes	Riva/WB	1983
	Stills Young Band	Long May You Run	Reprise	1976
	(Credited as "associate producer")			
w. Jerry Wexler	Ira Sullivan	Horizons	Discovery	1983
	Narada Michael Walden	Garden Of Love Light	Atlantic	1974
	Jerry Jeff Walker	Mr. Bojangles	Atco	1968
	Jerry Jeff Walker	Bein' Free	Atco	1970
	Wet Willie	Dixie Rock	Capricorn	1974
	Wet Willie	Keep On Smilin	Capricorn	1974
w. Jerry Wexler	Tony Joe White	The Train I'm On	WB	1972
	Tony Joe White	Home Made Ice Cream	WB	1973
w. Jerry Wexler	Wishbone Ash	Locked In	MCA	1976
	Young Rascals	Young Rascals	Atlantic	1966
	Young Rascals	Collections	Atlantic	1966

D047 Gary Downey

	Ron Elliott	The Candlestick Maker	WB	1970

D048 Pete Drake

	Larry Ballard	Young Blood and Sweet Country Music	Elektra	1974
	Marshall Chapman	Marshall	Epic	1979
	Linda Hargrove	Music Is Your Mistress	Elektra	1973
	Linda Hargrove	Blue Jean Country Queen	Elektra	1974
	Tommy James	My Head, My Bed, My Red Guitar	Roulette	1973
	Ronnie Prophet	Phantom Of The Opry	Cachet	1979
	Ringo Starr	Beaucoups Of Blues	Apple	1970
	B J Thomas	New Looks	Cleve-Int	1983
	B J Thomas	The Great American Dream	Cleve-Int	1983
	Ernest Tubb	The Legend And The Legacy Volume 1	Cachet	1979

D049 Gus Dudgeon

	Joan Armatrading	Whatever's For Us	Cube/A&M	1972
	Audience	The House On The Hill	Char/Elek	1971
	Bagatelle	Bagatelle	Polydor	1981
	Bonzo Dog Do Dah Band	Gorilla	Liberty	1967
	Bonzo Dog Do Dah Band	The Doughnut In Granny's Greenhouse	Liberty	1968
	Bonzo Dog Do Dah Band	Tadpoles	Liberty	1969
	Colin Blunstone	Planes	Epic/Rock	1976
	Johnny Bristol	Free To Be Me	Handshake	1981
w. Clive Franks	Elkie Brooks	I've Got The Music In Me	Rocket	1976
	Michael Chapman	Rainmaker	Harvest	1969
	Michael Chapman	Fully Qualified Survivor	Harvest	1970
	Michael Chapman	Window	Harvest	1970
	Roy Hill	Roy Hill	Arista	1978
	Elton John	Elton John	DJM/MCA	1970

Elton John	*Tumbleweed Connection*	DJM/MCA	1970
Elton John	*17-II-1970*	DJM/MCA	1971

(The date of Bert Muirhead's 21st birthday !)

Elton John	*Madman Across The Water*	DJM/MCA	1971
Elton John	*Honky Chateau*	DJM/MCA	1972
Elton John	*Don't Shoot Me I'm Only The Piano Player*	DJM/MCA	1972
Elton John	*Goodbye Yellow Brick Road*	DJM/MCA	1973
Elton John	*Caribou*	DJM/MCA	1974
Elton John	*Captain Fantastic and The Brown Dirt Cowboy*	DJM/MCA	1974
Elton John	*Rock Of The Westies*	DJM/MCA	1975
Elton John	*Here And There*	DJM/MCA	1976
Elton John	*Blue Moves*	Rocket/MCA	1976
Davey Johnstone	*Smiling Face*	Rocket	1973
Lindisfarne	*Back And Fourth*	Mercury	1978
Ralph McTell	*Revisited*	Tra	1970
Ralph McTell	*You Well-Meaning Brought Me Here*	Famous/ABC	1971
Magna Carta	*Songs From Wasties Orchard*	Vertigo	1971
John Miles	*Play On*	EMI	1983
Chris Rea	*Deltics*	Magnet/UA	1979
Shooting Star	*Shooting Star*	Virgin	1980
Steeleye Span	*Sails Of Silver*	Chry/Tak	1981
Gilbert O'Sullivan	*Off Centre*	Epic	1980
Sinceros	*Pet Rock*	CBS	1981
Strawbs	*Strawbs*	A&M	1969
Bernie Taupin	*Bernie Taupin*	Elektra	1971
w. Mike Vernon	Ten Years After	*Ten Years After*	Deram	1967
Voyager	*Halfway Hotel*	Elektra	1979
Voyager	*Act Of Love*	RCA	1980

D050 Jimmy Duncan

Cupid's Inspiration	*Yesterday Has Gone*	NEMS	1969
Gordon Haskell	*Sailing In My Boat*	CBS	1969

D051 Donald "Duck" Dunn

w. Steve Cropper	Crimson Tide	*Reckless Love*	Capitol	1979
Delaney and Bonnie	*At Home*	Stax	1970
Isaac Hayes	*In The Beginning*	Atlantic	1972
Levon Helm	*Levon Helm*	ABC	1978
Albert King	*King Does The King's Thing*	Stax	1968

D052 Bob Dylan

Barry Goldberg	*Barry Goldberg*	Atlantic	1974

E001 Mitch Easter

Richard Barne and James Mastro	*Nuts and Bolts*	Passport	1983
R.E.M.	*Murmur*	IRS	1983
w. Don Dixon	R.E.M.	*Reckoning*	IRS	1984

(Album also known as "File Under Water")

w. Alan Betrock
and Chris Stamey

Sneakers	*In The Red*	Car	1978
Chris Stamey	*It's A Wonderful Life*	Albion	1983

E002 Duane Eddy

Phil Everly	*Star Spangled Springer*	RCA	1973

E003 John Eden

Graham Bonnet	*Line Up*	Vertigo	1981
Climax Blues Band	*Sample And Hold*	Epic	1983
Andy Fraser	*Fine Fine Line*	Island	1984
Grand Prix	*Samurai*	Chrysalis	1983
Nutz	*Live Cutz*	A&M	1977
Status Quo	*Just Supposin'*	Vertigo	1980
Status Quo	*Never Too Late*	Vertigo	1981

E004 Dave Edmunds

Brinsley Schwarz	*The New Favourites Of Brinsley Schwarz*	UA	1974
Ducks De Luxe	*Taxi To The Terminal Zone*	RCA	1975
Dave Edmunds	*Rockpile*	EMI	1971
Dave Edmunds	*Subtle As A Flying Mallet*	Rockfield	1975
Dave Edmunds	*Get It*	Swansong	1977
Dave Edmunds	*Tracks On Wax 4*	Swansong	1978
Dave Edmunds	*Repeat When Necessary*	Swansong	1979
Dave Edmunds	*Twangin'*	Swansong	1981
Dave Edmunds	*DE 7*	Arista	1982
Dave Edmunds	*Information*	Arista	1983
Flamin' Groovies	*Shake Some Action*	Sire	1976
Flamin' Groovies	*Now*	Sire	1978
King Kurt	*Ooh Wallah Wallah*	Stiff	1983
Love Sculpture	*Forms And Feelings*	EMI	1969
Polecats	*Are Go*	Mercury	1981
Polecats	*Make A Circuit With*	Mercury	1983
Shakin' Stevens	*A Legend*	EMI	1970
Del Shannon	*.. And The Music Plays On (1 track)*	Sunset	1978
Stray Cats	*Stray Cats*	Arista	1981
Stray Cats	*Built For Speed (5 tracks; US compilation)*	EMI-Amer	1982
Stray Cats	*Rant And Rave With The Stray Cats*	Arista	1983

E005 Esmond Edwards

Mose Allison	*Middle Class White Boy*	Elektra	1982
Chuck Berry	*London Sessions*	Chess	1972
Chuck Berry	*Bio*	Chess	1973
Bobby Bland and B.B.King	*Together Again...Live*	Impulse	1976
Jackie Byard	*Giant Steps*	Prestige	1979
King Curtis	*King Soul*	New Jazz	1960
King Curtis	*Best Of King Curtis*	Prestige	1968
King Curtis	*One More Time*	Prestige	1968
Eric Dolphy	*Fire Waltz (from 1960)*	Prestige	1979

	Keith Jarrett	*Mysteries*	ABC/Imp	1976
	Keith Jarrett	*Shades*	ABC/Imp	1976
	Keith Jarrett	*Byablue*	ABC/Imp	1977
	Roosevelt Sykes	*Honeydripper*	Bluesville	1960
	Phil Upchurch	*Name Of The Game*	Jam	1984

E006 Kenny Edwards

	Karla Bonoff	*Karla Bonoff*	CBS	1977
	Karla Bonoff	*Restless Nights*	CBS	1979
	Karla Bonoff	*Wild Heart Of The Young*	CBS	1982
w. Greg Ladanyi	David James Holster	*Chinese Honeymoon*	CBS	1979
	Graham Shaw and The Sincere Serenaders	*Graham Shaw and The Sincere Serenaders*	Capitol	1980

E007 Kevin Eggers

	John Lee Hooker	*The Cream*	Tomato	1978
w. Jack Clement	Townes Van Zandt	*Our Mother The Mountain*	Poppy	1969
	Townes van Zandt	*High Low And In Between*	Poppy	1971
	Townes Van Zandt	*The Late Great*	UA/Poppy	1973
w. Jack Clement	Townes Van Zandt	*Townes Van Zandt*	Tomato	1978
	Doc and Merle Watson	*Now And Then*	Poppy	1973

E008 Brian Elliott

	Skip Battin	*Navigator*	Appaloosa	1981

E009 Ron Elliott

	Levitt and McClure	*Living In The Country*	WB	1969
	Stoneground	*Family Album*	WB	1971

E010 Terry Ellis

	Clouds	*Water Colour Days*	Chrysalis	1971
	Jethro Tull	*This Was*	Chrysalis	1968
	Jethro Tull	*Stand Up*	Chrysalis	1969

E011 Kevin Elson

w. G.Workman	Journey	*Departure*	CBS	1980
w. Mike Stone	Journey	*Escape*	CBS	1981
w. Mike Stone	Journey	*Frontiers*	CBS	1983
	Eric Martin Band	*Sucker For A Pretty Face*	Elektra	1983
	Shooting Star	*III Wishes*	Virg/Epic	1982
	Shooting Star	*Burning*	Virg/Epic	1983
	Johnny Van Zandt Band	*Round Two*	Polydor	1981

E012 Geoff Emerick

	Badfinger	*No Dice*	Apple	1970
	Elvis Costello	*Imperial Bedroom*	F-Beat/CBS	1982
	Nick Heyward	*North Of A Miracle*	Arista	1983
	Split Enz	*Dizrythmia*	Chrysalis	1977
	Robin Trower	*Long Misty Days*	Chrysalis	1976
	Robin Trower	*Victims Of The Fury*	Chrysalis	1980
	Gino Vannelli	*Gist Of The Gemini*	A&M	1980

E013 Brian Eno

	Harold Budd	*Pavilion Of Dreams*	Obscure	1980
	Devo	*Are We Not Men*	Virgin/WB	1980
	Eno	*Here Come The Warm Jets*	Island	1973
	Eno	*Taking Tiger Mountain By Strategy*	Island	1974
w. Rhett Davies	Eno	*Another Green World*	EG	1975
	Eno	*Ambient 1-Music For Airports*	EG	1975
w. Rhett Davies	Eno	*Before And After Science*	EG	1977
w. Rhett Davies	Eno	*Music For Films*	EG/Ant	1978
	Eno	*Ambient 4-On Land*	EG	1982
w. Don Landis	Eno	*Apollo Atmospheres*	EG/Jem	1983
	Brian Eno and John Hassell	*Possible Musics*	EG	1980
	Brian Eno and David Byrne	*My Life In The Bush Of Ghosts*	EG	1981
	Fripp and Eno	*No Pussyfooting*	EG	1973
	Fripp and Eno	*Evening Star*	EG	1975
	Hobbs/Adams/Bryars	*Ensemble Pieces*	Obscure	1975
	Pacesetters	*Edikanfo*	EG	1982
	Portsmouth Sinfonia	*Hallelujah*	Tra	1979
	Talking Heads	*More Songs About Buildings And Food*	Sire	1978
	Talking Heads	*Fear Of Music*	Sire	1979
	Talking Heads	*Remain In Light*	Sire	1980
	Ultravox	*Ultravox !*	Island	1977
	various artists	*No New York*	Antilles	1979

E014 John Entwistle

	Fabulous Poodles	*The Fabulous Poodles*	Pye	1977

E015 Greg Errico

	Betty Davis	*Betty Davis*	Just Sun	1975
	Funkadelic	*Connections and Disconnections*	LAX	1981
	Giants	*Giants*	LAX	1978
	Lee Oskar	*Lee Oskar*	MCA	1976
	Lee Oskar	*Before The Rain*	MCA/LAX	1978
	Lee Oskar	*Our Road, Your Road*	Elektra	1981

E0I6 Ahmet Ertegun

	Apache	*Apache*	Atco	1981
	Barnaby Bye	*Room to Grow*	Atlantic	1973
	Batdorf and Rodney	*Off The Shelf*	Atlantic	1972
	Mike Corbett and Jay Hirsh	*Mike Corbett and Jay Hirsh*	Atlantic	1971
	Country	*Country (featuring Tom Snow)*	Clean/Atl	1971
	Bobby Darin	*For Teenagers Only*	Atlantic	1959
	Nicholas Lampe	*It Happened A Long Time Ago*	Cottilion	1970
	Manhattan Transfer	*The Manhattan Transfer*	Atlantic	1975
	Blind Willie McTell	*Atlanta 12 String*	Atlantic	1972

	Danny O'Keefe	*Danny O'Keefe*	Cotillion	1970
	Professor Longhair	*New Orleans Piano*	Atlantic	1972
w. Wally Harper	Twiggy and Tommy Tune	*My One And Only*	Atlantic	1983
	Jimmy and Mama Yancey	*Chicago Piano Vol. 1*	Atlantic	1972

E017 Nesuhi Ertegun

	King Curtis	*Have Tenor Will Blow*	Atco	1959
	Wilson Pickett	*Midnight Mover*	Atlantic	1968

E018 Bob Esty

	Brooklyn Dreams	*Sleepless Nights*	RCA/Casab	1979
	Cher	*Prisoner*	Casab	1979
	Ava Cherry	*Take Me Home*	Capitol	1982
	Ava Cherry	*Streetcar Named Desire*	Capitol	1982
	Paul Jabara	*Keeping Time*	Casab	1978
w. G.Moroder	Roberta Kelly	*Gettin' The Spirit*	Casb	1978
	D.C.La Rue	*Confessions*	Pye/Casab	1978
	D.C.La Rue	*Forces Of The Night*	Casab	1979
	soundtrack	*Roller Boogie*	Casab	1979

E019 Mal Evans

	Badfinger	*Magic Christian Music*	Apple	1970
	Badfinger	*No Dice (2 tracks)*	Apple	1970

E020 Jeff Eyrich

	T-Bone Burnett	*Proof Through The Night*	S.Eff/Wb	1983
	Plimsouls	*Everywhere At Once*	Geffen	1983
	Rank And File	*Long Gone Dead*	Slash	1984

E021 Bob Ezrin

w. B.Christian	Babys	*The Babys*	Chrysalis	1977
	Alice Cooper	*Killer*	WB	1971
	Alice Cooper	*School's Out*	WB	1972
	Alice Cooper	*Billion Dollar Babies*	WB	1973
	Alice Cooper	*Welcome To My Nightmare*	Anchor/Atl	1975
	Alice Cooper	*Goes To Hell*	WB	1976
w. B.Christian	Alice Cooper	*The Alice Cooper Show*	WB	1977
	Alice Cooper	*Lace & Whiskey*	WB	1977
	Alice Cooper	*Da-Da*	WB	1983
	Tim Curry	*Read My Lips*	A&M	1978
	Detroit	*Detroit*	Paramount	1972
	(Group featured Mitch Ryder)			
	Flo and Eddie	*Flo and Eddie*	WB	1973
	Peter Gabriel	*Peter Gabriel One*	Char/Atco	1977
	David Gilmour	*About Face*	Harv/CBS	1984
	Steve Hunter	*Swept Away*	Atco	1977
	Kings	*The Kings*	Elektra	1980
	Kings	*Amazon Beach*	Elektra	1981
	Kiss	*Destroyer*	Casab	1976
	Kiss	*The Elder*	Casab	1976
	Nils Lofgren	*Nils*	A&M	1979
	Murray McLauchlan	*Storm Warning*	Asylum	1981

w. Roger Waters and Dave Gilmour	Pink Floyd	*The Wall*	Harv/CBS	1979
	Lou Reed	*Berlin*	RCA	1973
	Telephone	*Telephone*	Virgin	1982
w. B.Christian	Richard Wagner	*Richard Wagner*	Atlantic	1978

F001 Bruce Fairbairn

	Blue Oyster Cult	*The Revolution By Night*	CBS	1983
	Ian Lloyd	*Goose Bumps*	Atl/Scotti	1979
	Ian Lloyd	*Third Wave Civilization*	Scotti	1980
	Loverboy	*Loverboy*	CBS	1980
	Loverboy	*Get Lucky*	CBS	1981
	Loverboy	*Keep It Up*	CBS	1983
	Prism	*See Forever Eyes*	Ariola	1978
	Prism	*Armageddon*	Capitol	1979
	Prism	*Young And Restless*	Capitol	1980
	Shanghai	*Shanghai*	Chrysalis	1982
	Strange Advance	*Worlds Away*	Capitol	1983
	Kasim Sulton	*Kasim*	Emi-Amer	1982

F002 Adam Faith

w. D.Courtney	Roger Daltrey	*Roger Daltrey*	Track	1973
	Lonnie Donnegan	*Puttin' On The Style*	Chrysalis	1978
	Lonnie Donnegan	*Sundown*	Chrysalis	1978
w. D.Courtney	Leo Sayer	*Silverbird*	Chry/WB	1973
w. D.Courtney	Leo Sayer	*Just A Boy*	Chry/WB	1974

F003 Joe Falsia

	Tim Buckley	*Look At The Moon*	DiscReet	1974
	Joanne Mackell	*Joanne Mackell*	UA	1978
	Stephen Sinclair	*Stephen Sinclair*	UA	1977
	Small Talk	*Small Talk*	MCA	1981

F004 Cyrus Faryar

	Firesign Theatre	*How Can You Be In Two Places At The One Time*	CBS	1968

F005 Barry Fasman

	Pieces	*Pieces*	UA	1979
	James Lee Stanley	*James Lee Stanley*	W.Nickel	1973
	James Lee Stanley	*Too*	W.Nickel	1973
	Stringcheese	*Stringcheese*	RCA	1971
	The Kids From Fame	*Again*	RCA/MGM	1982
	The Kids From Fame	*Sing For You*	BBC	1983

F006 Ricky Fataar

w. M.Murray	Tim Finn	*Escapade*	Epic	1984

F007 Mike Finesilver

	Flys	*Waikiki Beach Party*	EMI	1978
	Gonzalez	*Our Only Weapon Is Our Music*	EMI	1975
w. Pete Ker	Love Sculpture	*Forms And Feelings*	EMI	1968
	Ross	*Ross*	RSO	1974

F008 John Fischbach

Flying Burritos	*Airborne*	CBS	1976
Carole King	*Writer*	Ode	1970

F009 Matthew Fisher

Bandit	*Partners In Crime*	Arista	1977
Roderick Falconer	*New Nation*	UA	1976
Procol Harum	*A Salty Dog*	RZ/A&M	1969
Tir Na Nog	*Strong In The Sun*	Chrysalis	1973
Robin Trower	*Twice Removed From Yesterday*	Chrysalis	1973
Robin Trower	*Bridge Of Sighs*	Chrysalis	1974
Robin Trower	*For Earth Below*	Chrysalis	1975

F010 Morgan Fisher

Hybrid Kids	*Claws*	Cherry	1980

F011 Reggie Fisher

T-Bone Burnett	*Truth Decay*	Chrysalis	1980
T-Bone Burnett	*Trap Door*	WB	1982

F012 Mike Flicker

Chilliwack	*Chilliwack*	Sire	1974
Clocks	*Clocks*	Boulevard	1982
Dixon House Band	*Fighting Alone*	Infinity	1979
Dixon House	*Masked Madness*	A&M	1981
Heart	*Dreamboat Annie*	Arista	1976
Heart	*Magazine*	Arista	1978
Heart	*Little Queen*	Portrait	1977
Heart	*Dog and Butterfly*	Portrait	1978
Heart	*Bebe Le Strange*	Epic	1980
Heart	*Live*	Epic	1980
Randy Meisner	*Randy Meisner*	CBS	1982
Poco	*Under The Gun*	MCA	1980
Poco	*Blue and Grey*	MCA	1981
Poco	*Cowboys and Englishmen*	MCA	1982
Silver Condor	*Silver Condor*	CBS	1981
St.Paradise	*St.Paradise*	WB	1979
T.K.O.	*Let It Roll*	Infinity	1979
Wendy Waldman	*Strange Company*	WB	1978

F013 Flo & Eddie (Mark Volman and Howard Kaylan)

DMZ	*DMZ*	Sire	1978
Phlorescent Leech and Eddie	*Phlorescent Leech and Eddie*	WB	1972
Flo and Eddie	*Moving Targets*	CBS	1976
Good Rats	*From Rats To Riches*	Passport	1978
w. John Stronach Roadmaster	*Fortress*	Mercury	1980

F014 Dan Fogelberg

Michael Brewer	*Beauty Lies*	Full Moon	1983

F015 John Fogerty

Blue Ridge Rangers	*Blue Ridge Rangers*	Fantasy	1973
John Fogerty	*John Fogerty*	Fant/Asy.	1975

(Fogerty produced every Creedence Clearwater Revival album)

F016 Tom Fogerty

	Ruby	*Ruby*	PBR	1977
	Ruby	*Rock 'n' Roll Madness*	PBR	1978
	Merl Saunders	*Heavy Turbulence*	Fantasy	1977

F017 Richard Foos (see under entry for Harold Bronson)

F018 Mickey Foote

	Clash	*The Clash*	CBS	1977

F019 Martyn Ford

	Nasty Pop	*Mistaken I.D.*	Polydor	1977
	Sky King	*Secret Sauce*	CBS	1975

F020 Gordon Fordyce

	Motley Crue	*Too Fast For Love*	Elektra	1982
	The World	*Break The Silence*	WB	1983

F021 David Foster

w. Jay Graydon	Airplay	*Airplay*	RCA	1979
	Peter Allen	*Bi-Coastal*	A&M	1980
	AWB	*Volume 8*	Atlantic	1980
	AWB	*Shine*	RCA/Arista	1980
	Bill Champlin	*Single*	Full Moon	1978
	Bill Champlin	*Runaway*	Elektra	1981
	Chicago	*XVI*	WB-F.Moon	1982
	Chicago	*17*	WB-F.Moon	1984
	Alice Cooper	*From The Inside*	WB	1978
	Hall and Oates	*Along The Red Ledge*	RCA	1978
	Hall and Oates	*X-Static*	RCA	1979
	Ray Kennedy	*Ray Kennedy*	ARC	1980
w. Jay Lewis	Danny Peck	*Heart and Soul*	Arista	1977
w. Lionel Richie	Lionel Richie	*Can't Slow Down (1 track only)*	Motown	1983
w. Harvey Mason	Lee Ritenour	*Rit*	Elektra	1981
	Tavares	*Supercharged*	Capitol	1980
	Tubes	*Completion Backwards Principle*	Capitol	1981
	Tubes	*Outside Inside*	Capitol	1983
w. Ray Parker	Deniece Williams	*When Love Comes Calling*	CBS	1979

F022 Kim Fowley

	A.B.Skhy	*Ramblin' On*	MGM	1970
	Cherie Currie	*Beauty's Only Skin Deep*	Mercury	1978
	Dyan Diamond	*In The Dark*	MCA	1979
	Flash Cadillac and The Continetal Kids	*Flash Cadillac and The Continental Kids*	Epic	1972
	Kim Fowley	*Born To Be Wild*	Imperial	1968
	Kim Fowley	*International Heroes*	Capitol	1973
	Kim Fowley	*Animal God Of The Street*	Skydog	1974
	Kim Fowley	*Visions Of The Future*	Capitol	1974
	Kim Fowley	*Sunset Boulevard*	Illegal	1978
	Kim Fowley	*Snake Document Masquerade*	Island	1979

w. M.Lloyd	St. John Green	*St. John Green*	MGM	1970
	Industrials	*The Industrials*	CBS	1980
	Original Modern	*The Original Modern*		
	Lovers	*Lovers*	Bomp	1981
	Orchids	*The Orchids*	MCA	1980
	The Quick	*Mondo Deco*	Mercury	1976
w. E.Mankey	Helen Reddy	*Ear Candy*	Capitol	1977
	Helen Reddy	*We'll Sing In The Sunshine*	Capitol	1978
	Runaways	*The Runaways*	Mercury	1976
	Runaways	*Queens Of Noise*	Mercury	1977
	Runaways	*Waitin' For The Night*	Mercury	1977
	Seeds	*Future (1 track)*	GNP	1967
w. M.Lloyd	Smoke	*The Smoke*	Capitol	1969
	Steel Breeze	*Steel Breeze*	RCA	1982
	Steven T.	*West Coast Confidential*	*Dream*	1978
	Underground All Stars	*Extremely Heavy*	Dot	1969
	various artists	*Vampires From Outer Space*	Bomp	1979
	Venus and The Razorblades	*Songs From The Sunshine Jungle*	Spark/Bomp	1977

F023 Keith Forsey

	Keith Forsey	*Dynamite*	Carrere	1980
	Generation X	*Kiss Me Deadly*	Chrysalis	1981
w. G.Moroder	Nina Hagen	*Fearless*	CBS	1983
w. Iva Davies	Ice House	*Primitive Man*	Chrysalis	1982
w. Iva Davies	Ice House	*Love In Motion*	Chrysalis	1983
	Billy Idol	*Billy Idol*	Chrysalis	1982
	Billy Idol	*Rebel Yell*	Chrysalis	1983
	Psychedelic Furs	*Mirror Moves*	CBS	1984

F024 Fred Foster

	Brush Arbor	*Page One*	Monument	1976
	Brush Arbor	*Straight*	Monument	1977
	Larry Gatlin	*High Time*	Monument	1973
	Larry Gatlin	*Rain Rainbow*	Monument	1974
	Larry Gatlin	*Broken Lady*	Monument	1976
	Larry Gatlin	*Oh Brother*	Monument	1978
	Roy Orbison	*Regeneration*	Monument	1976
	Clay Smith	*Decoupage*	Monument	1977

F025 Rob Fraboni

	Blondie Chaplin	*Blondie Chaplin*	Asylum	1977
	Eric Clapton	*No Reason To Cry*	RSO	1976
	Joe Cocker	*Stingray*	A&M	1976
	Rick Danko	*Rick Danko*	Arista	1978
w. R.Robertson	Bob Dylan	*Planet Waves*	Asylum	1974
	Renee Geyer	*Renee Geyer*	Portrait	1982
	Max Gronenthal	*Max*	Chrysalis	1980
w. Andy Johns	Hughes/Thrall	*Hughes/Thrall*	CBS/Boul	1982
	Ian McLagan	*Jump In The Night*	Mercury	1981
	Pure Prairie League	*Something In The Night*	Casab	1981
	Bonnie Raitt	*Green Light*	WB	1982

| | Tonio K | *Life On The Food Chain* | Full Moon | 1979 |
| | Jennifer Warnes | *Shot Through The Heart* | Arista | 1979 |

F026 Ron Frangipane

	Beckies	*The Beckies*	Sire	1976
	Janis Ian	*Miracle Row*	CBS	1977
	Janis Ian	*Night Rains*	CBS	1979
	Grace Slick	*Dreams*	RCA	1980
	Grace Slick	*Welcome To The Wrecking Ball*	RCA	1981
w. M.Cuscuna	Chris Smither	*I'm A Stranger Too*	Poppy	1973
w. Al Steckler	Stanky Brown Group	*The Stanky Brown Group*	Sire	1976
	Townes Van Zandt	*Delta Momma Blues*	Tomato	1978

F027 Clive Franks

w. Elton John	Blue	*Another Night Time Flight*	Rocket	1977
	Blue	*Fools Party (3 tracks)*	Rocket	1979
w. Elton John	Kiki Dee	*Loving And Free*	Rocket	1973
w. Elton John	Kiki Dee	*Kiki Dee*	Rocket	1977
w. Gus Dudgeon	Kiki Dee Band	*I've Got The Music In Me*	Rocket	1976
w. Elton John	Elton John	*A Single Man*	Rocket	1978
w. Elton John	Elton John	*21 At 33*	Rocket	1980
w.Chris Thomas & Elton John	Elton John	*The Fox (5 tracks)*	Rocket	1981

F028 Freebo (Dan Friedberg)

	Catfish Hodge Band	*Eyewitness Blues*	Adelphi	1979

F029 Ed Freeman

	Roy Buchanan	*Rescue Me*	Polydor	1974
	Tim Hardin	*Bird On A Wire*	CBS	1971
	Don McLean	*American Pie*	UA	1971
	Don McLean	*Don McLean*	UA	1972
	Don McLean	*Playin' Favorites*	UA	1973
	Tom Rush	*Tom Rush*	CBS	1970

F030 Rob Freeman

w. R.Gotterher	Go-Go's	*Beauty And The Beast*	IRS	1980
	Larry Gowan	*Gowan*	CBS	1982
	Single Bullet Theory	*Single Bullet Theory*	Nemperor	1983

F031 Toxey French

	Chi Coltrane	*Chi Coltrane*	CBS	1972
	Dunn and McCashen	*Dunn and McCashen*	Capitol	1970
	Flash Cadillac	*There's No Face Like Chrome*	Epic	1974
	Flash Cadillac	*Sons Of Beaches*	P.Stock	1975

F032 Glenn Frey

	Lou Ann Barton	*Lou Ann Barton*	Asylum	1981
	Fools Gold	*Fools Gold*	Arista	1976
w. Allan Blazek & Jim Ed Norman	Glenn Frey	*No Fun Aloud*	Asylum	1982

w. Allan Blazek	Jack Mack and The Heart Attack	*Cardiac Party*	Full Moon	1982

F033 Barry Friedman

	Kaliedoscope	*Side Trips*	Epic	1967

F034 Don Friedman

	Lenny Bruce	*At Carnegie Hall*	UA	1972

(Has a sleeve note by "Elvis" author Albert Goldman.)

F035 Michael Friedman

	Jesse Frederick	*Jesse Frederick*	WB	1971
	Gordon Lightfoot	*Shadows*	WB	1982

F036 Steven Friedman

	Blue Ash	*Front Page News*	Playboy	1977

F037 Tim Friese-Green

	Blue Zoo	*Two By Two*	Magnet	1983
	City Boy	*Heads Are Rolling*	Phonog/Atl	1980
	Dirty Looks	*Dirty Looks*	Stiff/Epic	1980
	Thomas Dolby	*Blinded By Science*	EMI/Harv	1982
	Night	*Long Distance*	Planet	1980
	Praying Mantis	*Time Tells No Lies*	Arista	1981
	Quincy	*Quincy*	CBS	1980
w. Mutt Lange	Records	*Shades In Bed*	Virgin	1970
	Peter Straker	*The Changeling*	EMI	1978
	Talk Talk	*It's My Life*	EMI	1984
	Tight Fit	*Tight Fit*	Jive	1982
	Zones	*Under Influence*	Arista	1979

F038 Ken Friesen

	American Flyer	*Spirit Of A Woman*	UA	1977
	Gordon Lightfoot	*Shadows*	WB	1982

F039 Robert Fripp

	Fripp and Eno	*No Pussyfooting*	EG	1973
	Fripp and Eno	*Evening Star*	EG	1975
	Robert Fripp	*Exposure*	EG	1979
	Robert Fripp	*Under Heavy Manners*	EG	1980
	Robert Fripp	*Let The Power Fall*	EG	1981
	Robert Fripp	*League Of Gentlemen*	EG	1981
	Peter Gabriel	*Peter Gabriel Two*	Char/Atco	1978
	Daryl Hall	*Sacred Songs*	RCA	1980
	Roches	*The Roches*	WB	1979
	Roches	*Keep On Doing*	WB	1982
	Andy Summers and Robert Fripp	*I Advance Masked*	A&M	1982

F040 John Fry

	Big Star	*#1 Record*	Ardent	1972
	Big Star	*Radio City*	Ardent	1974

F041 Fritz Fryer

	CMU	*Space Cabaret*	Tra	1972
	Lee Fardon	*Stories Of Adventure*	Aura	1981

Global Village Trucking Company	*Global Village Trucking Company*	Virgin	1975
Horslips	*Dance Hall Sweethearts*	RCA	1974
Horslips	*The Unfortunate Cup Of Tea*	RCA	1975
Motorhead	*On Parole*	UA	1976
Nucleus	*Under The Sun*	Vertigo	1974
Prelude	*After The Goldrush*	Island	1974
Rock Workshop	*The Very Last Time*	CBS	1971
Skin Alley	*Two Quid Deal*	Tra	1972
Stackridge	*Stackridge*	MCA	1971

F042 Jerry Fuller

Butts Band	*Hear And Now*	B.Thumb	1975
Knickerbockers	*Lies*	Challenge	1966

F043 Lew Futterman

	Dirty Angels	*Dirty Angels*	A&M	1978
	If	*If*	Isl/Cap	1970
	If	*If 2*	Isl/Cap	1970
	If	*If 3*	UA/Cap	1971
	If	*If 4*	UA	1972
	If	*Not Just Another Bunch Of Pretty Faces*	Gull/Cap	1974
	If	*Teabreak Over, Back On Your Heads*	Gull/Cap	1975
	Brother Jack McDuff	*A Change Is Gonna Come*	Atlantic	1966
	Brother Jack McDuff	*Tobacco Road*	Atlantic	1967
	Ted Nugent	*Tooth, Fang & Claw*	WB	1974
	Ted Nugent	*Call Of The Wild*	WB	1975
w. Tom Werman	Ted Nugent	*Ted Nugent*	Epic	1975
w. Tom Werman	Ted Nugent	*Free For All*	Epic	1976
w. Tom Werman	Ted Nugent	*Cat Scratch Fever*	Epic	1977
w. Tom Werman	Ted Nugent	*Double Live Gonzo*	Epic	1978
w. Tom Werman	Ted Nugent	*Weekend Warriors*	Epic	1978
	Ted Nugent	*State Of Shock*	Epic	1979

G001 Pete Gage

Joan Armatrading	*Back To The Night*	A&M	1975
Barracudas	*Mean Time*	Closer	1983
Hustler	*High Street*	A&M	1974
Movies	*The Movies*	A&M	1975
Sassafras	*Riding High*	Chrysalis	1976

G002 Phil Galdston

Robin Williams	*Throbbing Python Of Love*	Casab	1983

G003 Stephan Galfas

	Philip D'Arrow	*Philip D'Arrow*	Polydor	1979
	Good Rats	*Rat City In Blue*	Platinum	1976
w. Flo and Eddie	Good Rats	*From Rats To Riches*	Passport	1978
w. John Jansen	Good Rats	*Birth Comes To Us All*	Passport	1979
	Intergalactic Touring Band	*Intergalactic Touring Band*	Char/Pass	1977

(features an early singing appearance by Meatloaf.)

	Magnet	*Worldwide Attraction*	A&M	1979
	Meatloaf	*Deadringer*	CBS	1981
	Pezband	*Pezband*	Passport	1977
	Quacky Duck	*Media Push*	WB	1974
	Rollers	*Ricochet*	Epic	1981
	Southside Johnny	*Reach Up And Touch The Sky*	Mercury	1981
	Didi Stewart	*Begin Here*	Kirshner	1982
	John Tropea	*To Touch You Again*	TK	1979
	Martha Velez	*American Heartbeat*	Sire	1977

G004 Mickey Gallagher

	Pearl Harbour	*Don't Follow Me I'm Lost Too*	WB	1980

G005 Don Galluci

	Crabby Appleton	*Crabby Appleton*	Elektra	1970
	Stooges	*Fun House*	Elektra	1970

G006
Albhy Galuten (see also under Karl Richardson)

	Jesse "Ed" Davis	*Ululu*	Atco	1972
w. Tom Dowd	Jo Mama	*J Is For Jump*	Atlantic	1971
w. Tom Dowd	James Montgomery Band	*High Roller*	Capricorn	1974

G007 Thomas Earnest Gamache

	American Patrol	*Back Seat Boogie*	Vanity	1983
	D.B.Cooper	*Buy American*	WB	1980
	D.B.Cooper	*Dangerous Curves*	WB	1981
	Dr. Demento	*Dr. Demento's Delights*	WB	1976

G008 Joe Gannon

	Greg Allman	*The Greg Allman Tour*	Capricorn	1974

G009 Don Gant

w. Ron Chancey	Bobby Bland	*Get On Down*	ABC	1975
	Bobby Braddock	*Between The Lines*	Elektra	1979
	Bobby Braddock	*Love Bomb*	Elektra	1980
	Jimmy Buffett	*A White Sport Coat And A Pink Crustaecian*	ABC	1974
	Jimmy Buffett	*A.1.A*	ABC	1974
	Jimmy Buffett	*Living And Dying In 3/4 Time*	ABC	1974
	Jimmy Buffett	*Havana Daydreaming*	ABC	1975
	Killough and Eckley	*Killough and Eckley*	Epic	1977
	John D.Loudermilk	*Elloree-Volume 1*	WB	1971
	Mickey Newbury	*The Sailor*	Hickory	1979
w. Ron Chancey	Rafe Van Hoy	*Prisoner Of The Sky*	MCA	1980

G010 Jerry Garcia

	Good Old Boys	*Pistol Packin' Mama*	Round	1975
	Robert Hunter	*Tiger Rose*	Round	1975

G011 Brian Gardner

Tom Fogerty	*Tom Fogerty*	Fantasy	1972

G012
Thomas "Snuff" Garrett

soundtrack	*Any Which Way You Can*	WB-Viva	1980
Boys In The	*The Boys In The*		
Bunkhouse	*Bunkhouse*	UA	1977
soundtrack	*Bronco Billy*	Elektra	1980
Glen Campbell	*It's The World Gone*		
	Crazy	Capitol	1980
Carol Chase	*Some Songs*	Casab	1979
Cher	*Cher*	MCA	1974
Cher	*Half-Breed*	MCA	1974
Crickets	*Rock Reflections*	UA	1971
John Durrill	*Just For The Record*	UA	1978
Phil Everly	*Living Alone*	Elektra	1978
soundtrack	*Every Which Way But*		
	Loose	Elektra	1978
David Frizell	*On My Own Again*	Viva	1983
David Frizell and	*Carrying On The*		
Shelly West	*Family Names*	WB-Viva	1982
David Frizell and			
Shelly West	*Our Best To You*	WB-Viva	1983
David Frizell and			
Shelly West	*In Session*	Viva	1984
Snuff Garrett	*Snuff Garrett's Texas*		
	Opera Company	Rainwood	1977
Brian Hyland	*The Joker Went Wild*	Philips	1968
Jerry Inman	*You Betchum*	Elektra	1976
Brenda Lee	*L.A. Sessions*	MCA	1977
Gary Lewis and The	*A Session With Gary*		
Playboys	*Lewis and The Playboys*	Liberty	1965
Gary Lewis and The			
Playboys	*Everybody Loves A Clown*	Liberty	1965
Gary Lewis and The			
Playboys	*This Diamond Ring*	Liberty	1965
Gary Lewis and The			
Playboys	*She's Just My Style*	Liberty	1966
Gary Lewis and The	*You Don't Have To*		
Playboys	*Paint Me A Picture*	Liberty	1967
Larry Mahan	*King Of The Rodeo*	WB	1976
Ray Price	*Master Of The Art*	WB-Viva	1983
Telly Savalas	*Telly*	MCA	1974
soundtrack	*Sharky's Machine*	WB	1981
Shandi Sinnamon	*Shandi Sinnamon*	Asylum	1976
soundtrack	*Smokey and The Bandit 2*	MCA	1980
Sonny And Cher	*All I Ever Need Is You*	MCA	1974
Travel Agency	*The Travel Agency*	Dot	1967
(The Travel Agency featured a young J.J.Cale.)			
Tanya Tucker	*Tanya*	MCA	1975
Tanya Tucker	*Live*	MCA	1982
Bobby Vee	*Meets The Crickets*	Liberty	1962
Bobby Vee	*Tribute To Buddy Holly*	Liberty	1963
w. B.Reisdorff Bobby Vee	*Meets The Crickets*	Liberty	1963

	Porter Wagoner	*Viva Porter Wagoner*	WB-Viva	1983
w. Steve Dorff	Dottie West	*New Horizons*	Liberty	1983
w. Steve Dorff	Shelly West	*West By West*	WB-Viva	1983
w. Steve Dorff	Shelly West	*Red Hot*	Viva	1983

(In addition to producing over 25 US Top Ten singles, Garrett has produced albums for Julie London, Gene McDaniels as well as his marathon series of "The 50 Guitars Of Tommy Garrett" albums. As a publisher he owns the rights to "Summertime Blues" and "Young Girl"

G013 Val Garay

	Joan Armatrading	*The Key*	A&M	1983
	Marty Balin	*Lucky*	EMI-Amer	1983
	Kim Carnes	*Mistaken Identity*	EMI-Amer	1981
	Kim Carnes	*Voyeur*	EMI-Amer	1982
	Craig Fuller and Eric Kaz	*Craig Fuller/Eric Kaz*	CBS	1978
	Richie Furay	*I Still Have Dreams*	Asylum	1979
	Mr. Big	*Photographic Smile*	Arista	1976
w. Russ Kunkel	Leah Kunkel	*Leah Kunkel*	CBS	1979
	Randy Meisner	*One More Song*	CBS	1980
	Motels	*All Four One*	Capitol	1982
	Motels	*Little Robbers*	Capitol	1983
	Pablo Cruise	*Lifeline*	A&M	1978
	Pan	*Pan*	CBS	1973

(Group featured Ron Elliott, former Beau Brummel.)

	Dolly Parton	*The Great Pretender*	RCA	1984
	Ronin	*Ronin*	Mercury	1980
	Volunteers	*Volunteers (3 tracks)*	Arista	1976

G014 Russ Gary

	Doug Clifford	*Doug "Cosmo" Clifford*	Fantasy	1972
w. R.DaShiell	Crowfoot	*Crowfoot*	Paramount	1970
w. R.DaShiell	Crowfoot	*Find The Sun*	Paramount	1971
	Tom Fogerty	*Myopia*	Fantasy	1974
	Tom Fogerty	*Zephyr National*	Fantasy	1974
	Redwing	*Redwing*	Fantasy	*1971*
	Redwing	*What This Country Needs*	Fantasy	1972

G015 Terry Garthwaite

	Ferron	*Shadows Of A Dime*	Lucy	1984

G016 Nick Garvey

w. Rick Chertoff	A's	*A Woman's Got The Power*	Arista	1981
	Dirty Looks	*Turn It Up*	Stiff/Epic	1981
	Fingerprintz	*Distinguishing Marks*	Virgin	1980
	Nick Garvey	*Blue Skies*	Virgin	1982
w. Peter Ker	Motors	*Approved By The Motors*	Virgin	1978
w. Peter Ker	Bram Tchaikovsky	*Strange Man, Changed Man*	Radar	1979
	Bram Tchaikovsky	*Funland*	Arista	1981

G017 David Gates

	Pleasure Fair	*The Pleasure Fair*	Uni	1967

(David Gates, of course, produced the bulk of Bread's albums as well as his own solo albums after Bread split up.)

G018 Bob Gaudio

	Alessi Brothers	Words and Music	A&M	1979
	Chris Christian	Chris Christian	Boardwalk	1981
	Neil Diamond	I'm Glad You're Here With Me Tonight	CBS	1977
	Neil Diamond	You Don't Bring Me Flowers	CBS	1978
	Neil Diamond	September Morn	CBS	1979
	Richard Fagan	Richard Fagan	Mercury	1979
	Four Seasons	Genuine Imitation Life Gazette	Philips	1968
	Four Seasons	Chameleon	Mowest	1975
	Four Seasons	Who Loves You	WB	1975
	Four Seasons	Helicon	WB	1977
w. C.Calello	Four Seasons	Reunited-Live	WB	1981
	Frank Sinatra	Watertown	Reprise	1970
	Stoneground	Hearts Of Stone	WB	1978
	Frankie Valli	Close-Up (4 tracks)	P.Stock	1975
	Frankie Valli	Valli	P.Stock	1977
	Frankie Valli	Frankie Valli Is The Word	WB-Curb	1978
w. Bob Crewe	Frankie Valli	Heaven Above Me	MCA	1980

G019 Don Gehman

	John Cougar	American Fool	Riva	1982
	John Cougar	Uh-Huh	Riva	1983
	Billy Satellite	Billy Sattelite	Capitol	1984
	Stephen Stills	Illegal Stills	CBS	1976
	Stills-Young Band	Long May You Run	Reprise	1976

G020 Lowell George

	Tret Fure	Tret Fure	Uni	1973
	Lowell George	Thanks I'll Eat It Here	WB	1979
	Grateful Dead	Shakedown Street	Arista	1978
	Howdy Moon (Featured Valerie Carter)	Howdy Moon	A&M	1974
	Little Feat	Dixie Chicken	WB	1973
	Little Feat	Feats Don't Fail Me Now	WB	1974
	Little Feat	The Last Record Album	WB	1975
	Little Feat	Waiting For Columbus	WB	1978
	Little Feat	Down On The Farm	WB	1979
w.Audie Ashworth	John Starling	Long Time Gone	Sugar Hill	1980

G021 Neil Geraldo

w. P.Coleman	Pat Benatar	Get Nervous	Chrysalis	1982
	Pat Benatar	Live From Earth	Chrysalis	1983
	John Waite	Ignition	Chrysalis	1982

G022 Phil Gernhard

	Arrogance	Suddenly	WB	1980
w. Tony Scott	Bellamy Brothers	Let Your Love Flow	WB	1976
	Bellamy Brothers	Plain And Fancy	WB	1977
	Dion	Dion	Laurie	1969
	Dion	Sit Down Old Friend	WB	1970

	Dion	*You're Not Alone*	WB	1971
	Dion	*Sanctuary*	WB	1971
	Dion	*Born To Be With You*	PSI	1975
	Lobo	*Of A Simple Man*	Philips	1974
	Lobo	*Calumet*	Philips	1974
	Lobo	*Just A Singer*	Big Tree	1975
	Royal Guardsmen	*Snoopy Vs. The Red Baron*	Laurie	1966
	Royal Guardsmen	*Snoopy And His Friends*	Laurie	1967
	Royal Guardsmen	*Snoopy For President*	Laurie	1968
	Royal Guardsmen	*Return Of The Red Baron*	*Laurie*	1968
	Snuff	*Snuff*	Elek-Curb	1982
	Jim Stafford	*Jim Stafford*	MGM	1974
w. Lobo	Jim Stafford	*Spiders and Snakes*	MGM	1974
w. Lobo	Jim Stafford	*Not Just Another Pretty Fool*	MGM	1975
	Hank Williams, Jnr	*Family Tradition (1 tr)*	*Elektra*	1979

G023 Steve Gibson

	Gene Cotton	*Rain On*	ABC	1976
	Gene Cotton	*Save The Dancer*	Ariola	1978

G024 Voyle Gilmore

	John Stewart	*Signals Through The Glass*	Capitol	1968

G025 David Gilmour

w. Roger Waters	Syd Barrett	*The Madcap Laughs*	Harvest	1969
w. Rick Wright	Syd Barrett	*Barrett*	Harvest	1970

G026 Chuck Glaser

	Kinky Friedman	*Sold American*	Vanguard	1973

G027 Dick Glasser

	Everley Brothers	*In Our Image*	WB	1966
	Everley Brothers	*Sing*	WB	1967
	Everley Brothers	*Beat And Soul*	WB	1965
	Gary Puckett	*The New Gary Puckett Album*	CBS	1969
	Ventures	*Walk Don't Run Vol.2*	Liberty	1964
	Ventures	*Knock Me Out*	Liberty	1965
	Ventures	*On Stage*	Liberty	1965
	Hank Williams, Jnr	*Hank Williams, Jnr And Friends*	MGM	1975
	Mason Williams	*Music*	WB	1969
	Mason Williams	*Hand Made*	WB	1970

G028 Ted Glasser

	Mars Bonfire	*Faster Than The Speed Of Life*	CBS	1968
	Gentlehood	*Gentlehood*	CBS	1973

G029 Nick Glennie-Smith

	Ian Gomm	*The Village Voice*	Albion	1983

G030 The Glimmer Twins (Mick Jagger and Keith Richard)

Rolling Stones	*It's Only Rock 'n' Roll*	RSR	1974
Rolling Stones	*Love You Live*	RSR	1977
Rolling Stones	*Some Girls*	RSR	1978
Rolling Stones	*Emotional Rescue*	RSR	1980
Rolling Stones	*Tattoo You*	RSR	1981
Rolling Stones	*Still Life*	RSR	1982
Rolling Stones	*Under Cover*	RSR	1983

G031 Jeff Glixman

	Paul Barrere	*On My Own Two Feet*	WB	1983
	Blind Date	*Blind Date*	Windsong	1979
	(a.k.a. The Ratz, from San Francisco.)			
	Boxer	*Absolutely*	Epic	1977
	Gambler	*Teenage Magic*	EMI-Amer	1979
	Head East	*A Different Kind Of Crazy*	A&M	1979
	Kansas	*Song For America*	Epic/Kir	1975
	Kansas	*Leftoverture*	Kirshner	1976
	Kansas	*Point Of Know Return*	Kirshner	1978
	Magnum	*Chase The Dragon*	Jet	1982
	Gary Moore	*Corridors Of Power*	Virgin	1982
	Gary Moore	*Victims Of The Future*	Vir/Mirage	1984
	Mothers Finest	*Iron Age*	Epic	1981
	Saxon	*The Power And The Glory*	Carrere	1983
	Paul Stanley	*Paul Stanley*	Casab	1978
w. S.Lillywhite	Urban Verbs	*Early Damage*	WB	1981

G032 Mick Glossop

	Ashra	*Correlations*	Virgin	1979
	Camel	*Reckless*	Decca	1979
	Ian Gillan	*Magic*	Virgin	1982
	Hambi and The Dance	*Heartache*	Virgin	1982
	Interview	*Snakes And Losers*	Virgin	1980
	Lurkers	*Fulham Fallout*	B.Banquet	1978
	Passions	*Sanctuary*	Polydor	1982
	Ruts	*The Crack*	Virgin	1979
	Skids	*The Absolute Game*	Virgin	1980
	UFO	*Making Contact*	Chrysalis	1983
	Wanderers	*Only Lovers Left Alive*	Polydor	1981
	Waysted	*Vices*	Chrysalis	1983

G033 Henry Glover

Paul Butterfield	*Put It In Your Ear*	Bearsville	1976
Dave "Baby" Cortez	*In Orbit With*	Roulette	1965
Tommy James	*It's Only Love*	Roulette	1967

G034 John Glover

Amazing Blondel	*Inspiration*	DJM	1975
Amazing Blondel	*Bad Dreams*	DJM	1976
Amazing Blondel	*Live In Tokyo*	DJM	1977

G035 Roger Glover

David Coverdale	*Northwinds*	Purple	1978
Elf	*Carolina County Ball*	Purple	1974
Roger Glover	*The Butterfly Ball*	Purple	1974

Roger Glover	*Elements*	Polydor	1978
Grand Theft	*Have You Seen This Band*	EMI	1978
Maciver/Hine	*Pick Up A Bone*	Purple	1974
Judas Priest	*Sin After Sin*	CBS	1977
Nazareth	*Loud 'n' Proud*	Mooncr/A&M	1973
Nazareth	*Razamanazz*	Mount/A&M	1973
Nazareth	*Rampant*	Mount/A&M	1974
Rainbow	*Down To Earth*	Polydor	1979
Rainbow	*Difficult To Cure*	Polydor	1981
Rainbow	Straight Between The *Eyes*	Poly/Merc	1982
Rainbow	*Bent Out Of Shape*	Poly/Merc	1983
Michael Schenker Group	*Michael Schenker Group*	Chrysalis	1980
Strapps	*Strapps*	Harvest	1976
Whitesnake	*Snakebite*	UA	1978
Young And Moody	*Young And Moody*	Magnet	1977

G036 Godley and Creme

Blue Rondo A La Turk	*Chewing The Fat*	Virgin	1982
Mickey Jupp	*Long Distance Romancer*	Chrysalis	1979

G037 Andrew Gold

Karla Bonoff	*Live*	CBD	1980
Rita Coolidge	*Heartbreak Radio*	A&M	1981
Nicolette Larson	*All Dressed Up And No Place To Go*	WB	1982
Moon Martin	*Mystery Ticket*	Capitol	1982

G038 Ritchie Gold

Harvey Andrews	*Fantasies From A Corner Seat*	Tra	1975
Mae McKenna	*Everything That Touches Me*	Tra	1975
Mae McKenna	*Walk On Water*	Tra	1977
Meal Ticket	*Three Times A Day*	Logo	1977
Pasadena Roof Orchestra	*Isn't It Romantic*	Tra	1976
Pasadena Roof Orchestra	*On Tour*	Tra	1976
Sadista Sisters	*Sadista Sisters*	Tra	1976
various artists	*A Poke In The Eye With A Sharp Stick*	Tra	1975

G039 Wally Gold

Kansas	*Kansas*	CBS/Kir	1974
Neil Sedaka	*Emergence*	RCA	1972

G040 Barry Goldberg

David Blue	*Cupid's Arrow*	Asylum	1976
Mother Earth	*Living With The Animals*	Mercury	1968
Charley Musselwhite	*Stone Blues*	Vanguard	1968
Rockets	*The Rockets*	W.Whale	1968

G041 Jim Golden

w. Bob Monaco	Cryan Shames	*Sugar and Spice*	CBS	1966
w. Bob Monaco	Cryan Shames	*A Scratch In The Sky*	CBS	1967
	Cryan Shames	*Synthesis*	CBS	1968

G042 Stephen R. Goldman

Flamin' Groovies	*Supersnazz*	Epic	1969
Dirk Hamilton	*Alias*	ABC	1977
Van Dyke Parks	*Jump*	WB	1984

G043 George Goldner

Joey Dee	*Dance, Dance, Dance*	Roulette	1963

G044 Jerry Goldstein

Eric Andersen	*Avalanche*	WB	1970
Blood, Sweat & Tears	*Nuclear Blues*	LAX	1980
Tim Buckley	*Greetings From L.A.*	WB	1974
Eric Burdon Band	*Sun Secrets*	Capitol	1974
Eric Burdon Band	*Stop*	Capital	1975
Eric Burdon and War	*The Black Man's Burdon*	Liberty	1970
Eric Burdon and War	*Eric Burdon Declares War*	Polydor	1970
Circle Jerks	*Golden Shower Of Hits*	Alleg	1983
Dick Glass	*Glass Derringer*	LAX	1976
McCoys	*Hang On Sloopy*	Bang	1965
Lee Oskar	*Lee Oskar*	MCA	1976
Tanya Tucker	*T.N.T.*	MCA	1978
War	*War*	UA	1971
War	*All Day Music*	UA	1971
War	*The World Is A Ghetto*	Isl/UA	1973
War	*Deliver The Word*	Isl/UA	1973
War	*Why Can't We Be Friends*	Isl/UA	1975
War	*Platinum Funk*	Isl/UA	1977
War	*Love Is All Around*	MCA/ABC	1976
War	*Galaxy*	MCA	1978
War	*Music Band*	MCA	1979
War	*Music Band 2*	MCA	1979
War	*Outlaw*	RCA	1982
War	*Life Is So Strange*	RCA	1983
Jimmy Witherspoon	*Life Is A Five Letter Word*	Capitol	1975

G045 Giorgio Gomelsky

	Blossom Toes	*If Only For A Moment*	Marmalade	1969
	Julie Driscoll	*Streetnoise*	Marmalade	1969
	Gong	*Angel's Egg*	Virgin	1973
	John McLaughlin	*Extrapolation*	Marmalade	1969
	Magma	*Mechanik*	A&M	1973
	Magma	*Live*	RCA	1975
w. G.Chkiantz	Julie Tippetts	*Sunset Glow*	Utopia	1975
	Yardbirds	*Five Live Yardbirds*	EMI	1964

G046 Dave Goodman

Eater	*The Album*	The Label	1977

G047 Steve Goodman

John Prine	*Bruised Orange*	Asylum	1978

G048 Miles Goodwyn

Teaze	*One Night Stands*	Capitol	1979

(As leading member of April Wine, Goodwyn has produced all of April Wine's output since 1976, more recently co-producing with Mike Stone.)

G049 Al Gorgoni

Eric Andersen	*More Hits From Tin Can Alley*	Vanguard	1968

G050 Alan Gorrie

U.K. Players	*No Way Out*	A&M	1982

G051 Arthur Gorson

Ars Nova	*Sunshine And Shadows*	Atlantic	1969
David Blue	*David Blue*	Elektra	1966
Tom Rush	*The Circle Game*	Elektra	1968
White Lightnin'	*File Under Rock*	Olympic	1969
White Lightnin'	*Fresh Air*	Polydor	1970

G052 Richard Gotterher

	Joan Armatrading	*Me Myself I*	A&M	1980
	Aum	*Bluesvibes*	Sire	1969
	Blondie	*Blondie*	P.Stock	1977
	Blondie	*Plastic Letters*	Chrysalis	1977
	Bongos	*Numbers With Wings*	RCA	1983
	Joe "King" Carrasco	*Party Weekend*	MCA	1983
w. Craig Leon	Chilliwack	*Rockerbox*	Sire	1975
	Climax Chicago	*Rich Man*	Sire	1972
	Climax Chicago	*Sense Of Direction*	Polydor	1974
	Marshall Crenshaw	*Marshall Crenshaw*	WB	1982
	Darling	*Put It Down To Experience*	Charisma	1979

(Group featured Hal Lindes, later to join Dire Straits.)

	Dirty Angels	*Kiss Tomorrow Goodbye*	P.Stock	1977
	Dr. Feelgood	*Private Practice*	UA	1978
	Paul Geremia	*Paul Geremia*	Sire	1970
w. Rob Freeman	Go-Go's	*Beauty And The Beat*	IRS	1981
	Go-Go's	*Vacation*	IRS	1982
	Robert Gordon	*Robert Gordon with Link Wray*	P.Stock	1977
	Robert Gordon	*Fresh Fish Special*	P.Stock	1978
	Robert Gordon	*Rock Billy Boogie*	RCA	1979
	Robert Gordon	*Bad Boy*	RCA	1980
	Richard Hell and The Voidoids	*Blank Generation*	Sire	1977
	Holly and The Italians	*The Right To Be Italian*	Virgin	1981
	Peter Kelley	*Dealin' Blues*	Sire	1971
	McCoys	*Hang On Sloopy*	Bang	1965
	Renaissance	*Turn Of The Cards*	BTM	1974

	Regina Richards and Red Hot	*Regina Richards and Red Hot*	1&M	1981
	Tim Scott	*Swear*	Sire	1983
	Martha Velez	*Matinee Weepers*	Sire	1973
	Link Wray	*Bullshot*	Char/Inst	1979
w. T.Panunzio	Link Wray	*Live At El Paradiso*	Instant	1980
	Yachts	*Yachts*	Radar	1979

G053 Graham Gouldman

	Gilbert O'Sullivan	*Life And Rhymes*	CBS	1980
	Ramones	*Pleasant Dreams*	Sire	1981
	various	*Animalympics*	Mercury	1980

G054 Nick Gravenites

	Big Brother	*Be A Brother*	CBS	1970
w. M.Melford	Michael Bloomfield	*It's Not Killing Me*	CBS	1969
	Brewer and Shipley	*Weeds*	K.S	1969
	Brewer and Shipley	*Tarkio*	K.S.	1971
	Danny Cox	*Danny Cox*	Dunhill	1971
	Nick Gravenites and John Cipollina	*Monkey Medicine*	Big Beat	1982
	Nick Gravenites and Mike Bloomfield	*Steelyard Blues*	WB	1972
	Sam Lay	*In Bluesland*	B.Thumb	1970
w. Harvey Brooks and Pete Welding	Quicksilver Messenger Service	*Quicksilver Messenger Service*	Capitol	1968
w. John Kahn	Southern Comfort	*Southern Comfort*	CBS	1969
	various artists	*Mill Valley Jam Session*	Polydor	1972

G055 Nigel Gray

	Code Blue	*Code Blue*	WB	1980
	Danse Society	*Heaven Is Waiting*	Arista	1984
	Gas	*Emotional Warfare*	Polydor	1981
	Girls School	*Screaming Blue Murder*	Bronze	1982
	Sonja Kristina	*Sonja Kristina*	Chopper	1980
	Hazel O' Connor	*Sons and Lovers*	Albion/A&M	1981
	Passions	*30,000 Feet Over China*	Polydor	1981
	Planets	*Spot*	Rialto	1980
	Police	*Regatta de Blanc*	A&M	1979
	Police	*Zenyatta Mondatta*	A&M	1980
	Professionals	*I Didn't See It Coming*	Virgin	1981
	Fay Ray	*Contact You*	WEA/Elek	1982
	Siousxie and The Banshees	*Kaleidoscope*	Polydor	1980
	Siousxie and The Banshees	*Ju Ju*	Polydor	1981
	Roy Sundholm	*East To West*	Ensign	1981
	Tank	*Power Of The Hunter*	Kamaflage	1982
	Wishbone Ash	*Number The Brave*	MCA	1981

G056 Jay Graydon

w. David Foster	Airplay	*Airplay*	RCA	1979
	Sheena Easton	*Well Kept Secret*	EMI	1983
	Herbie Hancock	*Lite Me Up*	CBS	1982

	Al Jarreau	*This Time*	WB	1980
	Al Jarreau	*Breakin' Away*	WB	1981
	Al Jarreau	*Jarreau*	WB	1983
	Marc Jordan	*Blue Desert*	WB	1979
	Steve Kipner	*Knock The Walls Down*	Elektra	1979
	Manhattan Transfer	*Extensions*	Atlantic	1979
	Manhattan Transfer	*Mecca For Moderns*	Atlantic	1981
	Pages	*Pages*	Capitol	1981
	David Roberts	*All Dressed Up*	Elektra	1982

G057 John Grazier

| | Blue Ash | *No More, No Less* | Mercury | 1973 |

G058 Mick Green

| | Shanghai | *Shanghai* | WB | 1974 |
| | Shanghai | *Fallen Heroes* | WB | 1976 |

G059 Bill Greene

| | Taj Mahal | *Satisfied 'n' Tickled Too* | CBS | 1975 |

G060 Charles Greene

w. Brian Stone	Apache	*Apache*	Emerald	1981
w. Brian Stone	Buffalo Springfield	*Buffalo Springfield*	Atlantic	1967
w. Tom Dowd	Dr. John	*Remedies*	Atlantic	1970
	Dr. John	*The Sun, The Moon and The Herbs*	Atco	1971
w. C.Underwood	Dr. John	*Anytime, Anyplace*	Scepter	1974
	High Mountain Hoedown	*High Mountain Hoedown*	Atco	1970
w. Brian Stone	Rose Garden	*The Rose Garden*	Atco	1968
	Sail	*Steppin' Out On A Saturday Night*	UA	1978
	Alan Toussaint	*Toussaint*	DJM	1970

G061 Marlin Greene

| | John Hammond | *Southern Fried* | Atlantic | 1970 |
| w. Jann Wenner | Boz Scaggs | *Boz Scaggs* | Atlantic | 1972 |

G062 Mitch Greenhill

	Robin Flower	*First Dibs*	F.Fish	1984
	John Renbourn Group	*Live In America*	F.Fish	1982
	Dave Van Ronk	*Somebody Else, Not Me*	Philo	1980
	Doc and Merle Watson	*Look Away*	UA	1978
	Doc and Merle Watson	*Live and Pickin'*	UA	1979
	Doc and Merle Watson	*Guitar Album*	UA	1983

G063 Dale Griffin

	Def Leppard	*On Through The Night*	Mercury	1980
w. O.Watts	Hanoi Rocks	*Back To Mystery City*	Lick	1983
	Slaughter	*Bite Back*	DJM	1980

G064 Nick Griffiths

| | Cozy Powell | *Octopuss* | Polydor | 1983 |
| | T.V. Smith's Explorers | *Last Words Of The The Great Explorer* | Epic | 1981 |

G065 Stefan Grossman

Duck Baker	*When You Wore A Tulip*	K.Mule	1977
Duck Baker	*The Art Of Finger Style Guitar*	K.Mule	1979
Duck Baker	*The King Of Bongo Bong*	K.Mule	1977
Mickey Baker	*Jazz Rock Guitar*	K.Mule	1978
David Cohen	*How To Play Folk Guitar*	K.Mule	1976

(David Cohen was formerly in Country Joe and The Fish)

Peter Finger	*Acoustic Rock Guitar*	K.Mule	1977
Davey Graham	*Dance For Two People*	K.Mule	1979
Sam Mitchell	*Bottleneck and Slide Guitar*	K.Mule	1976
Sam Mitchell	*Follow You Down*	K.Mule	1978
Charlie Musselwhite	*Harmonica According To Charlie Musselwhite*	K.Mule	1978
Tom Paley	*Hard Luck Papa*	K.Mule	1978
Leo Wijnkamp,Jnr	*Return Of Dr. Hackenbush*	K.Mule	1979
various artists	*Blues Guitar Workshop*	K.Mule	1979
various artists	*Kicking Mule's Flat Picking Guitar Festival*	K.Mule	1979

G066 James William Guercio

w. B.Johnston

Beach Boys	*L.A.(Light Album)*	CBS	1979
Blood, Sweat and Tears	*Blood, Sweat and Tears*	CBS	1968
Buckinghams	*Portraits*	CBS	1968
Buckinghams	*Time And Changes*	CBS	1970
Chicago	*Chicago Transit Authority*	CBS	1968
Chicago	*Chicago*	CBS	1970
Chicago	*3*	CBS	1971
Chicago	*4*	CBS	1971
Chicago	*5*	CBS	1972
Chicago	*6*	CBS	1973
Chicago	*7*	CBS	1974
Chicago	*8*	CBS	1975
Chicago	*9 (Greatest Hits)*	CBS	1975
Chicago	*10*	CBS	1976
Chicago	*11*	CBS	1977
Gerard	*Gerard*	Caribou	1976
Illinois Speed Press	*The Illinois Speed Press*	CBS	1968
Illinois Speed Press	*Duet*	CBS	1970

(Group featured Paul Cotton, later to star in Poco.)

Lake	*Ouch !*	Caribou	1981
Sailor	*Dressed For Drowning*	Caribou	1980
soundtrack	*Electra Glide In Blue*	UA	1973
Carl Wilson	*Carl Wilson*	CBS	1982

G067 John Guerin

David Blue	*Comin' Back For More*	Asylum	1975
Keith Carradine	*Easy*	Asylum	1979
Terry Garthwaite	*Hand In Glove*	Fantasy	1978

G068 James Guthrie

	Ambrosia	*Road Island*	WB	1982.
	Heatwave	*Candles*	GTO	1980
	Judas Priest	*Killing Machine*	CBS	1978
	Movies	*Double A*	GTO	1977
	Movies	*Bullets Through The Barrier*	A&M	1978
w. M.Kamen	Pink Floyd	*The Final Cut*	Harv/CBS	1983
	Runner	*Runner*	Acrobat	1979

H001 John Haeny

	Ned Doheny	*Ned Doheny*	Asylum	1973
	Tom Jans	*Through The Eyes Of An Only Child*	CBS	1975
	Ohio Knox	*Ohio Knox*	Reprise	1971
	Jim Morrison and The Doors	*An American Prayer*	Elektra	1978
	Roxy	*Roxy*	Elektra	1969
	(Featuring Bob Segarini and Randy Bishop.)			
	Sanford and Townsend	*Duo Glide*	WB	1978
	Savage Grace	*2*	Reprise	1971
	Richard Torrance	*Bareback*	Capitol	1977

H002 Ron Haffkine

	City Streets	*Livin' In The Jungle*	RCA	1070
	Mac Davis	*Thunder In The Afternoon*	CBS	1977
	Dr. Hook	*Doctor Hook*	CBS	1972
	Dr. Hook	*Sloppy Seconds*	CBS	1972
	Dr. Hook	*Belly Up*	CBS	1973
	Dr. Hook	*Bankrupt*	Capitol	1975
	Dr. Hook	*A Little Bit More*	Capitol	1976
	Dr. Hook	*Makin' Love And Music*	Capitol	1977
	Dr. Hook	*Pleasure and Pain*	Capitol	1978
	Dr. Hook	*Sometimes You Win*	Capitol	1979
	Dr. Hook	*Live In The UK*	Capitol	1981
	Dr. Hook	*Rising*	Mercury	1980
	Dr. Hook	*Players In The Dark*	Mer/Casab	1982
	Helen Reddy	*Take What You Find*	Capitol	1980
	Ray Sawyer	*Ray Sawyer*	Capitol	1977
	Shel Silverstein	*Freakin' At The Freakers Ball*	CBS	1972
	Shel Silverstein	*Songs And Stories*	Parachute	1978

H003 Stephen Hague

	Gleaming Spires	*Songs Of The Spires*	Posh Boy	1982
	Gleaming Spires	*Walk On Well Lighted Streets*	PVC	1983
	Slow Children	*Slow Children*	Ensign	1981

H004 Lew Hahn

	Judy Collins	*Times Of Our Lives*	Elektra	1982
w. James Taylor	Kate Taylor	*Kate Taylor*	CBS	1978

H005 Roy Halee

	Big Wha-Koo	*The Big Wha-Koo*	ABC	1977
	Blue Angel	*Blue Angel*	Polydor	1980
	(Cyndi Lauper's first group.)			
	Blood Sweat & Tears	*3*	CBS	1970
	Blood Sweat & Tears	*Brand New Day*	ABC	1977
	Art Garfunkel	*Angel Clare*	CBS	1973
	Art Garfunkel	*Scissors Cut*	CBS	1981
w. Don Potter	Dan Hill	*If Dreams Had Wings*	Epic	1980
	Journey	*Journey*	CBS	1977
	Littlejohn	*Littlejohn*	Epic	1971
	Willie Nile	*Willie Nile*	Arista	1980
	Laura Nyro	*New York Tendaberry*	CBS	1969
	David Pomeranz	*The Truth Of Us*	Pacific	1980
	Roches	*Nurds*	WB	1980
	Rufus and Chaka Khan	*Street Player*	ABC	1978
	Rufus	*Numbers*	ABC	1979
	Boz Scaggs	*My Time*	CBS	1972
	Simon and Garfunkel	*Bookends*	CBS	1967
	Simon and Garfunkel	*Bridge Over Troubled Water*	CBS	1970
w. Phil Ramone	Simon and Garfunkel	*Reunion In Central Park*	Geffen	1982
	Paul Simon	*Paul Simon*	CBS	1972
	Paul Simon	*There Goes Rhymin' Simon (4 tracks only)*	CBS	1973
w. Russ Titelman	Paul Simon	*Hearts and Bones*	WB	1983

H006 Rick Hall

Clarence Carter	*This Is Clarence Carter*	Atlantic	1968
Clarence Carter	*The Dynamic Clarence Carter*	Atlantic	1968
Clarence Carter	*Testifyin'*	Atlantic	1969
Clarence Carter	*Patches*	Atlantic	1970
Clarence Carter	*60 Minutes With*	Fame	1974
Mac Davis	*Mac Davis*	CBS	1973
Travis Wammack	*Travis Wammack*	Fame	1972
Travis Wammack	*Not For Sale*	Capricorn	1975

H007 Daryl Hall

Stephen Dees	*Hip Shot*	RCA	1977

H008 Don Hall

Jimmy Campbell	*Half-Baked*	Vertigo	1970
Curt Newbury	*Half A Month Of Maydays*	Verve	1969

H009 John Hall

Pacheco and Alexander	*Pacheco and Alexander*	CBS	1971
Bonnie Raitt	*Takin' My Time*	WB	1973

H010 Bill Halverson

Batdorf and Rodney	*Batdorf and Rodney*	Asylum	1972
Blue Mountain Eagle	*Blue Mountain Eagle*	Atco	1970
Blues Image	*Blues Image*	Atco	1969

	Jack Bruce	*How's Tricks*	RSO	1977
	Highway Robbery	*For Love Or Money*	RCA	1972
	High Wind	*High Wind*	EMI	1979
	Alvin Lee	*Ride On*	RSO	1979
	Mason Proffit	*Bareback Rider*	WB	1973
	Roger McGuinn	*Peace On You*	CBS	1974
	Graham Nash and David Crosby	*Crosby and Nash*	Atlantic	1972
	REO Speedwagon	*Ridin' The Storm Out*	Epic	1973
	REO Speedwagon	*Lost In A Dream*	Epic	1979
	Spellbound	*Spellbound*	EMI-Amer	1978
	Stephen Stills	*Stephen Stills*	Atlantic	1970
	Stephen Stills	*Stephen Stills 2*	Atlantic	1972
w. Ron and Howie Albert	Stephen Stills	*Stills*	CBS	1975
	Richard Supa	*Tall Tales*	Polydor	1978
	Talbot Brothers	*The Talbot Brothers*	WB	1974
	Clifford T. Ward	*New England Days*	Mercury	1977
	Bobby Whitlock	*One Of A Kind*	Capricorn	1975
	Zephyr	*Zephyr (early Tommy Bolin group.)*	Probe	1970

H011 Bill Ham

	Jay Boy Adams	*Jay Boy Adams*	Atlantic	1977
	Jay Boy Adams	*Fork In The Road*	Atlantic	1978
	Point Blank	*Point Blank*	Arista	1976
	Point Blank	*Second Season*	Arista	1977
	Point Blank	*Airplay*	MCA	1979
	Point Blank	*The Hard Way*	MCA	1980
	Point Blank	*American Express*	MCA	1981
	Point Blank	*On A Roll*	MCA	1982
	Z.Z. Top	*First Album*	London	1970
	Z.Z. Top	*Rio Grande Mud*	London	1972
	Z.Z. Top	*Tres Hombres*	London	1973
	Z.Z. Top	*Fandango*	London	1975
	Z.Z. Top	*Tejas*	London	1976
	Z.Z. Top	*Deguello*	WB	1979
	Z.Z. Top	*El Loco*	WB	1981
	Z.Z. Top	*Eliminator*	WB	1983

H012 Peter Hammill

	Random Hold	*The View From Here*	Polydor	1980
	Random Hold	*Etceteraville*	Passport	1980

H013 John Hammond

	Addis and Crofut	*Eastern Ferris Wheel*	CBS	1968
w. Bob Porter	Kenny Burrell	*Bluesin' Around*	CBS	1983
	Bob Dylan	*Bob Dylan*	CBS	1962
	Bob Dylan	*The Freewheelin'*	CBS	1963
	Allen Ginsberg	*First Blues*	JHR	1982
	Son House	*Father Of Folk Blues*	CBS	1966
	Alberta Hunter	*Amtrak Blues*	CBS	1980

Alberta Hunter	*The Glory Of Alberta Hunter*	CBS	1982
Alberta Hunter	*Look For The Silver Lining*	CBS	1983
Stevie Ray Vaughan	*Texas Flood*	Epic	1983

(Listed as "executive producer".Similar credit on 1984 release.)

Lester Young	*Evening Of A Basie-ite*	CBS	1980

H014 Jeff Hanna

	Dirt Band	*The Dirt Band*	UA	1978
w. Bob Edwards	Dirt Band	*An American Dream*	UA	1979
	Dirt Band	*Make A Little Magic*	UA	1979
	Dirt Band	*Jealousy*	UA	1981

H015 Martin Hannett

	A Certain Ratio	*To Each...*	Factory	1980
	A Certain Ratio	*Sextet*	Factory	1981
	Basement Five	*1965-1980*	Island	1980
	Basement Five	*In Dub*	Island	1980
	John Cooper Clarke	*Disguise In Love*	Epic	1978
w. Steve Hopkins	John Cooper Clarke	*Snap,Crackle,Bop*	Epic	1980
w. Steve Hopkins	John Cooper Clarke	*Zip Style Method*	Epic	1982
	Durutti Column	*The Return Of The Durutti Column*	Factory	1979
	Joy Division	*Unknown Pleasures*	Factory	1979
	Joy Division	*Closer*	Factory	1980
	Joy Division	*Still*	Factory	1981
	Magazine	*The Correct Use Of Soap*	Virgin	1980
	New Order	*Movement*	Factory	1982
	Pauline Murray and The Invisible Girls	*Pauline Murray and The Invisible*	RSO	1980
	Psychedelic Furs	*The Psychedelic Furs (2 tracks only.)*	CBS	1980
	Section 25	*Always Now*	Factory	1981

H016 Mark Henry Harman

	Poco	*Head Over Heels*	ABC	1975
	Poco	*Live*	Epic	1976
	Poco	*Rose Of Cimarron*	ABC	1976
	Poco	*Indian Summer*	ABC	1978
	Neil Young	*On The Beach (3 tracks)*	Reprise	1979

H017 Bob Harris

	Druid	*Towards The sun*	EMI	1975

H018 Emmylou Harris

	Delia Bell	*Delia Bell*	WB	1983

H019 Roger Harris

	Steve Fromholz	*A Rumour In My Own Time*	Capitol	1976

H020 George Harrison

	Badfinger	*Straight Up*	Apple	1972

	George Harrison	*Wonderwall Music*	Apple	1968
	George Harrison	*Electronic Sound*	Zapple	1969
	George Harrison	*Living In The Material World*	Apple	1973
	George Harrison	*Dark Horse*	Apple	1974
	George Harrison	*Extra Texture*	Apple	1975
	George Harrison	*33 1/3rd*	Dark Horse	1976
w. Russ Titelman	George Harrison	*George Harrison*	Dark Horse	1979
w. Ray Cooper	George Harrison	*Somewhere In England*	Dark Horse	1981
w. Ray Cooper	George Harrison	*Gone Troppo*	Dark Horse	1982
	Jackie Lomax	*Is This What You Want*	Apple	1969
	Billy Preston	*That's The Way God Planned It*	Apple	1969
	Billy Preston	*Encouraging Words*	Apple	1970
	Radha Krsna Temple	*The Radha Krsna Temple*	Apple	1974
	Ravi Shankar	*Music Festival From India*	Dark Horse	1975
	Shankar Family and Friends	*Shankar Family and Friends*	Dark Horse	1974
	Splinter	*The Place I Love*	Dark Horse	1974
	Ringo Starr	*Stop And Smell The Roses (1 track)*	RCA/Board	1981

H021 Mickey Hart

	Diga Rhythm Band	*Diga*	Round	1976
	Rhythm Devils	*Play River Music*	Passport	1980

H022 Dan Hartman

	Average White Band	*Cupid's In Fashion*	RCA	1982
	Dan Hartman	*Images*	Blue Sky	1976
	Dan Hartman	*Instant Replay*	Blue Sky	1979
	Dan Hartman	*Relight My Fire*	Blue Sky	1979
	Dan Hartman	*It Hurts To Be In Love*	Blue Sky	1979
	Neil Sedaka	*Come See About Me*	MCA	1984
	38 Special	*38 Special*	A&M	1977
	38 Special	*Special Delivery*	A&M	1978

H023 Geoffrey Haslam

	Jan Akkerman	*Tabernakel*	Atlantic	1973
	Badger	*One Live Badger*	Atlantic	1973
	Burlesque	*Burlesque*	Arista	1977
	Cactus	*Hot And Sweaty*	Atco	1972
	Kevin Coyne	*Matching Head And Feet*	Virgin	1975
	Delbert and Glen	*Clean*	Atlantic	1973
	J.Geils Band	*Live-Full House*	Atlantic	1972
	Bill Haley	*Welcome Home Bill*	Antic	1974
	Eddie Harris	*I Need Some Money*	Atlantic	1975
	MC5	*High Times*	Atlantic	1971
	Herbie Mann	*London Underground*	Atlantic	1974
	George Melly	*Is At It Again*	Reprise	1976
	Ramatam	*In April Came The Dawning Of The Red Suns*	Atlantic	1973
	Jess Roden Band	*You Can Keep Your Hat On*	Island	1976
	Jess Roden Band	*Play It Dirty, Play It Class*	Island	1976

	Peter Skellern	*Kissing In The Cactus*	Mercury	1977
w. Shel Kagan	Velvet Underground	*Loaded*	Atlantic	1972
	Velvet Underground	*Live At Max's*	Atlantic	1972

H024 Alex Hassilev

	Hoyt Axton	*My Griffin Is Gone*	CBS	1974
	Cosmic Sounds	*The Zodiac*	Elektra	1967
	Dick Rosmini	*A Genuine Rosmini*	Imperial	1968
	Ananda Shankar	*Ananda Shankar*	Reprise	1970
	Richard Twice	*Richard Twice*	Philips	1969

H025 Dave Hassinger

	Electric Prunes	*Underground*	Reprise	1967
	Electric Prunes	*Mass In F Minor*	Reprise	1968
	Grateful Dead	*The Grateful Dead*	WB	1967
	Grateful Dead	*Anthem Of The Sun*	WB	1968

H026 Tony Hatch

	Searchers	*Meet The Searchers*	Pye	1963
	Searchers	*Sugar and spice*	Pye	1963
	Searchers	*It's The Searchers*	Pye	1964
	Searchers	*Sounds Like The Searchers*	Pye	1965
	Searchers	*Take Me For What I'm Worth*	Pye	1965
w. Des Parton	Sweet Sensation	*Sweet Sensation*	Pye	1975

H027 Dan Healy

	Charlatans	*The Charlatans*	Philips	1969
w. Bob Weir	Kingfish	*Kingfish*	Round	1976
	Doug Sahm	*Hell Of A Spell*	Takoma	1980

H028 Mike Hedges

	Associates	*Sulk*	B.Banquet	1982
	Creatures	*Feast*	Wonderland	1983
	Cure	*Seventeen Seconds*	Fiction	1980
	Cure	*Faith*	Fiction	1981

(Released in the USA as a compilation double album entitled "Happily Ever After" on A&M.)

	Diamond Head	*Borrowed Time*	MCA	1982
	Robert Gorl	*Night Full Of Tension*	Mute	1984
	Music For Pleasure	*Into The Rain*	Polydor	1982
	Southern Death Cult	*Southern Death Cult*	B.Banquet	1982

H029 Richard Heenan

	Crazy Horse	*Crazy Moon*	RCA	1978

H030 Zeus B. Held

	Dead Or Alive	*Sophisticated Boom Boom*	Epic	1984
	Fashion	*Fabrique*	Arista	1982
	Fashion	*Twilight Of Idols*	Epic	1984
	John Foxx	*The Golden Section*	Virgin	1983
	Gina X Performance	*Nice Mover*	EMI	1979

H031 Fred Hellerman

Arlo Guthrie	*Alice's Restaurant*	Reprise	1967
Arlo Guthrie	*Arlo*	Reprise	1968

H032 Bill Henderson

Headpins	*Turn It Loud*	Atlantic	1982
Toronto	*Lookin' For Trouble*	A&M	1980

H033 Peter Henderson

	Climax Blues Band	*Shine On*	WB/Sire	1978
	Lion	*Running All Night*	A&M	1980
	Rush	*Grace Under Pressure*	Mercury	1984
	Supertramp	*Breakfast In America*	A&M	1979
	Supertramp	*Paris*	A&M	1980
	Supertramp	*Famous Last Words*	A&M	1982
w. Rikki Farr	Tubes	*The Tubes Live*	A&M	1978

H034 Jimi Hendrix

Cat Mother	*The Street Giveth and The Street Taketh Away*	Polydor	1969
Eire Apparent	*Sunrise*	Buddah	1969

H035 Don Henley

w. Jim Ed Norman	Glenda Griffith	*Glenda Griffith*	Ariola	1977

H036 David Hentschel

Tony Banks	*A Curious Feeling*	Charisma	1979
Genesis	*A Trick Of The Tail*	Char/Atco	1976
Genesis	*Wind and Wuthering*	Char/Atco	1977
Genesis	*Seconds Out*	Char/Atl	1977
Genesis	*Then There Were Three*	Char/Atl	1978
Genesis	*Duke*	Char/Atl	1980
(All co-produced with Genesis.)			
David Hentschel	*Startling Music*	Ring O'	1975
David Hentschel	*Educating Rita*	Mercury	1983
Mike Oldfield	*QE2*	Virgin	1978
Kai Olsson	*Once In A While*	EMI	1975
Renaissance	*A Song For All Seasons*	WB/Sire	1978
Renaissance	*Azure D'Or*	WB/Sire	1979
Mike Rutherford	*Smallcreep's Day*	Charisma	1980
Marti Webb	*I'M Not That Kind Of Girl*	Polydor	1982

H037 Andy Hernandez

Coati Mundi	*The Former 12 Year Old Genius*	Virgin	1983
Palais Schaumberg	*Lupa*	Phonogram	1982

H038 John Hewlett

Dickies	*The Incredible Shrinking Dickies*	A&M	1979

H039 Simon Heyworth

Gong	*You*	Virgin	1974
Steve Hillage	*Fish Rising*	Virgin	1975

H040 Tony Hicks

Taggett	*Taggett*	EMI	1973

H041 Andy Hill

Bucks Fizz	*Bucks Fizz*	RCA	1981
Bucks Fizz	*Are You Ready*	RCA	1982
Bucks Fizz	*Hand Cut*	RCA	1983

H042 Steve Hillage

Robyn Hitchcock	*Groovy Decay*	Albion	1982
Ken Lockie	*The Impossible (9 tracks)*	Virgin	1981
Simple Minds	*Sister Feelings Call*	Virgin	1981
Simple Minds	*Sons And Fascination*	Virgin	1981

H043 Jimmy Hilliard

Everly Brothers	*Rock 'n' Soul*	WB	1965

H044 Chris Hillman

Dan McCorison	*Dan McCorison*	MCA	1977
Rick Roberts	*She Is A Song*	A&M	1973

H045 Rupert Hine

After The Fire	*Laser Love*	CBS	1979
Kevin Ayers	*Confessions Of Dr. Dream*	Island	1972
Cafe Jacques	*Round The Back*	Epic	1977
Cafe Jacques	*International*	Epic	1978
Camel	*I Can See Your House From Here*	Decca	1979
Chris De Burgh	*The Getaway*	A&M	1983
Chris De Burgh	*Man On The Line*	A&M	1984
Yvonne Elliman	*Food Of Love*	Purple	1973
Fixx	*Shuttered Room*	MCA	1982
Fixx	*Reach The Beach*	MCA	1983
Dave Greenslade	*Cactus Choir*	WB	1976
Rupert Hine	*Immunity*	A&M	1981
Rupert Hine	*Waving Not Drowning*	A&M	1982
Howard Jones	*Human's Lib*	WEA/Elek	1984
Jonesey	*Growing*	Dawn	1973
Little Heroes	*Watch The World*	Capitol	1983
Members	*1980, The Choice Is Yours*	Virgin	1980
No Dice	*Two-Faced*	EMI/Cap	1979
Nova	*Blink*	Arista	1975
Anthony Phillips	*Wise After The Event*	Arista	1978
Anthony Phillips	*Sides*	Arist/Pass	1979
Anthony Phillips	*Private Parts And Pieces Volume 2*	PVC	1980
Quantum Jump	*Quantum Jump*	Electric	1976
Quantum Jump	*Barracuda*	Electric	1977
Saga	*Worlds Apart*	Portrait	1982

Saga	*Heads Or Tails*	Portrait	1983
Wildlife	*Burning*	Chrysalis	1980

H046 Eddie Hinton

John Hammond	*Can't Beat The Kid*	Capricorn	1975

H047 Larry Hirsch

Alpha Band	*The Alpha Band*	Arista	1976
Alpha Band	*The Statue Makers Of Hollywood*	Arista	1978
Jules & The Polar Bears	*Got No Breeding*	CBS	1978

H048 David Hitchcock

Camel	*The Snow Goose*	Decca/Jan	1975
Camel	*A Live Record*	Decca	1978
Caravan	*Land Of Grey And Pink*	Decca/Lon	1971
Caravan	*Waterloo Lily*	Decca/Lon	1972
Caravan	*For Girls Who Grow Plump In The Night*	Decca/Lon	1973
Caravan	*Caravan And The New Symphonia Live*	Decca/Lon	1974
Caravan	*Cunning Stunts*	Decca	1975
Caravan	*Blind Dog At St. Dunstans*	BTM	1966
Curved Air	*Live*	BTM	1975
East Of Eden	*East Of Eden*	Decca	1970
East Of Eden	*Snafu*	Decca	1970
Genesis	*Foxtrot*	Charisma	1972
Nazareth	*Nazareth*	Mount/WB	1971
Pink Fairies	*Kings Of Oblivion*	Polydor	1973

H049 Hitmen Productions (A production team featuring the talents of Larrie Londin, Reggie Young, Bobby Thompson and Joe Osborn.)

Sonny Curtis	*Sonny Curtis*	Elektra	1979
Sonny Curtis	*Love Is All Around*	Elektra	1980
Sonny Curtis	*Rollin'*	Elektra	1981
Frankie Miller	*Easy Money*	Chrysalis	1980

H050 Suzi Jane Hokom

International Submarine Band	*Safe At Home*	LHI	1968
The Kitchen Cinq	*Everything But The Kitchen Cinq*	LHI	1968

H051 Ed Hollis

Eddie & The Hot Rods	*Teenage Depression*	Island	1976
Eddie & The Hot Rods	*Life on The Line*	Island	1977
Johnny G	*Natural Sharp*	B.Banquet	1979

H052 Danny Holloway

Plimsouls	*Zero Hour*	Beat	1980
Plimsouls	*The Plimsouls*	Planet	1981

H053 Rupert Holmes

	Lindsey De Paul	*Tigers and Fireflies*	Polydor	1979
	Rupert Holmes	*Pursuit Of Happiness*	P.Stock	1978
	Rupert Holmes	*Partners In Crime*	MCA/Infin	1979
	Rupert Holmes	*Adventure*	MCA	1980
	Rupert Holmes	*Full Circle*	MCA	1981
	John Miles	*Stranger In The City*	Decca/Lon	1976
	John Miles	*Zaragon*	Decca/Aris	1978
	No Dice	*Two Faced*	EMI	1979
w. J.Lesser	Orchestra Luna	*Orchestra Luna*	Epic	1974
	Sparks	*Big Beat*	Island	1976
w. J.Lesser	Strawbs	*Deep Cuts*	Polydor	1976
w. J.Lesser	Barbra Streisand	*Lazy Afternoon*	CBS	1975

H054 Jac Holzman

w. P.Rothchild	Tim Buckley	*Tim Buckley*	Elektra	1966
	Harry Chapin	*Heads And Tails*	Elektra	1976
w. M.Abramson	Judy Collins	*Judy Collins Concert*	Elektra	1964
w. M.Abramson	Judy Collins	*#3*	Elektra	1965
	Erik Darling	*Erik Darling*	Bounty	1974
w. P.Rothchild	Koerner,Ray & Glover	*The Return Of Koerner, Ray & Glover*	Elektra	1965
w. M.Abramson	Love	*Love*	Elektra	1966
w. B.Botnick	MC5	*Kick Out The Jams*	Elektra	1969
w. M.Abramson	Phil Ochs	*In Concert*	Elektra	1966

H055 David Hood

w. J.Johnson	Blackfoot	*No Reservations*	Island	1975
	Jackson Highway	*Jackson Highway*	MSS	1980
	Smith,Perkins Smith	*Smith Perkins Smith*	Island	1972

H056 Trevor Horn

	ABC	*The Lexicon Of Love*	Neutron	1982
	Art Of Noise	*Into Battle*	ZTT/Island	1984
w. Geoff Downes	Buggles	*The Age Of Plastic*	Island	1980
w. Geoff Downes	Buggles	*Adventures In Modern Recording*	Carrere	1980
	Philip Japp	*Philip Japp*	A&M	1983
	Malcolm McLaren	*Duck Rock*	Char/Isl	1983
	Malcolm McLaren	*Scratchin' (mini LP)*	Charisma	1984
	Yes	*90125*	Atlantic	1983

H057 Paul Hornsby

	Cooder Browne	*Cooder Browne*	Lone Star	1978
	Charlie Daniels	*Fire On The Mountain*	K.S.	1974
	Charlie Daniels	*Nightrider*	K.S.	1975
	Charlie Daniels	*Saddle Tramp*	Epic	1976
	Charlie Daniels	*High Lonesome*	Epic	1977
	Charlie Daniels	*Volunteer Jam*	Capricorn	1976
	Charlie Daniels	*Volunteer Jam 3 and 4*	Epic	1978
	Grinderswitch	*Honest To Goodness*	Capricorn	1974
	Grinderswitch	*Macon Tracks*	Capricorn	1975
	Grinderswitch	*Pullin' Together*	Capricorn	1976
	Grinderswitch	*Redwing*	Atco	1977
	Randy Howard	*All-American Redneck*	WB-Viva	1983

Marshall Tucker Band	*A New Life*	Capricorn	1974
Marshall Tucker Band	*Marshall Tucker Band*	Capricorn	1974
Marshall Tucker Band	*Searchin' For A Rainbow*	Capricorn	1975
Marshall Tucker Band	*Where We All Belong*	Capricorn	1975
Marshall Tucker Band	*Long Hard Ride*	Capricorn	1976
Marshall Tucker Band	*Carolina Dreams*	Capricorn	1977
Marshall Tucker Band	*Together Forever*	Capricorn	1978
Target	*Captured*	A&M	1977
Eric Quincy Tate	*Drinking Man's Friend*	Capricorn	1972
Two Guns	*Balls Out*	Capricorn	1977
Wet Willie	*The Wetter The Better*	Capricorn	1976
Wet Willie	*Left Coast Live*	Capricorn	1977
Bobby Whitlock	*Rock Your Sox Off*	Capricorn	1976

H058 Jimmy Horowitz

Air Supply	*Love And Other Bruises*	CBS	1977
Long John Baldry	*Good To Be Alive*	GM	1973
Long John Baldry	*Baldry's Out*	EMI-Amer	1979
Lesley Duncan	*Sing Children Sing*	CBS	1971
Lesley Duncan	*Earth Mother*	CBS	1972
Lesley Duncan	*Everything Changes*	GM	1974
Lesley Duncan	*Moonbathing*	GM	1975
Lesley Duncan	*Maybe It's Lost*	GM	1977
Steve Harley	*The Candidate*	EMI	1979
Tim Hardin	*Nine*	GM	1973

H059 Dill House

w. Jim Seiter	Rocky Burnette	*Son Of Rock And Roll*	EMI-Amer	1980
w. Jim Seiter	Rocky Burnette	*Rocky Burnette*	EMI	1982
w. Jim Seiter	Rocky Burnette	*Heart Stopper*	Goods	1982
	Hitmen	*Aim For The Feet*	Urgent	1980
	Bill House	*Dancing With A Smile*	Decca	1979
	Moon Martin	*Mystery Ticket*	Capitol	1982
	Pirates	*Happy Birthday Rock 'n' Roll*	Cube/P.Art	1980

(Released in the USA with the title "Hard Ride".)

Michael Smotherman	*Michael Smotherman*	CBS	1982

H060 James Newton Howard

	Black Rose	*Black Rose*	Casab	1980

(Featured Cher, Les Dudek and Mike Finnigan.)

	Valerie Carter	*Wild Child*	CBS	1978
w. E.Scheiner	Richard Cocciante	*Sincerely*	Virgin	1984
w. Andy Johns	DFK Band	*Dudek, Finnigan and Kreuger*	CBS	1980

H061 Ashley Howe

Duke Jupiter	*You Make It Look Easy*	CTC	1983
Hawkwind	*Live 1979*	Bronze	1979
Hawkwind	*Levitation*	Bronze	1980
Ted Nugent	*Penetrator*	Atlantic	1983
Sally Oldfield	*Easy*	Bronze	1979
Uriah Heep	*Abominog*	Bronze	1982
Uriah Heep	*Head First*	Bronze	1983
Wishbone Ash	*Twin Barrells Burning*	AVM	1982

H062 Dayton "Bones" Howe

Alessi	*Alessi*	A&M	1976
Association	*Windy*	Valiant	1967
Association	*Birthday Party*	WB	1968
Carnival	*The Carnival*	Lib/W.Pac	1970
Andy Desmond	*Andy Desmond*	Ariola	1978
Barbara Dickson	*Sweet Oasis*	Epic	1978
Free Flight	*Soaring*	P.Alto	1983
Fifth Dimension	*Stoned Soul Picnic*	Liberty	1968
Fifth Dimension	*The Magic Garden*	Liberty	1968
Fifth Dimension	*The Age Of Aquarius*	Liberty	1969
Ahmad Jamal	*One*	20th Cent	1978
Jerry Lee Lewis	*Jerry Lee Lewis*	Elektra	1979
Martin Mull	*Near Perfect/Perfect*	Elektra	1979
Juice Newton and Silver Spur	*Juice Newton and Silver Spur*	RCA	1975
w. Alan Abrahams Juice Newton	*After The Dust Settles*	RCA	1975
Alan Price	*Rising Sun*	Jet	1980
Johnny Rivers	*Realization*	Imperial	1968
Sandpipers	*A Gift Of Song*	A&M	1971
Timberline	*The Great Timber Rush*	CBS	1977
Turtles	*You Baby*	W.Whale	1966
Turtles	*Happy Together*	Lon/W.W.	1967
Turtles	*Wooden Head*	W.Whale	1970
Tom Waits	*Heart Of A Saturday Night*	Asylum	1974
Tom Waits	*Nighthawks At The Diner*	Asylum	1975
Tom Waits	*Small Change*	Asylum	1976
Tom Waits	*Foreign Affairs*	Asylum	1977
Tom Waits	*Blue Valentine*	Asylum	1978
Tom Waits	*Heart Attack and Vine*	Asylum	1980

H063 Jimmie Howell

Terry Allen	*Juarez*	Landfall	1975

H064 Mike Howlett

A Flock Of Seagulls	*A Flock Of Seagulls*	Jive/Aris	1982
A Flock Of Seagulls	*Listen*	Jive/Aris	1983
Any Trouble	*Wheels In Motion*	Stiff	1981
Berlin	*Love Life*	Geffen	1984
Blancmange	*Happy Families*	Decc/Isl	1982
Jo Broadberry and The Standouts	*Jo Broadberry and The Standouts*	Revenge	1980
China Crisis	*Possible Pop Songs*	Virgin	1983
China Crisis	*Working With Fire And Steel*	Virgin	1984
Comsat Angels	*Land*	Jive/Aris	1983
Fischer-Z	*Word Salad*	UA	1979
Fischer-Z	*Going Deaf For A Living*	UA	1980
Gong	*Live,etc*	Virgin	1977
Hunters And Collectors	*Hunters And Collectors*	Virgin	1983
Martha And The Muffins	*Metro Music*	Virgin	1980

	Martha Muffins	*Dance Trance*	Virgin	1980
	OMID	*Organisation*	DinDisc	1980
	Original Mirrors	*Heart Twango and Raw Beat*	Phonogram	1981
	Penetration	*Race Against Time*	Virgin	1978
	Punishment Of Luxury	*Laughing Academy*	UA	1979
	Revillos	*Rev Up*	DinDisc	1980
	Sniff 'n' The Tears	*Love Action*	Chiswick	1981
	Straight Eight	*Shuffle 'n' Cut*	Logo/RCA	1980
	Teardrop Explodes	*Kiliminjaro (2 tracks)*	Mercury	1980
	Thompson Twins	*In The Name Of Love (one track only)*	Hansa	1981

H065 Garth Hudson

	The Bengali Bauls	*At Big Pink*	Buddah	1968

H066 John Hug

	Marty Balin	*Balin*	EMI-Amer	1981
	Jesse Barrish	*Mercury Shoes*	RCA	1980
	Commander Cody	*Flying Dreams*	Arista	1978
	Brad Love	*Brad Love*	MCA	1983
w. Noah Shark	Dwight Twilley	*Jungle*	EMI-Amer	1983
	Tim Weisberg	*Party Of One*	MCA	1980
	Tim Weisberg	*Travelin' Light*	MCa	1981

H067 Bob Hughes

	Fleetwood Mac	*Heroes Are Hard To Find*	Reprise	1974
w. Jim Dickson	Flying Burrito Brothers	*The Flying Burrito Brothers*	A&M	1971
	Paris	*Big Town*	Capitol	1976

H068 Chris Hughes

	Adam and The Ants	*Kings Of The Wild Frontier*	CBS	1981
	Adam and The Ants	*Prince Charming*	CBS	1981
w. Ross Cullum	Tears For Fears	*The Hurting*	Mercury	1983
w. Ross Cullum	Wang Chung	*Points On The Curve*	Geffen	1984

H069 Simon Humphrey

	Drones	*Further Temptations*	Valer	1977
	Jags	*Evening Standards*	Island	1980

H070 Ian Hunter

w. Mick Ronson	Ellen Foley	*Nightout*	CBS	1979
	Generation X	*Valley Of The Dolls*	Chrysalis	1979

H071 Mike Hurst

	P.P. Arnold	*The First Lady Of Immediate (6 tracks)*	Immediate	1967
	Alan Bown	*Outward Bown*	MGM	1968
	David Clayton-Thomas	*Tequila Sunrise*	CBS	1972

Fancy	*Wild Thing*	Antic	1974
Fancy	*Something To Remember*	Arista	1977
Terry Mace	*Confessions Of A Sinner*	Mercury	1979
Nirvana	*To Markos III*	Pye	1970
Showaddywaddy	*Step Two*	Bell	1975
Showaddywaddy	*Trocadero*	Bell	1976
Cat Stevens	*Cat Stevens*	Deram	1967
Cat Stevens	*Matthew And Son*	Deram	1967
Shakin' Stevens	*Take One*	Epic	1979
Bruce Woolley	*English Garden*	Epic	1979

H072 Chris Huston

Aim	*Aim For The Highest*	B.Thumb	1969
Robben Ford	*Schizophonic*	LAX	1976
Jeff Simmons	*Lucille Has Messed Up My Mind*	Straight	1970

I001 Jimmy Ienner

Bay City Rollers	*Dedication*	Arista	1976
Blood Sweat & Tears	*New City*	CBS	1975
Eric Carmen	*Eric Carmen*	Arista	1976
Grand Funk	*Caught In The Act*	Capitol	1975
Grand Funk	*All The Girls In The World Beware*	Capitol	1975
Grand Funk	*Born To Die*	Capitol	1976
Murphy's Law	*Urban Renewal*	ABC	1975
J.F. Murphy and Salt	*The Last Illusion*	CBS	1973
Raspberries	*Raspberries*	Capitol	1972
Raspberries	*Fresh*	Capitol	1973
Raspberries	*Side 3*	Capitol	1973
Raspberries	*Starting Over*	Capitol	1974
Sha Na Na	*Sha Na Now*	K.S.	1975
Three Dog Night	*Hard Labor*	ABC	1974
Three Dog Night	*Comin' Down Your Way*	ABC	1975

I002 Pat Ieraci

Joey Covington	*Fat Fandango*	Grunt	1973
Hot Tuna	*The Phosphorescent Rat*	Grunt	1973
Hot Tuna	*America's Choice*	Grunt	1975

I003 Neil Innes

w. Viv Stanshall	Bonzo Dog Do Dah Band	*Keynsham*	UA	1969
w. Viv Stanshall	Bonzo Dog Do Dah Band	*Let's Make Up And Be Friendly*	UA	1979
w. Roger Gough	Grimms	*Grimms*	Island	1973
	Neil Innes	*How Sweet To Be An Idiot*	UA	1973
	Neil Innes	*The Innes Book Of Records*	Polydor	1979
w. Steve James	John Otway	*Where Did I Go Right*	Polydor	1979
	Rutles	*The Rutles*	WB	1978
	The World	*Lucky Planet*	Liberty	1970

I004 Tony Iommi

Quartz	*Quartz*	Jet	1977
Quartz	*Deleted*	Jet	1977

I005 Jimmy Iovine

w. Jon Small	D. L. Byron	*This Day And Age*	Arista	1980
W. M.Knopfler	Dire Straits	*Makin' Movies*	Vert/WB	1980
	Mark Farner Band	*No Frills*	Atlantic	1978
	Flame	*Too Many Cooks*	RCA	1978
	Flame	*Queen Of The Neighborhood*	RCA	1977
	Robert Fleischmann	*Perfect Stranger*	Arista	1979
	Golden Earring	*Grab It For A Second*	MCA	1978
	Mothers Finest	*Live*	Epic	1979
	Motors	*Tenement Steps*	Virgin	1980
	Stevie Nicks	*Belladonna*	Modern	1981
	Stevie Nicks	*The Wild Heart*	Modern	1983
	Graham Parker	*The Up Escalator*	Stiff/Aris	1980
	Tom Petty and The Heartbreakers	*Damn The Torpedoes*	Backstreet	1979
	Tom Petty and The Heartbreakers	*Hard Promises*	Backstreet	1981
	Tom Petty and The Heartbreakers	*Long After Dark*	Backstreet	1982
	Bob Seger	*The Distance*	Capitol	1982
	Patti Smith	*Easter*	Arista	1978
	U2	*Under A Blood Red Sky*	Island	1983

I006 Clayton Ivey and Terry Woodford

Robert Byrne	*Blame It On The Night*	Mercury	1979
FCC	*Baby I Want You*	F.Flight	1978
Hoodoo Rhythm Devils	*All Kidding Aside*	Fantasy	1978
Thelma Houston	*Any Way You Like It*	Motown	1976
John Kay	*All In Good Time*	Mercury	1978
Mac MacNally	*All In Good Time*	RCA	1980
Roy Orbison	*Laminar Flow*	Elektra	1979

J001 Joe Jackson

The Keys	*The Keys Album*	A&M	1981
soundtrack	*Mike's Murder*	A&M	1983

J002 Michael James Jackson

Mimi Farina and Tom Jans	*Take Heart*	A&M	1971
Max Gronenthal	*Whistling In The Dark*	Chrysalis	1979
Steve Harley (1 track only.)	*Hobo With A Gun*	EMI/Cap	1978
Kiss	*Killers*	Casabl	1982
Kiss	*Creatures Of The Night*	Casabl	1982
Kiss	*Lick It Up*	Mercury	1983
Tim Moore	*White Shadows*	Polydor	1977
Pablo Cruise	*Pablo Cruise*	A&M	1975
Red Rider	*Don't Fight It*	Capitol	1980
Tom Snow	*Tom Snow*	Capitol	1976
Paul Williams	*Just An Old Fashioned Love Song*	A&M	1971
Paul Williams	*Life Goes On*	A&M	1972
Lauren Wood	*Lauren Wood*	WB	1979
Jess Colin Young	*The Perfect Stranger*	Elektra	1982

J003 Ron Jacobs

various	A Child's Garden Of Grass (A Pre-Legalization Comedy	Elektra	1971

J004 Mick Jagger (see also Glimmer Twins)

P.P.Arnold	The First Lady Of Immediate (3 tracks)	Immediate	1967
Chris Farlowe	The Art Of Chris Farlowe	Immediate	1966

J005 Eric Jakobsen

Blue Velvet Band	Sweet Moments With The Blue Velvet Band	WB	1969
Brian Elliott	Brian Elliott	WB	1978
Norman Greenbaum	Spirit In The Sky	Reprise	1970
Norman Greenbaum	Back Home Again	Reprise	1970
Norman Greenbaum	Petaluma	Reprise	1972
Tim Hardin	One	MGM	1966
Tim Hardin	4	MGM	1969
Lovin' Spoonful	Daydream	KS	1966
Lovin' Spoonful	Do You Believe In Magic	KS	1966
Lovin' Spoonful	You're A Big Boy Now	KS	1967
Leonard Schaeffer	A Boy And His Dog	WB	1967
John Sebastian	The Tarzana Kid	Reprise	1974
Sopwith Camel	Hello Hello	KS	1973
Sopwith Camel	The Miraculous Hump	WB	1983
Tazmanian Devils	The Tazmanian Devils	WB	1980
Tazmanian Devils	Broadway Hi-Life	WB	1981
William Truckaway	Breakaway	Reprise	1971

J006 Bob James

	Blood,Sweat & Tears	More Than Ever	CBS	1976
	Eric Gale	Ginseng Woman	CBS	1977
	Eric Gale	Multiplication	CBS	1977
	Steve Kahn	Tightrope	CBS/T.Z.	1977
w. Phil Ramone	Kenny Loggins	Celebrate Me Home	CBS	1977
	Kenny Loggins	Nightwatch	CBS	1978
w. Jay Chattaway	Wilbert Longmire	Sunny Side Up	CBS/T.Z.	1978
w. Jay Chattaway	Wilbert Longmire	Champagne	CBS/T.Z.	1979
w. Jay Chattaway	Wilbert Longmire	With All My Love	CBS/T.Z.	1980
	Richard Tee	Strokin'	CBS/T.Z.	1979
	Richard Tee	Natural Ingredients	CBS/T.Z.	1980

J007 Peter James

Nikki & The Corvettes	Nikki & The Corvettes	Bomp	1980

J008 Nick Jameson

	Better Days	Better Days	Bearsv	1973
	Foghat	Rock And Roll Outlaws	Bearsv	1974
	Foghat	Fool For The City	Bearsv	1976
	Foghat	Girls To Chat, Boys To Bounce	Avat/Bearsv	1981
w. Tony Outeda	Foghat	In The Mood For Something Rude	Bearsv	1982

	Tim Moore	*Tim Moore*	Mooncrest	1974
w. Paul Leka	Tim Moore	*Behind The Eyes*	Pooydor	1975

J009 Chas Jankel

	Alberto Y Los Trios Paranois	*Skite*	Logo	1978
w. S.Stanley	Ian Dury	*Lord Upminster*	Polydor	1981
	Streetband	*London*	Logo	1978

J010 John Jansen

	Coast Road Drive	*Delicious And Refreshing*	Decca	1979
w. S.Galfas	Good Rats	*Birth Comes To Us All*	Passport	1978
w. E.Kramer	Jimi Hendrix	*Rainbow Bridge*	Reprise	1971
w. E.Kramer	Jimi Hendrix	*Hendrix In The West*	Poly/Rep	1972
w. E.Kramer	Jimi Hendrix	*War Heroes*	Poly/Rep	1973
	Lou Reed	*New Sensations*	RCA	1984
	Television	*Adventure*	Elektra	1978
	Yipes	*Yipes*	Millenium	1979

J011 Rick Jarrard

	David Cassidy	*Dreams Are Nothing More Than Wishes*	Bell	1973
	Family Tree	*Miss Butters*	RCA	1968
	Jose Feliciano	*In Concert At The Palladium*	RCA	1969
	Jose Feliciano	*Feliciano*	RCA	1968
	Jose Feliciano	*10 To 23*	RCA	1969
	Jose Feliciano	*Fireworks*	RCA	1970
	Jose Feliciano	*Romance In The Night*	Motown	1983
	John Hartford	*John Hartford*	RCA	1969
	John Hartford	*Iron Mountain Depot*	RCA	1970
	John Hurley	*Sings About People*	RCA	1970
	John Hurley	*One More Hallelujah*	Bell	1972
	John Hurley	*Children's Dreams*	Bell	1973
	Jefferson Airplane	*Surrealistic Pillow*	RCA	1967
	Jefferson Airplane	*Early Flight*	Grunt	1974
	Loading Zone	*The Loading Zone*	RCA	1967
	Rick Moses	*Face The Music*	20th Cent	1976
	Nilsson	*Pandemonium Shadow Show*	RCA	1967
	Nilsson	*Aerial Ballet*	RCA	1968
	Nilsson	*Harry (4 tracks)*	RCA	1967
	Silverado	*Silverado*	RCA	1976
	Tom Snow	*Taking It All In Stride*	Capitol	1976
	Stone Country	*Stone Country*	RCA	1968
	(Group included Steve Young.)			

J012 Felton Jarvis (Charles Felton Jarvis 1934-1981)

	James Burton	*The Guitar Sounds Of James Burton*	A&M	1971
	John Hartford	*Looks At Life*	RCA	1967
	John Hartford	*Housing Project*	RCA	1968
	John Hartford	*The Love Album*	RCA	1968
w. James Ritz	Ronnie McDowell	*"Elvis" soundtrack*	RCA	1979

Mike Nesmith	Magnetic South	RCA	1970
Mickey Newbury	Funny Familiar Forgotten Feelings	RCA	1968
Mickey Newbury	Sings His Own	RCA	1972
Elvis Presley	How Great Thou Art	RCA	1967
Elvis Presley	Double Trouble	RCA	1967
Elvis Presley	Clambake	RCA	1967
Elvis Presley	Speedway	RCA	1968
Elvis Presley	NBC TV Special	RCA	1968
Elvis Presley	From Elvis In Memphis	RCA	1969
Elvis Presley	From Memphis To Vegas	RCA	1970
Elvis Presley	On Stage February 1970	RCA	1970
Elvis Presley	In Person At The International	RCA	1970
Elvis Presley	That's The Way It Is	RCA	1971
Elvis Presley	Elvis Country; I'm 10,000 Years Old	RCA	1971
Elvis Presley	Love Letter From Elvis	RCA	1971
Elvis Presley	Elvis Now	RCA	1971
Elvis Presley	Live At Madison Square Gardens	RCA	1972
Elvis Presley	Aloha From Hawaii	RCA	1973
Elvis Presley	Good Times	RCA	1974
Elvis Presley	Live On Stage In Memphis	RCA	1974
Elvis Presley	Having Fun On Stage	RCA	1974
Elvis Presley	Promised Land	RCA	1974
Elvis Presley	Today	RCA	1975
Elvis Presley	From Elvis Presley Boulevard	RCA	1976
Elvis Presley	Welcome To My World	RCA	1976
Elvis Presley	Moody Blue	RCA	1977
Elvis Presley	Guitar Man	RCA	1981
Tommy Roe	Sheila	ABC	1962

J013 Steve Jarvis

Commander Cody	Country Casanova	Paramount	1973
Commander Cody	Live From Deep In The Heart Of Texas	Paramount	1974

J014 Garland Jeffreys

Outsets	The Outsets	Plexus	1983

J016 Peter Jenner

Alberto Y Los Trios Paranoias	Alberto Y Los Trios Paranoias	Tra	1976
Alberto Y Los Trios Paranoias	Italians From Outer Space	Tra	1977
Kevin Ayers	Shooting At The Moon	Harvest	1970
Edgar Broughton Band	Sing Brother Sing	Harvest	1969
Edgar Broughton Band	Wasa Wasa	Harvest	1970
John Gorman	Go Man Gorman	DJM	1972
Grimms	Sleepers	DJM	1975
Roy Harper	Flat Baroque And Berserk	Harv/Chry	1970
Roy Harper	Stormcock	Harv/Chry	1971

Roy Harper	*Lifemask*	Harv/Chry	1973
Roy Harper	*Valentine*	Harv/Chry	1974
Roy Harper	*Flashes From The*		
	Archives Of Oblivion	Harv/Chry	1974
Roy Harper	*H.Q.*	Harv/Chry	1975
(Released in the USA as "When An Old Cricketer Leaves The Crease".)			
Philip Rambow	*Shooting Gallery*	EMI	1979
Sharks	*Jab It In Yore Eye*	Isl/MCA	1974

J016 Elton John (see also Clive Franks)

Blue	*Another Night Time*		
	Flight	Rocket	1977
Blue	*Fool's Party (3 tr.)*	Rocket	1979
Kiki Dee	*Loving And Free*	Rocket	1973
Kiki Dee	*Kiki Dee*	Rocket	1974

J017 Jeremy Andrew "Andy" Johns

Axis	*Circus World*	RCA/Holog	1978
Jack Bruce	*Out Of The Storm*	RSO	1974
Detective	*Detective*	Swansong	1977
Les Dudek	*Ghost Town Parade*	CBS	1978
DFK Band	*The Dudek,Finnigan*		
	Kreuger Band	CBS	1980
Free	*Free Live*	Island	1971
Bobby Keys	*Bobby Keys*	WB	1972
Kids	*Anvil Chorus*	Atco	1975
Bobby Price	*Sundego's Travelling*		
	Orchestra	CBS	1972
Riggs	*Riggs*	Full Moon	1982
Danny Spanos	*Danny Spanos*	Windsong	1980
Rod Stewart	*Foolish Behaviour*	Riva/WB	1980
String Driven Thing	*Keep Yer Hand On It*	Charisma	1975
Television	*Marquee Moon*	Elektra	1977
West,Bruce and Laing	*Why Dontcha*	CBS/Windf	1972
West,Bruce and Laing	*Whatever Turns You On*	RSO	1973
Bobby Whitlock	*Bobby Whitlock*	CBS	1972
Bobby Whitlock	*Raw Velvet (1 tr)*	CBS	1972
Ron Wood	*1-2 3 4*	CBS	1981
Gary Wright	*Extraction*	A&M	1970

J018 Glyn Johns

Joan Armatrading	*Joan Armatrading*	A&M	1976
Joan Armatrading	*Show Some Emotion*	A&M	1977
Joan Armatrading	*To The Limit*	AA&M	1978
Joan Armatrading	*Steppin' Out*	AM	1979
Marc Benno	*Lost In Austin*	AM	1979
Danny Joe Brown	*Danny Joe Brown and The*		
	Danny Joe Brown Band	Epic	1981
Buckacre	*Morning Comes*	MCA	1976
Eric Clapton	*Slowhand*	RSO	1977
Eric Clapton	*Backless*	RSO	1978
Clash	*Combat Rock*	CBS	1982
Tim Davis	*Take Me As I Am*	Metro	1972
Eagles	*The Eagles*	Asylum	1972
Eagles	*Desperado*	Asylum	1973

	Eagles	*On The Border*	Asylum	1974
	Faces	*A Nod's As Good As A Wink To A Blind Horse*	WB	1971
	Faces	*Ooh La La*	WB	1973
	Andy Fairweather-Low	*La Booga Rooga*	A&M	1975
	Andy Fairweather-Low	*Be Bop 'n' Holla*	A&M	1976
w. John Gilbert	Family	*Family Entertainment*	Reprise	1969
	Fairport Convention	*Rising For The Moon*	Island	1971
	Georgie Fame	*Georgie Fame*	Island	1974
	Fools Gold	*Fools Gold*	Arista	1976
	Gallagher and Lyle	*Gallagher and Lyle*	Capitol	1972
	Gallagher and Lyle	*Willie and The Lapdog*	A&M	1973
	Gallagher and Lyle	*Seeds*	A&M	1973
	Gallagher and Lyle	*The Last Cowboy*	A&M	1974
	Jools Holland and The Millionaires	*Jools Holland and The Millionaires*	A&M/IRS	1981
	Nicky Hopkins, Ry Cooder, etc.	*Jamming With Edward*	RSR	1972
w. Rob Fraboni	Hughes/Thrall	*Hughes/Thrall*	CBS/Boul	1982
	Humble Pie	*Humble Pie*	A&M	1970
	Humble Pie	*Rock On*	A&M	1971
w. D.Anderle	Lambert and Nuttycombe	*At Home*	A&M	1969
	Ronnie Lane	*Anymore For Anymore*	GM	1974
	Lazy Racer	*Lazy Racer*	A&M	1979
	Lazy Racer	*Formula 2*	A&M	1980
	Bernie Leadon	*Natural Progressions*	Asylum	1976
	Live Wire	*Live Wire*	A&M	1979
	Local Boys	*Moments Of Madness*	Island	1983
	McGuinness Flint	*McGuinness Flint*	Capitol	1971
	McGuinness Flint	*Happy Birthday Ruthy Baby*	Capitol	1971
	Steve Miller Band	*Children Of The Future*	Capitol	1968
	Steve Miller Band	*Sailor*	Capitol	1969
	Steve Miller Band	*Brave New World*	Capitol	1969
	Steve Miller Band	*Your Saving Grace*	Capitol	1970
	Nine Below Zero	*Don't Point Your Finger*	A&M	1981
w. Andy Fairweather-Low	Craig Nuttycombe	*It's Just A Life Time*	A&M	1978
w. D.Anderle	Ozark Mountain Daredevils	*The Ozark Mountain Daredevils*	A&M	1974
w. D.Anderle	Ozark Mountain Daredevils	*It'll Shine When It Shines*	A&M	1974
	Tim Renwick	*Tim Renwick*	CBS	1980
	Brian Rogers Orchestra	*Plays The Melodies Of Gallagher and Lyle ...*	A&M	1977
	Rolling Stones	*Get Your Ya Ya's Out*	Decca	1970
	Boz Scaggs	*Boz Scaggs And Band*	CBS	1971
	Boz Scaggs	*Moments*	CBS	1971
	Pete Townshend and Ronnie Lane	*Rough Mix*	Polydor	1977
	various artists	*The Legend Of Jesse James*	A&M	1980
	various artists	*White Mansions*	A&M	1978

The Who	*By Numbers*	Poly/MCA	1975
The Who	*Who Are You*	Poly/MCA	1978
The Who	*It's Hard*	Polydor	1982
Ron Wood and Ronnie Lane	*Mahoney's Last Stand*	Atlantic	1976

J019 Jimmy Johnson (see also Barry Beckett for co-productions.)

	Amazing Rhythm Aces	*Amazing Rhythm Aces*	ABC	1979
	Amazing Rhythm Aces	*How Do You Spell Rhythm*	WB	1980
w. David Hood	Blackfoot	*No Reservations*	Island	1975
	Blackfoot	*Flying High*	Epic	1975
w. Dale Morris	Billy "Crash" Craddock	*Changes*	Capitol	1980
w. David Hood	Jackson Highway	*Jackson Highway*	MSS	1980
w. Tim Smith	Lynyrd Skynyrd	*First and Last*	MCA	1978

J020 Bob Johnston

Hoyt Axton	*Less Than The Song*	A&M	1973
Bell And Arc	*Bell And Arc*	Charisma	1971
Graham Bell	*Graham Bell*	Charisma	1972
Byrds	*Dr.Byrds and Mr.Hyde*	CBS	1969
China	*China*	Epic	1979
Jimmy Cliff	*Give Thanks*	WB	1978
Leonard Cohen	*Songs From A Room*	CBS	1967
Leonard Cohen	*Live Songs*	CBS	1973
Bob Dylan	*Highway 61 Revisited*	CBS	1965
Bob Dylan	*Blonde On Blonde*	CBS	1966
Bob Dylan	*John Wesley Harding*	CBS	1968
Bob Dylan	*Nashville Skyline*	CBS	1969
Bob Dylan	*Self Portrait*	CBS	1970
Bob Dylan	*New Morning*	CBS	1970
Bob Dylan	*Dylan*	CBS	1973
Joe Ely	*Down On The Drag*	MCA	1979
Flatt and Scruggs	*Nashville Airplane*	CBS	1968
Mac Gayden	*McGavock Gayden*	EMI	1973
Dan Hicks	*Original Recordings*	Epic	1969
Doug Kershaw	*The Louisiana Man*	WB	1978
L.A. Jets	*The L.A. Jets*	RCA	1976
Alvin Lee	*Rocket Fuel*	RSO	1978
Lindisfarne	*Fog On The Tyne*	Char/Elek	1971
Lindisfarne	*Dingly Dell*	Char/Elek	1972
John Mayall	*Bottom Line*	DJM	1979
Moby Grape	*Truly Fine Citizen*	CBS	1970
Michael Murphey	*Geronimo's Cadillac*	A&M	1972
Michael Murphey	*Cosmic Cowboy Souvenir*	EMI/A&M	1973
Michael Murpkey	*Michael Murphey*	EMI/Epic	1974
Michael Murphey	*Blue Sky Night Thunder*	Epic	1975
Michael Murphey	*Swans Against The Sun*	Epic	1975
Tracey Nelson	*Tracey Nelson*	Atlantic	1974
Tracey Nelson	*Sweet Soul Music*	MCA	1975
Rab Noakes	*Rab Noakes*	A&M	1972
NRPS	*Oh What A Mighty Time*	CBS	1975
NRPS	*New Riders*	MCA	1976
NRPS	*Who Are These Guys*	MCA	1977
Earl Scruggs Revue	*Anniversary Special*	CBS	1975
Earl Scruggs Revue	*Super Jammin'*	CBS	1984
Billy Joe Shaver	*When I Get My Wings*	Capricorn	1976

	Simon and Garfunkel	*Sounds Of Silence*	CBS	1966
	Dino Valente	*Dino Valente (2 tracks)*	Epic	1968
	Loudon Wainwright III	*Attempted Mustache*	CBS	1973

J021 Bruce Johnston

w. J.W.Guercio	Beach Boys	*L.A.(Light Album)*	CBS	1979
	Beach Boys	*Keeping The Summer Alive*	CBS	1980
	David Cassidy	*The Higher They Climb*	RCA	1975
	David Cassidy	*Home Is Where The Heart Is*	RCA	1976
	Barry Mann	*Survivor*	RCA	1975
	Terry Melcher	*Terry Melcher*	Reprise	1974
	Terry Melcher	*Royal Flush*	RCA	1976
w. Curt Becher	Sailor	*Checkpoint*	Epic	1977
	Sunrise	*Sunrise*	Buddah	1978

J022 Stanley Johnston

	Crosby,Stills & Nash	*Daylight Again*	Atlantic	1982
	Crosby Stills & Nash	*Allies*	Atlantic	1983
w. Graham Nash	Hollies	*What Goes Around*	Atlantic	1983
	various artists	*No Nukes*	Asylum	1979
	(Credited as "executive producer".)			

J023 Booker T. Jones

	William Bell	*Bound To Happen*	Pye	1976
w. D.Anderle	Rita Coolidge	*Love Me Again*	A&M	1978
w. D.Anderle	Rita Coolidge	*Satisfied*	A&M	1979
	Priscilla Coolidge Jones	*Flying*	Capricorn	1979
	Booker T. Jones	*Try And Love Again*	A&M	1979
	Earl Klugh	*Magic In Your Eyes*	UA	1979
	Memphis Horns	*High On Music*	RCA	1976
	Willie Nelson	*Stardust*	CBS	1978
	Willie Nelson	*Pretty Paper*	CBS	1979
	Willie Nelson	*Without A Song*	CBS	1983
	Billy Swan	*You're OK,I'm OK*	A&M	1978
	Bill Withers	*Just As I Am*	Sussex	1971

J024 Hugh Jones

	Clock DVA	*Advantage*	Polydor	1983
	Damned	*Strawberries (7 tracks)*	Bronze	1982
	Echo and The Bunnymen	*Heaven Up Here*	Kor/Sire	1981
	Essential Logic	*Beat Rhythm News*	R.Trade	1979
	Icicle Works	*The Icicle Works*	B.Banquet	1984
	Modern English	*After The Snow*	Poly/Sire	1983
	Monsoon	*Third Eye*	MSC	1983
	Mothmen	*One Black Dot*	Do It	1982
	Softies	*Nice and Nasty*	Charly	1982
	Sound	*From The Lion's Mouth*	Korova	1981

J025 Mick Jones

	Ellen Foley	*Spirit Of St.Louis*	Epic	1981
w. Mick Ronson	Ian Hunter	*Short Back And Sides*	Chrysalis	1981
	Theatre Of Hate	*Westworld*	B.Rome	1982

J026 Pardo Jones

Christ Child	*Christ Child*	Buddah	1978
Papa John Creach	*In Phasion*	DJM	1978

J027 Quincy Delight Jones, Jnr.

Patti Austin	*Patti Austin*	Qwest	1983
George Benson	*Give Me The Night*	WB	1983
Brothers Johnson	*Look Out For #1*	A&M	1976
Brothers Johnson	*Light Up The Night*	A&M	1980
Aretha Franklin	*Hey Now Hey, The Other Side Of The Sky*	Atlantic	1973
Lesley Gore	*Lesley Gore's Party*	Philips	1964
James Ingram	*It's Your Night*	Qwest	1983
Michael Jackson	*Off The Wall*	Epic	1979
Michael Jackson	*Thriller*	Epic	1982
Rufus	*Masterjam*	MCA	1979
various artists	*The Wiz*	Motown	1978

In addition to having recorded over 40 albums under his own name,
Quincy Jones has provided original soundtrack music for
the following films:
All Nudity Will Be Punished (1972)/The Anderson Tapes (1971)/Banning
(1967)/Blood Kin (1969)/Bob and Carol and Ted and Alice (1969)/Brother
John (1971)/Cactus Flower (1969)/Come Back Charleston Blue (1972)/
The Counterfeit Killer (1968)/A Dandy In Aspic (19)/The Deadly Affair
(1966)/Dig (1972)/The Heist (a.k.a. Dollars) (1971)/Duke Ellington-We
Love You Madly (1973)/Eggs (1970)/Enter Laughing (1967)/For Love of
Ivy (1968)The Getaway (1972)/The Hell With Heroes (1968)/Honky
(1971)/The Hot Rock (1971)/In Cold Blood (1967)/In The Heat Of The
Night (1967)/Ironside-TV Movie (1967)/The Italian Job (1969)/Jigsaw
(1968)/John And Mary (1969)/Killer By Night (1971)/The Lost Man
(1969)/ Mackenna's Gold (1968)/ Man And Boy (1971)/ Mirage (1965)/
New Centurians (1972)/ Of Men And Demons (1970)/ The Out Of
Towners (1969)/ The Pawmbroker (1964)/ Boy In The Tree (1961)/Rise
And Fall Of Ivor Dickie (1967)/ Roots (1977)/ The Slender Thread (1965)/
The Split (1968)/ Split Second To An Epitaph (the second Ironside
movie)(1968)/ They Call Me Mister Tibbs (1970)/ The Toy Grabbers
(1970)/ Walk, Don't Run (1966)/ The Wiz (1978).
And the following television series:
Hey Landlord (31 episodes) 1966/67
Ironside (198 episodes) 1967/74
Sandford and Townsend (136 episodes) 1972/77

J028 Richard Jones

Gonzalez	*Haven't Stopped Dancing*	Sidewalk	1979
Gloria Jones	*Windstorm*	Sidewalk	1978

J029 Dave Jordan

Fun Boy Three	*Fun Boy Three*	Chrysalis	1982
w.Jerry Dammers			
Specials	*More Specials*	Two Tone	1980

K001 John Kahn

	Jerry Garcia	*Garcia*	Round	1974
w. E.Mazer	Jerry Garcia	*Reflections*	Round	1976
	Jerry Garcia	*Run For The Roses*	Arista	1982
w. Bill Vitt	Saunders,Garcia, Kahn and Vitt	*Live At The Keystone*	Fantasy	1973
	Southern Comfort	*Southern Comfort*	CBS	1970

K002 David Kahne

Humans	*Happy Hour*	IRS	1981
Pearl Harbor and The Explosions	*Pearl Harbor and The Explosions*	WB	1980
Jorma Kaukonen	*Barbecue King*	RCA	1980
Rank And File	*Sundown*	RT/Slash	1982
Red Rockers	*Good As Gold*	CBS	1983
Romeo Void	*It's A Condition*	415	1981
Translator	*Heartbeats And Triggers*	ARC	1982
Translator	*No Time Like Now*	CBS/415	1983
Wire Train	*In A Chamber*	CBS/415	1984

K003 Michael Kamen

w.Dick Wagner	Tim Curry	*Fearless*	A&M	1979
	Tim Curry	*Simplicity*	A&M	1981
	Jimmy Destri	*Heart On A Wall*	Chrysalis	1982
w. James Guthrie	Pink Floyd	*The Final Cut*	Harv/CBS	1983
	Roger Waters	*The Pros And Cons Of Hitchiking*	Harv/CBS	1984

K004 Pete Kameron

Cumberland Three	*Civil War Almanac Volume 1 (Yankees)*	Roulette	1960
Cumberland Three	*Civil War Almanac Volume 2 (Rebels)*	Roulette	1960

(John Stewart was a member of this group.)

K005 Gary Katz

	Joe Cocker	*Civilised Man*	Capitol	1984
	Eye To Eye	*Eye To Eye*	Auto/WB	1982
	Eye To Eye	*Shakespeare Stole My Baby*	WB	1983
	Donald Fagen	*The Nightfly*	WB	1983
	Dirk Hamilton	*You Can Sing On The Left*	ABC	1976
	James House	*James House*	Atlantic	1983
	Marc Jordan	*Mannequin*	WB	1978
	Thomas Jefferson Kaye	*Thomas Jefferson Kaye*	ABC	1976
	Thomas Jefferson Kaye	*First Grade*	ABC	1974
	Root Boy Slim and His Sex Change Band	*Root Boy Slim and His Sex Change Band*	Illegal/WB	1978
w. Ray Parker,Jnr	Diana Ross	*Ross*	RCA	1983
	Steely Dan	*Can't Buy A Thrill*	ABC	1972
	Steely Dan	*Countdown To Ecstasy*	ABC	1973

Steely Dan	*Pretzel Logic*	ABC	1974
Steely Dan	*Katy Lied*	ABC	1975
Steely Dan	*The Royal Scam*	ABC	1976
Steely Dan	*Aja*	ABC	1977
Steely Dan	*Gaucho*	MCA	1980

K006 Jerry Katz and Jerry Kasenetz (better known as Kasenetz-Katz)

Crazy Elephant	*Crazy Elephant*	Buddah	1969
Finders Keepers	*Salt Water Taffy*	Buddah	1969
Kasenetz-Katz Singing Orchestral Circus	*Kasenetz-Katz Singing Orchestral Circus*	Buddah	1968
Kasenetz-Katz Super Circus	*Quick Joey Small*	Buddah	1969
Five Stairsteps and Cubie	*Our Family Portrait*	Buddah	1968
Lemon Pipers	*Jungle Marmalade*	Buddah	1968
Lt. Garcia's Magic Music Box	*Cross The Border*	Buddah	1969
Music Explosion	*Little Bit O' Soul*	Laurie	1968
1910 Fruitgum Company	*Goody Goody Gum Drops*	Buddah	1968
1910 Fruitgum Company	*1-2-3 Red Light*	Buddah	1968
1910 Fruitgum Company	*Simon Says*	Buddah	1968
1910 Fruitgum Company	*Indian Giver*	Buddah	1969
1910 Fruitgum Company	*Hard Ride*	Buddah	1970
Ohio Express	*Ohio Express*	Buddah	1968
Ohio Express	*Chewy Chewy*	Buddah	1968
Ohio Express	*Mercy*	Buddah	1969
Ram Jam	*Ram Jam*	Epic	1977
Ram Jam	*Portrait Of The Artist As A Young Ram*	Epic	1978
Speedway Boulevard	*Speedway Boulevard*	Epic	1978

(Members of the Kasenetz-Katz production team included, at various times Joey Levine, Artie Resnick, M.Gutowski, B.Carl, R.Whitelaw and S.Trimachi. The most notable effort by those six was The Third Rail's "ID Music" on Epic in the late 1960's which was produced by Levine and Resnick.)

K007 Matthew Katz

Jefferson Airplane	*Takes Off*	RCA	1966
Jefferson Airplane	*Early Flight*	Grunt	1974

K008 Steve Katz

Rory Block	*Rory Block*	RCA	1975
Graf	*Graf*	Precision	1981
Horslips	*The Man Who Built America*	DJM	1979
Horslips	*Short Stories, Tall Tales*	DJM	1979
Horslips	*The Belfast Gigs*	Oats/Mer	1980
Elliott Murphy	*Nightlights*	RCA	1976
Lou Reed	*Sally Can't Dance*	RCA	1974
Lou Reed	*Rock 'n' Roll Animal*	RCA	1974
Lou Reed	*Live*	RCA	1975

K009 Matthew King Kaufman

w.Glen Kolotkin	Earthquake	*Live*	Beserkley	1975
w.Glen Kolotkin	Earthquake	*Leveled*	Beserkley	1977
w.Glen Kolotkin	Earthquake	*8.5*	Beserkley	1976
w.Glen Kolotkin	Earthquake	*Rockin' The World*	Beserkley	1975
w.Kenny Laguna	Earthquake	*Two Years In A Padded Cell*	Beserkley	1979
w.Glen Kolotkin	Greg Kihn	*Greg Kihn*	Beserkley	1976
w.Glen Kolotkin	Greg Kihn	*Greg Kihn Again*	Beserkley	1977
w.Glen Kolotkin and Kenny Laguna	Greg Kihn	*Next Of Kihn*	Beserkley	1978
w.Glen Kolotkin and Kenny Laguna	Greg Kihn	*With The Naked Eye*	Beserkley	1979
	Greg Kihn	*Glass House Rock*	Beserkley	1980
	Greg Kihn	*Rockihnroll*	Beserkley	1981
	Greg Kihn	*Kihntinued*	Beserkley	1982
	Greg Kihn	*Kihnspiracy*	Beserkley	1983
	Greg Kihn	*Kihntagious*	Beserkley	1984
w.Glen Kolotkin	Modern Lovers	*The Modern Lovers*	Beserkley	1976
w. Kenny Laguna	Modern Lovers	*Live*	Beserkley	1977
w.Glen Kolotkin	Jonathan Richman and The Modern Lovers	*Jonathan Richman and The Modern Lovers*	Beserkley	1976
	Jonathan Richman and The Modern Lovers	*Rock And Roll With The Modern Lovers*	Beserkley	1977
w.Kenny Laguna & Glen Kolotkin	Jonathan Richman and The Modern Lovers	*Back In Your Life*	Beserkley	1979
w.Glen Kolotkin & Gary Phillips	Rubinoos	*The Rubinoos*	Beserkley	1977
w.Glen Kolotkin & Gary Phillips	Rubinoos	*Back To The Drawing Board*	Besrekley	1979
w.Glen Kolotkin & Kenny Laguna	Spitballs	*The Spitballs*	Beserkley	1978
w.Kenny Laguna	Tyla Gang	*Moonproof*	Beserkley	1978
w.Glen Kolotkin	various artists	*Beserk Times*	Beserkley	1978

K010 Lenny Kaye

Kingpins	*Rockin' With Cindy*	Hoo Ha	1982
Sidewinders	*The Sidewinders*	RCA	1972
various artists	*Nuggets*	Elektra	1972

K011 Thomas Jefferson Kaye

Mike Bloomfield,John Hammond,Dr.John	*Triumvirate*	CBS	1973
Gene Clark	*No Other*	Asylum	1974
Gene Clark	*Two Sides To Every Story*	RSO	1977
Hassles	*Hour Of The Wolf*	UA	1969
(Group featured a young Billy Joel.)			
Jay And The Americans	*Wax Museum*	UA	1970
Jay And The Americans	*Capture The MOment*	UA	1970
Mistress	*Mistress*	RSO	1979
Bob Neuwirth	*Bob Neuwirth*	Asylum	1974
Loudon Wainwright III	*Album III*	CBS	1972

K012 John "Speedy" Keen

Heartbreakers	*L.A.M.F.*	Track	1977
Speedy Keen	*Y'Know What I Mean*	Island	1975
Speedy Keen	*Previous Convictions*	MCA	1973
Motorhead	*Motorhead*	Chiswick	1977

K013 Jon Kelly

Kate Bush	*Never For Ever*	EMI	1980
Chris Rea	*Chris Rea*	Mag/CBS	1983
Ali Thompson	*Take A Little Rhythm*	A&M	1980
Ali Thompson	*Deception Is An Art*	A&M	1981

K014 Peter Ker

	Bill Barclay	*Viva Dunbar*	Pye	1976
	Bay City Rollers	*Elevator*	Arista	1979
	DP's	*If You Know What I Mean*	Barn	1978
	Eddie and The Hot Rods	*Thriller*	Island	1979
	Elektriks	*Current Events*	Capitol	1980
	Headboys	*The Headboys*	RSO	1979
	Laughing Dogs	*Meet Their Makers*	CBS	1980
	Love Sculpture	*Forms And Feelings*	EMI	1969
w. Nick Garvey	Motors	*Approved By The Motors*	Virgin	1978
w. Nick Garvey	Bram Tchaikovsky	*Strange Man, Changed Man*	Radar	1979

K015 Kenny Kerner (all co-produced with Richie Wise except where indicated.)

	Elkie Brooks	*Rich Man's Woman*	A&M	1975
	Danny Cox	*Feels So Good*	Casab	1971
	Dust	*Dust*	K.S.	1971
	(Featured a pre-Ramones Marc Bell.)			
	Emperor	*Emperor*	P.Stock	1977
	Faragher Brothers	*Family Ties*	ABC	1977
	Jose Feliciano	*And The Feeling's Good*	RCA	1974
	KGB	*Motion*	MCA	1976
	Kiss	*Kiss*	Casab	1974
	Gladys Knight and The Pips	*Imagination (4 tracks)*	Buddah	1973
	Gladys Knight and The Pips	*2nd Anniversary (4 tr.)*	Buddah	1975
	Pets	*Wet Behind The Ears*	Arista	1978
	Steve Marriott	*Marriott*	A&M	1976
w. Steven Kramer	Stingers	*The Stingers*	Peliades	1983
	Stories	*About Us*	K.S.	1973
	(1 track; the US hit version of "Brother Louie".)			
	Stories	*Travelling Underground*	K.S.	1973

K016 Neil Kernon

Jon Anderson	*Animation*	Polydor	1982
Brand X	*Product*	Charisma	1979
Brand X	*Do They Hurt*	Charisma	1980
Flicks	*Go For The Effect*	Ariola	1979
Hall & Oates	*H_2O*	RCA	1982

Kansas	*Drastic Measures*	Epic	1983
Spys	*Spys*	WMI-Amer	1982
Streets	*First*	Atlantic	1983
Tom Teeley	*Tales Of Glamour And Distress*	A&M	1984

K017 David Kershenbaum

Any Trouble	*Any Trouble*	EMI-Amer	1983
Hoyt Axton	*Fearless*	A&M	1976
Lisa Bade	*Suspicion*	A&M	1982
Joan Baez	*Diamonds And Rust*	A&M	1975
Joan Baez	*From Every Stage*	A&M	1976
Joan Baez	*Blowin' Away*	Portrait	1977
Elkie Brooks	*Shooting Star*	A&M	1978
Peter Frampton	*Breaking All The Rules*	A&M	1981
Johnny G and The Distractions	*Let It Rock*	A&M	1981
Gallagher and Lyle	*Breakaway*	A&M	1976
Gallagher and Lyle	*Love On The Airwaves*	A&M	1977
Lani Hall	*Double Or Nothing*	A&M	1979
Richie Havens	*The End Of The Beginning*	A&M	1976
Robert Hazard	*Wing Of Fire*	RCA	1984
Hues Corporation	*Love Corporation*	RCA	1975
Joe Jackson	*Look Sharp*	A&M	1979
Joe Jackson	*I'm The Man*	A&M	1979
Joe Jackson	*Night And Day*	A&M	1982
Joe Jackson	*Body And Soul*	A&M	1984
Jerry Knight	*Jerry Knight*	A&M	1980
Jerry Knight	*Perfect Fit*	A&M	1981
Ozark Mountain Daredevils	*Don't Look Down*	A&M	1977
Graham Parker	*The Real Macaw*	RCA/Aris	1983
R.A.F.	*R.A.F.*	A&M	1980
Reds	*The Reds*	A&M	1979
Stephen Michael Schwarz	*Stephen Michael Schwarz*	RCA	1974
Sterling	*City Kids*	A&M	1979
Cat Stevens	*Izitso*	Island/A&M	1977
B.W.Stevenson	*B.W.Stevenson*	RCA	1972
B.W.Stevenson	*Lead Free*	RCA	1972
B.W.Stevenson	*My Maria*	RCA	1973
B.W.Stevenson	*Calabasas*	RCA	1973
Tarney-Spencer Band	*Three's a Crowd*	A&M	1978
Tarney-Spencer Band	*Run For Your Life*	A&M	1979
Randy Vanwarmer	*The Things That You Dream*	Bearsv	1983

K018 Abe "Voco" Kesh

Blue Cheer	*Inside Out*	Philips	1968
Harvey Mandel	*Cristo Redentor*	Philips	1968
Harvey Mandel	*Righteous*	Philips	1969
Harvey Mandel	*Games Guitars Play*	Philips	1970
Harvey Mandel	*Baby Batter*	Janus	1971
various artists	*Lights Out San Francisco*	B.Thumb	1969

K019 Stan Kessler

Sam The Sham	*Wooly Bully*	MGM	1965
Sam The Sham	*Their Second Album*	MGM	1965
Sam The Sham	*Li'l Red Riding Hood*	MGM	1966
Sam The Sham	*The Sam The Sham Revue*	MGM	1966
Sam The Sham	*Ten Of Pentacles*	MGM	1968

K020 Adam Kidron

Delta 5	*Whirls*	Pre	1981
Ian Dury	*4000 Weeks Holiday*	Polydor	1983
Orange Juice	*You Can't Hide Your Love Forever*	Polydor	1982
Orchestre Rouge	*More Passion Fodder*	RCA	1983
Panther Burns	*Blow Your Top*	Animal	1982
Pere Ubu	*Song Of The Bailing Man*	R.Trade	1981
Raincoats	*Odyshape*	R.Trade	1981
w. Mayo Thompson Red Crayola	*Kangaroo*	R.Trade	1981
Rip,Rig & Panic	*Attitude*	Virgin	1983
Scritti Politti	*Songs To Remember*	R.Trade	1982

K021 Chris Kimsey

Carillo	*Rings Around The Moon*	Atlantic	1978
Jimmy Cliff	*Special*	CBS	1982
Dice	*The Dice*	Mercury	1984
Peter Frampton	*Where I Should Be*	A&M	1979
Mike Harrison	*Rainbow Rider*	Island	1975
Doc Holliday	*Doc Holliday*	Metro	1973

(Not to be confused with the more recent Doc Holliday's on A&M or the German group of the early 1980's.)

Fingerprintz	*Beat Noir*	Virg/Stiff	1981
Novo Combo	*Novo Combo*	Polydor	1981
Terry Reid	*Rogue Waves*	Capitol	1979
w.Glimmer Twins Rolling Stones	*Emotional Rescue*	RSR	1980
w.Glimmer Twins Rolling Stones	*Tattoo You*	RSR	1981
w.Glimmer Twins Rolling Stones	*Under Cover*	RSR	1983
Chris Stainton	*Tundra*	Decca	1976
Strapps	*Secret Damage*	EMI	1977
Peter Tosh	*Mama Africa*	EMI	1983
Widowmaker	*Too Late To Cry*	Jet	1977
Jerry Williams	*Gone*	WB	1979
Bill Wyman	*Bill Wyman*	A&M	1982

K022 Jonathan King

Genesis	*From Genesis To Revelation*	Decca	1969
Tina Harvey	*Tina Harvey*	UK	1977

K023 Dennis Kirk

Bette Midler	*Divine Madness*	Atlantic	1980

K024 Gary Klein

Judy Collins	*Hard Times For Lovers*	Elektra	1979
Glen Campbell	*Southern Nights*	Capitol	1978

w.Snuff Garrett	Glen Campbell	*It's The World Gone Crazy*	Capitol	1980
	Glen Campbell	*Something 'Bout You Baby I Like*	Capitol	1980
	Charlie Daniels	*Te John, Grease and The Wolfman*	KS	1972
	Mac Davis	*Burning Thing*	CBS	1974
	Dr. Buzzard	*Dr. Buzzard Goes To Washington*	Elektra	1979
	Sandy Farina	*All Alone In The Night*	MCA	1980
	Tim Hardin	*Tim Hardin 3-Live In Concert*	MGM	1968
	Tim Hardin	*Suite For Susan Moore And Damion*	CBS	1969
	Janis Ian	*Restless Eyes*	CBS	1981
	Gladys Knight	*The First Solo Album*	Buddah	1978
	Cheryl Ladd	*Cheryl Ladd*	Capitol	1978
	Cheryl Ladd	*Dance Forever*	Capitol	1979
	Gary Lewis	*Listen*	Liberty	1968
	Stephanie Mills	*Merciless*	Casab	1983
	Nana Mouskouri	*Nana*	Mercury	1984
	Dolly Parton	*Dolly*	RCA	1978
	Dolly Parton	*Heartbreaker*	RCA	1978
	Dolly Parton	*Dolly Dolly Dolly*	RCA	1980
	Plant And See	*Plant And See*	W.Whale	1968
	Samantha Sang	*Emotion*	P.Stock	1978
	Barbra Streisand	*Superman*	CBS	1978
	Barbra Streisand	*Songbird*	CBS	1978
	Barbra Streisand	*The Eyes Of Laura Mars (soundtrack)*	CBS	1978
	Barbra Streisand	*Wet*	CBS	1979
	Wright Brothers	*Made In The USA*	WB	1982

K025 Mark Klingman

	Bette Midler	*Songs For The New Depression*	Atlantic	1976

K026 Terry Knight

	Faith	*Faith*	Brown Bag	1973
	Grand Funk	*On Time*	Capitol	1969
	Grand Funk	*Grand Funk Railroad*	Capitol	1970
	Grand Funk	*Closer To Home*	Capitol	1970
	Grand Funk	*Live Album*	Capitol	1971
	Mom's Apple Pie	*Mom's Apple Pie*	Brown Bag	1973

K027 Mark Knopfler

	Bob Dylan	*Infidels*	CBS	1983

K028 Tom Knox

	Toto	*Hydra*	CBS	1979

K029 Glen Kolotkin (see under Matthew King Kaufman and Kenny Laguna for co-production credits.)

w. R.Cordell	Doug And The Slugs	*Music For The Hard Of Thinking*	RCA	1983
	Duke Jupiter	*1*	CTC	1981

	Duke Jupiter	*White Knuckle Ride*	Morocco	1984
	Earthquake	*Live*	Beserkley	1975
	Earthquake	*Rocking The World*	Beserkley	1975
	Earthquake	*8.5*	Beserkley	1976
	Eathquake	*Levelled*	Beserkley	1977
	Greg Kihn	*Greg Kihn*	Beserkley	1976
	Greg Kihn	*Greg Kihn Again*	Beserkley	1977
	Greg Kihn	*Next Of Kihn*	Beserkley	1978
	Greg Kihn	*With The Naked Eye*	Beserkley	1979
	Modern Lovers	*The Modern Lovers*	Beserkley	1976
w.Hilly Kristel	Pet Clams	*The Pet Clams*	Handshake	1981
	Jonathan Richman and The Modern Lovers	*Jonathan Richman and The Modern Lovers*	Beserkley	1976
	Jonathan Richman and The Modern Lovers	*Back In Your Life*	Beserkley	1979
	Rubinoos	*The Rubinoos*	Beserkley	1977
	Rubinoos	*Back To The Drawing Board*	Beserkley	1979
w.R.Cordell	Shrapnel	*Shrapnel*	Elektra	1984
	Spitballs	*The Spitballs*	Beserkley	1978
w.R.Cordell	Stompers	*The Stompers*	Boardwalk	1983
	various artists	*Beserk Times*	Beserkley	1978

K030 Al Kooper

	Appaloosa	*Appaloosa*	CBS	1969
w. Andy Kulberg	Blues Project	*Reunion In Central Park*	MCA	1973
	Mike Bloomfield,Al Kooper,Stephen Stills	*Super Session*	CBS	1967
	Mike Bloomfield and Al Kooper	*The Live Adventures Of Mike Bloomfield And Al Kooper*	CBS	1968
	Marshall Chapman	*Jaded Virgin*	Epic	1978
	Sweet Linda Devine	*Sweet Linda Devine*	CBS	1969
	Eddie and The Hot Rods	*Fish And Chips*	EMI	1981
	Elijah	*Fanfares*	SOTS	1973
	David Essex	*Be-Bop The Future*	Mercury	1981
	Four On The Floor	*Four On The Floor*	Casab	1979
	Freddy Henry	*Get It Out In The Open*	Clouds	1979
	Mose Jones	*Get It Right*	MCA	1973
	Phil Judd (Ex-Split Enz.)	*The Swinger*	MCA	1983
	Al Kooper	*Kooper Session (introducing Shuggie Otis)*	CBS	1969
	Al Kooper	*I Stand Alone*	CBS	1967
	Al Kooper	*You Never Know Who Your Friends Are*	CBS	1969
	Al Kooper	*Easy Does It*	CBS	1970
	Al Koper	*A Possible Projection Of The Future*	CBS	1971
	Al Kooper	*New York City (You're A Woman)*	CBS	1971
	Al Kooper	*The Landlord soundtrack*	UA	1971
	Al Kooper	*Naked Songs*	CBS	1972

	Al Kooper	Act Like Nothing's Wrong	UA	1976
	Nils Lofgren	Cry Tough	A&M	1976
	Lynyrd Skynyrd	Lynyrd Skynyrd	MCA	1973
	Lynyrd Skynyrd	Second Helping	MCA	1974
	Lynyrd Skynyrd	Nuthin' Fancy	MCA	1975
	Tubes	The Tubes	A&M	1975
	Johnny Van Zandt Band	No More Dirty Deals	Polydor	1980
	Johnny Van Zandt Band	Last Of The Wild Ones	Polydor	1982

K031 Charles Koppelman and Don Rubin

	Critters	Touch 'n' Go	T.Sound	1968
	Tim Hardin	2	MGM	1967
	Gary Lewis	New Directions	Liberty	1967

(See also entries for Eric Jacobsen and Gary Klein both of whom worked with Koppelman-Rubin over the years.)

K032 Artie Kornfeld

	Barbara Barrow and Mike Smith	Mickey And Babs Get Hot	Bell	1974
	The Wind In The Willows	The Wind In The Willows	Capitol	1968

(Early Debbie Harry appearance on record.)

K033 Danny Kortchmar (aka Danny Kootch)

	Louise Goffin	Kid Blue	Asylum	1979
	Louise Goffin	Louise Goffin	Asylum	1981
w. Greg Ladanyi	Don Henley	I Can't Stand Still	Asylum	1982
w. R.Appere	Danny Kortchmar	Kootch	WB	1973
	Danny Kortchmar	Innuendo	Asylum	1980

K034 Edwin H.Kramer

	Air Raid	Air Raid	20th Cent	1981
	Amboy Dukes	Marriage On The Rocks	Polydor	1969
	Angel	On Earth As It Is In Heaven	Casab	1977
	April Wine	Live At El Mocambo	Decca/Aqu	1977
	Brownsville Station	Brownsville Station	P.Stock	1977
	Duke And The Drivers	Cruisin'	ABC	1975
	Fastway	Fastway	CBS	1983
	Foghat	Stone Blue	Bearsv	1978
	Fotomaker	Fotomaker	Atlantic	1978
	Peter Frampton	The Art Of Control	A&M	1982
	Ace Frehley	Ace Frehley	Casab	1978
w.Mitch Mitchell	Jimi Hendrix	Cry Of Love	Poly/Rep	1971
w.Mitch Mitchell & John Jansen	Jimi Hendrix	Rainbow Bridge	Reprise	1971
w.John Jansen	Jimi Hendrix	Hendrix In The West	Poly/Rep	1972
w.John Jansen	Jimi Hendrix	War Heroes	Poly/Rep	1973
	Kiss	Rock And Roll Over	Casab	1976
	Kiss	Kiss Alive	Casab	1976
	Kiss	Love Gun	Casab	1977
	Kiss	Alive 2	Casab	1977

	J.F.Murphy and Salt	*J.F.Murphy and Salt*	Elektra	1971
	Mott	*Shouting And Pointing*	CBS	1976
	Music	*Music*	Buddah	1971
	(Group featured Buzzy Linhart.)			
	NRBQ	*Scraps*	KS	1970
	NRBQ	*Workshop*	KS	1972
	Sha Na Na	*Sha Na Na*	KS	1971
	Michael Stanley Band	*North Coast*	EMI-Amer	1981
	Stories	*About Us*	KS	1973
	Wendy Waldman	*Which Way To Main Street*	Epic	1982

K035 Bob Krasnow

w.Richard Perry	Captain Beefheart	*Safe As Milk*	Pye/K.S.	1967
	Captain Beefheart	*Strictly Personal*	B.Thumb	1968
	Captain Beefheart	*Mirror Man*	Buddah	1971

K036 Murray Krugman and Sandy Pearlman

	Blue Oyster Cult	*Blue Oyster Cult*	CBS	1971
	Blue Oyster Cult	*Tyranny and Mutation*	CBS	1973
	Blue Oyster Cult	*Secret Treaties*	CBS	1974
	Blue Oyster Cult	*On Your Feet Or On Your Knees*	CBS	1975
	Blue Oyster Cult	*Agents Of Fortune*	CBS	1976
	Blue Oyster Cult	*Spectres*	CBS	1977
	Blue Oyster Cult	*Some Enchanted Evening*	CBS	1978
	Dictators	*Go Girl Crazy*	Epic	1975
	Dictators	*Manifest Destiny*	Asylum	1977
	Dictators	*Blood Brothers*	Asylum	1978
	Pavlov's Dog	*Pampered Menial*	CBS	1975
	Pavlov's Dog	*At The Sound Of The Bell*	CBS	1976

K037 Murray Krugman

	Mahavishnu Orchestra	*Live*	CBS	1973

K038 Dick Kunc

	Tim Buckley	*Lorca*	Elektra	1970
	Spanky and Our Gang	*Live*	Mercury	1970

L001 Jeff Labes

	Jesse Colin Young	*American Dreams*	Elektra	1978

L002 Greg Ladanyi

w. J.Browne	Jackson Browne	*Hold Out*	Asylum	1980
w. J.Browne	Jackson Browne	*Lawyers In Love*	Asylum	1983
w. D.Kortchmar	Don Henley	*I Can't Stand Still*	Asylum	1982
w. K.Edwards	David James Holster	*Chinese Honeymoon*	CBS	1979
w. J.Browne	David Lindley	*El Rayo-X*	Asylum	1981
	David Lindley	*Win This Record*	Asylum	1982
w. R.Cannata	Phoebe Snow	*Rock Away*	Mirage	1981
	Warren Zevon	*Bad Luck Streak In The Dancing School*	Asylum	1980
	Warren Zevon	*Stand In The Fire*	Asylum	1980

w. W.Wachtel	Warren Zevon	*The Envoy*	Asylum	1982

L003 Gary Ladinsky

	American Noise	*American Noise*	Planet	1980
	Fotomaker	*Vis-a-Vis*	Atlantic	1978

L004 Kenny Laguna (see also Matthew King Kaufman for co-productions)

	Advertising	*Advertising Jingles (4 tracks only)*	EMI	1978
	Bethnal	*Dangerous Times*	Vertigo	1978
	Bow Wow Wow	*I Want Candy*	EMI	1982
	Earthquake	*Two Years In A Padded Cell*	Beserkley	1979
	Steve Gibbons	*Any Road Up*	Polydor	1976
	Steve Gibbons	*Rollin' On*	Polydor	1977
	Steve Gibbons	*Caught In The Act*	Polydor	1977
w. R.Cordell	Tommy James	*In Touch*	Fantasy	1976
w. R.Cordell	Joan Jett	*Joan Jett*	Ariola	1980
w. R.Cordell	Joan Jett	*Bad Reputation*	Boardwalk	1981
w. R.Cordell	Joan Jett	*I Love Rock And Roll*	Epic/Board	1982
	Joan Jett	*Album*	Epic/MCA	1983
	Greg Kihn	*Next Of Kihn*	Beserkley	1978
	Greg Kihn	*With The Naked Eye*	Beserkley	1979
	Modern Lovers	*Live*	Beserkley	1977
	Jonathna Richman's Modern Lovers	*Back In Your Life*	Beserkley	1979
	Spitballs	*The Spitballs*	Beserkley	1978
	Tyla Gang	*Moonproof*	Beserkley	1978

L005 Bob Lamb

	UB40	*Signing Off*	Grad/Epic	1980

L006 Dennis Lambert

	Dennis Edwards	*Don't Look Any Further*	Gordy	1984
w. Steve Barri	Temptations	*Surface Thrills*	Gordy	1983

L007 Dennis Lambert and Brian Potter

	Glen Campbell	*Bloodline*	Capitol	1976
w. Steve Barri	Four Tops	*Mainstreet People*	ABC	1973
	Cuba Gooding	*First Album*	Motown	1978
	Gayle McCormick	*Gayle McCormick*	Dunhill	1971
	Player	*Danger Zone*	RSO	1978
	Gene Redding	*Blood Brother*	Haven	1974
	Righteous Brothers	*Give It To The People*	Capitol	1974
	Righteous Brothers	*The Sons Of Mrs Righteous*	Capitol	1975
	Rock Rose	*Rock Rose*	CBS	1979
	Santana	*Inner Secrets*	CBS	1978
w. Steve Barri	Dusty Springfield	*Cameo*	Phil/ABC	1973
	Tavares	*Check It Out*	Capitol	1974
	Tavares	*Hard Core Poetry*	Capitol	1975
	Tavares	*In The City*	Capitol	1975

L008 Kit Lambert

w. Vicki Wickham	Labelle	*Labelle*	WB	1971
	The Who	*A Quick One*	Reac/Decca	1966

	The Who	*The Who Sell Out*	Track/Dec	1967
	The Who	*Magic Bus*	Decca	1968
	The Who	*Tommy*	Track/MCA	1969

L009 Jon Landau

	Jackson Browne	*The Pretender*	Asylum	1976
	MC5	*Back In The USA*	Atlantic	1970
	Bruce Springsteen	*Born To Run*	CBS	1975
	Bruce Springsteen	*Darkness On The Edge Of Town*	CBS	1978
w.Miami Steve	Bruce Springsteen	*The River*	CBS	1980
w.Miami Steve & Chuck Plotkin	Bruce Springsteen	*Born In The USA*	CBS	1984
	Livingston Taylor	*Echoes*	Capricorn	1979

L010 Richard Landis

	Peter Allen	*Not The Boy Next Door*	Arista	1983
	Crimson Tide	*Crimson Tide*	Capitol	1978
	Desmond Child and Rouge	*Desmond Child and Rouge*	Capitol	1979
	Desmond Child and Rouge	*Runners In The Night*	Capitol	1979
	King Of Hearts	*Close But No Cigar*	Capitol	1978
	Juice Newton	*Juice*	Capitol	1981
	Juice Newton	*Quiet Lies*	Capitol	1982
	Juice Newton	*Dirty Looks*	Capitol	1983
	Nielsen/Pearson	*Nielsen/Pearson*	Capitol	1980
	Nitty Gritty Dirt Band	*Let's Go*	Liberty	1983
	Gary O'Connor	*Gary O*	Capitol	1981
	Red Rider	*As Far As Siam*	Capitol	1981

L011 Gary Langan

	ABC	*Beauty Stab*	Phonogram	1983
	RPM	*Phonogenic*	WB	1984

L012 Robert John "Mutt" Lange

	AC/DC	*Highway To Hell*	Atlantic	1979
	AC/DC	*Back In Black*	Atlantic	1980
	AC/DC	*For Those About To Rock*	Atlantic	1981
	Boomtown Rats	*The Boomtown Rats*	Ensign	1977
	Boomtown Rats	*Tonic For The Troops*	Ensign	1978
	Boomtown Rats	*The Fine Art Of Surfacing*	Ensign	1979

(Album includes "I Don't Like Mondays" which was produced by Phil Wainman.)

	Broken Home	*Broken Home*	Sire	1980
	Cars	*Heartbeat City*	Elektra	1984
	Clover	*Unavailable*	Vertigo	1977
	Clover	*Love On The Wire*	Vertigo	1977
	City Boy	*City Boy*	Vert/Mer	1976
	City Boy	*Young Men Gone West*	Vert/Mer	1977
	City Boy	*Dinner At The Ritz*	Vert/Mer	1978
	City Boy	*Book Early*	Vert/Mer	1978

	City Boy	*The Day The Earth Caught Fire*	Vertigo	1979
	Kevin Coyne	*In Living Black And White*	Virgin	1976
	Deaf School	*English Boys/Working Girls*	WB	1970
	Def Leppard	*High 'n' Dry*	Vert/Mer	1981
	Def Leppard	*Pyromania*	Vert/Mer	1982
w. Mick Jones	Foreigner	*4*	Atlantic	1981
	Motors	*1*	Virgin	1977
	Outlaws	*Playing To Win*	Arista	1978
	Graham Parker and The Rumour	*Heat Treatment*	Vert/Mer	1976
	Graham Parker and The Rumour	*The Parkerilla*	Vert/Mer	1978
w.T.Friese-Green	Records	*Shades In Bed*	Virgin	1979
	Rumour	*Max*	Vert/Mer	1977
	Savoy Brown	*Savage Return*	London	1978
	Michael Stanley Band	*Cabin Fever*	Arista	1978
	Supercharge	*Horizontal Refreshment*	Virgin	1976
	Supercharge	*Body Rhythm*	Virgin	1979
	Tycoon	*Tycoon*	Arista	1979

L013 Clive Langer

	Teardrop Explodes	*Wilder*	Mercury	1981

L014 Clive Langer and Alan Winstanley

	Blue Rondo A La Turk	*Chewing The Fat*	Virgin	1982
	Bette Bright	*Rhythm Breaks The Ice*	Korova	1981
	Elvis Costello	*Punch The Clock*	F-Beat/CBS	1983
	Elvis Costello	*Goodbye Cruel World*	F-Beat/CBS	1984
	Dexys Midnight Runners	*Too-Rye-Ay*	Mercury	1982
	Haysi Fantayzee	*Battle Hymns For Children Singing (2 tr)*	Regard	1983
	Clive Langer	*Splash*	F-Beat	1980
	Madness	*One Step Beyond*	Stiff/Sire	1979
	Madness	*Absolutely*	Stiff/Sire	1980
	Madness	*7*	Stiff	1981
	Madness	*Rise And Fall*	Stiff	1982
	Madness	*Keep Moving*	Stiff/Geff	1984
	Nitecaps	*Go To The Line*	Sire	1982
	Teardrop Explodes	*Kiliminjaro (2 tracks)*	Mercury	1980

L015 Bob Last

	Fire Engines	*Aufgeladen*	Fast	1981
	Mekons	*The Quality Of Mercy*	Virgin	1979

L016 Laurie Latham

	Jimmy Hibbert	*Heavy Duty*	Logo	1980
	Philip Rambow	*Jungle Law*	EMI	1981
	Paul Young	*No Parlez*	CBS	1983

L017 Nick Launay

	Inxs	*The Swing*	Atco	1984
	Spear Of Destiny	*Grapes Of Wrath*	B.Rome	1983

L018 Derek Lawrence

w. Big Jim Sullivan	Angel	*Angel*	Casab	1976
w.Big Jim Sullivan	Angel	*Helluva Band*	Casab	1976
	Richie Blackmore	*Green Bullfrog*	ECY	1981
	Deep Purple	*Book Of Taliesyn*	Harvest	1969
	Deep Purple	*Deep Purple*	Harvest	1970
	Dragonfly	*Almost Abandoned*	EMI	1974
	Fist	*Turn On The Hell*	MCA	1980
	Flash	*Flash*	EMI	1972
	Garnet Mimms	*Live*	UA	1967
	Wishbone Ash	*Wishbone Ash*	MCA	1970
	Wishbone Ash	*Argus*	MCA	1972
	Wishbone Ash	*Pilgrimage*	MCA	1974
	Wishbone Ash	*No Smoke Without Fire*	MCA	1978

L019 Trevor Lawrence

	Ace	*No Strings*	Anchor	1977
	Jimmy Cliff	*Follow My Mind*	Reprise	1976
	Country Joe McDonald	*Rock 'n' Roll From Planet Earth*	Fantasy	1978
w. Bill Belmont	Country Joe McDonald	*Childs Play*	Rag Baby	1983
	Joe Farrell	*Night Dancing*	WB	1978
	Bobby Lyle	*Night Fire*	Capitol	1979
	McRarys	*On The Other Side*	Portrait	1979
	McRarys	*Loving Is Living*	Portrait	1983
	Geoff Muldaur	*Motion*	WB	1976
	Nilsson	*That's The Way It Is*	RCA	1976
w. Andy Wickham	Van Dyke Parks	*Clang Of The Yankee Reaper*	WB	1975
	Jon Stevens	*Jon Stevens*	MCA	1982
w. G.Mekler	Goldie Zelkowitz	*Goldie Zelkowitz*	Janus	1974

L020 Ken Laxton

	Steve Fromholz	*Jus' Playin' Along*	Lone Star	1978
	Don King	*Lonely Hotel*	Epic	1980
	Red,White & Blue	*Red White & Blue Grass*	GRC	1973

L021 Jim Lea and Noddy Holder

	Girl School	*Play Dirty*	Bronze	1983

L022 Mike Leander

	Gary Glitter	*Touch Me*	Bell	1973
	Gary Glitter	*Glitter*	Bell	1974
	Gary Glitter	*Silver Star*	Arista	1977
	Glitter Band	*Hey*	Bell	1974
	Glitter Band	*Rock And Roll Dudes*	Bell	1975
	Glitter Band	*Listen To The Band*	Bell	1975
	G Band	*Paris Match*	CBS	1976

	Hello	*Keep Us Off The Streets*	Bell	1976
w. T. MacAuley	London Cast	*Godspell*	Bell	1971

L023 Chuck Leavell

	Duke Jupiter	*Sweet Cheeks*	Mercury	1978

L024 John Leckie

	Adverts	*Crossing The Red Sea With The Adverts*	Bright	1978
	After The Fire	*Laser Love*	CBS	1979
	Be-Bop Deluxe	*Modern Music*	Harvest	1976
	Be-Bop Deluxe	*Sunburst Finish*	Harvest	1976
	Be-Bop Deluxe	*Live In The Air Age*	Harvest	1977
	Be-Bop Deluxe	*Drastic Plastic*	Harvest	1978
	Cuban Heels	*Cuban Heels*	Virgin	1981
	Doctors Of Madness	*Figments Of Emancipation*	Polydor	1976
	The Doll	*Listen To The Silence*	B.Banquet	1977
	Roy Harper	*Bullinamingvase*	Harv/Chry	1977
	Roger McGough	*Summer with Monika*	Island	1978
	Magazine	*Real Life*	Virgin	1978
	Bill Nelson	*Sound On Sound*	Harvest	1979
	Mr.Partridge (Andy Partridge of XTC.)	*Take Away*	Virgin	1980
	Proof	*It's Safe*	Nemperor	1980
	Simple Minds	*Life In A Day*	Zoom	1979
	Simple Minds	*Real To Real Cacophony*	Zoom	1979
	Simple Minds	*Empires And Dance*	Arista	1980
	XTC	*White Music*	Virgin	1978
	XTC	*Go 2*	Virgin	1978

L025 Geddy Lee

	Boys Brigade	*The Boys Brigade*	Capitol	1983

L026 Mark Lee

	Kenny and The Kasuals	*Live At The Studio Club*	Mark	1977
	Kenny and The Kasuals	*Garage Kings*	Mark	1979

L027 Kyle Lehning

w. S.Gibson	Bobby Bare	*Sleeper Wherever I Fall*	CBS	1978
	England Dan and John Ford Coley	*Nights Are Forever*	Big Tree	1976
	England Dan and John Ford Coley	*Dowdy Ferry Road*	Big Tree	1977
	England Dan and John Ford Coley	*Some Things Don't Come Easy*	Big Tree	1978
	England Dan and John Ford Coley	*Dr.Heckle and Mr.Jive*	Big Tree	1979
w. Ron and Howie Albert	Firefall	*Undertow*	Atlantic	1979
	Firefall	*Clouds Across The Sun*	Atlantic	1980
	Parker McGee	*Parker McGee*	Big Tree	1977

	Tom Powers	*Love And Learn*	Big Tree	1977
	Dan Seals	*Stones*	Atlantic	1980
	Dan Seals	*Harbinger*	Atlantic	1982
	Dan Seals	*Rebel Heart*	Liberty	1983
	Thunder	*Thunder*	Atco	1980
w. Don Cobb	Thunder	*Headphones For Cows*	Atco	1981
	Wilson Bros	*Another Night*	Atlantic	1979

L028 Leiber and Stoller

	Elkie Brooks	*Two Days Away*	A&M	1976
	Jerry Butler	*Need To Belong*	Vee Jay	1964
	Coasters	*The Coasters*	Atco	1957
	Coasters	*One By One*	Atco	1960
	Coasters	*On Broadway*	King	1963
	Dino & Sembello	*Dino & Sembello*	A&M	1974
	Dixie Cups	*The Dixie Cups*	Red Bird	1964
	Exciters	*Tell Him*	UA	1962
	Jay and The Americans	*She Cried*	UA	1962
	Ben E.King	*Spanish Harlem*	Atco	1961
	Peggy Lee	*Mirrors*	A&M	1975
	Leiber-Stoller Big Band	*Yakety Yak*	Atlantic	1961
	Procol Harum	*Procol's Ninth*	Chrysalis	1975
	Steve Rossi	*Try To Remember*	Red Bird	1965
	Shangri La's	*Bulldog*	Red Bird	1965
	Stealers Wheel	*Stealers Wheel*	A&M	1973
	Stealers Wheel	*Ferguslie Park*	A&M	1973
	Joan Tolliver	*Joan Tolliver*	Kapp	1964
	Sammy Turner	*Lavender Blue Moods*	Big Top	1959
	Leslie Uggams	*What's An Uggams*	Atlantic	1968
	T-Bone Walker	*Very Rare*	WB	1973
	Billy Ed Wheeler	*A New Bag Of Songs*	Kapp	1962

L029 Paul Leka

	Aztec Two-Step	*Second Step*	RCA	1975
	Harry Chapin	*Short Stories*	Elektra	1973
	Harry Chapin	*Portrait Gallery*	Elektra	1975
	Harry Chapin	*Greatest Stories Live*	Elektra	1976
	Randle Chowning Band	*Hearts On Fire*	A&M	1978
	Left Banke	*Too*	Smash	1968
	Lemon Pipers	*Green Tambourine*	Buddah	1968
	Lori Lieberman	*Letting Go*	Millenium	1978
	R.E.O.Speedwagon	*R.E.O.Speedwagon*	Epic	1971
	R.E.O.Speedwagon	*Two*	Epic	1972
	Maggie Ryder	*Maggie Ryder*	Polydor	1978
	Silverbird	*Getting Together*	CBS	1972
	Jimmy Spheeris	*Isle Of View*	CBS	1971

L030 John Lennon

w. Yoko Ono	Elephant's Memory	*Elephant's Memory*	Apple	1972
w. Yoko Ono	John Lennon and Yoko Ono	*Two Virgins:Unfinished Music No. 1*	Apple	1968
w. Yoko Ono	John Lennon and Yoko Ono	*Unfinished Music:Life With The Lions*	Apple	1969

w. Yoko Ono	John Lennon and Yoko Ono	*Wedding Album*	Apple	1969
w. Yoko Ono	John Lennon and Yoko Ono	*Live Peace In Toronto*	Apple	1970
w. Yoko Ono and Phil Spector	John Lennon	*Plastic Ono Band*	Apple	1970
w. Yoko Ono and Phil Spector	John Lennon	*Imagine*	Apple	1971
w. Yoko Ono and Phil Spector	John Lennon	*Sometime In New York City*	Apple	1972
	John Lennon	*Mind Games*	Apple	1973
	John Lennon	*Walls And Bridges*	Apple	1974
	John Lennon	*Rock And Roll*	Apple	1975
	(4 tracks produced by Phil Spector.)			
w. Yoko Ono and Jack Douglas	John Lennon/Yoko Ono	*Double Fantasy*	Geffen	1980
w. Yoko Ono	John Lennon	*Milk And Honey*	Polydor	1984
	Nilsson	*Pussy Cats*	RCA	1974
w. Yoko Ono	Yoko Ono	*Fly*	Apple	1971
w. Yoko Ono	Yoko Ono	*Approximately Infinite Universe*	Apple	1972
	David Peel	*The Pope Smokes Dope*	Apple	1973

L031 Craig Leon

	Willie Alexander and The Boom Boom Band	*Willie Alexander and The Boom Boom Band*	MCA	1978
	Willie Alexander	*Meanwhile... Back In The States*	MCA	1978
	Lisa Burns	*Lisa Burns*	MCA	1978
w. R.Gottehrer	Chilliwack	*Rockerbox*	Sire	1975
	City Lights	*Silent Dancing*	Sire	1975
	Rodney Crowell	*But What Will The Neighbours Think*	WB	1980
	Garfeel Ruff	*Garfeel Ruff*	Capitol	1979
	The Kind	*Pain and Pleasure*	ThreeSixty	1983
	Moon Martin	*Shots From A Cold Nightmare*	Capitol	1978
	Moon Martin	*Escape From Domination*	Capitol	1979
	Ramones	*The Ramones*	Sire	1976
	Records	*Crashes*	Virgin	1980
w. Cassell Webb	Sir Douglas Quintet	*Border Wave*	Chrysalis	1981
w. Marty Thau	Suicide	*Suicide*	Red Star	1977
w. Bob Marley	Martha Velez	*Escape From Babylon*	Sire	1976

L032 Eddie Leonetti

	Artful Dodger	*Babes On Broadway*	CBS	1977
w. Jack Douglas	Artful Dodger	*Honor Among Thieves*	CBS	1976
	Angel	*White Hot*	Casab	1977
	Angel	*Sinful*	Casab	1979
	Angel	*Live-Without A Net*	Casab	1980
	Gus	*Convicted*	Nemperor	1980
	Legs Diamond	*A Diamond Is A Hard Rock*	Mercury	1977
	Network	*Nightwork*	Epic	1978
	Private Eye	*Private Eye*	Capitol	1979

	Skyhooks	*Guilty Until Proven Insane* UA		1979

L033 Jeffrey Lesser

w. B.Goldberg	Coup	*Coup De Grace*	A&M	1984
	Head East	*Head East*	A&M	1978
	Head East	*Live*	A&M	1978
	Hounds	*Puttin' On The Dog*	CBS	1979
	Rupert Holmes	*Widescreen*	Epic	1974
	Rupert Holmes	*Rupert Holmes*	Epic	1975
	Invisible Zoo	*Invisible Zoo (12"EP)*	Vanity	1983
	Hilly Michaels	*Lumia*	WB	1981
w. Rupert Holmes	Orchestra Luna	*Orchestra Luna*	Epic	1974
	Sailor	*Trouble*	Epic	1975
	Sailor	*The Third Step*	Epic	1976
	Starcastle	*Real To Reel*	Epic	1978
	Straight Lines	*Run For Cover*	Epic	1982
w. Rupert Holmes	Strawbs	*Deep Cuts*	Polydor	1976
	Strawbs	*Burning For You*	Polydor	1977
	Strawbs	*Deadlines*	Arista	1978
w. Rupert Holmes	Barbra Streisand	*Lazy Afternoon*	CBS	1975
	Pat Travers	*Heat In The Street*	Polydor	1978
	Vivabeat	*Party In The War Zone*	Charisma	1980

L034 Hank Levine

	Davy Jones	*Davy Jones*	Colpix	1967
	Jim Webb	*Sings Jim Webb*	CBS	1968

L035 Steve Levine

	Angelic Upstarts	*Still From The Heart*	EMI	1982
	China Crisis	*Difficult Shapes*	Virgin	1982
	Culture Club	*Kissing To Be Clever*	Virgin	1982
	Culture Club	*Colour By Numbers*	Virgin	1983
w. S.Humphrey	Dance People	*Fly Away*	Satril	1979
	David Grant	*David Grant*	Chrysalis	1983
	Gary Moore	*Corridors Of Power*	Virg/Mir	1983

L036 Stewart Levine

w. Rik Pekkonen	Arthur Adams	*Love My Lady*	A&M	1979
	soundtrack	*Casey's Shadow*	CBS	1978
	Joe Cocker	*Civilized Man (1 side)*	Capitol	1984
	Randy Crawford	*Everything Must Change*	WB	1976
	Dixie Dregs	*Freefall*	Capricorn	1976
	Charlie Dore	*Listen*	Chrysalis	1981
	Crusaders	*One*	ABC	1972
	Crusaders	*Unsung Heroes*	ABC	1973
	Crusaders	*Scratch*	ABC	1974
	Crusaders	*Southern Comfort*	ABC	1974
	Crusaders	*Those Southern Knights*	ABC	1976
	Crusaders	*Free As The Wind*	ABC	1977
	Jiva	*Jiva*	Dark Horse	1975
	B.B.King	*Midnight Believer*	ABC	1978
	B.B.King	*Take It Home*	MCA	1979
	B.B.King	*There Must Be A Better World Somewhere*	MCA	1981
	B.B.King	*Love Me Tender*	MCA	1982
	Marshall Tucker	*Together Forever*	Capricorn	1978
	Marshall Tucker	*Running Like The Wind*	WB	1979

	Marshall Tucker	*Tenth*	WB	1980
	Hugh Masekala	*Techno-Bush*	Jive	1984
w. Herb Alpert	Letta Mbulu	*Letta*	A&M	1978
	Moon	*Too Close For Comfort*	Epic	1976
	Minnie Ripperton	*Adventures In Paradise*	Epic	1975
	Brenda Russell	*Love Life*	A&M	1981
	Sea Level	*Sea Level*	Capricorn	1977
	Sea Level	*Cats On The Coast*	Capricorn	1977
	Sea Level	*On The Edge*	Capricorn	1978
	Sly and The Family Stone	*Ain't But The One Way*	WB	1983
	Womack And Womack	*Love Wars*	Elektra	1984

L037 Jacques Levy

	Philip D'Arrow	*Sub Zero*	Polydor	1980

L038 Jay Lewis

	Attitudes	*Good News*	Dark Horse	1977
	Highway	*Highway 1*	Epic/RSO	1979
	Mighty Flyers	*Too You To Have Fun*	Takoma	1984
w. D.Foster	Danny Peck	*Heart And Soul*	Arista	1977
	Lorna Wright	*Circle Of Love*	Rocket	1978
	Morning	*Morning*	Liberty	1970
	Morning	*Struck Like Silver*	UA	1972
	Danny O'Keefe	*The Global Blues*	WB	1979
	Paul Waroff	*California Son*	Casab	1980

L039 Marty Lewis

w.N.Putnam	Dan Fogelberg	*Phoenix*	Full Moon	1980
	Dan Fogelberg	*The Innocent Age*	Full Moon	1981
	Dan Fogelberg	*Windows And Walls*	Full Moon	1984

L040 Stan Lewis

	John Fred and His Playboys	*John Fred And His Playboys*	Paula	1968
	John Fred and His Playboys	*34.40 Of John Fred*	Paula	1969

L041 Henry Lewy

	Joan Armatrading	*How Cruel (12" EP)*	A&M	1979
	Hoyt Axton	*Southbound*	A&M	1975
	Joan Baez	*Here's To Life*	A&M	1974
w. Stuart Love	Batteaux	*Batteaux*	CBS	1973
	Stephen Bishop	*Careless*	ABC	1976
w. Bob Rafkin	David Blue	*Stories*	Asylum	1971
	John Braden	*John Braden*	A&M	1968
	Leonard Cohen	*Recent Songs*	CBS	1979
w. Larry Marks	Flying Burritos	*The Gilded Palace Of Sin*	A&M	1969
w. Jim Dickson	Flying Burritos	*Burrito Deluxe*	A&M	1970
	Honk	*Honk*	Epic	1974
	Kittyhawk	*Race For The Oasis*	EMI-Amer	1981
	Leah Kunkel	*I Run With Trouble*	CBS	1980
	Van Morrison	*The Common One*	Mercury	1980
	Paxton Brothers	*The Paxton Brothers*	ABC	1975
	Minnie Ripperton	*Minnie*	Capitol	1979

w. Jim Pons	Judee Sill	*Judee Sill*	Asylum	1972
	Judee Sill	*Heart Food*	Asylum	1973
	Jimmy Spheeris	*The Dragon Is Dancing*	CBS	1975
	Buffy St.Marie	*Sweet America*	ABC	1976
	Timber	*Part Of What You Hear*	Kapp	1970
	Neil Young	*Harvest (1 track only)*	Reprise	1972

L042 Mark Liggett and Chris Barbosa

	Shannon	*Let The Music Play*	Mirage	1984

L043 Steve Lillywhite

	Joan Armatrading	*Walk Under Ladders*	A&M	1981
	Joan Armatrading	*The Key*	A&M	1983
	Joan Armatrading	*Track Record*	A&M	1983
	Big Country	*The Crossing*	Merc/Sire	1983
	Brains	*Electronic Eden*	Mercury	1981
	Buzzards	*Jellied Eels To Record Deals*	Chrysalis	1979
	Marshall Crenshaw	*Field Day*	WB	1983
w. Ed Hollis	Eddie and The Hot Rods	*Life On The Line*	Island	1977
w. Stan Shaw	Bruce Foxton	*Touch Sensitive*	Arista	1984
	Peter Gabriel	*Peter Gabriel 3*	Char/Mer	1980
	Members	*The Members At The Chelsea Nightclub*	Virgin	1979
	Penetration	*Coming Up For Air*	Virgin	1979
	Psychedelic Furs	*The Psychedelic Furs*	CBS	1980
	Psychedelic Furs	*Talk Talk*	CBS	1981
	Sector 27	*Sector 27*	Font/IRS	1980
	Simple Minds	*Sparkle In The Rain*	Virg/A&M	1983
	Snips	*Video King*	Jet	1978
	Thompson Twins	*In The Name Of Love*	Hansa	1981
	Thompson Twins	*Set*	Tee	1982
	Toyah	*The Changeling*	Safari	1982
	U2	*Boy*	Island	1980
	U2	*October*	Island	1981
	U2	*War*	Island	1981
	Ultravox	*Ultravox !*	Island	1977
	Urban Verbs	*Early Damage*	WB	1981
	XTC	*Drums And Wires*	Virgin	1979
	XTC	*Black Sea*	Virgin	1980

L044 Sandy Linzer

	Cory Daye	*Corey And Me*	New York	1979
	(Formerly a singer with Dr.Buzzard.)			
	Dr. Buzzard	*Dr. Buzzard's Original Savannah Band*	RCA	1976

L045 Tommy Lipuma

	George Benson	*Breezin'*	WB	1976
	George Benson	*Weekend In L.A.*	WB	1978
	George Benson	*Livin' Inside Your Love*	WB	1979

w.M.Mainieri	Stephen Bishop	*Red Cab To Manhattan*	WB	1980
	Randy Crawford	*Secret Combination*	WB	1981
	Randy Crawford	*Windsong*	WB	1982
	Randy Crawford	*Nightline*	WB	1983
	Nick De Caro	*Italian Graffiti*	B.Thumb	1974
	Deodato	*Love Island*	WB	1978
w.Hugh McCracken	Dr.John	*City Lights*	A&M	1978
w.Hugh McCracken	Dr.John	*Tango Palace*	A&M	1979
	Bill Evans	*You Must Believe In Spring*	WB	1981
	Michael Franks	*The Art Of Tea*	WB	1975
	Michael Franks	*Sleeping Gypsy*	WB	1977
	Michael Franks	*Burchfield Nines*	WB	1978
	Michael Franks	*One Bad Habit*	WB	1980
	Full Moon	*Full Moon (Buzz Feiten and Neil Larsen.)*	WB	1982
	Dan Hicks	*Where's The Money*	B.Thumb	1971
	Dan Hicks	*Striking It Rich*	B.Thumb	1972
	Dan Hicks	*Last Train To Hicksville*	B.Thumb	1973
	Dan Hicks	*It Happened One Bite*	WB	1978
	Paul Humphrey	*America,Wake Up*	B.Thumb	1974
	Al Jarreau	*Glow*	WB	1976
	Al Jarreau	*Live In Europe*	WB	1977
	Neil Larsen	*Jungle Fever*	A&M	1978
	Neil Larsen	*High Gear*	A&M	1979
	Larsen-Feiten Band	*The Larsen-Feiten Band*	WB	1980
	Mark-Almond	*Other People's Rooms*	A&M	1975
	Dave Mason	*Alone Together*	B.Thumb	1970
	Dave Mason	*Headkeeper*	B,Thumb	1972
	Dave Mason	*Dave Mason Is Alive*	B.Thumb	1972
	Roger Nicholls	*A Small Circle Of Friends*	A&M	1967
	Claus Ogerman and Michael Brecker	*Cityscape*	WB	1982
	Brenda Russell	*Two Eyes*	WB	1983
	Seawind	*Light The Light*	A&M	1979
	Southwind	*Ready To Ride*	B.Thumb	1970
	B. W. Stevenson	*We Be Sailing*	WB	1975
	Phil Upchurch	*Lovin' Feeling*	B.Thumb	1971
	Phil Upchurch	*Darkness Darkness*	B.Thumb	
	various artists	*Casino Lights-Live At Montreux 1981*	WB	1982
	Yellowjackets	*Yellowjackets*	WB	1981
	Yellowjackets	*Mirage A Trois*	WB	1983

L046 John Lissauer

	Leonard Cohen	*New Skin For The Old Ceremony*	CBS	1974
	Lewis Furey	*Lewis Furey*	A&M	1975
	Lewis Furey	*The Sky Is Falling*	Aquarius	1979
	Loudon Wainwright III	*Final Exam*	Arista	1978

L047 Scott Litt

	DB's	Repercussion	Albion	1982
w. Lance Quinn	Robert Gordon	Are You Gonna Be The One	RCA	1981

L048 Michael Lloyd

	Automatic Man	Visitors	Island	1977
	Axe	Axe	MCA	1979
	Scott Baio	The Boys Are Out Tonight	RCA	1983
	Bellamy Brothers	Beautiful Friends	WB	1978
	Bellamy Brothers	The Two And Only	WB	1979
	Bellamy Brothers	You Can Get Crazy	WB	1980
	Bellamy Brothers	Sons Of The Sun	WB	1980
	Burrito Brothers	Hearts On The Line	CBS	1981
	Burrito Brothers	Sunset Sundown	CBS	1982
	Shaun Cassidy	Da Doo Ron Ron	WB	1977
	Shaun Cassidy	Born Late	WB	1977
	Shaun Cassidy	Under Wraps	WB	1978
	Shaun Cassidy	Room Service	WB	1979
	Shaun Cassidy	Live	WB	1979
	Dalton And Dubarri	Good Head	CBS	1974
	Kim Fowley	Love Is Alive And Well	Tower	1967
	Leif Garret	Leif Garrett	Scotti	1978
	Leif Garrett	Feel The Need	Scotti	1978
	Leif Garrett	Same Goes For You	Scotti	1980
	St John Green	Live	Flick Disc	1970
	Lisa Hartman	Hold On	Kirshner	1979
	Hero	Boys Will Be Boys	20th Cent	1978
	Hudson	Damn These Kids	Elektra	1980
	Jimmy and The Mustangs	Jimmy And The Mustangs	MCA	1984
	Maureen McGovern	Maureen McGovern	WB-Curb	1979
	Bill Medley	Sweet Thunder	Liberty	1981
	Pink Lady	Pink Lady	Elektra	1979
w. Kim Fowley	Smoke	The Smoke	Capitol	1969
	Simon Stokes and The Nighthawks	Simon Stokes and The Nighthawks	MGM	1971

L049 Steve Loeb (and Billy Arnell)

Riot	Rock City	Firesign	1978
Riot	Narita	Elektra	1980
Riot	Fire Down Under	Elektra	1981
Riot	Restless Breed	Elektra	1982

L050 Nils Lofgren

Charlie and The	Pep Boys	Daddy's Girl	A&M	1976

L051 Dan Loggins

Starry Eyed and Laughing	Starry Eyed and Laughing	CBS	1974
Starry Eyed and Laughing	Thought Talk	CBS	1975

(Dan Loggins is the brother of Kenny and David Loggins.)

L052 Roger Lomas

Bad Manners	*Ska 'n' B*	Magnet	1980
Bad Manners	*Loonee Tunes*	Magnet	1980
Bad Manners	*Gosh It's Bad Manners*	Magnet	1981
Bad Manners	*Forging Ahead*	Magnet	1982
Bad Manners	*Klass*	MCA	1983
Mo-Dettes	*The Story So Far*	Decca	1980
Reluctant Stereotypes	*The Label*	WEA	1980
Selecter	*Celebrate The Bullet*	Chrysalis	1981

L053 Alan Lorber

Free Beer	*Highway Robbery*	RCA	1977
Free Beer	*Nouveau Chapeau*	RCA	1978
Orpheus	*Ascending*	MGM	1968
Ultimate Spinach	*The Ultimate Spinach*	MGM	1968

L054 David Lord

Peter Gabriel	*Peter Gabriel 4*	Char/Geff	1982
(Released in the USA as "Security".)			
various artists	*WOMAD-Music And Rhythm*	WEA	1982

L055 Jack Lothrop

Eric Andersen	*A Country Dream*	Vanguard	1961
Country Gentlemen	*The Country Gentlemen*	Vanguard	1973
Jerry Jeff Walker	*Driftin' way Of Life*	Vanguard	1969
Doc Watson	*On Stage*	Vanguard	1971

L056 Stuart Alan Love

w. D.Chackler	Flower	*Flower*	UA	1977
	Nick Gilder	*You Know Who You Are*	Casab	1977
w. S.Barncard	Jiva	*Still Life*	Polydor	1978
	Michael Quatro	*Dancers,Romancers ..*	Prodigal	1976
w. Ray Ruff	Michael Quatro	*Gettin' Ready*	Prodigal	1977
w. D.Chackler	Shotgun	*Good,Bad and Funky*	ABC	1978
w. Craig Hillis	Traveller	*Lost In The Late Late Show*	ABC	1978
	Bobbi Walker	*Diamond In The Rough*	Casab	1980

L057 Nick Lowe

	Paul Carrack	*Suburban Voodoo*	CBS	1982
	Carlene Carter	*Musical Shapes*	F-Beat	1980
	Carlene Carter	*Blue Nun*	F-Beat	1981
	Elvis Costello	*My Aim Is True*	Stiff/CBS	1977
	Elvis Costello	*This Year's Model*	Radar/CBS	1978
	Elvis Costello	*Armed Forces*	Radar/CBS	1979
	Elvis Costello	*Get Happy*	F-Beat/CBS	1980
	Elvis Costello	*Elvis Costello*	CBS	1980
w.R.Bechirian	Elvis Costello	*Trust*	F-Beat/CBS	1981
	Damned	*Damned,Damned,Damned*	Stiff	1977
	Dr.Feelgood	*Be Seeing You*	UA	1977
	Dr.Feelgood	*A Case Of The Shakes*	UA/Stiff	1980
	Fabulous Thunderbirds	*T-Bird Rhythm*	Chrysalis	1982
	John Hiatt	*Riding With The King*	Geffen	1983
	Mickey Jupp	*Juppanese (side one)*	Stiff	1978

Nick Lowe	*Jesus Of Cool*	Radar/CBS	1978

(Released in the USA as "Pure Pop For Now People".)

Nick Lowe	*Labour Of Lust*	Radar/CBS	1979
Nick Lowe	*Nick The Knife*	F-Beat/CBS	1982
Nick Lowe	*The Abominable Showman*	F-Beat/CBS	1983
Moonlighters	*Rush Hour*	Demon	1983
Graham Parker and The Rumour	*Heat Treatment (1 tr.)*	Vert/Mer	1976
Graham Parker and The Rumour	*Howlin' Wind*	Vert/Mer	1976
Graham Parker and The Rumour	*Stick To Me*	Vert/Mer	1979
Pretenders	*The Pretenders (1 tr.)*	Real/Sire	1979
Wreckless Eric	*Wreckless Eric*	Stiff	1978

L058 David Lucas

Alessi	*All For A Reason*	A&M	1977
Blue Oyster Cult	*Agents Of Fortune*	CBS	1976
Blue Oyster Cult	*Spectres*	CBS	1977

(Both BOC albums co-produced with Krugman and Pearlman.)

L059 Robin Lumley

Rod Argent	*Moving Home*	MCA	1978
Brand X	*Masques*	Charsima	1978
Brand X	*Is There Anything About*	CBS	1982
Bill Bruford	*Feels Good To Me*	Polydor	1977
Dave Greenslade	*The Pentateuch*	EMI	1979
Eddie Howell	*The Eddie Howell Gramophone Record*	WB	1975
Jack Lancaster	*Skinnigrove Bay*	Kamera	1981
Nova	*Vimara*	Arista	1976
Orleans	*Orleans*	MCA	1980

L060 John Luongo

Blancmange	*Mange Tout*	London	1984
Jimmy Maelen	*Beats Workin'*	CBS	1980
Quick	*Fascinating Rhythm (2 tracks only)*	Epic	1982
Sorrows	*Teenage Heartbreak*	CBS	1980
Sly Stone	*Ten Years Too soon*	Epic	1979
THP 2	*Tender Is The Night*	Rocket	1979

L061 Gary Lyons

	Aerosmith	*A Night In The Ruts*	CBS	1979
	Aviary	*Aviary*	Epic	1979
	Champion	*Champion*	CBS	1978
	Crawler	*Snake,Rattle and Roll*	Epic	1978
w. J.Sinclair	Foreigner	*Foreigner*	Atlantic	1977
	Gamma	*Gamma 2*	Elektra	1980
w. Cliff Davies	Grand Funk	*What's Funk*	Full Moom	1983
	Grateful Dead	*Go To Heaven*	Arista	1980
	Humble Pie	*Go For The Throat*	Atco	1981
	Kevin Lamb	*Sailing Down The Years*	Arista	1978

143

	Robin Lane and The Chartbusters	*Imitation Life*	WB	1981
	Lone Star	*Firing On All Six*	Epic	1977
w. Alan Parsons	John Miles	*Sympathy*	Arista	1980
	Nutz	*Hard Nutz*	A&M	1977
	Outlaws	*Ghost Rider*	Arista	1981
	Outlaws	*Los Hombres Malo*	Arista	1982
	Trillion	*Trillion*	Epic	1978
	UFO	*Mechanix*	Chrysalis	1982
	Bob Weir	*Bobby and The Midnites*	Arista	1981
	Wet Willie	*Manorisms*	Epic	1977

L062 Leo Lyons

	Bogey Boys	*Friday Night*	Chrysalis	1979
	Magnum	*II*	Jet	1979
	Magnum	*Marauder*	Jet	1979
	Brian Protheroe	*Leave Him To Heaven*	Chrysalis	1976
	Bridget St.John	*Jumblequeen*	Chrysalis	1974
	UFO	*Phenomemnon*	Chrysalis	1974
	UFO	*Force It*	Chrysalis	1975
	UFO	*No Heavy Petting*	Chrysalis	1976

M001 Robin McBride

	Doug Sahm	*Rough Edges*	Mercury	1973

M002 Paul McCartney

	Mary Hopkin	*Postcard*	Apple	1969
	Mary Hopkin	*Those Were The Days (4 tracks only.)*	Apple	1972
	Paul McCartney	*McCartney*	Apple	1970
	Paul McCartney	*Ram*	Apple	1971
	Paul McCartney	*McCartney 2*	Parl/CBS	1980
	Mike McGear	*McGear*	WB	1974
	soundtrack	*The Family Way*	Decca	1967
	Ringo Starr	*Stop And Smell The Roses (3 tracks)*	RCA/Bdwlk	1981
	Wings	*Wild Life*	Apple	1971
	Wings	*Red Rose Speedway*	Apple	1973
	Wings	*Band On The Run*	Apple	1973
	Wings	*Venus And Mars*	Capitol	1975
	Wings	*Wings At The Speed Of Sound*	Parl/Cap	
	Wings	*Wings Over America*	Parl/Cap	1976
	Wings	*London Town*	Parl/Cap	1978
w. Chris Thomas	Wings	*Back To The Egg*	MPL/CBS	1979

M003 Matthew McCauley

w. Fred Mollin	America	*Alibi*	Capitol	1980
w. Fred Mollin	Randy Bishop	*Bishop And Gwinn*	Infinity	1979
w. Fred Mollin	Randy Edelman	*You're The One*	2oth Cent	1979
w. Fred Mollin	First Fire	*First Fire*	Tortoise	1978
w. Fred Mollin	Dan Hill	*Dan Hill*	20th Cent	1976
w. Fred Mollin	Dan Hill	*Hold On*	20th Cent	1977
w. Fred Mollin	Dan Hill	*Longer Fuse*	20th Cent	1978
w. Fred Mollin	Dan Hill	*Frozen In The Night*	20th Cent	1978
	Bat McGrath	*From The Blue Eagle*	Amherst	1976
	Bat McGrath	*The Spy*	Amherst	1978
w. Fred Mollin	Jimmy Webb	*Angel Heart*	CBS/Lori	1982

M004 John McClure

John Cale and Terry Riley	Church Of Anthrax	CBS	1971
Flock	Dinosaur Swamps	CBS	1970
New York Rock Ensemble	Freedomburger	CBS	1972

(Group featured Michael Kamen:see entry.)

M005 Ian McDonald

Fireball	Night On Bald Mountain	Passport	1975

M006 Michael McDonald
w.P.Henderson

Amy Holland	Amy Holland	Capitol	1980
Amy Holland	One Your Every Word	Capitol	1983

M007 Phil McDonald

Squeeze	Sweets From A Stranger	A&M	1982
John Weider	John Weider	Anchor	1976

(An early example of the engineering art of Roger Bechirian.)

M008 Allan McDougall

Hoyt Axton	Life Machine	A&M	1974
Spencer Davis	Crossfire	Allegiance	1984

M009 William E. McEuen (Aspen Recording Society)

Steve Martin	Let's Get Small	WB	1977
Steve Martin	A Wild And Crazy Guy	WB	1978
Steve Martin	Comedy Is Not Pretty	WB	1979
Steve Martin	The Steve Martin Brothers	WB	1981
Nitty Gritty Dirt Band	Uncle Teddy and His Dog Teddy	Liberty	1970
Nitty Gritty Dirt Band	All The Good Times	UA	1972
Nitty Gritty Dirt Band	Will The Circle Be Unbroken	UA	1972
Nitty Gritty Dirt Band	Stars And Stripes Forever	UA	1974
Nitty Gritty Dirt Band	Dream	UA	1975

M010 John McFee

Tim Goodman	Footsteps	CBS	1981

M011 Earl McGrath

Jim Carroll Band	Catholic Boy	Atco	1980
Jim Carroll Band	Dry Dreams	CBS/Atco	1982
Jim Carroll Band	I Write Your Name	Atlantic	1984
Amy Kantner	The Other Girl	Atlantic	1982

M012 Jim McGuire

Mike Auldridge	Dobro	Takoma	1974

M013 Malcolm McLaren

Bow Wow Wow	I Want Candy	EMI	1982

M014 Ian McLintock

Be-Bop Deluxe	*Axe Victim*	Harvest	1974

M015 Teo Macero

Auracle	*Glider*	Chrysalis	1978
Gato Barbieri	*Gato..Para Los Amigos*	Dr. Jazz	1984
Miles Davis	*Bitches brew*	CBS	1970
Miles Davis	*Agartha*	CBS	1975
Miles Davis	*Water Babys*	CBS	1976
Miles Davis	*The Man With The Horn*	CBS	1981
Miles Davis	*Live At The Plugged Nickel l965*	CBS	1982
Miles Davis	*We Want Miles*	CBS	1982
Miles Davis	*Star People*	CBS	1983
Tal Farlow	*Trilogy*	I.City	1981
John Hammond	*Little Big Man (soundtrack album)*	CBS	1971
Ramsey Lewis	*Sun Goddess*	CBS	1981
Lounge Lizards	*The Lounge Lizards*	EG	1981
Thelonius Monk	*Live At The Jazz Workshop 1964*	CBS	1982
Thelonius Monk	*Monk*	Pausa	1983
Thelonius Monk	*Tokyo Concert*	CBS	1984
Jimmy Rushing	*Mr Five By Five*	CBS	1980
soundtrack	*Betrayal*	I.City	1978
various artists	*The Third Isle Of Wight Festival*	CBS	1971

M016 Mack (James L. Mack)

	After The Fire	*80f*	CBS	1980
	After The Fire	*Batteries Not Included*	CBS	1982
	Doc Holliday	*Modern Romance*	A&M	1983
w. Brian May	Heavy Pettin'	*Lettin' Loose*	Polydor	1983
w. Leo Graham	Kokomo	*Kokomo*	CBS	1982
	Ramsey Lewis	*Legacy*	CBS	1978
	Ramsey Lewis	*Ramsey*	CBS	1979
	Queen	*The Game*	EMI/Elek	1980
w. Brian May	Queen	*Flash Gordon Soundtrack*	EMI/Elek	1980
	Queen	*The Works*	EMI/Cap	1984
	Sparks	*Whomp That Sucker*	WhyFi/RCA	1981
	Sparks	*Angst In My Pants*	Atlantic	1982
	Billy Squier	*Don't Say No*	Capitol	1981
	Billy Squier	*Emotions In Motion*	Capitol	1982
	Peter Straker	*Real Natural Man*	Rocket	1980
	Violinski	*Stop Cloning Around*	Jet	1980

M017 Dave Mackay

	Blue Mink	*Fruity*	EMI	1974
	Tony Cole	*Magnificently Mad*	20th Cent	1972
	Dame Edna Everage	*Last Night Of The Poms*	EMI	1981
	Johnny Logan	*Johnny Logan*	Epic	1980
	Meal Ticket	*Take Away*	Logo	1978
	Frankie Miller	*Falling In Love*	Chrysalis	1979
w. Barry Guard	Kai Olsson	*Crazy Love*	Chrysalis	1979
	Gene Pitney	*Pitney '75*	Bronze	1975
	Plain Sailing	*Dangerous Times*	Chrysalis	1980
	Demis Roussos	*Man Of The World*	Mercury	1980
	Tarney & Spencer	*Tarney & Spencer*	Bradleys	1976

Bonnie Tyler	*The World Starts Tonight*	RCA	1977
Bonnie Tyler	*It's A Heartache*	RCA	1978
Florence Warner	*Another Hot Night*	Mercury	1981

M018 Dennis Mackay

Tommy Bolin	*Private Eyes*	CBS	1976
Brand X	*Unorthodox Behaviour*	Charisma	1976
Brand X	*Moroccan Roll*	Charisma	1977
Cowboys International	*The Original Sin*	Virgin	1979
Curved Air	*Airborne*	RCA	1976
Al Di Meola	*Electric Rendezvous*	CBS	1982
Al Di Meola	*Tour De Force Live*	CBS	1982
Al Di Meola	*Scenario*	CBS	1983
805	*Stand In Line*	RCA	1982
Gong	*Gazeuse*	Virgin	1976
Eddie Howell	*The Eddie Howell Gramophone Record*	WB	1978
Ironhorse	*Everything Is Grey*	Scotti	1980
Judas Priest	*Stained Class*	CBS	1978
Kayak	*Phantom Of The Night*	Janus	1978
Johnny McLaughlin	*Electric Guitarist*	CBS	1978
Mahavishnu Orchestra	*Inner Worlds*	CBS	1976
Bob Sargeant	*First Starring Role*	RCA	1974
Screen Idols	*Premiere*	Cobra	1979
Shooting Star	*Hang On For Your Life*	Virgin	1981
Pat Travers	*Crash And Burn*	Polydor	1980
Pat Travers	*Radio Active*	Polydor	1981
Tygers Of Pan Tang	*Crazy Nights*	MCA	1981
Stomu Yamashta	*Go*	Island	1976
Stomu Yamashta	*Go 2*	Arista	1977

M019 Steve Mackay

Commander Cody	*Lose It Tonight*	Line	1980

M020 Brent Maher

w. Steve Gibson	Michael Johnson	*The Michael Johnson Album*	EMI-Amer	1978
w. Steve Gibson	Michael Johnson	*Dialogue*	EMI-Amer	1979
w. Steve Gibson	Michael Johnson	*You Can Call Me Blue*	EMI-Amer	1980
	Dave Loggins	*One Way Ticket To Paradise*	Epic	1977
	Dave Loggins	*David Loggins*	Epic	1979
w. M.Lloyd	Bill Medley	*Sweet Thunder*	Liberty	1981

M021 Vic Maile

Brinsley Schwarz	*Please Don't Ever Change*	UA	1973
Dr.Feelgood	*Down By The Jetty*	UA	1975
Dr.Feelgood	*Malpractice*	UA	1975
Dr.Feelgood	*As It Happens*	UA	1979
Dr.Feelgood	*Fast Women And Slow Horses*	Chiswick	1982
Eddie and The Hot Rods	*Teenage Depression*	Island	1976

Girlschool	*Demolition*	Bronze	1980
Girlschool	*Hit And Run*	Bron/Stiff	1981
Inmates	*First Offence*	Radar	1979
Inmates	*Shot In The Dark*	Radar	1980
Kursaal Flyers	*Five Live Kursaals*	CBS	1977
Motorhead	*Ace Of Spades*	Bron/Mer	1980
Motorhead	*No Sleep 'Til Hammersmith*	Bron/Mer	1981
999	*The Biggest Prize In Sport*	Polydor	1980
999	*Concrete*	Albion	1981
101-ers	*Elgin Avenue Breakdown (4 tracks only.)*	Andalucia	1981
Pirates	*Out Of Their Skulls*	WEA	1977
Pirates	*Skull Wars*	WEA	1978
Rock Goddess	*Rock Goddess*	A&M	1983
Vibrators	*2*	Epic	1978

M022 Mike Mainieri

w. Tommy Lipuma	Stephen Bishop	*Red Cab To Manhattan*	WB	1980
	Brecker Brothers	*Blue Montreux 2*	Arista	1979
	David Liebman	*What It Is*	CBS	1980
	Ben Sidran	*The Cat And The Hat*	A&M	1979
	Ben Sidran	*Bop City*	Antilles	1983
	Carly Simon	*Come Upstairs*	WB	1980
	Carly Simon	*Torch*	WB	1981
	Carly Simon	*Hello Big Man*	WB	1983
	David Spinozza	*Spinozza*	A&M	1978

M023 Eric Malamud

	Skip Battin	*Skip Battin*	Signpost	1972
w. J.Palladino	Jackie De Shannon	*Songs*	Capitol	1971
w. Jerry Lawson	Persuasions	*More Than Before*	A&M	1974

M024 Gary Mallaber

Steve Miller	*Abracadabra*	Mercury	1982

M025 David Malloy

Badfinger	*Airwaves*	Elektra	1979
Creed	*Creed*	Elektra	1978
Stella Parton	*Love Ya*	Elektra	1979
Eddie Rabbitt	*Rocky Mountain Music*	Elektra	1976
Eddie Rabbitt	*Rabbitt*	Elektra	1978
Eddie Rabbitt	*Loveline*	Elektra	1979
Eddie Rabbitt	*Horizon*	Elektra	1981
Eddie Rabbitt	*Step By Step*	Mercury	1982
Eddie Rabbitt	*Radio Romance*	Mercury	1983
Bruce Roberts	*Cool Fool*	Elektra	1980
Tanya Tucker	*Changes*	Arista	1982

M026 Will Malone

Aviator	*Turbulence*	Harvest	1980
Iron Maiden	*Iron Maiden*	Harvest	1980

M027 Harvey Mandel

Freddie Roulette	*Sweet Funky Steel*	Janus	1973

M028 Earle Mankey

	Arthur Brown	*Requiem*	Remote	1982
	Dream 6	*Dream 6*	H.Hermit	1983
	Walter Egan	*The Last Stroll*	Edge/CBS	1981
	Elevators	*Frontline*	Arista	1980
	Earle Mankey	*Earle Mankey (12" EP)*	Select	1981
	Paley Brothers	*The Paley Brothers*	Sire	1978
	The Pop	*Go*	Arista	1979
w. Kim Fowley	The Quick	*Mondo Deco*	Mercury	1976
w. Kim Fowley	Helen Reddy	*Ear Candy*	Capitol	1977
w. Kim Fowley	Runaways	*Queens Of Noise*	Mercury	1977
	20/20	*20/20*	Epic	1979

M029 Manfred Mann

	McGuiness,Flint, Coulson and Dean	*Lo And Behold*	DJM	1972

(An album of "Basement Tape"-era Bob Dylan cover versions.)

M030 Terry Manning

	Cargoe	*Cargoe*	Ardent	1972
	Hot Dogs	*Say What You Mean*	Ardent	1973
	Terry Manning	*Home Sweet Home*	Enterprise	1974

M031 Ken Mansfield

w. W.Jennings	Jesse Colter	*Diamond In The Rough*	Capitol	1976
w. W,Jennings	Jesse Colter	*Jessi*	Capitol	1976
	Jesse Colter	*Miriam*	Capitol	1977
	Marty Cooper	*A Minute Of Your Time*	Barnaby	1972
	Rick Cunha	*Songs*	GRC	1973
	Rick Cunha	*Moving Pictures*	CBS	1975
	Nick Gilder	*Rock America*	Casab	1980
	Tompall Glaser	*Tompall Glaser And His Outlaw Band*	ABC	1977
	Waylon Jennings	*Are You Ready For The Country*	RCA	1976
	La Costa	*Changin' All The Time*	Capitol	1980
	O.X.O.	*O.X.O.*	Geffen	1983
	Carter Robinson	*Shoot The Moon*	ABC	1978
	Sand	*Sand*	Barnaby	1973
	Robb Strandlund	*Robb Strandlund*	Polydor	1976

(Has written songs for The Eagles and The Funky Kings.)

w. Larry Murray	Swampwater	*Swampwater*	RCA	1971

M032 Tony Mansfield

	Captain Sensible	*Women And Captains First*	A&M	1982
	Captain Sensible	*The Power Of Love*	A&M	1983
	Philip Jap	*Philip Jap*	A&M	1983
	Naked Eyes	*Burning Bridges*	EMI	1983
	New Musik	*From A To B*	GTO	1980
	New Musik	*Anywhere*	GTO	1981
	New Musik	*Warp*	Epic	1982
	Rescue	*Messages*	A&M	1984
	Mari Wilson	*Showpeople*	Compact	1983

M033 Richard Manwaring

Budgie	*Impeckable*	A&M	1978
Fischer-Z	*Red Skies Over Paradise*	UA	1981
Human League	*Travelogue*	Virgin	1980
Ken Lockie	*The Impossible (7 tr.)*	Virgin	1981
Orchestral Manoeuvres In The Dark	*Architecture And Morality*	DinDisc	1981
John Watts	*One More Twist*	EMI	1982

M034 Ray Manzarek

X	*X*	Slash	1980
X	*Wild Gift*	Slash	1981
X	*Under The Big Black Sun*	Elektra	1982
X	*More Fun In The Big World*	Elektra	1983

M035 Arif Mardin

	Average White Band	*Average White Band*	Atlantic	1974
	Average White Band	*Cut The Cake*	Atlantic	1975
	Average White Band	*Soul Searching*	Atlantic	1977
	Average White Band	*Person To Person*	Atlantic	1977
	Average White Band	*Warmer Communications*	RCA/Atl	1978
	Average White Band and Ben E.King	*Benny And Us*	Atlantic	1977
	Average White Band etc.	*The Atlantic Family Live At Montreux*	Atlantic	1978
	Bee Gees	*Mr. Natural*	RSO	1974
	Bee Gees	*Main Course*	RSO	1975
	Maggie Bell	*Queen Of The Night*	Poly/Atl	1974
	George Benson	*In Your Eyes*	WB	1983
	Brook Benton	*Today*	Atlantic	1970
	Brook Benton	*The Gospel Truth*	Atlantic	1971
	Brook Benton	*Home style*	Atlantic	1970
	Bugatti and Musker	*The Dukes*	WEA	1982
	Cher	*3614 Jackson Highway*	Atlantic	1969
	Judy Collins	*Judith*	Elektra	1975
	Judy Collins	*Bread And Roses*	Elektra	1976
	King Curtis	*Sweet Soul*	Atlantic	1968
	King Curtis	*Live At Fillmore West*	Atlantic	1971
w. Tom Dowd	Jackie De Shannon	*Jackie*	Atlantic	1972
w. Joel Dorn	Roberta Flack	*Roberta Flack and Donny Hathaway*	Atlantic	1972
w.Jerry Wexler	Aretha Franklin	*Live At The Fillmore West*	Atlantic	1971
	Aretha Franklin	*Young,Gifted And Black*	Atlantic	1972
	Aretha Franklin	*Amazing Grace*	Atlantic	1972
	Aretha Franklin	*With Everything I Feel In Me*	Atlantic	1974
	Aretha Franklin	*Love All The Hurt Away*	Arista	1981
	Steve Goodman	*Somebody Else's Troubles*	Buddah	1972
	Hall and Oates	*Whole Oates*	Atlantic	1972
	Hall and Oates	*Abandoned Lunceonette*	Atlantic	1973
	Richard Harris	*The Prophet Kahil Gibran*	Atlantic	1974

	Gordon Haskell	*It Is And It Isn't*	Atco	1972
	Donny Hathaway	*Donny Hathaway*	Atlantic	1970
	Donny Hathaway	*Extension Of A Man*	Atlantic	1973
w.Jerry Wexler	Donny Hathaway	*In Performance*	Atlantic	1980
	Margie Joseph	*Margie Joseph*	Atlantic	1973
	Margie Joseph	*Sweet Surrender*	Atlantic	1974
	Margie Joseph	*Feeling My Way*	Atlantic	1976
	Chaka Khan	*Chaka*	WB	1978
	Chaka Khan	*Naughty*	WB	1980
	Chaka Khan	*What Cha Gonna Do For Me*	WB	1981
	Chaka Khan	*Chaka Khan*	WB	1982
	Charles Lloyd	*Dream Weaver*	Atlantic	1966
	Liner	*Liner*	Atlantic	1979
	Lulu	*Melody Fair*	Atco	1970
	Mama's Pride	*Mama's Pride*	Atlantic	1976
	Melissa Manchester	*Emergency*	Arista	1983
w.Tom Dowd	Arif Mardin	*Glass Onion*	Atlantic	1969
	Arif Mardin	*Journey*	Atlantic	1974
w.B.Manilow	Bette Midler	*Bette Midler*	Atlantic	1973
	Bette Midler	*Thighs And Whispers*	Atlantic	1979
	Modern Jazz Quartet	*Plastic Dreams*	Atlantic	1972
w.David Briggs	Willie Nelson	*Shotgun Willie*	Atlantic	1973
	Willie Nelson	*The Troublemaker*	CBS	1976
w.F.Cavaliere	Laura Nyro	*Christmas And The Beads Of Sweat*	CBS	1970
	Danny O'Keefe	*O'Keefe*	Signpost	1972
	Danny O'Keefe	*Breezy Stories*	Atlantic	1973
	Andy Pratt	*Resolution*	Nemperor	1976
	Andy Pratt	*Shiver In The Night*	Nemperor	1977
	John Prine	*John Prine*	Atlantic	1971
	John Prine	*Diamonds In The Rough*	Atlantic	1972
	John Prine	*Sweet Revenge*	Atlantic	1974
	Doug Sahm	*Doug Sahm and Band*	Atlantic	1973
	Leo Sayer	*World Radio*	Chrysalis	1982
	Leo Sayer	*Have You Ever Been In Love*	Chrysalis	1983
	Carly Simon	*Boys In The Trees*	Elektra	1978
	Carly Simon	*Spy*	Elektra	1979
	Sir Douglas Band	*Texas Tornado*	Atlantic	1973
w.Tom Dowd and Jerry Wexler	Dusty Springfield	*In Memphis*	Atlantic	1968
	Ringo Starr	*Ringo's Rotogravure*	Poly/Atl	1976
	Ringo Starr	*Ringo The 4th*	Poly/Atl	1977
	Sonny Stitt	*Stitt Plays bird*	Atlantic	1966
w.Tom Dowd	Tony Joe White	*The Train I'm On*	Atlantic	1972

M036 Robert Margouleff

	Buckwheat	*Pure Buckwheat Honey*	Buddah	1970
	Caldara	*A Moog Mass*	K.S.	1972
	Devo	*Freedom Of Choice*	Virgin/WB	1980
	Inner Circle	*Ready For The World*	Capitol	1977
	Innocents	*The Innocents*	Boardwalk	1982
	Jamie James	*The Big One*	Vanity	1984
	Lothar and The Hand People	*Presenting Lothar and The Hand People*	Capitol	1968

Gary Myrick	*Language*	Epic	1983
Oingo Boingo	*Good For Your Soul*	IRS	1983
Michael Pinder	*The Promise*	Threshold	1976
Billy Preston	*It's My Pleasure*	A&M	1975
Billy Preston	*Billy*	A&M	1976
Christopher Rainbow	*Home Of The Brave*	Polydor	1975

M037 Bob Markley

Goodness And Mercy	*Goodness And Mercy*	MGM	1969
West Coast Pop Art Band	*Where's My Daddy*	Amos	1969

M038 Larry Marks

	Gene Clark and The Gosdin Brothers	*Gene Clark and The Gosdin Brothers*	CBS	1967
	Doug Dillard and Gene Clark	*The Fantastic Expedition Of Dillard And Clark*	A&M	1968
	Doug Dillard and Gene Clark	*Through The Morning Through The Night*	A&M	1969
	Doug Dillard and Gene Clark	*Kansas City Southern*	Ariola	1975
	Craig Doerge	*Craig Doerge*	CBS	1973
w. H.Lewy	Flying Burrito Brothers	*The Gilded Palace Of Sin*	A&M	1969
	Merry-Go-Round	*You're A Very Lovely Woman*	A&M	1967
	(Emitt Rhodes first recordings.)			
	Lee Michaels	*Carnival Of Life*	A&M	1968
	Lee Michaels	*Lee Michaels*	A&M	1969
	Lee Michaels	*Barrel*	A&M	1970
	Liza Minnelli	*Live At The Olympia In Paris*	A&M	1972
	Phil Ochs	*easures Of The Harbor*	A&M	1967
	Helen Reddy	*Helen Reddy*	Capitol	1972
	Emitt Rhodes	*The American Dream*	A&M	1971
	Thirty Days Out	*Thirty Days Out*	Reprise	1971

M039 Bill Martin and Phil Coulter

Arrows	*First Hit*	Rak	1976
Bay City Rollers	*Rollin'*	Bell	1974
Beggars Opera	*Act One*	Vertigo	1970
Christian	*Shine It On*	Polydor	1978
Kenny	*The Sound Of Super K*	Rak	1975
Slik	*Slik*	Bell	1976

M040 George Martin

Action	*The Ultimate Action*	Edsel	1980
America	*Holiday*	WB	1974
America	*Hearts*	WB	1975
America	*History*	WB	1975
America	*Hideaway*	WB	1976
America	*Harbor*	WB	1977
America	*Live*	WB	1977
America	*Silent Letter*	Capitol	1979
American Flyer	*American Flyer*	UA	1976
Beatles	*Please Please Me*	Parlophone	1963
Beatles	*With The Beatles*	Parlophone	1963

Beatles	*A Hard Day's Night*	Parlophone	1964
Beatles	*Beatles For Sale*	Parlophone	1964
Beatles	*Help !*	Parl/Cap	1965
Beatles	*Rubber Soul*	Parl/Cap	1965
Beatles	*Revolver*	Parl/Cap	1966
Beatles	*A Collection Of Oldies*	Parlophone	1966
Beatles	*Sgt. Pepper*	Parl/Cap	1967
Beatles	*Magical Mystery Tour*	Apple/Cap	1968
Beatles	*The Beatles (White Album)*	Parl/Apple	1968
Beatles	*Yellow Submarine*	Apple	1968
Beatles	*Abbey Road*	Apple/Cap	1969
Beatles	*Let It Be*	Apple	1970
Beatles	*1962-1966*	Parl/Cap	1973
Beatles	*1967-1970*	Parl/Cap	1973
Beatles	*Rock And Roll Music*	Parl/Cap	1976
Beatles	*At The Hollywood*	EMI/Cap	1977
Beatles	*Love Songs*	Parl/Cap	1977
Beatles	*Rarities*	Parl/Cap	1980
Beatles	*20 Greatest Hits*	Parl/Cap	1982
Beatles	*Reel Music*	Parl/Cap	1982
Jeff Beck	*Blow By Blow*	Epic	1975
Jeff Beck	*Wired*	Epic	1976
Cilla Black	*Cilla*	Parlophone	1965
Cilla Black	*Sher-oo !*	Parlophone	1968
Cilla Black	*Surround Yourself With Cilla Black*	Parlophone	1969
Cilla Black	*Sweet Inspiration*	Parlophone	1970
Cilla Black	*Images*	Parlophone	1971
Cilla Black	*Day By Day*	Parlophone	1973
Gary Brooker	*No More Fear Of Flying*	Chrysalis	1979
Billy J. Kramer	*Listen to Billy J. Kramer*	Parlophone	1963
Billy J.Kramer	*Billy Boy*	Parlophone	1965
Little River Band	*Time Exposure*	Capitol	1981
Paul McCartney	*Tug Of War*	Parl/CBS	1982
Paul McCartney	*Pipes Of Peace*	Parl/CBS	1983
John McLaughlin	*Apocalypse*	CBS	1974
George Martin Orchestra	*Off The Beatle Track*	Parlophone	1964
George Martin Orchestra	*The Beatle Girls*	UA	1966
Sea Train	*Sea Train*	Capitol	1971
Neil Sedaka	*A Song*	Polydor	1977
various artists	*Sergeant Pepper (soundtrack)*	A&M/RSO	1978
Stackridge	*Do The Stanley*	MCA	1973
Stackridge	*Man In The Bowler Hat*	MCA	1974
Ringo Starr	*Sentimental Journey*	Apple	1970
Temperance Seven	*Direct From The Balls Pond Rio*	Parlophone	1962
Temperance Seven	*Family Album*	Parlophone	1964
various artists	*That Was The Week That Was*	Parlophone	1964
UFO	*Nowhere To Run*	Chrysalis	1980

Ultravox	*Quartet*	Chrysalis	1983
Jimmy Webb	*El Mirage*	Atlantic	1977
Paul Winter Consort	*Icarus*	A&M	1971

M041 Nick Martinelli

Loose Ends	*A Little Spice*	Virgin	1984

M042 Eddie Martinez

Papa John Creach	*I'm The Fiddle Man*	Buddah	1975
Papa John Creach	*Rock Father*	Buddah	1976

M043 John Martyn

Scullion	*Balance And Control*	WEA	1980

M044 Harry Maslin

	Air Supply	*The One That You Love*	Arista	1981
	Air Supply	*Now And Forever*	Arista	1982
	Bay City Rollers	*It's A Game*	Arista	1977
	Bay City Rollers	*Strangers In The Wind*	Arista	1978
	David Bowie	*Young Americans*	RCA	1975
	David Bowie	*Station To Station*	RCA	1976
	Eric Carmen	*Tonight You're Mine*	Arista	1980
	Hollywood Stars	*The Hollywood Stars*	Arista	1977
	Hot Tuna	*Hoppkorv*	Grunt	1976
w. Leon Ware	Melissa Manchester	*Don't Cry Out Loud*	Arista	1978
	Nervous Eaters	*Nervous Eaters*	Elektra	1980
	Camilo Sesto	*Camilo*	Arista	1983
	Earl Slick	*The Earl Slick Band*	Capitol	1976
	Michael Stanley Band	*Greatest Hints*	Arista	1979
	Striker	*Striker*	Arista	1978

M045 Dave Mason

Family	*Music In A Doll's House*	Reprise	1968
Gordon Jackson	*Thinking Back*	Marmalade	1969

M046 Jim Mason

	Cate Brothers Band	*The Cate Brothers Band*	Asylum	1977
	Firefall	*Firefall*	Atlantic	1976
	Firefall	*Luna Sea*	Atlantic	1977
	Richie Furay	*Dance A Little Light*	Asylum	1978
	Lowry Hamner and The Cryers	*Midnight Run*	Mercury	1979
	Chris Hillman	*Free Sailin'*	Asylum	1977
	Mama's Pride	*Uptown And Lowdown*	Atlantic	1977
w.J.Richardson	Poco	*A Good Feelin' To Know*	Epic	1972
	Racing Cars	*Bring On The Night*	Chrysalis	1978
	Rhinestones	*The Rhinestones*	20th Cent	1975
	David Soul	*Band Of Friends*	Energy	1980
	Volunteers	*Volunteers*	Arista	1976
	Rusty Wier	*Stoned, Slow, Rugged*	ABC	1974

M047 Nick Mason

Damned	*Music For Pleasure*	Stiff	1977
Gong	*Shamal*	Virgin	1975
Steve Hillage	*Green*	Virgin	1978

| | Robert Wyatt | *Rock Bottom* | Virgin | 1974 |
| | Robert Wyatt | *Ruth Is Stranger Than Richard* | Virgin | 1975 |

M048 George Massenburg

| | Valerie Carter | *Just A Stone's Throw Away* | CBS | 1977 |
| | Little Feat | *Hoy Hoy* | WB | 1982 |

M049 Greg Mathieson

w. Trevor Veitch	Toni Basil	*Word Of Mouth*	Radial	1981
w. Jack White	Laura Branigan	*Branigan*	Atlantic	1982
w. Jay Graydon	Sheena Easton	*Best Kept Secret*	EMI	1983
w. Trevor Veitch	Lee Ritenour	*Banded Together*	Elektra	1984
w. Jay Graydon	David Roberts	*All Dressed Up*	Elektra	1982

M050 Anton Matthews

| | Alkatraz | *Doing A Moonlight* | Rockfield | 1976 |
| | Neutrons | *Black Hole Star* | UA | 1974 |

M051 Bob Matthews

| | Grateful Dead | *Workingman's Dead* | WB | 1970 |

M051 Richard Mazda

	Alternative TV	*Strange Kicks*	IRS	1981
	The Fall	*Hex Enduction Hour*	Kamera	1982
	Fleshtones	*Roman Gods*	IRS	1981
	Fleshtones	*Hexbreaker*	IRS	1983
	Tom Robinson	*North By Northwest*	Panic/IRS	1982
	Suburban Lawns	*Baby*	IRS	1983
	Wall Of Voodoo	*Call Of The West*	IRS	1982

M052 Elliot F. Mazer

	Area Code 615	*Area Code 615*	Polydor	1969
	Blue	*Life In The Navy*	RSO	1974
	Barclay James Harvest	*Time Honoured Ghosts*	Polydor	1975
	Mike D'Abo	*Down At Rachel's Place*	A&M	1974
	Dingoes	*Five Times The Sun*	A&M	1977
w. Ron Nagle	Durocs	*The Durocs*	Capitol	1979
	Andy Fairweather-Low	*Spider Jiving*	A&M	1974
w. John Kahn	Jerry Garcia	*Reflections*	Round	1976
	Janis Joplin	*Farewell Song*	CBS	1982
	Ken Lauber	*Contemplation*	Polydor	1970
	Frankie Miller	*The Rock*	Chrysalis	1975
	Rab Noakes	*Red Pump Special*	WB	1973
	Rab Noakes	*Never Too Late*	WB	1975
	Juice Newton	*Come To Me*	Capitol	1977
	Jack Nitzsche	*St. Giles Cripplegate*	Reprise	1972
	Paupers	*Ellis Island*	Verve	1968
	Linda Ronstadt	*Silk Purse*	Capitol	1970
	David Soul	*David Soul*	P.Stock	1976
	Jerry Jeff Walker	*Five Years Gone*	Atlantic	1969
	Neil Young	*Harvest (7 Tracks)*	Reprise	1972
	Neil Young	*Time Fades Away*	Reprise	1973

Neil Young	American Stars 'n' Bars	Reprise	1977
Neil Young	Everybody's Rockin'	Geffen	1983

M054 Huey P. Meaux

Cates Gang	Wanted	Metro	1970
Freddy Fender	If You Don't Love Me	Dot	
Freddy Fender	If You're Ever In Texas	Dot	
Freddy Fender	Rockin' Country	ABC	
Freddy Fender	Before The Next Teardrop Falls	ABC	1975
Freddy Fender	Are You Ready For Freddy	ABC	1975
Freddy Fender	Swamp Gold	ABC	1978
Freddy Fender	Tex Mex	ABC	1979
Freddy Fender	The Texas Balladeer	Starflite	1979
Freddy Fender and The Sir Douglas Quintet	Reunion Of The Cosmic Brothers	Crazy Caj	1975
Kinky Friedman	Lasso From El Paso	Epic	1976
The Good, The Bad and The Ugly	The Good, The Bad and The Ugly	Mercury	1970
Tommy McLain	Backwoods Bayou Adventure	Starflite	1979
Sir Douglas Quintet	Together After Five	Smash	1970
Sir Douglas Quintet	The Return Of Doug Saldana	Philips	1971
Sir Douglas and The Texas Tornados	Texas Rock For Country Rollers	ABC	1976
Wayne Talbert	Houston Nickel Kicks	Mercury	1970

M055 Hank Medress and Dave Appell

Beds	Beds	Elektra	1981
Cross Country	Cross Country	Atlantic	1971
Dawn	Tie A Yellow Ribbon	Bell	1973
Lenny and Squiggy	Lenny And The Squigtones	Casab	1979
Tony Orlando	Prime Time	Bell	1974
Tony Orlando	He Don't Love You	Elektra	1975
Tony Orlando	To Be With You	Elektra	1976
Tony Orlando	I Got Rhythm	Casab	1979
Tony Orlando	Livin' For The Music	Casab	1980
Pierce Arrow	Pierce arrow	CBS	1977
Pierce Arrow	Pity The Rich	CBS	1978
Pousette-Dart Band	3	Capitol	1978
Sam The Band	Play It Again Sam	Casab	1979
Terry Scott	Terry Scott	Elektra	1982
Stanky Brown Group	If The Lights Don't Get You The Helots Will	Sire	1977
Frankie Valli	Fallen Angel	P.Stock	1976

M056 Patrick Meehan

Black Sabbath	Volume 4	Vert/WB	1972

M057 Gabriel Mekler

Birtha	Birtha	ABC	1972

	David Blue	25 Days In September	Reprise	1968
	Blues Project	Blues Project	Capitol	1972
	David Clayton-Thomas	David Clayton-Thomas	RCA	1973
	Etta James	Come A Little Closer	Chess	1974
	Janis Joplin	I Got Dem Ol' Kozmic Blues Again Mama	CBS	1969
	Steppenwolf	Steppenwolf Live	ABC	1973
	Three Dog Night	Three Dog Night	Dunhill	1968
	Goldie Zelkowitz	Goldie Zelkowitz	Janus	1974

M058 Terry Melcher

	Byrds	Turn ! Turn ! Turn !	CBS	1966
	Byrds	Mr. Tambourine Man	CBS	1965
	Byrds	Ballad Of Easy Rider	CBS	1970
	Byrds	(Untitled)	CBS	1970
	Byrds	Byrdmaniax	CBS	1971
	Freeway	Freeway	Decca	1979
	Gentle Soul	Gentle Soul	Epic	1968
w. B.Johnston	Terry Melcher	Terry Melcher	Reprise	1974
w. B.Johnston	Terry Melcher	Royal Flush	RCA	1976
	Paul Revere and The Raiders	Here They Come	CBS	1965
	Paul Revere and The Raiders	Just Like Us	CBS	1966
	Paul Revere and The Raiders	Midnight Ride	CBS	1966
	Paul Revere and The Raiders	Spirit of '67	CBS	1967

M059 Michael Melford

	David Bromberg	Hillbilly Jazz	Sonet/FF	1975
	Vassar Clements	Crossing The Catskills	Rounder	1972
	Dillard Hartford Dillard	Dillard Hartford Dillard	F.Fish	1977
	Dillard Hartford Dillard	Permanent Wave	F.Fish	1980
	Buddy Emmons	Steel Guitar	F.Fish	1975
	Buddy Emmons	Sings Bob Wills	F.Fish	1977
	Buddy Emmons and Buddy Spicher	Two Buddies	F.Fish	1977
	Buddy Spicher	Buddy Emmons and Minors Aloud	F.Fish	1979
	Amos Garrett	Go Cat Go	Waterfront	1980
	John Hartford	All In The Name Of Love	F.Fish	1977
	John Hartford	Nobody Knows What You Do	F.Fish	1977
	John Hartford	Mark Twang	F.Fish	1978
	John Hartford	Headin' Down To The Mystery Below	F.Fish	1978
	John Hartford, Pat Burton, Benny Martin	Slumberin' On The Cumberland	F.Fish	1979
	Geoff Muldaur	Blues Boy	F.Fish	1979
	Shel Silverstein	The Great Conch Train Robbery	F.Fish	1980

M060 Chuck Mellone

Hoyt Axton	*A Rusty Old Halo*	Youngblood	1980
New Riders	*Feelin' Allright*	A&M	1980

M061 Barry Melton

Ghost Rides	*Ghost Rides*	Anthem	1981

M062 Robin Menken

Country Joe McDonald	*Hold On It's Coming*	Vanguard	1971

M063 Lewis Merenstein

	Association	*Waterbeds In Trinidad*	CBS	1972
	John Cale	*Vintage Violence*	CBS	1971
	Calliope	*Steamed*	Buddah	1968
	Cass Elliott	*The Road Is No Place For A Lady*	RCA	1972
	Cass Elliott	*Cass Elliott*	RCA	1972
	Barry Goldberg	*The Barry Goldberg Reunion*	Buddah	1968
	Barry Goldberg	*Two Jews Blues*	Buddah	1969
	Barry Goldberg	*Blasts From My Past*	Buddah	1971
	Barry Goldberg	*Barry Goldberg and Friends*	Buddah	1976
	Alexander Harvey	*Purple Crush*	Buddah	1977
	Lightning	*Lightning*	Casab	1979
	Van Morrison	*Astral Weeks*	WB	1968
	Biff Rose	*Biff Rose*	Buddah	1971
	Charlie Starr	*Tough And Tender*	Prophecy	1971
w. B.Johnston	Sunrise	*Sunrise*	Buddah	1978
	Michael Wendroff	*Michael Wendroff*	Buddah	1973

M064 Neil Merryweather

Lita Ford	*Out For Blood*	Mercury	1983

M065 Jim Messina

Boones Farm	*Boones Farm*	CBS	1972
Buffalo Springfield	*Last Time Around*	Atlantic	1972
Loggins & Messina	*Sittin' In*	CBS	1972
Loggins & Messina	*Loggins & Messina*	CBS	1972
Loggins & Messina	*Full Sail*	CBS	1973
Loggins & Messina	*On Stage*	CBS	1974
Loggins & Messina	*Motherlode*	CBS	1974
Loggins & Messina	*So Fine*	CBS	1975
Loggins & Messina	*Native Sons*	CBS	1976
Loggins & Messina	*Finale*	CBS	1977
Jimmy Messina	*Oasis*	CBS	1979
Jimmy Messina	*Messina*	WB	1981
Poco	*Pickin' Up The Pieces*	Epic	1969
Poco	*Deliverin'*	Epic	1970
Poco	*Poco*	Epic	1970

M066 Miami Steve (Steve Van Zandt) (a.k.a. Little Steven)

w. B.Springsteen	Gary U.S. Bonds	*Dedication*	EMI-Amer	1981
w. B.Springsteen	Gary U.S. Bonds	*On The Line*	EMI-Amer	1982

	Little Steven and The Disciples Of Soul	*Men Without Women*	EMI-Amer	1982
	Little Steven	*Voice Of America*	EMI-Amer	1984
	Southside Johnny	*I Don't Wanna Go Home*	Epic	1976
	Southside Johnny	*This Time It's For Real*	Epic	1977
	Southside Johnny	*Hearts Of Stone*	Epic	1978
w. Jon Landau	Bruce Springsteen	*The River*	CBS	1980
w. Jon Landau & Chuck Plotkin	Bruce Springsteen	*Born In The USA*	CBS	1984

M067 Jimmy Miller

	Ginger Baker's Air Force	*Ginger Baker's Air Force*	Polydor	1970
	Blind Faith	*Blind Faith*	Poly/Atco	1969
	Jim Capaldi	*The Contender (1 tr.)*	Polydor	1978
	Delaney and Bonnie	*On Tour*	Atlantic	1970
	Billy Falcon	*Falcon Around*	MCA	1980
w. Gary Wright	Steve Gibbons	*Short Stories*	Wizard	1971
	Kracker	*Kracker Brand*	RSR	1973
	Motorhead	*Overkill*	Bronze	1979
	Plasmatics	*New Hope For The Wretched*	Stiff	1980
	Rolling Stones	*Beggars Banquet*	Decca/Lon	1969
	Rolling Stones	*Let It Bleed*	Decca/Lon	1969
	Rolling Stones	*Sticky Fingers*	RSR	1971
	Rolling Stones	*Exile On Main Street*	RSR	1972
	Rolling Stones	*Goat's Head Soup*	RSR	1973
	Rolling Stones	*Metamorphosis*	Decca/ABK	1975
	Savage Rose	*Refugee*	RCA	1972
	Spooky Tooth	*It's All About*	Island	1968
	Spooky Tooth	*Spooky Two*	Island	1969
	Johnny Thunders	*Too Much Junkie Business*	ROIR	1983
	Johnny Thunders	*Diary Of A Lover*	PVC	1984
	Traffic	*Mr.Fantasy*	Island/UA	1967
	Traffic	*Traffic*	Island/UA	1968
	Traffic	*Last Exit*	Island/UA	1969
	Trapeze	*Hold On*	Aura/Paid	1979
	Bobby Whitlock	*Bobby Whitlock (1 tr)*	CBS	1972
w. Joe Zagarino	Bobby Whitlock	*Raw Velvet*	CBS	1972

M068 Russ Miller

	David Ackles	*Subway To The Country*	Elektra	1969
w. D.Anderle	David Ackles	*Road To Cairo*	Elektra	1969
w. M.Greene	Carol Hall	*Beads And Feathers*	Elektra	1972
	Lonnie Mack	*Whatever's Right*	Elektra	1969
	Lonnie Mack	*Hills Of Indiana*	Elektra	1971
w. M.Greene	Lonnie Mack	*Home At Last*	Capitol	1977
	Sweet Salvation	*Sweet Salvation*	Elektra	1972

M069 Jackie Mills

	Floating Bridge	*Floating Bridge*	Vault	1971
	Fuse	*Fuse*	Epic	1971
	(Early version of Cheap Trick.)			
	Kaleidoscope	*Incredible*	Epic	1969
	Kaleidoscope	*Bernice*	Epic	1970

C. K. Strong (featuring Lyn Carey.)	*C. K. Strong*	Epic	1969

M070 John Mills

Billy Falcon	*Billy Falcon*	Phonogram	1979
Poco	*Ghost Town*	Atlantic	1982

M071 Rodney Mills

38 Special	*Rockin' Into The Night*	A&M	1979
38 special	*Wild-Eyed Southern Boys*	A&M	1981
38 Special	*Special Forces*	A&M	1982
38 Special	*Tour De Force*	A&M	1983

M072 Terence Minogue

Crack The Sky	*Animal Notes*	Lifesong	1976
Crack The Sky	*White Music*	Lifesong	1980

M073 Willie Mitchell

Elizabeth Barraclough	*Hi*	Bearsv	1979
Paul Butterfield	*North South*	Bearsv	1980
Kenny Doss	*Movin' On A Feelin'*	Bearsv	1980
Al Green	*Green Is Blues*	Hi	1970
Al Green	*Al Green Gets Next To You*	London/Hi	1971
Al Green	*Let's Stay Together*	London/Hi	1971
Al Green	*I'm Still In Love With You*	London/Hi	1972
Al Green	*Call Me*	London/Hi	1973
Al Green	*Livin' For You*	London/Hi	1974
Al Green	*Explores Your Mind*	London/Hi	1974
Al Green	*Is Love*	London/Hi	1975
Al Green	*Full Of Fire*	London/Hi	1975
Al Green	*Have A Good Time*	London/Hi	1976
Anne Peebles	*Part Time Love*	Hi	1971
Anne Peebles	*Straight From The Heart*	London/Hi	1972
Anne Peebles	*I Can't Stand The Rain*	London/Hi	1974
Anne Peebles	*Tellin' It*	London/Hi	1976
Anne Peebles	*If This Is Heaven*	Hi	1978
Anne Peebles	*The Handwriting Is On The Wall*	Hi	1979
Jesse Winchester	*Talk Memphis*	Bearsv	1981
O.V.Wright	*Bottom Line*	Hi	1978
O.V.Wright	*Into Something I Can't Shake Loose*	Hi	1978
O.V.Wright	*We're Still Together*	Hi	1979

M074 Frazier Mohawk (pseudonym for a famous Elektra house producer.)

Holy Modal Rounders	*The Moray Eels Eat The Holy Modal Rounders*	Elektra	1969
John Koerner and Willie Murphey	*Running Jumping Standing Still*	Elektra	1970
Nico	*The Marble Index*	Elektra	1968

M075   Fred Mollin (see M003 for Matthew McCauley co-production credits.)

America	*Alibi*	Capitol	1980
Randy Bishop	*Bishop And Gwinn*	Infinity	1979
Randy Edelman	*You're The One*	20th Cent	1979
First Fire	*First Fire*	Tortoise	1978
Ronnie Hawkins	*A Legend In His Spare Time*	Quality	1981
Dan Hill	*Dan Hill*	20th Cent	1976
Dan Hill	*Hold On*	20th Cent	1977
Dan Hill	*Longer Fuse*	20th Cent	1978
Dan Hill	*Frozen In The Night*	20th Cent	1978
Marc Tanner Band	*Temptation (2 tracks only.)*	Elektra	1980
Jimmy Webb	*Angel Heart*	CBS/Lori	1982

M076 Chips Moman

w. Tommy Cogbill	Box Tops	*Dimensions*	Bell	1968
	Billy Burnette	*Billy Burnette*	Polydor	1979
	Billy Burnette	*Between Friends*	Polydor	1979
w. Bobby Emmons	Jessi Colter	*Rock And Roll Lullabye*	Triad	1984
	Paul Davis	*A Little Bit Of Paul Davis*	Bang	1974
	Gentrys	*Keep On Dancin'*	MGM	1965
	Gentrys	*Time*	MGM	1966
	Waylon Jennings	*Ol' Waylon*	RCA	1977
	Waylon Jennings	*Black On Black*	RCA	1982
	Waylon Jennings and Willie Nelson	*Waylon And Willie 2*	RCA	1982
	Waylon Jennings and Willie Nelson	*Take It To The Limit*	CBS	1983
	Willie Nelson	*Always On My Mind*	CBS	1982
	Paul Revere and The Raiders	*Going To Memphis*	CBS	1968
	Tommy Roe	*Full Bloom*	Monument	1977
	Earl Scruggs Revue	*Bold And New*	CBS	1978
	Gary Stewart	*Cactus And Rose*	RCA	1980
	B J Thomas	*Reunion*	ABC	1975
	B J Thomas	*Help Me Make It To My Rocking Chair*	ABC	1975
	B J Thomas	*Everybody Loves A Rain Song*	MCA	1978
	Townes Van Zandt	*Flyin' Shoes*	Tomato	1978
	Weinstein And Strodl	*Cook Me Up Your Taste*	Capitol	1969

M077 Bob Monaco

Cockrell and Santos	*New Beginnings*	A&M	1978
Crow	*Music*	Stateside	1970
Cryan Shames	*A Scratch In The Sky*	CBS	1967
Cryan Shames	*Sugar and Spice*	CBS	1966
Cryan Shames	*Synthesis*	CBS	1968
Lisa Dal Ballo	*Pretty Girls*	Talisman	1979
Freda Payne	*Out Of Payne Comes Love*	ABC	1975
Flora Purim	*Every Night*	WB	1978
Rufus	*Rufus*	ABC	1973
Rufus	*Rags To Rufus*	ABC	1974

	Rufus	*Rufusized*	ABC	1974
	Sweet Inspirations	*H-O-T Butterfly*	RSO	1979
	Three Dog Night	*American Pastime*	ABC	1976
	Tina Turner	*Rough*	UA	1978

M078 Bob Montgomery

	Eddy Arnold	*Somebody Loves You*	RCA	1979
	Razzy Bailey	*If Love Had A Face*	RCA	1979
	Razzy Bailey	*Feelin' Right*	RCA	1982
	Randy Crawford	*Miss Randy Crawford*	WB	1977
	Crickets	*Bubblegum, Bop, Ballads And Boogies*	Philips	1973
	Crickets	*Long Way From Lubbock*	Philips	1974
	Kenny Dale	*Only Love Can Break A Heart*	Capitol	1979
	Janie Fricke	*It Ain't Easy*	CBS	1982
	Janie Fricke	*Love Lies*	CBS	1983
w.S.Buckingham	Mark Gray	*Magic*	CBS	1984
	Lobo	*Lobo*	MCA	1979
	Johnny Rivers	*Road*	Atlantic	1974
	John Wesley Ryles	*Let The Night Begin*	MCA	1979
	B W Stevenson	*Lost Feeling*	WB	1977
	B J Thomas	*Shining*	CBS	1984
	Slim Whitman	*Angeline*	Epic	1984

M079 Anthony Moore

	Manfred Mann	*Angel Station*	Bronze	1978

M080 Daniel Moore

	Denny Brooks	*Denny Brooks*	WB	1969
	Kim Carnes	*St. Vincents Court*	EMI-Amer	1979
	Carp (Featuring Gary Busey.)	*Carp*	Epic	1967
	Colours	*Colours*	Dot	1968
	Colours	*Atmospheres*	Dot	1969
w. J.H. Burnett	Delbert and Glen (Delbert is Delbert McClinton.)	*Delbert and Glen*	Clean	1972
	East Side Kids	*The Tiger And The Lamb*	Uni	1970
	Daniel Moore	*Daniel Moore*	Probe	1971
	Don Preston	*Sacre Bleus*	Rag Baby	1981
	Sneaky Pete	*Cold Steel*	Ariola	1973
w. N.Putnam	Toby Beau	*More Than A Love Song*	RCA	1979

M081 Matthew Moore (brother of Daniel Moore)

	Moon	*The Moon*	Liberty	1967

M082 Pat Moran

	Airwaves	*New Day*	Mercury	1978
	Airwaves	*Next Step*	Mercury	1979
	Barracudas	*Drop Out*	Z	1981
	John Butcher Axis	*John Butcher Axis*	Polydor	1983
	Dodgers	*Love On the Rebound*	Polydor	1978
	Hawkwind	*Choose Your Masques*	RCA	1982
	Hobo	*Hobo*	UA	1976
	Searchers	*The Searchers*	Sire	1979
w. Ed Stasium	Searchers	*Play For Today*	Sire	1981

	Pete Stride and John Plain	*New Guitars In Town*	B.Banquet	1980

M083 Frank Morin

Shades Of Joy	*Shades Of Joy*	Philips	1969
various artists	*The Flying Bear Medicine Show*	Philips	1969

M084 Giorgio Moroder

	soundtrack	*American Gigolo*	Polydor	1980
	Berlin	*Love Life*	Geffen	1984
	Irene Cara	*What A Feelin'*	Geffen	1983
	soundtrack	*Cat People*	MCA/Backst	1982
	soundtrack	*Foxes*	Casab	1980
	Giorgio	*Knights In White Satin*	GTO	1976
	Giorgio	*From Here To Eternity*	GTO	1977
	Giorgio and Chris	*Love's In You, Love's In Me*	GTO	1978
w. Keith Forsey	Nina Hagen	*Fearless*	Epic	1983
	Janis Ian	*Night Rains (2 tracks)*	CBS	1979
	Madleen Kane	*Don't Want To Lose You*	Chalet	1981
	Roberta Kelly	*Zodiac Lady*	Oasis	1977
	Roberta Kelly –	*Gettin' The Spirit*	Oasis/Casa	1978
	Suzi Lane	*Ooh La La*	Elektra	1979
	soundtrack	*Midnight Express*	Casab	1978
w.H.Faltermeyer	Giorgio Moroder	*Music From Battlestar Galactica*	Casab	1978
w.H.Faltermeyer	Giorgio Moroder	*E=MC2*	Casab	1979
	Munich Machine	*Whiter Shade Of Pale*	Casab	1978
	Munich Machine	*Body Shine*	Casab	1979
	Sparks	*Number 1 In Heaven*	Virg/Elek	1978
	Sparks	*Terminal Jive*	Virgin	1980
	Donna Summer	*Four Seasons Of Love*	GTO	1976
	Donna Summer	*A Love Trilogy*	GTO	1976
	Donna Summer	*I Remember Yesterday*	GTO	1977
	Donna Summer	*Once Upon A Time*	Casab	1977
	Donna Summer	*Live And More*	Casab	1978
	Donna Summer	*Bad Girls*	Casab	1979
	Donna Summer	*The Wanderer*	Geffen	1980
	soundtrack	*Superman 3*	WB	1983
	Sylvers	*Disco Fever*	Casab	1979
	Three Degrees	*3-D*	Ariola	1980
	Three Degrees	*New Dimensions*	Ariola	1978

(See also Pete Bellotte for co-productions.)

M085 George "Shadow" Morton

Janis Ian	*Janis Ian*	MGM	1967
Janis Ian	*Society's Child*	MGM	1967
New York Dolls	*Too Much Too Soon*	Mercury	1974
Tom Pacheco	*Great American Heartland*	RCA	1976
Tom Pacheco	*The Outsider*	RCA	1976
Shangri La's	*Leader Of The Pack*	Red Bird	1965
Vanilla Fudge	*Vanilla Fudge*	Atlantic	1967
Vanilla Fudge	*The Beat Goes On*	Atlantic	1968
Vanilla Fudge	*Renaissance*	Atlantic	1968

M086 Wayne Moss

	Barefoot Jerry	*Southern Delight*	Capitol	1971
w. John Harris	Barefoot Jerry	*Barefoot Jerry*	WB	1973
w. Russ Hicks	Barefoot Jerry	*Watchin' TV*	Monument	1974
	Barefoot Jerry	*You Can't Get Off With Your Shoes On*	Monument	1975
	Barefoot Jerry	*Keys To The Country*	Monument	1976
	Barefoot Jerry	*Barefootin'*	Monument	1977
	Toni Brown and Terry Garthwaite	*Cross Country*	Capitol	1973

M087 Mickie Most

	Animals	*The Animals*	Col/MGM	1964
	Animals	*The Animals On Tour*	MGM	1964
	Animals	*Animal Tracks*	Col/MGM	1965
	Jeff Beck	*Truth*	Columbia	1968
	Jeff Beck	*Beck-Ola*	Columbia	1969
	Duncan Browne	*Duncan Browne*	Rak	1973
	CCS	*CCS*	Rak	1972
	CCS	*The Best Band In The Land*	Rak	1973
	Donovan	*Sunshine Superman*	Pye/Epic	1967
	Donovan	*Mellow Yellow*	Pye/Epic	1967
	Donovan	*Hurdy Gurdy Man*	Epic	1968
	Donovan	*Gift From A Flower To A Garden*	Pye/Epic	1968
	Donovan	*Barabajagal*	Epic	1968
	Donovan	*Cosmic Wheels*	Epic	1972
	Donovan	*Donovan*	Rak	1977
	Julie Felix	*Clotho's Web*	Rak	1972
	Heavy Metal Kids	*Kitsch*	Rak	1977
	Hermans Hermits	*Introducing Herman's Hermits*	Col/MGM	1964
	Herman's Hermits	*Herman's Hermits*	Col/MGM	1965
	Herman's Hermits	*Hold On (soundtrack)*	MGM	1966
	Herman's Hermits	*Both Sides Of Herman's Hermits*	Col/MGM	1966
	Herman's Hermits	*There's A Kind Of Hush*	Col/MGM	1967
	Herman's Hermits	*Mrs Brown You've Got A Lovely Daughter*	Col/MGM	1968
	Mary Hopkin	*Those Were The Days (5 tracks only.)*	Apple	1972
	Hot Chocolate	*Cicero Park*	Rak	1974
	Hot Chocolate	*Hot Chocolate*	Rak	1975
	Hot Chocolate	*Man To Man*	Rak	1976
	Hot Chocolate	*Everyone's A Winner*	Rak/Infin	1978
	Hot Chocolate	*Going Through The Motions*	Rak/Infin	1979
	Hot Chocolate	*Class*	Rak	1980
	Hot Chocolate	*Mystery*	Rak/EMI	1982
	Hot Chocolate	*Love Shot*	Rak	1983
	Lulu	*Lulu Loves To Love Lulu*	Columbia	1967
	Lulu	*Lulu's Album*	Columbia	1969
	New World	*Believe In Music*	Rak	1973
	Suzi Quatro	*Aggro-Phobia*	Rak	1977

Racey	Smash And Grab	Rak	1979
Terry Reid	Bang, Bang... You're Terry Reid	Epic	1969
Terry Reid	Move Over For Terry Reid	Epic	1969
Chris Spedding	Chris Spedding	Rak	1976
Chris Spedding	I'm Not Like Everybody Else	Rak	1980
Yardbirds	Little Games	Epic	1967

M088 Tom Moulton

Charo	Ole Ole	Salsoul	1979
Edge	Fame	Casab	1980
Grace Jones	Portfolio	Island	1977
Grace Jones	Fame	Island	1978
Robert Palmer	Double Fun (3 tracks)	Island	1978
Salsoul Orchestra	Street Sense	Salsoul	1979
Edgar Winter Group	The Edgar Winter Album	Blue Sky	1979

M089 Barry Mraz

Color Me Gone	Color Me Gone	A&M	1984
Fotomaker	Transfer Station	Atlantic	1979
David Johansen	Here Comes The Night	Blue Sky	1981
Benny Mardones	Never Run Never Hide	Polydor	1980
Siegel-Scwall	953 West	W.Nickel	1973
Pat Travers	Hot Shot	Polydor	1984

M090 Paul Muggleton

w. Mike Paxman	Judy Tzuke	Sports Car	Rocket	1980
	Judy Tzuke	The Phoenix	Rocket	1981
	Judy Tzuke	Shoot The Moon	Chrysalis	1982
	Judy Tzuke	Road Noise	Chrysalis	1982
w. Mike Paxman	Judy Tzuke	Ritmo	Chrysalis	1983
	Wendy and The Rockets	Dazed For Days	A&M	1983

M091 Tim Mulligan

Neil Young	Zuma (2 tracks)	Reprise	1975

(the following albums are co-produced with David Briggs and N.Y.)

Neil Young	American Stars 'n' Bars	Reprise	1977
Neil Young	Comes A Time	Reprise	1979
Neil Young	Rust Never Sleeps	Reprise	1979
Neil Young	Live Rust	Reprise	1979
Neil Young	Hawks And Doves	Reprise	1980
Neil Young	Re-Ac-Tor	Reprise	1981
Neil Young	Trans	Geffen	1982

M092 Mark Miller Mundy

	Marianne Faithfull	Broken English	Island	1979
w. C.Blackwell & S.Winwood	Marianne Faithfull	Dangerous Acquaintances	Island	1981
w. C.Blackwell	Steve Winwood	Steve Winwood	Island	1970

M093 Hugh Murphy

Sir John Betjeman	*Late Flowering Love*	Charisma	1974
Paul Brady	*Hard Station*	WEA/Poly	1982
Dave Cartwright	*Masquerade*	DJM	1979
Richard Digance	*Live At The Queen Elizabeth Hall*	Chrysalis	1978
Melanie Harrold	*Melanie*	DJM	1979
Mike Heron	*Mike Heron*	Casab	1979
Jack The Lad	*Jack The Lad*	Charsima	1974
Jack The Lad	*The Old Straight Track*	Charisma	1974
Ray Jackson	*In The Night*	Mercury	1980
Kilburn And The High Roads	*Handsome*	Pye	1975
Kursaal Flyers	*Chocs Away*	UK	1975
Lindisfarne	*The News*	Mercury	1979
Mark-Almond	*Mark-Almond*	Harvest	1971
Gerry Rafferty	*Can I Have My Money Back*	Tra/B.Th	1971
Gerry Rafferty	*City To City*	UA	1978
Gerry Rafferty	*Snakes and Ladders*	UA	1980
Raphael Ravenscroft	*Her Father Didn't Like Me Anyway*	Portrait	1979
Gary Shearston	*Dingo*	Charisma	1974
Ringo Starr, etc.,	*Scouse The Mouse*	Polydor	1977
Stray	*Stray*	Tra	1970
Stray	*Suicide*	Tra	1971
Sweet Thursday	*Sweet Thursday (with Nicky Hopkins/Jon Mark)*	Epic	1973
Bonnie Tyler	*Goodbye To The Island*	RCA	1981

M094 Ralph Murphy

April Wine	*April Wine*	Big Tree	1972
April Wine	*On Record*	Aquarius	1973
April Wine	*Electric Jewels*	Aquarius	1973
Larry Raspberry	*No Accident*	Mercury	1979

M095 Larry Murray

Severin Browne	*Severin Browne*	Motown	1973
Severin Browne	*New Improved*	Motown	1974

(Brother of Jackson Browne.)

Johnny Darrell	*California Stop-Over*	UA	1970
Swampwater	*Swampwater*	RCA	1971

(Larry Murray was the co-owner of the Blue Guitar music shop in San Diego, a fabled folkie meeting place.)

N001 Ron Nagle

w.Elliot Mazer	Durocs	*The Durocs*	Capitol	1979
w. S.Matthews	John Hiatt	*Riding With The King*	Geffen	1983

(1 side only; the other produced by Nick Lowe.)

w. S.Matthews	Paul Kantner	*Planet Earth Rock 'n' Roll*	RCA	1983

N002 John Nagy

Jeffrey Frederick	*Spiders in The Moonlight*	Rounder	1977
Giants	*Thanks For The Music*	Casab	1976

(Featured John Platania and Ron Elliott.)

Michael Hurley	*Have Moicy*	Rounder	1976
Michael Hurley	*Long Journey*	Rounder	1976
Nighthawks	*Hot Spot*	Varrick	1984
Andy Pratt	*Andy Pratt*	Epic	1973
George Thorogood and The Destroyers	*George Thorogood and The Destroyers*	Sonet/Roun	1978
George Thorogood and The Destroyers	*Move It On Over*	Sonet/Roun	1978
George Thorogood and The Destroyers	*More*	Sonet/Roun	1980

N003 Al Nalli

Axe	*Offering*	Atco	1982
Axe	*Nemesis*	Atco	1983
Blackfoot	*Strikes*	Atlantic	1979
Blackfoot	*Tomcattin'*	Atlantic	1980
Blackfoot	*Marauder*	Atlantic	1981
Blackfoot	*Highway Song-Live*	Atlantic	1982
Blackfoot	*Siogo*	Atlantic	1983
Brownsville Station	*Motor City Connection*	Big Tree	1975
More	*Warhead*	Atlantic	1981

N004 Simon Napier-Bell

	Marc Bolan	*The Beginning Of Doves*	Track	1974
	Marc Bolan	*You Scare Me To Death*	Cherry Red	1981
w. Ray Singer	Forever More	*Yours Forever More*	RCA	1970
w. Ray Singer	Fresh	*Fresh Out Of Borstal*	RCA	1970
w. Ray Singer	Fresh	*Fresh Today*	RCA	1970
w. Ray Singer	Clive Sarstedt	*Sarstedt*	RCA	1976
w.Paul Samwell-Smith	Yardbirds	*The Yardbirds*	Columbia	1966

(a.k.a. "Roger The Engineer", recently reissued on Edsel.)

N005 Graham Nash

David Blue	*Nice Baby And The Angel*	Asylum	1973
Steve Gillette	*A Little Warmth*	Regency	1980
Hollies	*What Goes Around*	Atlantic	1983
Graham Nash	*Songs For Beginners*	Atlantic	1971
Graham Nash	*Wild Tales*	Atlantic	1973
Graham Nash	*Earth and Sky*	Capitol	1979
Charles John Quarto	*Charles John Quarto*	Atlantic	1971
Terry Reid	*Seed Of Memory*	ABC	1976
Seemon and Marijke	*Son Of America*	A&M	1970

N006 Christopher Neil

	Andy Bown	*Good Advice*	EMI	1972
	Chorale	*Chorale*	Arista	1979
	Dollar	*Shooting Stars*	Carrere	1979
	Sheena Easton	*Take My Time*	EMI	1981
	Sheena Easton	*You Could Have Been With Me*	EMI	1981
	Sheena Easton	*Madness, Money And Music*	EMI	1982
w. Mike Batt	David Essex	*Imperial Wizard*	Mercury	1979
	Marshall Hain	*Free Ride*	Harv/Cap	1978
	Gerard Kenny	*Made It In The Rain*	RCA	1979

Gerard Kenny	*Living On Music*	RCA	1980
Hank Marvin	*All Alone With Friends*	Polydor	1983
Paul Nicholas	*Paul Nicholas*	RSO	1977
Gerry Rafferty	*Sleepwalking*	UA	1982
Leo Sayer	*Have You Ever Been In Love*	WB	1984
Shakin' Stevens	*The Bop Won't Stop*	Epic	1983
Dennis Waterman	*Dennis Waterman*	EMI	1980
Wavelength	*Hurry Home*	Ariola	1982

N007 Bill Nelson

Skids	*Days In Europa*	Virgin	1979

N008 Mike Nesmith

Garland Frady	*Pure Country*	Country	1973
Fresh	*Omniverse*	Prodigal	1978
Bert Jansch	*L.A. Turnaround*	Charisma	1974
Ian Matthews	*Valley Hi*	Elektra	1973
Mike Nesmith	*The Wichita Train Whistle Sings*	Dot	1968
Mike Nesmith	*The Loose Salute*	RCA	1970
Mike Nesmith	*Nevada Fighter*	RCA	1971
Mike Nesmith	*Tantamount To Treason*	RCA	1972
Mike Nesmith	*Pretty Much Your Standard Ranch Stash*	RCA	1972
Mike Nesmith	*The Hits Just Keep On Comin'*	RCA	1972
Mike Nesmith	*The Prison*	Pac Arts	1974
Mike Nesmith	*From A Radio Engine To A Photon Wing*	Pac Arts	1974
Mike Nesmith	*Live At The Palais*	Pac Arts	1978
Mike Nesmith	*Infinite Rider On The Big Dogma*	Pac Arts	1979
Red Rhodes	*Velvet Hammer In A Cowboy Band*	Country	1973

N009 Ron Nevison

	Babys	*Broken Heart*	Chrysalis	1977
	Babys	*Head First*	Chrysalis	1979
	Alex Call	*Alex Call*	Arista	1983
	Chilli Willi and The Red Hot Peppers	*Bongos Over Balham*	B&C	1974
	Mike Finnigan	*Black And White*	CBS	1978
w. Skip Taylor	Flo And Eddie	*Moving Targets*	CBS	1975
	Jefferson Starship	*Freedom At Point Zero*	Grunt	1979
	Jefferson Starship	*Modern Times*	Grunt	1981
	Jefferson Starship	*Nuclear Furniture*	Grunt	1984
	Dave Mason	*Flowing Free Forever*	CBS	1977
	Dave Mason	*Mariposo De Oro*	CBS	1978
	Eddie Money	*Playing For Keeps*	CBS	1980
	Michael Schenker Group	*Michael Schenker Group*	Chrysalis	1981
	Grace Slick	*Software*	RCA	1984
	Rex Smith	*Camouflage*	CBS	1983
	Thin Lizzy	*Night Life*	Vert/Mer	1974
	UFO	*Lights Out*	Chrysalis	1977
	UFO	*Obsession*	Chrysalis	1978
	UFO	*Strangers In The Night*	Chrysalis	1979

	various artists	*Reading Festival 1973*	GM	1973
	Wolf and Wolf	*Wolf and Wolf*	Morroco	1984

N010 Del Newman

	Catherine Howe	*Harry*	RCA	1974
	Longdancer	*Trailer For A Good Life*	Rocket	1974
	Max Merritt	*A Little Easier*	Arista	1975
	O Band	*The Knife*	UA	1977
	Brian Protheroe	*Pinball*	Chrysalis	1974
	Brian Protheroe	*Pick Up*	Chrysalis	1975
	Brian Protheroe	*I/You*	Chrysalis	1976
	Scott Walker	*Stretch*	CBS	1973
	Randy Vanwarmer	*Warmer*	Bearsv	1979

N011 Tom Newman

	Adverts	*Cast of 1000's*	RCA	1979
	Atomic Rooster	*Headline News*	Jem	1983
	Paul Brett	*Interlife*	RCA	1978
	Paul Brett	*Eclipses*	RCA	1979
	Doll By Doll	*Doll By Doll*	Magnet	1981
	Doll By Doll	*Grand Passion*	Magnet	1982
	Hatfield And The North	*Hatfield And The North*	Virgin	1974
	Henry Cow	*Legend*	Virgin	1973
	Neil Innes	*Taking Off*	Arista	1977
	Natasha	*Captured*	Towerbell	1982
	Mike Oldfield	*Tubular Bells*	Virgin	1972
	Mike Oldfield	*Hergest Ridge*	Virgin	1974
	Mike Oldfield	*Platinum*	Virgin	1979
	Sally Oldfield	*Celebration*	Bronze	1980
w. K.Harada	Snowy White	*White Flames*	Towerbell	1984

N012 Andy Newmark

	Nils Lofgren	*I Came To Dance*	A&M	1977
	Nils Lofgren	*Wonderland*	MCA/Backst	1983

N013 David Nichtern

	Kate and Anna McGarrigle	*Pronto Monto*	WB	1978
	Maria Muldaur	*Open Your Eyes*	WB	1979
	Maria Muldaur	*Sweet And Slow*	Tudor	1983

N014 Harry Nilsson

	various artists	*Popeye soundtrack*	Epic/Bdwlk	1980

N015 Jack Nitzsche

	soundtrack	*Blue Collar*	MCA	1978
	Crazy Horse	*Crazy Horse*	Reprise	1971
	soundtrack	*Cruisin'*	CBS	1980
w. Joe Wissert	Jackie De Shannon	*Me About You*	Liberty	1968
	Alan Gordon	*Alley And The Soul Sneakers*	Capitol	1978
	(Of the Bonner and Gordon songwriting team.)			
	Mick Jagger, etc.,	*Performance soundtrack*	WB	1970
	Mink De Ville	*Cabretta*	Capitol	1977
	Mink De Ville	*Return To Magenta*	Capitol	1978

	Mink De Ville	*Coup De Grace*	Atlantic	1978
	Ron Nagle	*Bad Rice*	WB	1970
	Rick Nelson	*Playing To Win*	Capol	1981
	Neville Brothers	*The Neville Brothers*	Capitol	1979
	soundtrack	*One Flew Over The Cuckoo's Nest*	Fantasy	1975
	Graham Parker	*Squeezing Out Sparks*	Vert/Aris	1979
	Michelle Phillips	*Victim Of Romance*	A&M	1977
	Sumner	*Sumner*	Asylum	1980
	Neil Young	*Harvest (2 tracks)*	Reprise	1972

N016 Don Nix

	Alabama State Troopers	*Road Show*	Elektra	1972
	Beck, Bogert and Appice	*Beck, Bogert and Appice*	Epic	1973
w.Donald Dunn	Delaney and Bonnie	*Home*	Stax	1970
	Danny Green	*Nightdog*	ABC	1978
	Carol Grimes	*Carol Grimes*	Goodear	1975
	Albert King	*Lovejoy*	Stax	1971
	Freddie King	*Getting Ready*	A&M/Shelt	1971
	John Mayall	*Ten Years Are Gone*	Polydor	1973
	Don Nix	*Living By The Days*	Elektra	1971
	Don Nix	*In God We Trust*	Shelter	1971
	Don Nix	*Hobos, Heroes. Street Corner Clowns*	Enterp	1973
	Don Nix	*Gone Too Long*	Cream	1976
	Don Nix	*Skywriter*	Cream	1979
	Paris Pilot	*Paris Pilot*	Hip	1970
	Larry Raspberry and The Highsteppers	*Highsteppin' and Fancy Dancin'*	Enterp	1974
	Skin Alley	*Skintight*	Tra	1973

N017 Jim Ed Norman

	C.Y.Walkin' Band	*Love The Way It Feels*	Parachute	1979
	Jackie De Shannon	*You're The Only Dancer*	Amherst	1977
	Glen Frey	*No Fun Aloud*	Asylum	1982
	Janie Fricke	*Sleeping With Your Memory*	CBS	1981
	Mickey Gilley	*That's All That Matters To Me*	Epic	1980
	Mickey Gilley	*You Don't Know Me*	Epic	1981
	Mickey Gilley	*Put Your Dreams Away*	Epic	1982
	Mickey Gilley	*Fool For Your Love*	Epic	1983
	Mickey Gilley	*You've Really Got A Hold On Me*	Epic	1983
	Glenda Griffith	*Glenda Griffith*	Ariola	1977
	Albert Hammond	*Your World And My World*	CBS	1981
	Johnny Lee	*Lookin' For Love*	Asylum	1980
	Johnny Lee	*Bet Your Heart On Me*	Full Moon	1981
	Johnny Lee	*Sounds Like Love*	Full Moon	1982
	Gary Morris	*Faded Blue*	WB	1984
	Michael Murphey	*Michael Martin Murphey*	EMI-Amer	1982
	Anne Murray	*I'll Always Love You*	Capitol	1979

Anne Murray	*A Country Collection*	Capitol	1980
Anne Murray	*Somebody's Waiting*	Capitol	1980
Anne Murray	*A Little Good News*	Capitol	1983
New Riders of The Purple Sage	*Marin County Line*	MCA	1978
Osmond Brothers	*One Way Rider*	WB-Curb	1984
T G Sheppard	*Slow Burn*	WB-Curb	1983
Jennifer Warnes	*Jennifer Warnes*	Arista	1977

N018 Max Norman

Coney Hatch	*Outa Hand*	Vertigo	1983
Ian Hunter	*All The Good Ones Are Taken*	CBS	1983
Ozzie Osbourne	*Diary Of A Madman*	Jet	1981
Ozzie Osbourne	*Talk Of The Devil*	Jet	1982
Ozzie Osbourne	*Bark At The Moon*	Jet/CBS	1983
Y&T	*Black Tiger*	A&M	1982

N019 Steve Nye

w.Simon Puxley	Bryan Ferry	*In Your Mind*	Poly/Atl	1977
	Bryan Ferry	*The Bride Stripped Bare*	Poly/Atl	1978
	Murray Head	*Shades*	Virgin	1982
	Murray Head	*Restless*	Virgin	1984
	Japan	*Tin Drum*	Virgin	1981
	David Sylvain	*Brilliant Trees*	Virgin	1984
	XTC	*Mummer*	Virgin	1983

O001 Tim O'Brien

Herman Brood	*Go Nutz*	Ariola	1980
Jerry Williams Group	*Down Home Boy*	CBS	1970

O002 Ric Ocasek

	Bad Brains	*Rock For Light*	Abst/PVC	1983
	Bebe Buell	*Covers Girl (12" EP)*	Rhino	1981
	Peter Dayton	*Love At First Sight*	Shoo Bop	1981
	Ric Ocasek	*Beattitude*	Geffen	1982
w. Ian Taylor	Romeo Void	*Never Say Never*	415	1982
	Alan Vega and Martin Rev (aka Suicide)	*Alan Vega and Martin Rev*	Ze	1980
	Alan Vega	*Saturn Drive*	Ze	1983

O003 Phil Ochs

Sammy Walker	*Song For Patty*	Folkways	1975

O004 Michael O'Connor

Fine Wine	*Fine Wine*	Polydor	1976

(Fine Wine comprised former Moby Grape members and were managed by O'Connor who also managed Chris Darrow and co-produced several Darrow albums: see Darrow entry.)

O005 Alan O'Duffy

Horslips	*Happy To Meet, Sorry To Part*	Oats/Atco	1972
Horslips	*The Tain*	Oats/Atco	1973

Horslips	*A Celtic Symphony*	DJM	1976
Horslips	*Aliens*	DJM	1977
Incantations	*On The Wings Of A Condor*	B.Banquet	1983
Pookie	*Beach Party*	Hep-Note	1982
Alan Price	*England, My England*	Jet	1978
various	*Andy Capp Soundtrack*	Key	1982

O003 Eddie Offord

Art In America	*Art In America*	Pavillion	1983
Baker Gurvitz Army	*Hearts On Fire*	Mountain	1976
Blackjack	*World's Apart*	Polydor	1980
Dregs	*Industry Standard*	Arista	1982
Steve Howe	*Beginnings*	Atlantic	1975
Idle Race	*Birthday Party*	Liberty	1968
Lindisfarne	*Happy Daze*	WB	1974
Pallas	*The Sentinel*	Harvest	1984
Andy Pratt	*Motives*	Nemperor	1979
Terry Reid	*River (2 tracks)*	Atlantic	1973
Rozetta	*Where's My Hero*	20th Cent	
David Sancious and Tone	*True Stories*	Arista	1978
Billy Squier	*Tale Of The Tape*	Capitol	1980
Yes	*Fragile*	Atlantic	1971
Yes	*Close To The Edge*	Atlantic	1972
Yes	*Yessongs*	Atlantic	1973
Yes	*Tales From The Topographic Oceans*	Atlantic	1973
Yes	*Relayer*	Atlantic	1974
Yes	*Drama*	Atlantic	1980
Ziggurat	*Melodic Scandal*	Robox	1982

O007 Milton Okun

John Denver	*Rhymes And Reasons*	RCA	1969
John Denver	*Take Me To Tomorrow*	RCA	1970
John Denver	*Poems, Prayers and Promises*	RCA	1971
John Denver	*Aerie*	RCA	1971
John Denver	*Rocky Mountain High*	RCA	1972
John Denver	*Farewell Andromeda*	RCA	1973
John Denver	*Back Home Again*	RCA	1974
John Denver	*Denver Gift Box*	RCA	1975
John Denver	*Rocky Mountain Christmas*	RCA	1975
John Denver	*Windsong*	RCA	1975
John Denver	*An Evening With John Denver*	RCA	1975
John Denver	*Spirit*	RCA	1976
John Denver	*I Want To Live*	RCA	1977
John Denver	*A Christmas Together (with The Muppets)*	RCA	1979
John Denver	*John Denver*	RCA	1979
John Denver	*Autograph*	RCA	1980
John Denver	*Some Days Are Diamonds*	RCA	1981
Fat City	*Welcome To Fat City*	Paramount	1972
Liberty	*Liberty*	Windsong	1978
Laura Nyro	*The First Songs*	CBS	1973

Tom Paxton		*The Marvellous Toy and Other Gallimaufry*	C.Lane	1984

O008 Mike Oldfield

	David Bedford	*Star's End*	Virgin	1974

O009 Andrew Loog Oldham

	P.P.Arnold	*The First Lady Of Immediate (2 tracks)*	Immediate	1967
	P.P.Arnold	*Kafunta*	Immediate	1968
	Duncan Browne	*Give Me Take You*	Immediate	1968
	Jimmy Cliff	*In Concert, The Best Of Jimmy Cliff*	Reprise	1976
	Donovan	*Essence To Essence*	Epic	1973
	Humble Pie	*Street Rats*	A&M	1975
	Benny Mardones	*Thank God For Girls*	P.Stock	1978
	Andrew Oldham Orchestra	*Plays Maggie May*	Decca	1964
w.Eric Easton	Rolling Stones	*The Rolling Stones*	Decca/Lon	1964
	Rolling Stones	*No.2*	Decca/Lon	1965
	Rolling Stones	*Out Of Our Heads*	Decca/Lon	1965
	Rolling Stones	*Aftermath*	Decca/Lon	1965
	Rolling Stones	*Got Live If You Want It*	London	1967
	Rolling Stones	*Between The Buttons*	Decca/Lon	1967
	Rolling Stones	*Metamorphosis*	Decca/ABK	1975
	Del Shannon	*...And The Music Plays On*	Sunset	1978
	Sunday Funnies	*Sunday Funnies*	Rare Earth	1981
	Twice As Much	*That's all*	Immediate	1968
	Werewolves	*Werewolves*	RCA	1978
	Werewolves	*Ship Of Fools*	RCA	1978
w.James Gadson	Bobby Womack	*The Poet 2*	Motown	1984

O010 Keith Olsen

	Airborne	*Airborne*	CBS	1979
	Babys	*Union Jacks*	Chrysalis	1980
	Babys	*On The Edge*	Chrysalis	1980
	Russ Ballard	*At The Third Stroke*	Epic	1978
	Pat Benatar	*Crimes Of Passion*	Chrysalis	1980
w.Neil Geraldo	Pat Benatar	*Precious Time*	Chrysalis	1981
	Nickey Barclay	*Diamonds In A Junkyard*	Ari-Amer	1976
	Buckingham Nicks	*Buckingham Nicks*	Polydor	1973
	Cado Belle	*Cado Belle*	Anchor	1976
	Tane Cain	*Tane Cain*	RCA	1982
	Kim Carnes	*Cafe Racers*	EMI-Amer	1983
	Michael Dinner	*Tom Thumb The Dreamer*	Fantasy	1976
	Fleetwood Mac	*Fleetwood Mac*	Reprise	1975
	Fools Gold	*Mr.Lucky*	CBS	1977
	Foreigner	*Double Vision*	Atlantic	1978
	Geronimo Black	*Geronimo Black*	Uni	1972
	Grateful Dead	*Terrapin Station*	Arista	1977
	Sammy Hagar	*Standing Hampton*	Geffen	1981
	Sammy Hagar	*Three Lock Box*	Geffen	1982
	Heart	*Passion Works*	Epic	1983
	I-Ten	*Taking A Cold Look*	Epic	1983
w. Curt Becher	Millenium	*Begin*	CBS	1970
	Preview	*Preview*	Geffen	1983
	Jerry Riopelle	*Take A Chance*	ABC	1975

	Santana	*Marathon*	CBS	1979
	Santana	*Zeebop (3 tracks)*	CBS	1981
	Sheila	*Little Darlin'*	Carrere	1981
w. Curt Becher	Song	*Album*	MGM-Verve	????
	Sons Of Champlin	*A Circle Filled With Love*	Ariola	1976
w.Bill Drescher	Rick Springfield	*Working Class Dog*	RCA	1981
	Rick Springfield	*Success Hasn't Spoiled Me Yet*	RCA	1982
	Domminic Troiano	*Dom*	Mercury	1972
	Bob Weir	*Heaven Help The Fool*	Arista	1978

O011 Richard Olsen

	Michael Wilhelm	*Wilhelm*	ZigZag-UA	1976

(This record is earnestly recommended to anyone reading this book)

O012 Michael Omartian (see also Steve Barri for co-production credits)

	Kerry Chater	*Part Time Love*	WB	1977
	Cher	*I'd Rather Believe In You*	WB	1976
	Crackin'	*Special Touch*	WB	1978
	Christopher Cross	*Christopher Cross*	WB	1979
	Christopher Cross	*Another Page*	WB	1983
	Dion	*Streetheart*	WB	1976
w. Bill Schnee	Richie Furay Band	*I've Got A Reason*	Asylum	1976
	Jermaine Jackson	*Jermaine Jackson (1 tr)*	Arista	1984
	Tom Johnson	*Still Feels Good*	WB	1981
	Jim Kreuger	*Sweet Salvation*	CBS	1978
	Maxus	*Maxus*	WB	1981
	Michael Omartian	*White Horse*	ABC	1974
	Michael Omartian	*Adam Again*	Myrrh	1977
	Michael and Stormie Omartian	*Mainstream*	Sparrow	1982
	Stormie Omartian	*Excercise For Life*	Sparrow	1983
	Pratt and McClain	*Pratt and McClain*	ABC	1974
	Pratt and McClain	*Featuring Happy Days*	Reprise	1976
	Rod Stewart	*Camouflage*	WB	1984
	Donna Summer	*She Works Hard For The Money*	Mercury	1983
	Roger Voudouris	*Roger Voudouris*	WB	1978
	Roger Voudouris	*Radio Dreams*	WB	1979
	Scott Wilk	*Scott Wilk and The Walls*	WB	1980

O013 Genesis P. Orridge

	Alternative TV	*Live At The Rat Club '77*	ATV	1977

O014 Richard Sandford Orshoff

	Jackson Browne	*Jackson Browne*	Asylum	1972
	John Hall Band	*All Of The Above*	EMI-Amer	1981
	Craig Mirijian	*A Perfect Fit*	WB	1980
	Poco	*Legend*	ABC	1978

O015 Johnny Otis

	Sugarcane Harris	*Sugarcane Harris*	Epic	1970

Johnny Otis Show	*Live At Monterey*	Epic	1971
Johnny Otis Show	*The New Johnny*		
	Otis show	Sonet/Alli	1981
Shuggy Otis	*Freedom Flight*	Epic	1971

O016 Tony Outeda

	Foghat	*Boogie Motel*	Bearsv	1979
	Foghat	*Tight Shoes*	Bearsv	1980
w. Nick Jameson	Foghat	*In The Mood For*		
		Something Rude	Bearsv	1982

P001 Hugh Padgham

	Call	*The Call*	Mercury	1982
	Phil Collins	*Face Value*	Virg/Atl	1981
	Phil Collins	*Hello I Must Be Going*	Virg/Atl	1982
	Genesis	*Genesis*	Virg/Atl	1983
	Hall And Oates	*Rock And Soul Live;*		
		The Video	RCA	1984
w. Chris Thomas	Human League	*Hysteria*	Virg/A&M	1984
	Police	*Ghost In The Machine*	A&M	1981
	Police	*Synchronicity*	A&M	1983
	Split Enz	*Time And Tide*	A&M	1982
w. Chris Butler	Waitresses	*Bruiseology*	Polydor	1983
	XTC	*English Settlement*	Virgin	1982

P002 Larry Page

	Troggs	*From Nowhere*	Fontana	1966
	Troggs	*Trogglodynamite*	Page One	1967
	Troggs	*Cellophane*	Page One	1967
	Troggs	*Mixed Bag*	Page One	1968
	Troggs	*The Troggs*	P.Farthing	1974

P003 John Palladino

w. Eric Malamud	Jackie De Shannon	*Songs*	Capitol	1971
	Joy Of Cooking	*Joy Of Cooking*	Capitol	1971
	Joy Of Cooking	*Closer To The Ground*	Capitol	1971
	Joy Of Cooking	*Castles*	Capitol	1972
w. Ed Black	Bob Meighan Band	*Bob Meighan Band*	Capitol	1977
	Navarro	*Straight To The Heart*	Capitol	1978
	Juice Newton	*Well Kept Secret*	Capitol	1978
	Quicksilver			
	Messenger Service	*Solid Silver*	Capitol	1976
	Helen Reddy	*Helen Reddy*	Capitol	1978
	Shirts	*Inner Sleeve*	Capitol	1980
	Chip Taylor	*Saint Sebastian*	Capitol	1979

P004 Robert Palmer

	Peter Baumann	*Repeat Repeat*	Virgin	1982
	Desmond Dekker	*Compass Point*	Stiff	1981
	Moon Martin	*Mystery Ticket*	Capitol	1982
	Robert Palmer	*Double Fun*	Island	1978
	Robert Palmer	*Secrets*	Island	1979
	Robert Palmer	*Clues*	Island	1980
	Robert Palmer	*Maybe It's Live*	Island	1982
	Robert Palmer	*Pride*	Island	1983

P005 Tom Panunzio

	Elliot Murphy	*Affairs*	Courtisane	1981
	Willie Nile	*Golden Down*	Arista	1981
	Iggy Pop	*Party*	Arista	1981
w. R.Gotterher	Link Wray	*Live At El Paradiso*	Instant	1980

P006 Felix Pappalardi

	Back Door	*8th Street Nites*	WB	1973
	Bo Grumpus	*Before The War*	Atco	1968
	Jack Bruce	*Songs For A Tailor*	Polydor	1969
	Cream	*Disraeli Gears*	Reac/Atco	1967
	Cream	*Wheels Of Fire*	Poly/Atco	1968
	Cream	*Goodbye*	Poly/Atco	1969
	Cream	*Live Volume 2*	Poly/Atco	1972
	Dead Boys	*We Have Come For Your Children*	Sire	1978
	Hot Tuna	*Double Dose*	Grunt	1978
	Jolliver Arkansaw	*Home*	Bell	1969
	Kensington Market	*Avenue Road*	WB	1968
	Kensington Market	*Aardvark*	WB	1969
	Mountain	*Mountain*	Windfall	1970
	Mountain	*Climbing*	Bell/Wind	1970
	Mountain	*Nantucket Sleighride*	Isl/Windf	1971
	Mountain	*Flowers Of Evil*	Isl/Windf	1971
	Mountain	*Live*	Isl/Windf	1972
	Mountain	*The Road Goes On Forever*	Windfall	1972
	Mountain	*Avalanche*	Epic	1974
	Mountain	*Twin Peaks*	CBS	1976
	Natural Gas	*Natural Gas*	P.Stock	1976
(Featured Joey Molland, ex-Badfinger.)				
	Felix Pappalardi and Creation	*Felix Pappalardi and Creation*	A&M	1976
	David Rea	*By The Grace Of God*	CBS	1971
	Sierra	*Sierra*	Mercury	1977
(Featuring Sneaky Pete Kleinow and Gib Guilbeau.)				
	Jesse Colin Young	*Love On The Wing*	WB	1977
	Youngbloods	*Get Together*	RCA	1969

P007 Dean Parks

	Gordon Lightfoot	*Salute*	WB	1983
w. Greg Perry	Dolly Parton	*Great Balls Of Fire*	RCA	1982
	Tom Snow	*Hungry Nights*	Arista	1982

P008 Van Dyke Parks

	Ry Cooder	*Ry Cooder*	Rewprise	1970
w. Andy Wickham	Mighty Sparrow	*Hot And Sweet*	WB	1974
w. L.Waronker	Randy Newman	*Randy Newman*	WB	1968
	Phil Ochs	*Greatest Hits*	A&M	1970

P009 Chris Parry

	The Cure	*Three Imaginary Boys*	Fiction	1979
	The Cure	*Boys Don't Cry*	PVC	1980
w. Dave Allen	The Cure	*The Top*	Fiction	1984
w. Vic Smith	The Jam	*In The City*	Polydor	1977

	The Jam	*This Is The Modern World*	Polydor	1977
w. Vic Smith	The Jolt	*The Jolt*	Polydor	1978
	Passions	*Michael And Miranda*	Fiction	1980
	Purple Hearts	*Beat That !*	Fiction	1980

P010 Alan Parsons

	Cockney Rebel	*The Psychomodo*	EMI	1974
	Cockney Rebel	*The Best Years Of Our Lives*	EMI	1975
	Dean Ford	*Dean Ford*	EMI	1975
w. M.Hamlisch	soundtrack	*Ice Castles*	Arista	1979
	John Miles	*Rebel*	Decca/Lon	1976
	John Miles	*More Miles Per Hour*	Decca/Aris	1979
	John Miles	*Sympathy*	Decca/Aris	1980
	Pilot	*From The Album Of The Same Name*	EMI	1974
	Pilot	*Second Flight*	EMI	1975
	Pilot	*Two's A Crowd*	Arista	1977
	Al Stewart	*Modern Times*	CBS	1975
	Al Stewart	*Time Passages*	RCA/Aris	1978
	Lenny Zak	*Lenny Zak*	A&M	1979

P011 Andy Partridge

	Peter Blegvad	*The Naked Shakespeare*	Virgin	1983

P012 Don Paul

	Pete Atkin	*A King At Nightfall*	RCA	1972
	Carl Wayne	*Carl Wayne*	RCA	1972

P013 Gary S.Paxton

	Vern Gosdin	*Till The End*	Elektra	1979
	Vern Gosdin	*You've Got Somebody*	Elektra	1979
	Gary Paxton	*Anchored In The Rock Of Ages*	Pax	1978
	Bobby (Boris) Pickett	*Monster Mash*	London	1962
	Your Gang	*Your Gang*	Mercury	1967

P014 Tim Pearce

	Rezillos	*Mission Accomplished*	Sire	1979

P015 Sandy Pearlman

w. M.Krugman	Blue Oyster Cult	*Blue Oyster Cult*	CBS	1973
w. M.Krugman	Blue Oyster Cult	*Tyranny And Mutation*	CBS	1974
w. M.Krugman	Blue Oyster Cult	*Secret Treaties*	CBS	1974
w. M.Krugman	Blue Oyster Cult	*On Your Feet Or On Your Knees*	CBS	1975
w. M.Krugman	Blue Oyster Cult	*Agents Of Fortune*	CBS	1976
w. M.Krugman	Blue Oyster Cult	*Spectres*	CBS	1977
w. M.Krugman	Blue Oyster Cult	*Some Enchanted Evening*	CBS	1978
	Clash	*Give 'Em Enough Rope*	CBS	1983
w. M.Krugman	Dictators	*Go Girl Crazy*	Epic	1975
w. M.Krugman	Dictators	*Manifest Destiny*	Asylum	1977
w. M.Krugman	Dictators	*Blood Brothers*	Asylum	1978
	Dream Syndicate	*Medicine Show*	IRS	1984

w. M.Krugman	Pavlov's Dog	*Pampered Menial*	CBS	1975
w. M.Krugman	Pavlov's Dog	*At The Sound Of The Bell*	CBS	1976
	Shakin' Street	*Shakin' Street*	CBS	1980

P016 John Peel

w. Tony Reeves	Burnin' Red Ivanhoe	*Burnin' Red Ivanhoe*	Sonet	1970
	Greatest Show On Earth	*The Going's Easy*	Harvest	1970
	The Greatest Show On Earth	*Horizons*	Harvest	1970
	Mike Hart	*Mike Hart Bleeds*	Dandelion	1969
	Robert MacLeod	*Between The Poppy And The Snow*	Charisma	1976
	Medicine Head	*New Bottles, Old Medicine*	Dandelion	1970
	Occasional Word	*The Year Of The Great Leap Sideways*	Dandelion	1969
	Principal Edwards Magic Theatre	*Soundtrack*	Dand/Elek	1969
	Principal Edwards Magic Theatre	*The Asmoto Running Band*	Dand/Elek	1970
	Stackwaddy	*Bugger Off*	Dandelion	1972

P017 Dan Penn

	Box Tops	*The Letter/Neon Rainbow*	State/Bell	1968
	Box Tops	*Cry Like A Baby*	State/Bell	1968
	Box Tops	*Non Stop*	Bell	1968

P018 Richard Perry

	Anders and Poncia	*The Anders And Poncia Album*	WB	1969
	Theodore Bikel	*A New Day*	Elektra	1969
	Bones	*Bones*	Signpost	1972
w. Bob Krasnow	Captain Beefheart	*Safe As Milk*	Pye/KS	1967
	Burton Cummings	*Burton Cummings*	Portrait	1976
	Burton Cummings	*My Own Way To Rock*	Portrait	1977
	Fats Domino	*Fats Is Back*	Reprise	1968
	Fanny	*Fanny*	Reprise	1970
	Fanny	*Charity Ball*	Reprise	1971
	Fanny	*Fanny Hill*	Reprise	1972
	Ella Fitzgerald	*Ella*	Reprise	1969
	Full Swing	*Good Times Are Back*	Planet	1982
	Art Garfunkel	*Breakaway*	CBS	1975
	Holy Mackerel	*Holy Mackerel*	Reprise	1968
	Marva King	*Feels Right*	Planet	1981
	Manhattan Transfer	*Coming Out*	Atlantic	1976
	Bill Medley	*Right Here And Now*	Planet	1982
	Night	*Night*	Planet	1979
	Nilsson	*Nilsson Schmilsson*	RCA	1972
	Nilsson	*Son Of Schmilsson*	RCA	1972
	June Pointer	*Baby Sister*	Planet	1983
	Pointer Sisters	*Energy*	Planet	1978
	Pointer Sisters	*Priority*	Planet	1979
	Pointer Sisters	*Special Things*	Planet	1980
	Pointer Sisters	*Black And White*	Planet	1981
	Pointer Sisters	*So Excited*	Planet	1981

	Pointer Sisters	*Break Out*	Planet	1983
	Diana Ross	*Baby It's Me*	Motown	1977
	Martha Reeves	*Martha Reeves*	MCA	1974
	Sue Saad and The Next	*Sue Saad and The Next*	Planet	1980
	Mark Saffan	*Mark Saffan and*		
		The Keepers	Planet	1981
	Leo Sayer	*Endless Flight*	Chrys/WB	1976
	Leo Sayer	*Thunder In My Heart*	Chry/WB	1977
	Leo Sayer	*Leo Sayer*	Chrys/WB	1978
	Carly Simon	*No Secrets*	Elektra	1973
	Carly Simon	*Hot Cakes*	Elektra	1974
	Carly Simon	*Playing Possum*	Elektra	1975
	Ringo Starr	*Ringo*	Apple	1973
	Ringo Starr	*Goodnight Vienna*	Apple	1974
	Barbra Streisand	*Stoney End*	CBS	1970
	Barbra Streisand	*Barbra Joan Streisand*	CBS	1971
	Barbra Streisand	*Live At The Forum*	CBS	1972
	Tiny Tim	*God Bless Tiny Tim*	Reprise	1968
	Tiny Tim	*Second Album*	Reprise	1968
	Tiny Tim	*For All My Little*		
		Friends	Reprise	1969
	Lon and Derek Van			
	Eaton	*Who Do You Out Do*	A&M	1975
	Andy Williams	*Solitaire*	CBS	1973

P019 Norman Petty

	Baby	*Baby*	Mercury	1975
	Fireballs	*Bottle Of Wine*	Stateside	1968
	Fireballs	*Come On, React!*	Atco	1969

P020 Tom Petty

	Del Shannon	*Drop Down And Get Me*	Edsel/Elek	1981

P021 John Pilla

	Cobble Mountain Band	*Cobble Mountain Band*	Single	1980
w.L.Waronker	Arlo Guthrie	*Washington County*	Reprise	1970
w.L.Waronker	Arlo Guthrie	*Hobo's Lullaby*	Reprise	1972
w.L.Waronker	Arlo Guthrie	*Last Of The Brooklyn*		
		Cowboys	Reprise	1973
w.L.Waronker	Arlo Guthrie	*Arlo Guthrie*	Reprise	1974
	Arlo Guthrie	*Amigo*	Reprise	1976
	Arlo Guthrie	*One Night*	Reprise	1978
	Arlo Guthrie	*Outlasting The Blues*	Reprise	1979
	Arlo Guthrie	*Power Of Love*	WB	1981
	Arlo Guthrie and			
	Pete Seeger	*Together*	Reprise	1975
	Arlo Guthrie and			
	Pete Seeger	*Precious Friends*	WB	1982
	soundtrack	*Woody Guthrie, Hard*		
		Travellin'	Arloco	1984

P022 Konrad "Conny" Plank

	DAF	*Die Klienen Und Die*		
		Bosen	Mute	1980
	DAF	*Alles Ist Gut*	Virgin	1981
	DAF	*Gold Und Liebe*	Virgin	1981
	DAF	*Fur Immer*	Virgin	1982

	Gabi Delgado	*Mistress*	Virgin	1983
	Eurythmics	*In The Garden*	RCA	1981
	Hunters And Collectors	*The Fireman's Curse*	Virgin	1983
	Ideal	*Der Ernst Des Liebens*	WEA	1982
	Killing Joke	*Revelations*	EG	1982
	Killing Joke	*Ha !*	EG	1982
	Kowalski	*German Underground*	Virgin	1982
	La Dusseldorf	*La Dusseldorf*	Radar	1978
	Neu	*Neu '75*	UA	1975
	Time	*Time*	Buk	1975
	Tourists	*The Tourists*	Logo	1979
w. D.Hutchins	Ultravox	*Systems Of Romance*	Island	1978
	Ultravox	*Vienna*	Chrysalis	1980
	Ultravox	*Rage In Eden*	Chrysalis	1981

P023 Tony Platt

	AC/DC	*Flick Of The Switch*	Atlantic	1983
	Krokus	*One Vice At A Time*	Arista	1982
	Motorhead	*Another Perfect Day*	Bron/Mer	1983
	Samson	*Shock Tactics*	RCA	1981
	Trust	*Savage*	Epic	1982

P024 Charles Ira "Chuck" Plotkin

w. G.Prestopino	Laura Allen	*Laura Allen*	Elektra	1978
	Karen Alexander	*Isn't It Always Love*	Asylum	1975
	Harry Chapin	*Living Room Suite*	Elektra	1978
	Bob Dylan	*Shot Of Love*	CBS	1981
	Steve Ferguson	*Steve Ferguson*	Asylum	1973
	Andrew Gold	*Andrew Gold*	Asylum	1976
	John Hall	*John Hall*	Asylum	1978
	Jelly	*A True Story*	Asylum	1979
	Bette Midler	*No Frills*	Atlantic	1983
	Kai Olsson	*Once In A While*	EMI	1975
	Orleans	*Let There Be Music*	Asylum	1975
	Orleans	*Waking And Dreaming*	Asylum	1976
	Shakers	*Yankee Reggae*	Asylum	1976
w. Jon Landau & Little Steven	Bruce Springsteen	*Born In The USA*	CBS	1984
	Rod Taylor	*Rod Taylor*	Asylum	1973
	(Taylor would later reappear under the name Roderick Falconer.)			
	Tommy Tutone	*Tommy Tutone 2 (side 1)*	*1981*	
	Dwight Twilley	*Scuba Diver (2 tracks)*	EMI-Amer	1982
	Wendy Waldman	*Love Has Got Me*	WB	1973
	Wendy Waldman	*Gypsy Sympnohy*	WB	1974

P025 Richard Podolor

	Carmen Appice	*Carmine Appice*	WEA/Pasha	1981
	Black Oak Arkansas	*X-Rated*	MCA	1975
	Black Oak Arkansas	*Ain't Life Grand*	Atco	1975
	Blues Image	*Open*	Atco	1970
	Blues Image	*Red White and Blues Image*	Atco	1970
	Alice Cooper	*Special Forces*	WB	1981
	Dillards	*Roots And Branches*	Anthem	1972
	Glass Family	*Electric Band*	WB	1970

	Head East	*Gettin' Lucky*	A&M	1977
	Iron Butterfly	*Live*	Atlantic	1970
	Iron Butterfly	*Metamorphosis*	Atlantic	1971
	Jellyroll	*Jellyroll*	MCA	1970
	John Kay	*My Sporting Life*	ABC/Dunh	1973
	John Kay and Steppenwolf	*Wolftracks*	Allegiance	1983
	Rowan Brothers	*The Rowans*	Asylum	1975
	Phil Seymour	*Phil Seymour*	Boardwalk	1980
	Souther Hillman Furay Band	*The Souther Hillman Furay Band*	Asylum	1974
	S.S. Fools	*S.S. Fools*	CBS	1976
	Three Dog Night	*Naturally*	Dunhill	1970
	Three Dog Night	*Harmony*	Dunhill	1971
	Three Dog Night	*Captured Live At The Forum*	State/Dunh	1970
	Three Dog Night	*Seven Separate Fools*	Dunhill	1972
	Three Dog Night	*Cyan*	Probe/Dunh	1973
	Three Dog Night	*It's A Jungle*	Passport	1983
	20/20	*Look Out*	Portrait	1981

P026 Ray Pohlman

	Association	*Live*	WB	1970
	Association	*Stop Your Motor*	WB	1971
	Ian Whitcomb	*You*	Ember	1973

P027 Vini Poncia

	Aztec Two-Step	*Adjoining Suites*	RCA	1977
	Breaks	*The Breaks*	RCA	1983
	Lynda Carter	*Lynda Carter*	Epic	1978
	Peter Criss	*Peter Criss*	Casabl	1978
	Gino Cunico	*Gino Cunico*	KS	1975
	Gino Cunico	*Gino Cunico*	Arista	1976
	Fanny	*Rock And Roll Survivors*	Casabl	1974
	Faragher Brothers	*Faragher Brothers*	ABC	1976
	Faragher Brothers	*Open Your Eyes*	Polydor	1978
	Ellen Foley	*Another Breath*	Cleveland	1983
	Fools	*Heavy Mental*	EMI-Amer	1981
w. Pete Anders	Innocence	*The Innocence*	KS	1968
	Kiss	*Dynasty*	Casab	1979
	Kiss	*Unmasked*	Mercury	1980
	Melissa Manchester	*Home To Myself*	Arista	1974
	Melissa Manchester	*Bright Eyes*	Arista	1974
	Melissa Manchester	*Melissa*	Arista	1975
	Melissa Manchester	*Better Days And Happy Ending*	Arista	1977
	Melissa Manchester	*Help Is On The Way*	Arista	1977
	Melissa Manchester	*Singin'*	Arista	1977
	David Pomeranz	*It's In Every One Of Us*	Arista	1976
	Scandal	*Scandal*	CBS	1982
	Ringo Starr	*Bad Boy*	Poly/Port	1978
	Mary Travers	*Mary Travers*	Chrys	1978
	Tycoon	*Turn Out The Lights*	Arista	1981

P028 John Porter
w. D.Hentschel
& J.Gilbert

Charlie Ainley	Too Much Is Not Enough	Nemperor	1978
w. John Punter	Bryan Ferry	These Foolish Things	Polydor	1973
Dana Gillespie	Ain't Gonna Play No Second Fiddle	RCA	1974
Bryn Haworth	Let The Days Go By	Island	1974
The Smiths	The Smiths	R.T./Sire	1984

P029 Robbie Porter

Air Supply	Lost In Love	Arista	1980
Daddy Cool	Daddy Who?	Reprise	1971
Daddy Cool	Teenage Heaven	Reprise	1972
Daddy Cool	Live	Wizard	1980

P030 Mike Post

Peter Allen	I Could Have Been A Sailor (5 tracks)	A&M	1979
Bobby Doyle	Nine Songs	Bell	1973
Dolly Parton	9 to 5 and Other Odd Jobs	RCA	1981
Herb Pedersen	Southwest	CBS	1976
Herb Pedersen	Sandman	CBS	1977
Mike Post	Railhead Overture	MGM	1975
Mason Williams	Phonograph Record	WB	1969
w. Herb Pedersen Tom Wopat	Tom Wopat	CBS	1983

(Tom Wopat is one of the co-stars in "The Dukes Of Hazard".)

P031 Bob Potter

Grease Band	Amazing Grease	Good Ear	1975
Carol Grimes	Warm Blood	Virgin	1974
Paul Kossof	Back Street Crawler	Island	1973
Snafu	All Funked Up	Capitol	1975
Uncle Dog	Old Hat	Signpost	1972

P032 Brian Potter (see also: Lambert and Potter)

w. Steve Barri	Bobby King	Love In The Fire	Motown	1984

P033 Andrew Powell

Kate Bush	The Kick Inside	EMI	1978
Kate Bush	Lionheart	EMI	1978
Chris De Burgh	Crusader	A&M	1979

P034 Bill Price

Doll By Doll	Remember	Automatic	1979
Racing Cars	Downtown Tonight	Chrysalis	1976
w. Chris Thomas Sex Pistols	Never Mind The Bollocks	Virgin/WB	1977

P035 Jim Price

David Bromberg	Reckless Abandon	Fantasy	1978
Joe Cocker	I Can Stand A Little Rain	Cube/A&M	1974
Joe Cocker	Jamaica Say You Will	Cube/A&M	1975
KGB	KGB	MCA	1976
Jennifer Warnes	Jennifer Warnes	Arista	1977

P036 Bobby Pridden

Eric Clapton	*Rainbow Concert*	RSO	1973
Steve Gibbons Band	*Street Parade*	RCA	1981
Streetwalkers	*Live*	Vertigo	1977

P037 Spencer Proffer

	Randy Bishop	*Dangerous Infatuation*	Pasha	1982
	Allan Clarke	*I've Got Time*	EMI/Asy	1976
	Allan Clarke	*I Wasn't Born Yesterday*	Aura	1978
	Allan Clarke	*The Only One*	Aura	1980
	Allan Clarke	*Legendary Heroes*	Elektra	1980
	DNA	*Party Tested*	Pasha/Bdwk	1983
	Scott English	*Scott English*	EMI	1978
	Kick Axe	*Vices*	Pasha	1984
	Dave Lambert	*Framed*	Polydor	1979
	Peter Noone	*One Of The Glory Boys*	CBS	1982
	Devin Payne	*Excuse Me*	Casab	1980
	Quiet Riot	*Mental Health*	Pasha	1983
	Billy Thorpe	*Children Of The Sun*	Polydor	1979
	Billy Thorpe	*21st Century Man*	Elektra	1980
	Billy Thorpe	*Stimulation*	Pasha	1981
w. Denny Diante	Tina Turner	*Acid Queen*	UA	1975
	Vanilla Fudge	*Mystery*	Atco	1984
	soundtrack	*Up The Creek*	Pasha	1984

P038 Punch (a.k.a. Punch Andrews)

Barooga Bandit	*Come Softly*	Capitol	1979
Brownsville Station	*Brownsville Station*	WB	1970
Bob Seger	*Mongrel*	Capitol	1969
Bob Seger	*Noah*	Capitol	1969
Bob Seger	*Ramblin' Gamblin' Man*	Capitol	1970
Bob Seger	*Brand New Morning*	Capitol	1971
Bob Seger	*Smokin O.P.'s*	Palladium	1972
Bob Seger	*Back In '72*	Palladium	1973
Bob Seger	*Seven*	Reprise	1974
Bob Seger	*Beautiful Loser*	Capitol	1975
Bob Seger	*Live*	Capitol	1976
Bob Seger	*Night Moves (4 tracks)*	Capitol	1976
Bob Seger	*Stranger In Town (4 tracks only)*	Capitol	1978
Bob Seger	*Nine Tonight*	Capitol	1981

(all Seger albums co-produced with Bob Seger.)

PO39 John Punter

	Johnny Cougar	*A Biography*	Riva	1978
	Doctors Of Madness	*Late Night Movies*	Polydor	1976
w. John Porter	Bryan Ferry	*These Foolish Things*	Poly/Atl	1973
	Bryan Ferry	*Another Time, Another Place*	Poly/Atl	1974
	Gloria Mundi	*The Word Is Out*	RCA	1979
	Japan	*Quiet Life*	Ariola	1979
	Japan	*Gentlemen Take Polaroids*	Virgin	1980
	Japan	*Oil On Canvas*	Virgin	1983
	Marseille	*Marseille*	Vert/RCA	1977

	Mr.Big	*Sweet Silence*	EMI	1975
	Nazareth	*Snazz*	Nems/A&M	1981
	Nazareth	*2 x 5*	Nems	1982
	Osibisa	*Heads*	MCA	1972
	Re-Flex	*The Politics Of Dancing*	EMI/Cap	1983
	Roxy Music	*Country Life*	Isl/Atco	1974
	SAHB (without Alex)	*Fourplay*	Mountain	1977
	Sad Cafe	*Fanx Ta-ra*	RCA	1977
	Sad Cafe	*Misplaced Ideals*	RCA/A&M	1978
w. Jim Lea	Slade	*The Amazing Kamikaze Syndrome*	RCA/CBS	1983

(Released in the USA as "Keep Your Hands Off My Power Supply".)

w. Nick Tauber	Specimen	*Batastrophe*	Sire	1984
	Judy Tzuke	*Stay With Me 'Til Dawn*	Rocket	1979
	Judy Tzuke	*Welcome To The Cruise*	Rocket	1979
w. Mim Scala	Warsaw Pakt	*Needle Time*	Island	1977
	John Wetton	*Caught In The Act*	EG	1980

P040 Bernard Purdie

	Felix Pappalardi	*Don't Worry, Ma*	A&M	1979

P041 Jimmy Pursey

	Angelic Upstarts	*Teenage Warning*	WEA	1979
w. Peter Wilson	Cockney Rejects	*Greatest Hits Vol. 1*	EMI	1980

P042 Norbert Putnam

	Addrisi Brothers	*We've Got To Get It On Again*	CBS	1972
	Addrisi Brothers	*Addrisi Brothers*	Buddah	1977
	Eric Andersen	*Blue River*	CBS	1972
	Joan Baez	*Come From The Shadows*	A&M	1972
	Joan Baez	*Where Are You Now My Son*	A&M	1973
	Brewer and Shipley	*Welcome To Riddle Bridge*	Capitol	1975
	Jimmy Buffett	*Changes In Lattitudes, Changes In Attitudes*	ABC	1977
	Jimmy Buffett	*Son Of A Son Of A Sailor*	ABC	1978
	Jimmy Buffett	*You Had To Be There*	MCA	1978
	Jimmy Buffett	*Volcano*	MCA	1979
	Jimmy Buffett	*Coconut Telegraph*	MCA	1980
	Jimmy Buffett	*Somewhere Over China*	MCA	1981
	David Buskin	*David Buskin*	CBS	1972
	Carol Chase	*The Chase Is On*	Casab	1980
	Donovan	*7-Tease*	Epic	1974
	Flying Burritos	*Flying Again*	CBS	1975
	Dan Fogelberg	*Home Free*	CBS	1972
	Dan Fogelberg	*Netherlands*	Epic	1977
w. Marty Lewis	Dan Fogelberg	*Phoenix*	Epic	1979
	Tom Ghent	*Yankee's Rebel Son*	MCA	1972
w. Kris Kristofferson	Steve Goodman	*Steve Goodman*	Buddah	1971
	Jimmy Hall	*Touch You*	Epic	1980
	Richard Kerr	*Somewhere In The Night*	CBS	1976

	Kris Kristofferson	*To The Bone*	Monument	1981
w.Glen Spreen	Ian Matthews	*Go For Broke*	CBS	1976
	Mickey Newbury	*After All These Years*	Mercury	1981
	New Riders of The Purple Sage	*Panama Red*	CBS	1973
	Nitty Gritty Dirt Band	*Let's Go*	Liberty	1983
	Pousette-Dart Band	*Pousette-Dart Band*	Cap	1976
	Pousette-Dart Band	*Amnesia*	Capitol	1977
	Pousette-Dart Band	*Never Enough*	Capitol	1979
w. Joan Baez	Jerry Shurtleff	*State Farm*	A&M	1972
	Splinter	*Two Man Band*	Dark Horse	1977
	Buffy St.Marie	*Moonshot*	Vanguard	1974
	Buffy St.Marie	*Native North American Child (3 tracks)*	Vanguard	1974
	Buffy St.Marie	*Buffy*	Vanguard	1974
	Buffy St.Marie	*Changing Woman*	MCA	1975
w. Daniel Moore	Toby Beau	*More Than A Love Song*	RCA	1979
	Jesse Winchester	*A Touch On The Rainy Side*	Bearsv	1978

Q001 Lance Quinn (See also Tony Bongiovi for co-production credits.)

w.Meco Monardo	soundtrack	*An American Werewolf In London*	Casab	1981
	Bon Jovi	*Bon Jovi*	Mercury	1984
	Cindy Bullens	*Desire Wire*	UA	1978
	Carlene Carter	*Two Sidoo To Every Woman*	WB	1979
	Elektrics	*State Of Shock*	Capitol	1981
	Lita Ford	*Dancin' On The Edge*	Vertigo	1984
	Robert Gordon	*Are You Gonna Be The One*	RCA	1981
	Johnny's Dance Band	*Love Wounds,Flesh Wounds*	Windsong	1978
	Meco	*Music From The Empire Strikes Back*	RCA	1980
	Meco	*Star Wars Christmas Album*	RSO	1980
	Meco	*Swingtime's Greatest Hits*	Arista	1982
	Meco	*Pop Goes To The Movies*	Arista	1982
	Orphan	*Lonely At Night*	Portrait	1983
	Jorge Santana	*Jorge Santana*	Tomato	1978
	Sylvain Sylvain	*Sylvain Sylvain*	RCA	1979
	Talking Heads	*77*	Sire	1977
w. Sonny Lester	Joe Thomas	*Make Your Move*	TK	1979
	Tuff Darts	*Tuff Darts*	Sire	1978

R001 Jerry Ragovoy

	Peggy Blue	*I Got Love*	MCA	1980
	Butterfield Blues Band	*Keep On Movin'*	Elektra	1969
	Lorraine Ellison	*Stay With Me*	WB	1969
	Farquhar	*Farquhar*	Elektra	1971
	Major Harris	*How Do You Take Your Love*	RCA	1978

	Bonnie Raitt	*Streetlights*	WB	1974
	Howard Tate	*Get It While You Can*	MGM	1967
	Dionne Warwicke	*Then Came You*	WB	1975

R002 Mick Ralphs

	Midnight Flyer	*Midnight Flyer*	Swansong	1981
	(Group featured Maggie Bell on vocals.)			
	Wildlife	*Wildlife*	Swansong	1983

R003 Phil Ramone

	Brigati	*Lost In The Wilderness*	Elektra	1976
	Chicago	*Hot Streets*	CBS	1978
	Chicago	*Street Player*	CBS	1979
	Get Wet	*Get Wet*	Boardwalk	1981
	Heatwave	*Hot Property*	Epic	1979
	Billy Joel	*The Stranger*	CBS	1977
	Billy Joel	*52nd Street*	CBS	1978
	Billy Joel	*Glass Houses*	CBS	1980
	Billy Joel	*Songs In The Attic*	CBS	1981
	Billy Joel	*The Nylon Curtain*	CBS	1982
	Billy Joel	*An Innocent Man*	CBS	1983
	Michael Johnson	*There Is A Breeze*	Atco	1973
	Quincy Jones	*Smackwater Jack*	A&M	1971
w. Peter Yarrow	Lazarus	*Lazarus*	Bearsv	1971
w. Bob James	Kenny Loggins	*Celebrate Me Home*	CBS	1977
	Groucho Marx	*An Evening With Groucho Marx*	A&M	1972
	Stephanie Mills	*Merciless*	Casab	1983
	Original Cast album	*Chicago*	Arista	1975
	Original Cast album	*The Little Shop Of Horrors*	Geffen	1983
	soundtrack	*Reds*	CBS	1981
	David Sanborn	*Sanborn*	WB	1976
	Michael Sembello	*Bossa Nova Hotel*	WB	1983
w. Roy Halee	Simon and Garfunkel	*Reunion In Central Park*	Geffen	1982
	Paul Simon	*There Goes Rhymin' Simon (4 tracks)*	CBS	1973
	Paul Simon	*One Trick Pony*	WB	1980
	Phoebe Snow	*Second Childhood*	CBS	1976
	Phoebe Snow	*Never Letting Go*	CBS	1977
w. Barry Beckett	Phoebe Snow	*Against The Grain*	CBS	1978
	Barbra Streisand and Kris Kristofferson	*A Star Is Born*	CBS	1976
	Libby Titus	*Libby Titus*	CBS	1977
w. John Simon	soundtrack	*You Are What You Eat*	CBS	1968

R004 Elliott Randall

	J.Jocko	*That's The Song*	KS	1975
	(Jocko was one of the singers with Sha Na Na.)			

R005 Denny Randell

	Tim Buckley	*Sefronia*	DiscReet	1974
	Iron Butterfly	*Scorchin' Beauty*	MCA	1975
	Ruben and The Jets	*Con Safos*	Mercury	1973

R006 Genya Ravan

Dead Boys	*Young, Loud and Snotty*	Sire	1977
Ronnie Spector	*Siren*	Polish	1980

R007 Chris Rea

Alibi	*Friends*	Polydor	1980

R008 Malcolm Rebennack (a.k.a. Dr. John)

Van Morrison	*Period Of Transition*	WB	1977

R009 Lou Reed

Nelson Slater	*Wild Angel*	RCA	1976

R010 Jay Reich, Jnr

Roy Buchanan	*That's What I'm Here For*	Polydor	1973
Roy Buchanan	*Livestock*	Polydor	1974

R011 Lou Reizner

Ancient Grease	*Women And Children First*	Mercury	1968
Dick Campbell	*Sings Where It's At*	Mercury	1967
Group Therapy	*You're In Need Of Group Therapy*	Philips	1969
Buzzy Linhart	*Buzzy*	Philips	1969
Rod Stewart	*An Old Raincoat Will Never Let You Down*	Vert/Mer	1969
Rod Stewart	*Gasoline Alley*	Vert/Mer	1970
various artists	*All This And World War 2*	Riva	1976

R012 Keith Relf

Medicine Head	*Heavy On The Drum*	Dandelion	1971

R013 Joe Renzetti

Jesse Cutler	*Entertainment For All*	UA	1978
Steve Fromholz	*Frolicking In The Myth*	Capitol	1977
Max Merritt	*Out Of The Blue*	Arista	1976
Simon Stokes	*The Buzzard Of Love*	UA	1977

R014 Bernard Rhodes

Vic Goddard	*What's The Matter Boy*	MCA	1980

R015 Emitt Rhodes

Bim	*Thistles*	Elektra	1976

R016 Cliff Richard

Garth Hewitt	*Did He Jump Or Was He Pushed*	Patch	1979

R017 Keith Richard

Aranbee Symphony Orchestra	*Today's Pop Symphony*	Immediate	1966
Max Romeo	*Holding Out My Love To You*	Shanachie	1981

(see also Glimmer Twins.)

R018 Deke Richards

Black Oak Arkansas	*Race With The Devil*	Capricorn	1977
Black Oak Arkansas	*I'd Rather Be Sailing*	Capricorn	1978
Bonnie Bramlett	*Memories*	Capricorn	1978
Duke and The Drivers	*Rollin' On*	ABC	1976
Jackie Lomax	*Livin' For Lovin'*	Capitol	1976

R019 Ron Richards

Hollies	*In The Hollies Style*	Parlophone	1964
Hollies	*Evolution*	Parlophone	1967
Hollies	*The Hollies Sing Dylan*	Parlophone	1969
Hollies	*Another Night*	Polydor	1974
Hollies	*The Hollies*	Polydor	1974
Hollies	*531.7704*	Polydor	1979
Tom Paxton	*Saturday Night*	MAM	1976
Prelude	*Back Into The Night*	Pye	1976

R020 Karl Richardson and Albhy Galuten

	Bee Gees	*Children Of The World*	RSO	1976
	Bee Gees	*Here At Last Live*	RSO	1977
	Bee Gees	*Spirits Having Flown*	RSO	1979
	Bee Gees	*Living Eyes*	RSO	1981
	Terri De Sario	*Pleasure Train*	Casab	1978
	Frannie Gold	*Frannie Gold*	Portrait	1979
	Network	*Network*	Epic	1977
w. Barry Gibb	Kenny Rogers	*Eyes That See In The Dark*	RCA	1983
	soundtrack	*Staying Alive*	RSO	1983
w. Barry Gibb	Barbra Streisand	*Guilty*	CBS	1980
	Dionne Warwicke	*Heartbreaker*	Arista	1982

R021 Jack Richardson

w. S.Wittmark	Badfinger	*Say No More*	Radio	1981
	Richard T. Bear	*Red Hot And Blue*	RCA	1979
	Richard T. Bear	*Bear*	RCA	1979
	Joe Beck	*Watch The Time*	Polydor	1977
	Dickey Betts	*Atlanta's Burning Down*	Arista	1978
	Brecker Brothers	*Don't Stop The Music*	Arista	1977
	David Clayton-Thomas	*Clayton*	ABC	1978
	Alice Cooper	*Muscle Of Love*	WB	1973
	Papa John Creach	*The Cat And The Fiddle*	DJM	1977
	Guess Who	*Rockin'*	RCA	1972
	Guess Who	*Live At The Paramount*	RCA	1972
	Guess Who	*Flavours*	RCA	1974
	Guess Who	*Power In The Music*	RCA	1975
	Bob McBride	*Here To Sing*	MCA	1978
	Manowar	*Hail To England*	MFN	1984
	Moonlighters	*The Moonlighters*	Amherst	1977
	(former members of The Commander Cody Band.)			
	Moxy	*Under The Light*	Polydor	1978
	Noah	*Noah*	RCA	1970
w. Jim Mason	Poco	*A Good Feelin' To Know*	Epic	1972
	Poco	*Crazy Eyes*	Epic	1973
	Poco	*Seven*	Epic	1974

Rovers	*Pain In My Past*	Cleveland	1982
Bob Seger	*Night Moves (1 track)*	Capitol	1976
Starz	*Colisseum Rock*	Capitol	1978
Stormin' Norman and Suzy	*Ocean Of Love*	Polydor	1978
Malcolm Tomlinson	*Comin' Outta Nowhere*	A&M	1977
Tornader	*Hit It Again*	Polydor	1976
Tufano and Giammarese	*Other Side*	Ode	1976
Max Webster	*Universal Juveniles*	Mercury	1980
Wilderness Road	*Wilderness Road*	CBS	1972
Wilderness Road	*Sold For The Prevention Of Disease Only*	WB	1973

R022 Neil Richmond

Bishops	*The Bishops Live*	Chiswick	1978
Ken Elliott	*Body Music*	RCA	1979
John Spencer's Louts	*The Last LP*	B.Banquet	1978

R023 Paul Riley
w. Ron Nevison

Chilli Willi and The Red Hot Peppers	*Bongos Over Balham*	B&C	1974
Inner City Unit	*Pass Out*	Riddle	1980

R024 Artie Ripp

Burton and Cunico	*Strive, Seek, Find*	Paramount	1971
Critters	*Younger Girl*	Kapp	1966
Billy Joel	*Coldspring Harbour*	CBS	1971
Kyle	*Times That Try A Man's Soul*	Paramount	1970
w. Billy James Penny Nichols	*Penny's Arcade*	Buddah	1969
Sha Na Na	*Rock And Roll Is Here To Stay*	KS	1969

R025 Johnny Rivers

James Hendricks	*Songs Of James Hendricks*	Liberty	1969
Bob Ray	*Initiation Of A Mystic*	Soul City	1969

(Johnny Rivers has produced at least 10 of his own albums.)

R026 Travis Rivers

Mother Earth	*Satisfied*	Mercury	1970
Tracey Nelson	*Poor Man's Paradise*	Epic	1970
Tracey Nelson	*Homemade Songs*	F.Fish	1980
Tracey Nelson	*Come See About Me*	F.Fish	1980

R027 Paul Rodgers

Tommy Morrison	*Place Your Bets*	Real	1979

R028 Bruce Robb

Steve Cropper	*Playin' My Thang*	MCA	1981
Steve Cropper	*Night After Night*	MCA	1982
Burton Cummings	*Sweet Sweet*	Alfa	1981
w. Jerry Wexler Donovan	*Lady Of The Stars*	Allegiance	1983

189

R029 Ira Robbins

various artists	The Best Of America Underground	ROIR	1983

R030 Sandy Roberton

	Alan Ashworth-Jones	Al Jones	Parlophone	1969
w. A.Hutchings	Shirley Collins	No Roses	Mooncrest	1971
	Decameron	Say Hello To The Band	Vertigo	1973
	Everyone	Everyone (featuring Andy Roberts)	B&C	1971
	Hard Meat	Through A Window	WB	1970
	Legend	Legend	Bell	1969
	Liverpool Scene	St. Adrian Co, Broadway And Third	RCA	1970
w. Ian Matthews	Longdancer	If It Was So Simple	Rocket	1973
	John Martyn	Well Kept Secret	WB/Duke	1982
	Ian Matthews	Journeys From Gospel Oak	Mooncrest	1974
	Ian Matthews	Stealin' Home	Rockburgh	1978
	Ian Matthews	Siamese Friends	Rockburgh	1979
	Ian Matthews	Spot Of Interference	Rockburgh	1980
	Plainsong	In Search Of Amelia Earhart	Elektra	1972
	Andy Roberts	Homegrown	RCA	1970
	Andy Roberts	Urban Cowboy	Elektra	1973
	Andy Roberts	Andy Roberts And The Great Stampede	Elektra	1973
	Andy Roberts	Nina And The Dream Tree	Polydor	1977
	Spriguns	Time Will Pass	Decca	1977
	Steeleye Span	Please To See The King	B&C/B.Tree	1971
	Steeleye Span	Hark The Village Wait	Mooncrest	1970
	Steeleye Span	Ten Man Mop Or Mr. Reservoir Butler Rides Again	Mooncrest	1971
	Frank White	Nice To Be On Your Show	Fantasy	1973
	Gay and Terry Woods	The Time Is Right	Polydor	1976
	Gay and Terry Woods	Renowned	Polydor	1976
	Gay and Terry Woods	Tender Hooks	Rockburgh	1978

R031 Robbie Robertson

	The Band	The Last Waltz	WB	1978
w. Alex North	soundtrack	Carney	WB	1980
	Neil Diamond	Beautiful Noise	CBS	1976
	Neil Diamond	Love At The Greek	CBS	1977
w. Rob Fraboni	Bob Dylan	Planet Waves	Asylum	1974
	soundtrack	King Of Comedy	WB	1982
	Hirth Martinez	Hirth From Earth	WB	1976
	Jesse Winchester	Jesse Winchester	Ampex	1971

R032 Dave Robinson

	Bees Make Honey	Music Every Night	EMI	1973
	Brinsley Schwarz	Brinsley Schwarz	UA	1970
	Brinsley Schwarz	Despite It All	UA	1970

	Brinsley Schwarz	*Silver Pistol*	UA	1972
	Brinsley Schwarz	*Nervous On The Road*	UA	1972
	Clover	*Unavailable*	Vertigo	1977
	(listed as "executive producer".)			
	Ernie Graham	*Ernie Graham*	Liberty	1971
	Help Yourself	*Help Yourself*	Liberty	1971
	Frankie Miller	*Once In A Blue Moon*	Chrysalis	1972

R033 Richard Robinson

	Flamin' Groovies	*Flamingo*	KS	1970
	Flamin' Groovies	*Teenage Head*	KS	1971
	Flamin' Groovies	*Still Shakin'*	Buddah	1976
	David Johansen	*David Johansen*	Blue Sky	1978
	Lou Reed	*Lou Reed*	RCA	1972
	Lou Reed	*Street Hassle*	RCA	1978
w. Doc Cavalier	Yankees	*The Yankees*	Big Sound	1978

R034 Nile Rodgers

w. David Bowie	David Bowie	*Let's Dance*	EMI-Amer	1983
	Michael Gregory	*Station X*	Island	1983
	Inxs	*The Swing (1 track)*	Atco	1984
	Nile Rodgers	*Land Of The Good Groove*	Mirage	1983
	Southside Johnny	*Trash It Up*	Mirage	1983

R035 Nile Rodgers and Bernard Edwards

	Chic	*Chic*	Atlantic	1978
	Chic	*C'est Chic*	Atlantic	1978
	Chic	*Risque*	Atlantic	1979
	Chic	*Real People*	Atlantic	1980
	Chic	*Take It Off*	Atlantic	1981
	Chic	*Tongue In Chic*	Atlantic	1982
	Chic	*Believer*	Atlantic	1983
	Debby Harry	*Koo-Koo*	Chrysalis	1981
	Norma Jean	*Norma Jean*	Bearsv	1978
	Diana Ross	*Diana*	Motown	1980
	Shiela B and Devotion	*Sheila B and Devotion*	Carrere	1980
	Sister Sledge	*We Are Family*	Cotillion	1979
	Sister Sledge	*Love Somebody Today*	Cotillion	1980
	soundtrack	*Soup For One*	WEA/Mirage	1982

R036 Kenny Rogers

	Alex Harvey	*Alex Harvey*	Capitol	1973

R037 Lelan Rogers

	Billy Cox	*Nitro Function*	Pye	1971
	Lightnin' Hopkins	*Free Form Patterns*	IA	1968
	Lost And Found	*Everybody's Here*	IA	1967
	Red Crayola	*Parable Of The Arable Land*	IA	1967
	13th Floor Elevators	*The Pyschedelic Sounds Of The 13th Floor Elevators*	IA	1966
	13th Floor Elevators	*Easter Everywhere*	IA	1968

R038 Mick Ronson

	Dead Fingers Talk	*Storm The Reality Studios*	Pye	1978
w. David Bowie	Dana Gillespie	*Weren't Born A Man (2 tracks only)*	RCA	1973
	Ian Hunter	*Ian Hunter*	CBS	1975
	Ian Hunter	*You're Never Alone With A Schizophrenic*	Chrysalis	1979
	Ian Hunter	*Welcome To The Club*	Chrysalis	1980
w. Mick Jones	Ian Hunter	*Short Back And Sides*	Chrysalis	1981
	Iron City Houserockers	*Get Out Alive*	MCA	1980
	David Johansen	*In Style*	Blue Sky	1979
	Los Illegals	*Internal Exile*	A&M	1983
	Roger McGuinn	*Cardiff Rose*	CBS	1976
	Payolas	*No Stranger To Danger*	A&M	1982
	Payolas	*Hammer On A Drum*	A&M	1983
w. David Bowie	Lou Reed	*Transformer*	RCA	1972
	Rich Kids	*Ghosts Of Princes In Towers*	EMI	1978
	Mick Ronson	*Slaughter On 10th Avenue*	RCA	1974
	Mick Ronson	*Play, Don't Worry*	RCA	1974
	Bob Sargeant	*First Starring Role (3 tracks only.)*	RCA	1974

R039 Brian Ross

	Sean Bonniwell	*The Bonniwell Music Machine*	WB	1968
	The Music Machine	*Talk, Talk*	Orig. Sound	1966

R040 Errol Ross

	Selecter	*Too Much Pressure*	Two Tone	1980

R041 Francis Rossi

	Flying Squad	*Flying Squad*	Epic	1978
	Mickey Jupp	*Shampoo, Haircut and Shave*	A&M	1983

R042 Paul A. Rothchild

	Ars Nova	*Ars Nova*	Elektra	1968
w. Jac Holzman	Tim Buckley	*Tim Buckley*	Elektra	1966
w. Mark Abramson	Paul Butterfield Blues Band	*The Paul Butterfield Blues Band*	Elektra	1965
w. Mark Abramson	Paul Butterfield Blues Band	*East West*	Elektra	1966
	Butterfield Blues Band	*Sometimes I Just Feel Like Smilin'*	Elektra	1971
w. Peter Siegel	Charles River Valley Boys	*Beatle Country*	Elektra	1966
	Clear Light	*Clear Light*	Elektra	1967
	Cottonwood South	*Cottonwood South*	CBS	1974
	Doors	*The Doors*	Elektra	1967
	Doors	*Strange Days*	Elektra	1967

	Doors	*Waiting For The Sun*	Elektra	1968
	Doors	*Soft Parade*	Elektra	1969
	Doors	*Morrison Hotel*	Elektra	1970
	Doors	*Absolutely Live*	Elektra	1970
	Doors	*Alive She Cried*	Elektra	1983
	Everly Brothers	*Stories We Could Tell*	RCA	1972
	Fast Fontaine	*Fast Fontaine*	EMI-Amer	1981
	Funky Kings	*The Funky Kings*	Arista	1976
	Goodthunder	*Goodthunder*	Elektra	1972
	Joel Scott Hill/ Johnny Barbata and Chris Ethridge	*L.A. Getaway*	Atco	1971
	Freddie Hubbard	*High Energy*	CBS	1974
	Janis Joplin	*Pearl*	CBS	1971
	Janis Joplin	*Janis soundtrack*	CBS	1972
w. Jac Holzman	Koerner, Ray and Glover	*The Return Of Koerner, Ray And Glover*	Elektra	1965
	Love	*Da Capo*	Elektra	1967
	Bette Midler	*The Rose*	Atlantic	1979
	Elliott Murphy	*Lost Generation*	RCA	1975
	Fred Neil	*Bleeker and MacDougal*	Elektra	1965
	Fred Neil	*A Little Bit Of Rain*	Elektra	1965
	Steve Noonan	*Steve Noonan*	Elektra	1968
	Phil Ochs	*All The News That's Fit To Sing*	Elektra	1964
	Phil Ochs	*I Ain't Marching Anymore*	Elektra	1965
	Outlaws	*The Outlaws*	Arista	1975
	Outlaws	*Lady In Waiting*	Arista	1976
	Bonnie Raitt	*Home Plate*	WB	1975
	Bonnie Raitt	*Sweet Forgiveness*	WB	1977
	Tom Rush	*Got A Mind To Ramble*	Prestige	1963
	Tom Rush	*Tom Rush*	Elektra	1965
	John Sebastian	*John B. Sebastian*	Reprise	1970
	John Sebastian	*The Four Of Us*	Reprise	1971
	John Sebastian	*Cheapo Cheapo Productions Presents Real Live John Sebastian*	Reprise	1971
w. Peter Siegel	Mark Spoelstra	*State Of Mind*	Elektra	1966
	Valdy	*See How The Years Have Gone By*	A&M	1974

R043 Steve Rowland

	Babe Ruth	*Babe Ruth*	Harvest	1975
	Babe Ruth	*Stealin' Home*	Capitol	1975
	Babe Ruth	*Kid's Stuff*	Capitol	1976
	Capability Brown	*From Scratch*	Charisma	1972
	Capability Brown	*Liar (4 tracks)*	Charisma	1976
	Darien Spirit	*Elegy To Marilyn*	Charisma	1973
	Family Dogg	*The View From Rowland's Head*	Buddah	1972
	Herd	*Paradise Lost*	Fontana	1968
	Snafu	*Situation Normal*	WWA	1974

R044 David Rubinson and friends

	soundtrack	*Apocalypse Now*	Elektra	1979

Aum	Resurrection	Fillmore	1969
Gato Barbieri	Tropico	A&M	1978
Elvin Bishop Group	The Elvin Bishop Group	Fillmore	1969
Elvin Bishop Group	Feel It	Fillmore	1970
Jack Burns and Avery Schreiber	In One Head And Out The Other	CBS	1970
Chick Corea and Herbie Hancock	Chick Corea and Herbie Hancock	Polydor	1979
Terry Garthwaite	Terry	Arista	1975
Herbie Hancock	Man-Child	CBS	1975
Herbie Hancock	Secrets	CBS	1976
Herbie Hancock	Sunlight	CBS	1978
Herbie Hancock	An Evening With Herbie Hancock and Chick Corea		
Herbie Hancock	Feets Don't Fail Me Now	CBS	1979
Herbie Hancock	Monster	CBS	1980
Herbie Hancock	Mr. Hands	CBS	1980
Herbie Hancock	Magic Windows	CBS	1981
Herbie Hancock	Quartet	CBS	1982
Randy Hansen	Randy Hansen	Capitol	1980
(Randy Hansen is the famous Jimi Hendirix clone.)			
Heartsfield	Foolish Pleasures	Mercury	1975
Heartsfield	Collectors Item	CBS	1977
Hoodoo Rhythm Devils	The Barbecue Of De Ville	B.Thumb	1972
Hoodoo Rhythm Devils	What The Kids Want	B.Thumb	1972
Labelle	Chameleon	Epic	1976
Patti Labelle	Patti Labelle	Epic	1977
Patti Labelle	Tasty	Epic	1978
Malo	Malo	WB	1972
Malo	Dos	WB	1972
Malo	Evolution	WB	1973
Moby Grape	Moby Grape	CBS	1967
Moby Grape	Wow	CBS	1968
Moby Grape	Grape Jam	CBS	1968
Moby Grape	69	CBS	1969
Moby Grape	20 Granite Creek	CBS	1971
Peter, Paul and Mary	Reunion	WB	1978
Pointer Sisters	That's A Plenty	B.Thumb	1974
Pointer Sisters	The Pointer Sisters Live At The Opera House	ABC/B.Th	1974
Pointer Sisters	Steppin'	ABC/B.Th	1975
Pointer Sisters	Having A Party	ABC/B.Th	1977
The Quintet	V.S.O.P.	CBS	1977
Santana	Festival	CBS	1976
Santana	Amigos	CBS	1976
Santana	Swing Of Delight	CBS	1980
John Shine	Music For A Rainy Day	CBS	1975
Phoebe Snow	It Looks Like Snow	CBS	1976
Taj Mahal	Taj Mahal	CBS	1967
Taj Mahal	The Natch'll Blues	CBS	1968
Taj Mahal	Giant Step	CBS	1969
Taj Mahal	The Real Thing	CBS	1971
Taj Mahal	Happy To Be Like I Am	CBS	1972
various artists	Jazz At The Opera House	CBS	1983

Bobby Womack	Safety Zone	UA	1975
Victoria	Victoria	San Fran	1971
Victoria	Secrets Of The Bloom	Atlantic	1971

R045 Ray Ruff

Tattoo	Tattoo	Prodigal	1977
Them	Them	Happy T	1970
(Them after Van Morrison had left the group.)			
Hank Williams, Jnr	Family Tradition	Elektra	1975

R046 Todd Rundgren

American Dream	The American Dream	Ampex	1969
Badfinger	Straight Up	Apple	1972
Badfinger	Ass	Apple	1973
	(3 tracks only.)		
The Band	Stage Fright	Capitol	1970
Butterfield Blues Band	Live	Elektra	1976
Shaun Cassidy	Born Late	WB	1980
Shaun Cassidy	Wasp	WB	1980
Felix Cavaliere	Felix Cavaliere	Bearsv	1974
Cheap Trick	Next Position Please	Epic	1983
James Cotton Blues Band	Takin' Care Of Business	Capitol	1970
Rick Derringer	Guitars And Women	CBS	1979
Fanny	Mother's Pride	Reprise	1973
Grand Funk Railroad	We're An American Band	Capitol	1973
Grand Funk Railroad	Shinin' On	Capitol	1974
Halfnelson	Halfnelson	Bearsv	1971
(Later reissued as Sparks first album.)			
Hall and Oates	War Babies	Atlantic	1974
Hello People	The Hello People	Philips	1974
Hello People	Bricks	ABC	1975
Steve Hillage	L	Virgin	1976
Lords Of The New Church	Live For Today (12"EP)	IRS	1983
Meatloaf	Bat Out Of Hell	CBS/Cleve	1977
The Nazz	The Nazz	SGC	1968
The Nazz	Nazz Nazz	SGC	1969
The Nazz	Nazz 3	SGC	1970
New York Dolls	The New York Dolls	Mercury	1973
Psychedelic Furs	Forever Now	CBS	1982
Tom Robinson Band	TRB 2	EMI	1979
Rubinoos	Party Of Two	WB	1983
Todd Rundgren	Runt	Ampex	1970
Todd Rundgren	The Ballad Of Todd Rundgren	Ampex	1971
Todd Rundgren	Something/Anything ?	Bearsv	1972
Todd Rundgren	A Wizard, A True Star	Bearsv	1973
Todd Rundgren	Todd	Bearsv	1974
Todd Rundgren	Utopia	Bearsv	1974
Todd Rundgren	Initiation	Bearsv	1975
Todd Rundgren	Faithful	Bearsv	1976
Todd Rundgren	The Hermit Of Mink Hollow	Bearsv	1978

	Todd Rundgren	*Back To The Bars*	Bearsv	1978
	Todd Rundgren	*Healing*	Bearsv	1981
	Todd Rundgren	*The Tortured Artist*		
		Effect	Bearsv	1982
	Jules Shear	*Watchdog*	EMI-Amer	1983
	Jules Shear	*Jules*	EMI-Amer	1984
	Patti Smith	*Wave*	Arista	1979
	Sparks	*Sparks*	Bearsv	1974
	Jim Steinman	*Bad For Good*	Epic	1981
	Tubes	*Remote Control*	A&M	1979
	Utopia	*Another Live*	Bearsv	1975
	Utopia	*Ra*	Bearsv	1977
	Utopia	*Oops, Wrong Planet*	Bearsv	1977
	Utopia	*Adventures In Utopia*	Bearsv	1980
	Utopia	*Deface The Music*	Bearsv	1980
	Utopia	*Swing To The Right*	Bearsv	1982
	Utopia	*Utopia*	CBS/Netw	1982
	Utopia	*Oblivion*	WB/Passp	1983
	Jesse Winchester	*3rd Down, 110 To Go*	Bearsv	1972

R047 Ray Rush

	Bubble Puppy	*A Gathering Of*		
		Promises	Int.Arts	1968

R048 Martin Rushent

	Altered Images	*Pinky Blue*	Epic	1982
	J J Burnel	*Euroman Cometh*	UA	1979
		(2 tracks only.)		
	Buzzcocks	*Another Music In A*		
		Different Kitchen	UA	1978
	Buzzcocks	*Love Bites*	UA	1978
	Buzzcocks	*A Different Kind*		
		Of Tension	UA/IRS	1979
	Curved Air	*Air Cut*	WB	1973
	Tom Dickie and The	*Tom Dickie and The*		
	Desires	*Desires*	Mercury	1981
w. Tim Read	Fats Domino	*Live In Europe*	UA	1977
	Generation X	*Generation X*	Chrysalis	1978
	Go-Go's	*Talk Show*	IRS	1984
	Ian Gomm	*Gomm With The Wind*	ALbion	1979
	Ian Gomm	*What A Blow*	ALb/Stiff	1980
	Hey Elastica!	*In On The Off Beat*	Virgin	1984
	Human League	*Dare*	Virg/A&M	1981
	Human League	*Fascination*	A&M	1983
	Danny Kirwan	*Second Chapter*	DJM	1975
	Deke Leonard	*Before Your Very*		
		Eyes	UA	1979
	League Unlimited			
	Orchestra	*Love And Dancing*	Virgin	1982
	999	*High Energy Plan*	PVC	1978
	999	*Separates*	UA	1978
	Pinpoint	*A Third State*	Albion	1980
	Raybeats	*Guitar Beat*	DFOTM/PVC	1981
	Sammy	*Sammy*	Philips	1972
	Pete Shelley	*Homosapien*	Isl/Gen	1982
	Pete Shelley	*XL.1*	Gen/Arista	1983

	Straight Eight	*Straight To Your Heart*	Logo	1981
	Stranglers	*Rattus Norvegicus*	UA	1977
	Stranglers	*No More Heroes*	UA	1977
	Stranglers	*Black And White*	UA	1978
	Stranglers	*Live (X Cert)*	UA	1979
w. A.Winstanley	Rachel Sweet	*Protect The Innocent*	Stiff	1980
	Telephone	*Au Coeur De La Nuit*	Virgin	1980
	Trickster	*Find The Lady*	Jet	1977
	Trickster	*Trickster*	Jet	1978
	Yachts	*Without Radar*	Radar	1980

R049 Leon Russell

	Asylum Choir	*Look Inside The Asylum Choir*	Mercury	1968
	Asylum Choir	*Asylum Choir 2*	A&M	1971
w.Denny Cordell	Joe Cocker	*Joe Cocker*	R.Z/A&M	1970
w.Denny Cordell	Joe Cocker	*Mad Dogs And Englishmen*	A&M	1970
	Daughters Of Albion	*Daughters Of Albion*	Fontana	1968
	(Group included Kathy Dalton.)			
w. Don Nix	Freddie King	*Getting Ready*	A&M/Shelt	1971
w. Denny Cordell	Freddie King	*Texas Cannonball*	A&M/Shelt	1972
	Freddie King	*Woman Across The River*	A&M/Shelt	1973
	Jim Horn	*Through The Eyes Of A Horn*	Shelter	1972
w.Denny Cordell	Mary McCreary	*Jezebel*	Shelter	1974
w.Willie Nelson	Willie Nelson and Leon Russell	*One For The Road*	CBS	1979
w.Denny Cordell	Leon Russell	*Leon Russell*	Shelter	1970
	Leon Russell	*Leon Russell and The Shelter People*	Shelter	1971
	Leon Russell	*Carney*	Shelter	1972
	Leon Russell	*Hank Wilson's Back*	Shelter	1973
	Leon Russell	*Leon Live*	Shelter	1973
	Leon Russell	*Stop All That Jazz*	Shelter	1974
	Leon Russell	*Will Of The Wisp*	Shelter	1975
	Leon Russell	*Americana*	Paradise	1978
	Leon Russell	*Life And Love*	Paradise	1979
	Leon Russell with The New Grass Revival	*Live*	Paradise	1981
	Leon and Mary Russell	*Wedding Album*	Paradise	1976
	Leon and Mary Russell	*Make Love To The Music*	Paradise	1977

R050 John Ryan (The Chicago Kid)

	Allman Brothers	*Brothers Of The Road*	Arista	1981
	Black Oak Arkansas	*Ten Year Overnight Success*	MCA	1977
	Taka Boom	*Taka Boom*	Ariola	1979
	(Ms.Boom is the sister of Chaka Khan.)			
	Broken Edge	*Time For A Change*	Polydor	1984
	Climax Blues Band	*Flying The Flag*	WB	1980
	Climax Blues Band	*Lucky For Some*	WB	1981
	Doucette	*The Douce Is Loose*	Mushroom	1981

	Greg Guidry	Over The Line	CBS	1982
	Hawks	30 Seconds Over Otho	CBS	1982
	Larry Lee	Marooned	CBS	1982
	(Formerly with the Ozark Mountain Daredevils.)			
	Nova	Sun City	Arista	1978
	Pure Prairie League	Firin' Up	Casab	1980
	Billy Rankin	Growin' Up Too Fast	A&M	1984
	Rare Earth	Grand Slam	Prodigal	1978
	Rare Earth	Band Together	Prodigal	1978
	Santana	Shango	CBS	1982
w.Ted Templeman	Patrick Simmons	Arcade	WB	1983
	The States	Picture Me Without You	Boardwalk	1981
	Styx	Styx	W.Nickel	1972
	Styx	Styx 2	W.Nickel	1973
	Styx	Man Of Miracles	RCA	1974
	Tantrum	Rather Be Rockin'	Ovation	1979
	Target	Target	A&M	1976
	Bill Wray	Seize The Moment	Liberty	1983

S001 Alex Sadkin

	Classix Nouveau	Secret	Liberty	1983
w.C.Blackwell	Joe Cocker	Sheffield Steel	Island	1982
	Duran Duran	Seven And The Ragged Tiger	EMI/Cap	1983
	Vic Godard and The Subway Sect	Songs For Sale	Decca	1982
	Paul Haig	Rhythm Of Life	Crepuscule	1983
w. Kofi Ayivor	Hi-Tension	Hi-Tension	Island	1979
	Jags	No Tie Like A Present	Island	1981
w.C.Blackwell	Grace Jones	Warm Leatherette	Island	1980
w.C.Blackwell	Grace Jones	Night Clubbing	Island	1981
	Grace Jones	Living My Life	Island	1982
	Bob Marley and The Wailers	Uprising	Island	1979
w.C.Blackwell	Plastics	Come Back	Invitation	1981
	Bary Reynolds	I Scare Myself	Island	1983
	Suicide Romeo	Pictures	Ze	1980
w.Cory Wade	T-Connection	Magic	TK	1977
w.C.Blackwell	Third World	Journey To Addis	Island	1978
w.C.Blackwell	Third World	Prisoner In The Street	Island	1980
	Thompson Twins	Quick Step And Side Kick	Arista	1983
w. Tom Bailey	Thompson Twins	Into The Gap	Arista	1984
	Toots and The Maytals	Live	Isl/Mango	1980

S002 Ian Samwell

w. Jeff Dexter	America	America	WB	1971
	Georgie Fame	Fame At Last	EMI	1964
w. Jeff Dexter	Isaac Guillory	Isaac Guillory	Atlantic	1974
	Hummingbird	Hummingbird	A&M	1975
	Hummingbird	We Can't Go On Meeting Like This	A&M	1976
	Hummingbird	Diamond Nights	A&M	1977

Claudia Lennear	*Phew*	WB	1973
Linda Lewis	*Say No More*	Reprise	1971
Prelude	*Dutch Courage*	Pye 1974	
Maggie and Terre			
Roche	*Seductive Reasoning*	CBS	1975

S003 Paul Samwell-Smith

Chris De Burgh	*At The End Of A Perfect Day*	A&M	1977
Claire Hamill	*October*	Island	1973
Murray Head	*Say It Ain't So*	Island	1975
Murray Head	*How Many Ways*	MLC	1981
Illusion	*Illusion*	Island	1978
Jethro Tull	*The Broadsword And The Beast*	Chrysalis	1982
Renaissance	*Renaissance*	Island	1978
Cat Stevens	*Mona Bone Jakon*	Isl/A&M	1970
Cat Stevens	*Tea For The Tillerman*	Isl/A&M	1970
Cat Stevens	*Teaser And The Firecat*	Isl/A&M	1971
Cat Stevens	*Catch Bull At Four*	Isl/A&M	1972
Cat Stevens	*Buddha And The Chocolate Box*	Isl/A&M	1974
Cat Stevens	*Back To Earth*	Isl/A&M	1978
Yardbirds	*The Yardbirds*	Col/Epic	1966

S004 Ed Sanders

Fugs	*Second Album*	ESP	1966
Fugs	*The Belle Of Avenue A*	WB	1968
Fugs	*It Crawlewd Into My Hand, Honest*	WB	1969
Fugs	*Tenderness Junction*	WB	1968
Ed Sanders	*Sanders Truckstop*	WB	1970
Ed Sanders	*Beercans On The Moon*	WB	1972

S005 Johnny Sandlin

Allman Brothers	*Brothers And Sisters*	Capricorn	1973
Allman Brothers	*Win Lose Or Draw*	Capricorn	1975
Greg Allman	*The Greg Allman Tour*	Capricorn	1974
Greg Allman and Cher	*Allman And Woman*	WB	1977
Richard Betts	*Highway Call*	Capricorn	1974
Elvin Bishop	*Let It Flow*	Capricorn	1974
Elvin Bishop	*Juke Joint Jump*	Capricorn	1975
Bonnie Bramlett	*It's Time*	Capricorn	1974
Bonnie Bramlett	*Ladie's Choice*	Capricorn	1976
Cowboy	*Reach For The Sky*	Capricorn	1971
Cowboy	*5'll Getcha Ten*	Capricorn	1972
Cowboy	*Boyer and Talton*	Capricorn	1974
Hydra	*Land Of Money*	Capricorn	1975
w. D.Allman Johnny Jenkins	*Ton Ton Macoute*	Capricorn	1970
Billy Karloff and The Extremes	*Let Your Fingers Do The Talking*	WB	1981
Eddie Kendricks	*Love Keys*	Atlantic	1981
Kingfish	*Trident*	Jet	1978
Corky Laing	*Makin' It On The Street*	Elektra	1977

The Look	We're Gonna Rock	Plastic	1981
Delbert McClinton	Second Wind	Capricorn	1978
Delbert McClinton	Keeper Of The Flame	Capricorn	1979
Melting Pot	Burn, Cauldron Bubble	Ampex	1970
Matin Mull	Normal	Capricorn	1974
Rockets	Rockets	RSO	1979
Rockets	No Ballads	RSO	1980
Alex Taylor	Alex Taylor With Friends And Neighbours	Capricorn	1971
Tim Weisberg Band	Tim Weisberg Band	UA	1977
Tim Weisberg Band	Rotations	UA	1978

S006 Joe Saraceno

Gentlehood	Gentlehood	CBS	1973
Marketts	The Marketts Take To Wheels	WB	1963
Marketts	Out Of Limits	WB	1964
Marketts	Batman Theme	WB	1966
Sunshine Company	Happy Is The Sunshine Company	Imperial	1967
Sunshine Company	The Sunshine Company	Imperial	1968
Sunshine Company	Sunshine And Shadows	Imperial	1968
Ventures	Ventures A Go Go	Liberty	1965
Ventures	Guitar Freakout	Dolton	1966
Ventures	Go With The Ventures	Dolton	1966
Ventures	Where The Action Is	Dolton	1966
Ventures	Super Psychedelics	Liberty	1967
Ventures	Flights Of Fantasy	Liberty	1968
Ventures	The Horse	Liberty	1968
Ventures	Underground Fire	Liberty	1969
Ventures	Hawaii Five-O	Liberty	1969
Ventures	Jim Croce Songbook	UA	1974
Ventures	NASA 25th Anniversary Commemorative Album	Award	1984

(Several eminent producers began their careers as recording engineers on Ventures albums, they include Bruce Botnick, Henry Lewy and Al Schmitt.)

S007 Bob Sargeant

	The Beat	I Just Can't Stop It	Go-Feet	1980
	The Beat	Wha'ppen?	Go-Feet	1981
	The Beat	Special Beat Service	Go-Feet	1982
	Buzzards	Jellied Eels To Record Deals (1 track only)	Chrysalis	1979
	Carpettes	Frustration Paradise	B.Banquet	1979
	The Fall	Live At The Witch Trials	S.F/IRS	1979
	Haircut 100	Pelican West	Arista	1980
	Monochrome Set	Strange Boutique	DinDisc	1980
	Q-Tips	Q-Tips	Chrysalis	1980
w.Dave Mackay	Bob Sargeant	First Starring Role	RCA	1974
	Transmitters	Twenty Four Hours	Ebony	1978
	XTC	Mummer (1 track only)	Virgin	1983

S008 Boz Scaggs

Les Dudek	*Ghost Town Parade*	CBS	1976

S009 Al Schmitt

Jackson Browne	*Late For The Sky*	Asylum	1974
Paul Horn	*Dream Machine*	Tomato	1978
Hot Tuna	*Hot Tuna*	RCA	1970
Al Jarreau	*We Got By*	WB	1975
Al Jarreau	*Glow*	WB	1976
Al Jarreau	*Live In Europe*	WB	1977
Al Jarreau	*All Fly Home*	WB	1978
Jefferson Airplane	*Crown Of Creation*	RCA	1968
Jefferson Airplane	*Bless Its Pointed Little Head*	RCA	1969
Jefferson Airplane	*After Bathing At Baxters*	RCA	1970
Jefferson Airplane	*Volunteers*	RCA	1970
Spirit	*Farther Along*	Mercury	1976
Jack Traylor and Steelwind	*Child Of Nature*	Grunt	1971
Neil Young	*On The Beach*	Reprise	1974

S010 Bill Schnee

Colin Blunstone	*Never Even Thought*	Rocket	1978
Brick	*Stone Heart*	Bang	1979
Kiki Dee	*Stay With Me*	Rocket	1978
Randy Edelman	*Farewell Fairbanks*	20th Cent	1976
Randy Edelman	*If Love Is Real*	20th Cent	1977
Frankie and The Knockouts	*Makin' The Point*	MCA	1984
Richie Furay Band	*I've Got A Reason*	Asylum	1976
Gallagher and Lyle	*Showdown*	A&M	1978
Koinonia	*More Than A Feelin'*	Breaker	1983
Huey Lewis and The News	*Huey Lewis and The News*	Chtysalis	1980
Nielsen-Pearson	*Blind Luck*	EMI	1983
Pablo Cruise	*A Place In The Sun*	A&M	1977
Pablo Cruise	*World's Away*	A&M	1978
Pablo Cruise	*Part Of The Game*	A&M	1980
Boz Scaggs	*Middle Man*	CBS	1980
Russ Taff	*Walls Of Glass*	Myrrh	1983
w. Richard Parry Lon And Derek Van Eaton	*Who Do You Out Do*	A&M	1975

S011 Brinsley Schwarz

Carlene Carter	*Carelene Carter*	WB	1978

S012 Duane Scott
w. L.Buckingham & S.Nicks

Walter Egan	*Fundamental Roll*	UA/CBS	1977
Walter Egan	*Wild Exhibitions*	Backstreet	1983
Richard Torrance	*Eureka*	Shelter	1974
Richard Torrance	*Belle Of The Ball*	Shelter	1975
Richard Torrance	*Anything's Possible*	Capitol	1975

S013 Ken Scott

David Batteau	*Happy In Hollywood*	A&M	1976
Jeff Beck	*There And Back*	Epic	1980
David Bowie	*Hunky Dory*	RCA	1972
David Bowie	*Ziggy Stardust And The Spiders From Mars*	RCA	1972
David Bowie	*Pinups*	RCA	1973
Stanley Clarke	*Journey To Love*	Nemperor	1975
Stanley Clarke	*School Days*	Nemperor	1976
Billy Cobham	*Total Eclipse*	Atlantic	1974
Billy Cobham	*Crosswinds*	Atlantic	1974
Billy Cobham	*Shabazz*	Atlantic	1975
Devo	*Duty Now For The Future*	Virgin/WB	1979
Dixie Dregs	*What If*	Capricorn	1978
Dixie Dregs	*Night Of The Living Dregs*	Capricorn	1979
Esperanto	*Esperanto Rock Orchestra*	A&M	1973
Gamma	*Gamma 1*	Elektra	1979
Happy The Man	*Crafty Hands*	Arista	1978
Don Harrison	*Not Far From Free*	Mercury	1977
Kansas	*Vinyl Confessions*	Kirshner	1982
Mahavishnu Orchestra	*Visions Of The Emerald Beyond*	CBS	1975
Michalski and Oosterveen	*M & O*	CBS	1979
Missing Persons	*Spring Session M*	Capitol	1982
Tim Moore	*High Contact*	Asylum	1979
Pilot	*Pilot*	RCA	1972
(The Bruce Stephens/Micky Waller version.)			
Jamie Sheriff	*No Heroes*	Polydor	1980
Supertramp	*Crime Of The Century*	A&M	1974
Supertramp	*Crisis, What Crisis*	A&M	1975
3-D	*3-D*	Polydor	1980
Tubes	*Young And Rich*	A&M	1976

S014 Tommy Scott

Them	*Them*	Decca	1965
Them	*Them Again*	Decca	1976

S015 Randy Scruggs

Jessy Dixon	*Sanctuary*	Power	1984
Waylon Jennings	*It's Only Rock And Roll*	RCA	1983
Earl Scruggs	*Top Of The World*	CBS	1983
Earl Scruggs and Tom T. Hall	*The Storyteller and The Banjoman*	CBS	1982
Bill Troy	*First Time Out*	CMH	1981

S016 Barry Seidel

Billy Burnette	*Billy Burnette*	CBS	1980
w. Barry Beckett Billy Burnette	*Gimme You*	CBS	1981
Randy Burns and The Skydog Band	*Randy Burns and The Skydog Band*	Mercury	1971

	Randy Burns	*I'm A Lover Not A Fool*	Polydor	1972
	Fallen Angels	*The Fallen Angels*	Roulette	1968
	Taos	*Taos*	Mercury	1969

S017 Roy Segal

	Big Brother	*How Hard It Is*	CBS	1971
	Stoneground	*Flat Out*	Flat Out	1976

S018 Tom Sellers

	Assembled Multitude	*The Assembled Multitude*	Atlantic	1970
	Eric Andersen	*Be True To You*	Arista	1975
	Eric Andersen	*Sweet Surprise*	Arista	1976
	Batdorf and Rodney	*Life Is You*	Arista	1975
w. John Madara	Gulliver	*Gulliver*	Elektra	1969
	(Group included Daryl Hall and Tim Moore.)			
	Essra Mohawk	*Essra Mohawk*	Mooncr/Asy	1974
	Andy Robinson	*Break Out Of The City*	Janus	1971
	Silver	*Silver*	Arista	1976

S019 Jay Senter

	Michael Clark	*Free As A Breeze*	Capitol	1977
	Helmet Boy	*Helmet Boy*	Asylum	1980
	Bill La Bounty	*This Night Won't Last Forever*	WB	1978
	Bill La Bounty	*Rain In My Life*	WB	1979
w. Ray Manzarek	Nite City	*Nite City*	20th Cent	1977
	Spider	*Spider*	Capitol	1972

S020 Steve Severin

	Altered Images	*Happy Birthday*	Epic	1981

S021 Alan Shacklock

	The Alarm	*Declaration*	IRS	1984
	Babe Ruth	*First Base*	Harvest	1972
	Babe Ruth	*Amar Caballero*	Harvest	1974
	Steve Gibbons Band	*Saints And Sinners*	RCA	1981
	JoBoxers	*Like Gangbusters*	RCA	1983
	The Look	*The Look*	MCA	1980

S022 Brad Shapiro

	James Brown	*The Original Disco Man*	Polydor	1979
	Creative Source	*Consider The Source*	Polydor	1976
	Andy Fraser	*In Your Eyes*	CBS	1975
w.Dave Crawford	J.Geils Band	*The J.Geils Band*	Atlantic	1971
	Millie Jackson	*Caught Up*	Spring	1974
	Millie Jackson	*Still Caught Up*	Spring	1975
	Millie Jackson	*Lovingly Yours*	Spring	1976
	Millie Jackson	*Free And In Love*	Spring	1976
	Millie Jackson	*Feeling Bitchy*	Spring	1977
	Millie Jackson	*Get It Outcha System*	Spring	1978
	Millie Jackson	*Live And Uncensored*	Spring	1979
	Millie Jackson	*A Moment's Pleasure*	Spring	1979
	Millie Jackson	*Live*	Spring	1980
	Millie Jackson	*For Men Only*	Spring	1980

Millie Jackson	A Little Bit Country	Spring	1981
Millie Jackson	Live And Outrageous	Spring	1982
Millie Jackson	Hard Times	Spring	1982
Millie Jackson	E.S.P.	Sire/Spr	1983
Millie Jackson and			
Isaac Hayes	Royal Rappin's	Polydor	1979
Kokomo	Rise And Shine	CBS	1975
Jackie Moore	Make Me Feel Like		
	A Woman	Kayvette	1984
Wilson Pickett	Miz Lena's Boy	RCA	1973
Joe Simon	Mood, Heart And Soul	Polydor	1974
Johnnie Taylor	She's Killing Me	CBS	1979
Johnnie Taylor	New Day	CBS	1980

S023 Noah Shark

	Blue Steel	No More Lonely Nights	MCA	1979
w.D.Cordell	Tom Petty	You're Gonna Get It	Shelter	1978
	Dwight Twilley	Twilley	Aris/Shel	1979
	Dwight Twilley	Scuba Divers		
		(2 tracks only.)	EMI-Amer	1982
w. Mark Smith				
& John Hug	Dwight Twilley	Jungle	EMI-Amer	1983

S024 Stan Shaw

	Bruce Foxton	Touch Sensitive	Arista	1984

S025 Louie Shelton

	Alessi	Driftin'	A&M	1978
	Deardrof and Joseph	Deardrof and Joseph	Arista	1976
	England Dan and			
	John Ford Coley	I Hear The Music	A&M	1976
	Garfunkel	Fate For Breakfast,		
		Doubt For Dessert	CBS	1979
	Paul Parrish	Song For A Young Girl	ABC	1977
	Seals And Crofts	Diamond Girl	WB	1972
	Seals And Crofts	Summer Breeze	WB	1972
	Seals And Crofts	Unborn Child	WB	1974
	Seals And Crofts	I'll Play For You	WB	1975
	Seals And Crofts	Get Closer	WB	1976
	Seals And Crofts	Sudan Village	WB	1976
	Seals And Crofts	Takin' It Easy	WB	1978
	Seals And Crofts	The Longest Road	WB	1980

S026 Billy Sherrill

	Johnny Cash	The Baron	CBS	1981
	David Allan Coe	Human Emotions	CBS	1978
	David Allan Coe	Spectrum V11	CBS	1979
	David Allan Coe	Compass Point	CBS	1980
	David Allan Coe	I've Got Something		
		To Say	CBS	1980
	David Allan Coe	Invictus (Means		
		Unconquered)	CBS	1981
	David Allan Coe	Encore	CBS	1981
	David Allan Coe	Tenessee Whiskey	CBS	1981
	David Allan Coe	Rough Rider	CBS	1982
	David Allan Coe	D.A.C	CBS	1982

David Allan Coe	Castles In The Sand	CBS	1983
	(This album dedicated to Bob Dylan.)		
David Allan Coe	Hello In There	CBS	1983
David Allan Coe	Just Divorced	CBS	1984
Elvis Costello	Almost Blue	F-Beat/CBS	1981
Lacy J. Dalton	Lacy J. Dalton	CBS	1980
Lacy J. Dalton	Hard Times	CBS	1980
Lacy J. Dalton	Dream Baby	CBS	1983
Johnny Duncan	The Best Is Yet To Come	CBS	1978
Johnny Duncan	Straight From Texas	CBS	1979
Johnny Duncan	In My Dreams	CBS	1980
Johnny Duncan and Janie Fricke	Nice 'n' Easy	CBS	1980
Barbara Fairchild	This Is Me	CBS	1978
Janie Fricke	Janie Fricke	CBS	1978
Janie Fricke	Love Notes	CBS	1979
Janie Fricke	From The Heart	CBS	1980
Merle Haggard and George Jones	A Taste Of Yesterday's Wine	Epic	1982
Jim and Jesse	Berry Pickin'	Epic	1969
George Jones and Tammy Wynette	We Go Together	Epic	1971
George Jones	We Can Make It	Epic	1971
George Jones and Tammy Wynette	Me And The First Lady	Epic	1972
George Jones	A Picture Of Me Without You	Epic	1972
George Jones and Tammy Wynette	We Love To Sing About Jesus	Epic	1972
George Jones and Tammy Wynette	Let's Build A World Together	Epic	1973
George Jones	Nothing Ever Hurt Me Half As Bad (As Losing You)	Epic	1973
George Jones	In A Gospel Way	Epic	1974
George Jones and Tammy Wynette	We're Gonna Hold On	Epic	1973
George Jones	The Grand Tour	Epic	1974
George Jones, Tammy Wynette and Tina Jones	George, Tammy & Tina	Epic	1974
George Jones	Memories Of Us	Epic	1975
George Jones	The Battle	Epic	1976
George Jones	Alone Again	Epic	1976
George Jones and Tammy Wynette	Golden Ring	Epic	1976
George Jones	I Wanna Sing	Epic	1977
George Jones	Bartenders Blues	Epic	1978
George Jones	My Very Special Guests	Epic	1979
George Jones and Johnny Paycheck	Double Trouble	Epic	1980
George Jones	I Am What I Am	Epic	1980
George Jones and Tammy Wynette	Together Again	Epic	1980

George Jones	I'm Still The Same Old Me	Epic	1981
George Jones	Encore	Epic	1981
George Jones	Shine On	Epic	1983
George Jones	Jones Country	Epic	1983
George Jones	You've Still Got A Place In My Heart	Epic	1984
Scotty Moore	The Guitar That Changed The World	CBS	1964
Johnny Paycheck	Armed And Crazy	Epic	1978
Johnny Paycheck	Everybody's Got A Family, Meet Mine	Epic	1979
Johnny Paycheck	New York Town	Epic	1980
Johnny Paycheck	Mr. Hag Told My Story	Epic	1981
Remains	The Remains	Epic	1968
Marty Robbins	The Performer	CBS	1979
Marty Robbins	All Around Cowboy	CBs	1979
Johnny Rodriguez	What'll I Tell Virginia	Epic	1979
Johnny Rodriguez	Rodriguez	Epic	1979
Johnny Rodriguez	Through My Eyes	Epic	1981
Johnny Rodriguez	After The Rain	Epic	1981
Joe Stampley	I Don't Lie	Epic	1979
soundtrack	Take This Job And Shove It	Epic	1981
Tammy Wynette	D-I-V-O-R-C-E	Epic	1968
Tammy Wynette	Stand By Your Man	Epic	1969
Tammy Wynette	Inspiration	Epic	1969
Tammy Wynette	The Ways To Love A Man	Epic	1970
Tammy Wynette	Tammy's Touch	Epic	1970
Tammy Wynette	The First Lady	Epic	1970
Tammy Wynette	We Sure Can Love Each Other	Epic	1971
Tammy Wynette	Bedtime Story	Epic	1972
Tammy Wynette	Another Lonely Song	Epic	1974
Tammy Wynette	Woman To Woman	Epic	1975
Tammy Wynette	I Still Believe In Fairy Tales	Epic	1975
Tammy Wynette	You And Me	Epic	1976
Tammy Wynette	Til I Can Make It On My Own	Epic	1976
Tammy Wynette	Christmas With Tammy	Epic	1976
Tammy Wynette	Let's Get Together	Epic	1977
Tammy Wynette	Just Tammy	Epic	1979
Tammy Wynette	Womanhood	Epic	1979
Tammy Wynette	Only Lonely Sometimes	Epic	1980

S027 Peter Sherster

w. Ian Sippen	Clark-Hutchinson	A=MH2	Decca	1969

S028 Ralph Shuckett

	Clarence Clemmons	Clarence Clemmons and The Red Bank Rockers	CBS	1983
w. Ed Sprigg	Ellen Shipley	Ellen Shipley	RCA	1979
w. John Siegler	Joel Zoss	Joel Zoss	Arista	1975

206

S029 Gordon Shyrock

	Ronnie Barron	*Bon Ton Roulette*	Ace	1983
	Jimmy Lewis and The Checkers	*Yeah, Right !*	Bomp	1981
	Don Preston	*Bluse*	A&M	1968
	Don Preston	*Hot Air Through A Straw*	A&M	1969

S030 Peter Kieve Siegel

	Roy Buchanan	*Roy Buchanan*	Polydor	1972
	Roy Buchanan	*Second Album*	Polydor	1973
	Crow Dog's Paradise	*Songs Of The Sioux*	Elektra	1971
w.Paul Rothchild	Charles River Valley Boys	*Beatle Country*	Elektra	1966
	Earth Opera	*The Great American Eagle Tragedy*	Elektra	1969
	Pat Kilroy	*Light Of Day*	Elektra	1966
	Elliott Murphy	*Aquashow*	Polydor	1973
	David Peel and The Lower East Side	*The American Revolution*	Elektra	1970
w. Paul Nelson	Dave Ray	*Fine Soft Land*	Elektra	1967
	Paul Siebel	*Woodsmoke And Oranges*	Elektra	1970
w.Paul Rothchild	Mark Spoelstra	*State Of Mind*	Elektra	1966
	Wild Thing	*Partyin'*	Elektra	1969

S031 Raymond Silva

	Roy Buchanan	*You're Not Alone*	Polydor	1978

S032 John Simon

	The Band	*Music From Big Pink*	Capitol	1968
	The Band	*The Band*	Capitol	1969
	Elizabeth Barraclough	*Elizabeth Barraclough (3 tracks only.)*	Bearsv	1978
	Karen Beth	*New Moon Rising*	Buddah	1975
	Blood, Sweat & Tears	*Child Is Father To The Man*	CBS	1970
	Bobby Charles	*Bobby Charles*	Bearsv	1972
	Leonard Cohen	*The Songs Of Leonard Cohen*	CBS	1966
	Ducks	*The Ducks*	Just Sun	1973
	Gil Evans	*Priestess*	Antilles	1983
w.Harvey Brooks	Electric Flag	*American Music Band*	CBS	1969
	Cyrus Faryar	*Islands*	Elektra	1973
	Steve Forbert	*Jackrabbit Slim*	Nemperor	1979
	Michael Franks	*Tiger In The Rain*	WB	1979
	Galdston and Thom	*American Gypsies*	WB	1977
	John Hartford	*Morning Bugle*	WB	1972
	Janis Joplin	*Farewell Song (4 tracks only.)*	CBS	1982
	Al Kooper	*Act Like Nothing's Wrong*	UA	1976
	Birelli Lagrene	*15*	Antilles	1982
w.John Court	Gordon Lightfoot	*Did She Mention My Name ?*	UA	1968
	Jackie Lomax	*Three*	WB	1972

	Hirth Martinez	*Big Bright Street*	WB	1977
	Matrix	*Tale Of The Whale*	WB	1979
	David Sanborn	*Heart To Heart*	WB	1978
	Seals And Crofts	*Down Home*	Bell	1971
	John Simon	*John Simon's Album*	WB	1969
	John Simon	*Journey*	WB	1972
	soundtrack	*The Best Little Whorehouse In Texas*	MCA	1978
	Staton Brothers	*The Staton Brothers*	Epic	1972
w.Phil Ramone	soundtrack	*You Are What You Eat*	CBS	1968

S033 Pete Sinfield

	Esperanto	*Danse Macabre*	A&M	1974
w. Robert Fripp	King Crimson	*In The Wake Of Poseidon*	Isl/Atl	1970
	Roxy Music	*Roxy Music*	Isl/Atl	1972

S034 Ray Singer

w.S.Napier-Bell	Forever More	*Yours Forever More*	RCA	1970
w.S.Napier-Bell	Fresh	*Fresh Out Of Borstal*	RCA	1970
w.S.Napier-Bell	Fresh	*Fresh Today*	RCA	1970
	Japan	*Obscure Alternatives*	Hansa	1978
	Japan	*Adolescent Sex*	Hansa	1978
w.S.Napier-Bell	Clive Sarstedt	*Sarstedt*	RCA	1976
w. Jeff Dexter	Peter Sarstedt	*Tall Tree*	WB	1975

S035 John Sinclair

	Enid	*In The Region Of The Summer Stars*	Buk	1976
w. Gary Lyons	Foreigner	*Foreigner*	Atlantic	1977
w. Gary Lyons	Nutz	*Hard Nutz*	A&M	1977

S036 Neil Slaven

	Egg	*The Polite Force*	Deram	1970
	Robert John Godfrey	*The Fall Of Hyperion*	Charisma	1974
	Keef Hartley	*Halfbreed*	Deram	1969
	Keef Hartley	*Battle Of NW6*	Deram	1970
	Keef Hartley	*The Time Is Near*	Deram	1970
	Keef Hartley	*Overdog*	Deram	1971
	Keef Hartley	*Little Big Band*	Deram	1971
	Pink Fairies	*Never Never Land*	Polydor	1971
	Stray	*Hearts Of Fire*	Pye	1976
	Trapeze	*Hot Wire*	WB	1974

S037 Dallas Smith

	Canned Heat	*Boogie With Canned Heat*	UA	1968
	Five Man Electrical Band	*Coming Of Age*	Lionel	1971
	Five Man Electrical Band	*Sweet Paradise*	MGM	1972
	Gabriel	*Sweet Release*	ABC	1976
	Nitty Gritty Dirt Band	*The Nitty Gritty Dirt Band*	Liberty	1967
	Nitty Gritty Dirt Band	*Rare Junk*	Liberty	1967
	Nitty Gritty Dirt Band	*Pure Dirt*	Liberty	1968

Nitty Gritty Dirt Band	*Alive*	Liberty	1969
Alan O' Day	*Caress Me Pretty Music*	WB	1973
Oliver	*Prisms*	UA	1971
Bobby Vee	*Do What You Gotta Do*	Liberty	1968
Robert Thomas Velline	*Nothing Like A Sunny Day*	UA	1972

(This is Bobby Vee disguised under his real name.)

S038 Doug Smith

Whirlwind	*Blowin' Up A Storm*	Chiswick	1977

S039 Martyn Smith

Carlene Carter	*Carlene Carter*	WB	1978
Country Gazette	*What A Way To Make A Living*	R.Runner	1977

S040 Mike Smith

Applejacks	*The Applejacks*	Decca	1964
Brian Poole and The Tremeloes	*Big Hits Of '62*	Decca	1962
Jim Rafferty	*Don't Talk Back*	Decca	1978

S041 Norman "Hurricane" Smith

Kevin Coyne	*Heartburn*	Virgin	1976
Little Richard	*Get Down With It (2 tracks only.)*	Edsel	1982
Pink Floyd	*Piper At The Gates Of Dawn*	Col/Tower	1967
Pink Floyd	*Saucerful Of Secrets*	Col/Tower	1968
Pretty Things	*Parachute*	Harv/Rare	1968
Pretty Things	*S.F.Sorrow*	Col/Rare	1968
Pretty Things	*Silk Torpedo*	Swansong	1974
Pretty Things	*Savage Eye*	Swansong	1974

S042 Steve Smith

w.C.Blackwell	Jim Capaldi	*Short Cut Draw Blood*	Island	1975
	Clancy	*Seriously Speaking*	WB	1975
	Detective	*It Takes One To Know One*	Swansong	1978
	Elephant's Memory	*Angels Forever*	Polydor	1974
	Gillan	*Double Trouble*	Virgin	1981
	Chris Jagger	*The Adventures Of Valentine Vox*	Asylum	1974
w.C.Blackwell	Bob Marley and The Wailers	*Live*	Island	1975
	Pakala-Meredith	*Pakalameredith*	Elektra	1977
w. R.Wace and P.Brown	No Dice	*No Dice*	Capitol	1978
	Robert Palmer	*Sneakin' Salley Thru The Alley*	Island	1974
	Robert Palmer	*Pressure Drop*	Island	1975
	Robert Palmer	*Some People Can Do What They Like*	Island	1976

	Rough Diamond	*Rough Diamond*	Island	1977
	Toronto	*Girls Night Out*	SGR	1983
	Trapeze	*Trapeze*	WB	1975

S043 Vic Smith (a.k.a. Vic Coppersmith-Heaven)

	Cochise	*So Far*	UA	1972
	Europeans	*Vocabulary*	A&M	1983
w. Chris Parry	The Jam	*In The City*	Polydor	1977
w. Chris Parry	The Jam	*This Is The Modern World*	Polydor	1977
	The Jam	*All Mod Cons*	Polydor	1978
	The Jam	*Setting Sons*	Polydor	1979
	The Jam	*Sound Affects*	Polydor	1980
w. Chris Parry	The Jolt	*The Jolt*	Polydor	1978
	Snafu	*Snafu*	WWA	1973
	Vapors	*New Clear Days*	UA	1980
	Johnny Warman	*From The Jungle*	Rocket	1982
	Steve York	*Manor Live*	Virgin	1973

S044 Steven Soles

	Alpha Band	*Spark In The Dark*	Arista	1977
	Seventy Sevens	*Ping Pong Over The Abyss*	Exit	1983

S045 Pete Solley

	Bus Boys	*American Worker*	Arista	1982
	Gregg Clemons	*Gregg Clemons*	Nemperor	1980
	Fools	*Sold Out*	EMI-Amer	1980
	Steve Forbert	*Little Stevie Orbit*	Nemperor	1980
	Frankie and The Knockouts	*Below The Belt*	Millenium	1982
	Jo Jo Zep and The Falcons	*Screaming Targets*	Mushroom	1979
	Jo Jo Zep and The Falcons	*Step Lively*	CBS	1981
	Jo Jo Zep and The Falcons	*Cha*	A&M	1983
	Kix	*Cool Kids*	Atlantic	1983
	Oingo Boingo	*Only A Lad*	A&M	1981
	Henry Paul Band	*Henry Paul Band*	Atlantic	1982
	Romantics	*The Romantics*	Nemperor	1980
	Romantics	*National Breakout*	Nemperor	1980
	Romantics	*In Heat*	Nemperor	1983
	Sports	*Don't Throw stones*	Sire	1979
	Sports	*Suddenly*	Arista	1980
	Rachel Sweet	*And Then He Kissed Me*	CBS	1981
	Wreckless Eric	*The Wonderful World Of Wreckless Eric*	Stiff	1978

S046 Maynard Solomon

	Al Anderson	*Al Anderson*	Vanguard	1972
	Clean Living	*Clean Living*	Vanguard	1972
	Country Joe McDonald	*Country Joe*	Vanguard	1974
	John Hammond	*Big City Blues*	Vanguard	1964
	John Hammond	*So Many Roads*	Vanguard	1963

	Tom Paxton	*New Songs From The Briarpatch*	MAM	1977
w. Jeff Zaraya	Tom Paxton	*Heroes*	Vanguard	1978
	Buffy St.Marie	*Fire And Fleet And Candlelight*	Vanguard	1971
	Buffy St.Marie	*Native North American Child*	Vanguard	1974

S047 John David Souther

	Linda Ronstadt	*Don't Cry Now*	Asylum	1973

S048 Pete Spargo

	Appletree Theatre	*Playback*	Poly/MGM	1968
	soundtrack	*Blow Up*	MGM	1968
w.J.Pfeiffer	Hugo Montenegro	*Love Theme From The Godfather*	RCA	1972
	Max Morath	*In Jazz Country*	Vanguard	1979
	Tony Scott	*Music For Yoga Meditation*	MGM	1972
	Sweet Lightnin'	*Sweet Lightnin'*	RCA	1972

S049 Tony Spath

	David Knopfler	*Release*	P.River	1983

S050 Mark Spector

	Dudes	*We're No Angels*	CBS	1975
	Tom Rush	*Ladies Love Outlaws*	CBS	1974

S051 Phil Spector

	Beatles	*Let It Be*	Apple	1970
	Checkmates Ltd.,	*Love Is All We Have To Give*	A&M	1969
	Leonard Cohen	*Death Of A Ladies Man*	CBS	1977
	Crystals	*Twist Uptown*	Philles	1962
	Crystals	*He's A Rebel*	Philles	1963
	Crystals	*The Crystals Sing The Greatest Hits*	Philles	1963
	Dion	*Born To Be With You*	PSI	1975
	George Harrison	*All Things Must Pass*	Apple	1970
	George Harrison	*The Concert For Bangla Desh*	Apple	1972
	Barney Kessell	*Slow Burn*	PSI	1965
	John Lennon	*John Lennon/Plastic Ono Band*	Apple	1970
	John Lennon	*Imagine*	Apple	1971
	John Lennon	*Some Time In New York City*	Apple	1972
	John Lennon	*Rock 'n' Roll*	Apple	1974
		(4 tracks only)	Apple	1975
w. Yoko Ono	Yoko Ono	*Season Of Glass*	Geffen	1981
	Righteous Brothers	*Greatest Hits*	Philles	1963
	Ronettes	*Presenting The Fabulous Ronettes*	Philles	1964
	Ramones	*End Of The Century*	Sire	1980
	Bobb B. Soxx	*Zip-A-Dee-Doo-Dah*	Philles	1963
	Teddy Bears	*The Teddy Bears Sing*	Imperial	1959

	Ike and Tina Turner	*River Deep, Mountain High*	Philles	1970

S052 David Spinozza

	Arthur, Hurley and Gottlieb	*Arthur, Hurley and Gottlieb*	CBS	1973
	Garland Jeffreys	*Ghost Writer*	A&M	1977
	Garland Jeffreys	*One-Eyed Jack*	A&M	1978
	James Taylor	*Walking Man*	WB	1974

S053 Glenn Spreen

	Bearfoot	*Friends*	CBS	1973
	David Buskin	*He Used To Treat Her*	CBS	1973
w. N.Putnam	Flying Burritos	*Flying Again*	CBS	1975
	John Hiatt	*Overcoats*	CBS	1975
	Gerard Kenny	*City Living*	RCA	1981
	Dave Loggins	*Apprentice (In A Musical Workshop*	CBS	1974
w. N.Putnam	Ian Matthews	*Go For Broke*	CBS	1976
	John Reid	*Facade*	CBS	1976
	Robey, Falk & Bod	*Kentucky Rambler*	CBS	1973
	Sutherland Brothers	*When The Night Comes Down*	CBS	1979
w.Nat Jeffreys	Marc Tanner	*No Escape*	Elektra	1979
	Rusty Wier	*Don't It Make You Wanna Dance*	20th Cent	1974
	Rusty Wier	*Rusty Wier*	20th Cent	1975
	Rusty Wier	*Black Hat Saloon*	CBS	1976
	Rusty Wier	*Stacked Deck*	CBS	1977

S054 Bruce Springsteen

w. Miami Steve	Gary US Bonds	*Dedication*	EMI-Amer	1981
w. Miami Steve	Gary US Bonds	*On The Line*	EMI-Amer	1982

S055 Owsley Stanley

	Grateful Dead	*Bear's Choice*	WB	1973

S056 Steven Stanley

	B-52's	*Whammy*	Island	1983
	Lizzy Mercier Descloux	*Mambo Nassau*	Philips	1981
w.Dury/Jankel	Ian Dury	*Lord Upminster*	Polydor	1981
w. Sly & Robbie	Gwen Guthrie	*Gwen Guthrie*	Island	1982
	Tom Tom Club	*Tom Tom Club*	Island	1981
	Tom Tom Club	*Close To The Bone*	Island	1983

S057 Allen Stanton

w. J.Riopelle	Brewer and Shipley	*Down In L.A.*	A&M	1968
	Byrds	*5-D*	CBS	1966

S058 Ed Stasium

w.Marshall Chess	Alda Reserve	*Love Goes On*	Sire	1979
w.Liam Sternberg	Burning Rome	*Burning Rome*	A&M	1982
w.Tony Erdelyi	Ramones	*Road To Ruin*	Sire	1978
	Ramones	*It's Alive*	Sire	1979

	Ramones	Rock 'n' Roll High School (soundtrack)	Sire	1979
	Helen Schnieder	Helen Schnieder with The Kick	WB	1981

S059 Chris Stein

	Casino Music	Jungle Love	Ze	1979
	Gun Club	Miami	Animal	1982
	Iggy Pop	Zombie Birdhouse	Animal	1982
	Walter Steding	Walter Steding	Red Star	1980
	Walter Steding	Dancing In Heaven	Animal	1982
	Snuky Tate	Babylon Under Pressure	Animal	1982

S060 Jim Steinman

	Bonnie Tyler	Faster Than The Speed Of Night	Epic	1983

S061 Jim Stern

	Country Joe McDonald	Paradise With An Ocean View	Fantasy	1976
	Country Joe McDonald	Love Is A Fire	Fantasy	1976
	Terry and The Pirates	Doubtful Handshake	Line	1980

S062 Liam Sternberg

	Jane Aire and The Belvederes	Jane Aire and The Belvederes	Virgin	1979
w. Ed Stasium	Burning Rome	Burning Rome	A&M	1982
	Color Me Gone	Color Me Gone	A&M	1984
	Ratt	Ratt	Time Coast	1983
	Rachel Sweet	Fool Around	Stiff/Epic	1978
	Unknowns	Dream Sequence	Sire/Bomp	1981

S063 Eric Stevens

	Brownsville Station	A Night On The Town	Big Tree	1972
w. D. Morris	Brownsville Station	Smoking In The Boys Room	Philips	1973
	Damnation	The Damnation Of Adam Blessing	UA	1970
	Damnation	Which Is The Justice, Which Is The Thief	UA	1971

S064 Guy Stevens

	The Clash	London Calling	CBS	1979
	Free	Tons Of Sobs	Island/A&M	1967
	Hapshash and The Coloured Coat	Hapshash and The Coloured Coat	Liberty	1967
	Mighty Baby	Mighty Baby	Head	1969
	Mott The Hoople	Mott The Hoople	Isl/Atl	1969
	Mott The Hoople	Mad Shadows	Isl/Atl	1970
	Mott The Hoople	Brain Capers	Isl/Atl	1971
	Winkies	The Winkies	Chrysalis	1975

S065 Rob Stevens

	Bullseye	On Target	CBS	1979

	Crack The Sky	Safety In Numbers	Lifesong	1978
	Crack The Sky	Live	Lifesong	1978
	Dean Friedman	Dean Friedman	Lifesong	1977
	Dean Friedman	Well, Well Said The Rocking Chair	Lifesong	1978
	Lavender Hill Mob	Lavender Hill Mob	UA	1977

S066 Al Stewart

| | John Martyn | The Tumbler | Island | 1968 |
| | Shot In The Dark | Shot In The Dark | RSO | 1981 |

S067 Eric Stewart

| | Sad Cafe | Facades | RCA/A&M | 1979 |
| | Sad Cafe | Sad Cafe | RCA/Poly | 1980 |

S068 Ian Stewart

| | Rocket 88 | Rocket 88 | Atlantic | 1981 |

S069 Michael Stewart

	Angelo	Midnight Prowler	Fantasy	1978
	Cecilio and Kapono	Cecilio and Kapono	CBS	1974
	Jackie De Shannon	New Arrangement	CBS	1975
	Gale Force	Gale Force Two	Fantasy	1978
w. James Gadson	Thelma Houston	Breakwater Cat	RCA	1979
	Ahmed Jamal	Genetic Walk	20th Cent	1979
	Billy Joel	Piano Man	CBS	1973
	Billy Joel	Streetlife Serenade	CBS	1974
	Evie Sands	Suspended Animation	RCA	1979
	John Stewart	The Lonesome Picker Rides Again	WB	1971
	John Stewart	Sunstorm	WB	1972
	(John Stewart is Michael Stewart's brother.)			
	Toni Brown and Terry Garthwaite	The Joy	Fantasy	1977

S070 Robert Stigwood

w. Ossie Byrne	Bee Gees	1st	Poly/Atco	1967
	Bee Gees	Odessa	Poly/Atco	1969
	Cream	Fresh Cream	React/Atco	1966
	Marbles	The Marbles	Atlantic	1970

S071 Mike Stone

w. Myles Goodwyn	April Wine	Nature Of The Beast	Capitol	1981
w. Myles Goodwyn	April Wine	Power Play	Capitol	1982
w. Myles Goodwyn	April Wine	Animal Grace	Capitol	1984
	Asia	Asia	Geffen	1982
	Asia	Alpha	Geffen	1983
	Charlie	Fantasy Girls	Polydor	1976
	Sean Delaney	Highway	Casabl	1979
w. Kevin Elson	Journey	Escape	CBS	1981
	Journey	Frontiers	CBS	1983
w. Paul Stanley	New England	New England	Infinity	1979
w. John Fannon	New England	Explorer Suite	Elektra	1980

	Queen	*News Of The World*	EMI/Elek	1977
	Romantics	*Strictly Personal*	Nemperor	1981
	Shoes	*Present Tense*	Elektra	1979
	Simms Brothers Band	*The Simms Brothers Band*	E/A	1979

S072 Sly Stone

	Beau Brummels	*Volume 2*	Autumn	1965

S073 Richard Strange

	Nightingales	*Pigs On Purpose*	C.Red	1982

S074 John Stronach

	Atlantics	*Big City Rock*	ABC	1979
	Commander Cody	*Tales From The Ozone*	WB	1975
	Fools Gold	*Fools Gold*	Arista	1976
	Force Ten	*Force Ten*	WB	1981
	Jo Jo Gunne	*So Where's The Show*	Asylum	1974
	Alvin Lee	*Free Fall*	Avatar	1980
w. Skip Taylor	Love	*Reel To Real*	RSO	1974
	John Mayall	*No More Interviews*	DJM	1979
w. Skip Taylor	Keith Moon	*Two Sides Of The Moon*	Poly/MCA	1975
	Bill Quateman	*Night After Night*	RCA	1977
	REO Speedwagon	*REO*	Epic	1976
	REO Speedwagon	*You Get What You Play For*	Epic	1977
w. Flo & Eddie	Roadmaster	*Fortress*	Mercury	1980
	Rufus	*Party 'Til You're Broke*	MCA	1981
	Richard Supa	*Life Lines*	CBS	1976
	Tears	*Tears*	Backstreet	1979
	Joe Walsh	*So What*	ABC	1974

S075 Chad Stuart

	Ron Davies	*Silent Song Throughout The Land*	A&M	1970

(Davies wrote "It Ain't Easy" covered by Bowie on "Ziggy Stardust")

S076 Tim Summerhayes

	John Otway	*All Balls And No Willy*	Empire	1982
	Siousxie and The Banshees	*Nocturne*	Polydor	1983

S077 Tony Swain and Steve Jolley

	Bananarama	*Deep Sea Skiving*	London	1983
	Bananarama	*Bananarama*	London	1984
	Imagination	*Body Talk*	R&B/MCA	1982
	Imagination	*In The Heat Of The Night*	R&B/MCA	1982
	Imagination	*Nightdubbing*	R&B/MCA	1983
	Imagination	*Scandalous*	R&B	1983
	Imagination	*New Dimension*	Elektra	1984
	Spandau Ballet	*True*	Chrysalis	1983
	Spandau Ballet	*Parade*	Chrysalis	1984

S078 Billy Swan

	Tony Joe White	*Black And White*	Monument	1969

S079 Bill Szymczyk

w. Allan Blazek	Elvin Bishop	*Struttin' My Stuff*	Capricorn	1975
	Elvin Bishop	*Hometown Boy Makes Good*	Capricorn	1976
	Harvey Brooks	*How To Play Electric Bass*	Elektra	1967
	Albert Collins	*There's Gotta Be A Change*	Tumble	1972
	Rick Derringer	*All American Boy*	Blue Sky	1973
	Denny Doherty	*Watcha Gonna Do*	Dunhill	1970
	Eagles	*On The Border*	Asylum	1974
	Eagles	*One Of These Nights*	Asylum	1975
	Eagles	*Hotel California*	Asylum	1976
	Eagles	*The Long Run*	Asylum	1979
	Eagles	*The Eagles Live*	Asylum	1980
	Fabulous Rhinestones	*Freewheelin'*	Just Sun	1973
	Jay Ferguson	*All Alone In The End Zone*	Asylum	1976
	Jay Ferguson	*Thunder Island*	Asylum	1977
	Jay Ferguson	*Real Life Ain't This Way*	Asylum	1979

(credited as "executive producer".)

	Ford Theatre	*Time Changes*	Probe	1968
	J.Geils Band	*The Morning After*	Atlantic	1972
	J.Geils band	*Nightmares And Other Tales From The Vinyl Jungle*	Atlantic	1974
	J.Geils Band	*Bloodshot*	Atlantic	1973
w. Allan Blazek	J.Geils Band	*Hotline*	Atlantic	1974
	J.Geils Band	*Ladies Invited*	Atlantic	1972
w. Allan Blazek	J.Geils Band	*Blow Your Face Out*	Atlantic	1976
	Danny Holien	*Danny Holien*	Tumble	1971
	James Gang	*Yer Album*	ABC	1969
	James Gang	*Rides Again*	ABC	1970
	James Gang	*Thirds*	ABC	1971
	James Gang	*Live In Concert*	ABC	1972
	Jo Jo Gunne	*Bite Down Hard*	Asylum	1973
	Jo Jo Gunne	*Jumpin' The Gunne*	Asylum	1973
	B.B.King	*Live And Well*	Bluesway	1969
	B.B.King	*Completely Well*	ABC	1969
	B.B.King	*Indianola Mississippi Seeds*	ABC	1970
	B.B.King	*Live At Cook County Jail*	ABC	1970
	Al Kooper	*Championship Wrestling*	CBS	1982
	Pete McCabe	*The Man Who Ate The Plant*	Tumble	1973
	Outlaws	*Hurry Sundown*	Arista	1977
	REO Speedwagon	*This Time We Mean It*	CBS	1975

(credited as "executive producer".)

	Sanatana	*Zeebop*	CBS	1982
	Sanatana	*Shango*	CBS	1982
	Silk	*Smooth As Raw Silk*	TW	1969
	Michael Stanley	*Michael Stanley*	Tumble	1974

(This album sometimes referred to as "Rosewood Bitters".)

	Michael Stanley	*Friends and Legends*	MCA	1973

	Michael Stanley	You Break It ... You Bought It	Epic	1975
	Michael Stanley	Ladies Choice	Epic	1976
w. Allan Blazek and Ed Mashal	Michael Stanley	Stagepass	Epic	1977
	Dewey Terry	Chief	Tumble	1972
w. Allan Blazek	Mickey Thomas	Alive Alone	Elektra	1981
	Joe Vitale	Plantation Harbor	Asylum	1981
	Joe Walsh	Barnstorm	ABC	1972
	Joe Walsh	The Smoker You Drink The Player You Get	ABC	1973
	Joe Walsh	So What (1 track)	ABC	1974
	Joe Walsh	But Seriously Folks	Asylum	1978
	Joe Walsh	You Bought It ... You Name It	Full Moon	1983
	The Who	Face Dances	Polydor	1981
	Wishbone Ash	There's The Rub	MCA	1974
	soundtrack	Zachariah	Probe	1971

T001 Ben Tallent

	R.C. Bannon	Arrives	CBS	1978
	Marshall Chapman	Me, I'm Feeling Free	CBS	1977
	Alexander Harvey	Preshus Child	KS	1976

T002 Charlie Tallent

	Gene Cotton	For All The Young Writers	ABC	1976
	Dianne Davidson	Mountain Mama	Janus	1972

T003 Shel Talmy

	Amen Corner	The Return Of The Magnificent 7	Immediate	1971
	Blues Project	Lazarus	Capitol	1971
	Coven	Blood On The Tracks	Buddah	1974
	Creation	How Does It Feel To Feel?	Demon	1982
	Creation	Creation	Charisma	1973
	Easybeats	Good Friday	UA	1967
	Fumble	Poetry In Lotion	RCA	1974
	Roy Harper	Come Out Fighting Genghis Smith	CBS	1967
	Jon and The Niteriders	Splashback (EP)	Bomp	1982
	Kinks	The Kinks	Pye	1964
	Kinks	Kinda Kinks	Pye	1965
	Kinks	Kinks Kontroversy	Pye	1966
	Kinks	Face To Face	Pye/Rep	1966
	Kristine	I'm A Song (5 tracks)	P.Exchange	1976
	Pentangle	Sweet Child	Tra/Rep	1968
	Pentangle	Basket Of Light	Tra/Rep	1969
	Rumplestiltskin	Rumplestiltskin	Bell	1970
	Seanor and Koss	Seanor and Koss	Reprise	1972
	Sorrows	Love Too Late	Pavilion	1981
	Spreadeagle	The Piece Of Paper	Charisma	1972
	String Driven Thing	String Driven Thing	Charisma	1972
	String Driven Thing	The Machine That Cried	Charisma	1972

	Chris White	*Mouth Music*	Charisma	1976
	The Who	*My Generation*	Brunswick	1965

T004 Jack Tann

w. Was Brothers	Sweet Pea Atkinson	*Don't Walk Away*	Ze	1982
	Was (Not Was)	*Was (Not Was)*	Ze	1981
	Was (Not Was)	*Born To Laugh At Tornadoes*	Geffen-Ze	1983

T005 Paul Tannen

	David Blue	*Me, S.David Cohen*	Reprise	1969
	Eric Andersen	*Eric Andersen*	WB	1970
	Kingsmen	*Up And Away*	Wand	1966
	Steve Young	*Seven Bridges Road*	Son/Rep	1972

T006 Alan Tarney

	Bow Wow Wow	*See Jungle*	RCA	1981
	Barbara Dickson	*The Barbara Dickson Album*	Epic	1980
	Barbara Dickson	*You Know It's Me*	Epic	1981
w. Bruce Welch	Charlie Dore	*Where To Now*	Island	1979
w. T.Spencer	Peter Doyle	*Skin Deep*	RCA	1977
	Cliff Richard	*I'm No Hero*	EMI	1980
	Cliff Richard	*Wired For Sound*	EMI	1981
	Leo Sayer	*Living In A Fantasy*	Chry/WB	1980

T007 Nick Tauber

	Boys	*Boys Only*	Safari	1980
	Deep Purple	*Live In London*	Harvest	1982
	Adrian Lee	*The Magician (6 tracks)*	DJM	1982
	Marillion	*Script For A Jester's Tear*	EMI	1983
	Marillion	*Fugazi*	EMI/Cap	1984
	Secret Affair	*Business As Usual*	I-Spy	1982
	Slaughter and The Dogs	*Do It Dog Style*	Decca	1978
	Spear Of Destiny	*One Eyed Jacks*	Epic	1984
w. John Punter	Specimen	*Batastrophe (12" EP)*	Sire	1984
	Stampede	*Hurricane Town*	Polydor	1983
	Stiff Little Fingers	*Now Then*	Chrysalis	1982
	Thin Lizzy	*Vagabonds Of The Western World*	Decca	1973
	Bernie Torme	*Turn Out The Lights*	Kamaflage	1982
	Toyah	*Toyah, Toyah, Toyah*	Safari	1981
	Toyah	*Anthem*	Safari	1981
	Toyah	*Warrior Rock*	Safari	1982
	Toyah	*Love Is The Law*	Safari	1983

T008 Bernie Taupin

	David Ackles	*American Gothic*	Elektra	1972

T009 Chip Taylor

	Stoney Edwards	*Blackbird*	Capitol	1976
w. Al Gorgoni	Fabulous Farquahr	*Fabulous Farquahr*	MGM	1968
	Gorgoni, Martin and Taylor	*Gotta Get Back To Cisco*	Buddah	1971
	Gorgoni, Martin and Taylor	*Gorgoni, Martin and Taylor*	Buddah	1972

	Chip Taylor	*Gasoline*	Buddah	1972
	Chip Taylor	*Chip Taylor's Last Chance*	WB	1974
	Chip Taylor	*Some Of Us*	WB	1974
	Chip Taylor	*This Side Of The Big River*	WB	1975
	Chip Taylor	*Shoot Out The Jukebox*	CBS	1976
w. J.Palladino	Chip Taylor	*Saint Sebastian*	Capitol	1979

T010 Derek Taylor

	Nilsson	*A Little Touch Of Schmillson In The Night*	RCA	1973

T011 Skip Taylor

	Canned Heat	*Living The Blues*	Liberty/UA	1968
	Canned Heat	*Hallelujah*	Liberty	1969
	Canned Heat	*Future Blues*	Liberty	1970
	Canned Heat and John Lee Hooker	*Hooker And Heat*	Liberty	1971
	Canned Heat	*Live In Europe*	Liberty	1971
	Canned Heat	*New Age*	UA	1973
	Canned Heat	*Historical Figures and Ancient Heads*	UA	1972
w. Ron Novicon	Flo and Eddie	*Moving Targets*	CBS	1976
	Love	*Reel-To-Real*	RSO	1974
	Harvey Mandel	*The Snake*	Janus	1972
	Harvey Mandel	*Shangrenade*	Janus	1973
	Harvey Mandel	*Feel The Sound Of Harvey Mandel*	Janus	1974
w. John Stronach	Keith Moon	*Two Sides Of The Moon*	Poly/MCA	1975
	Jim Pulte	*Shimmy She Roll... Shimmy She Shake*	UA	1972
	Southwind	*What A Place To Land*	B.Thumb	1971

T012 Ted Templeman

w. L.Waronker	Beau Brummels	*The Beau Brummels*	WB	1975
	Captain Beefheart	*Clear Spot*	Reprise	1972
	Carrera	*Carrera*	WB	1983
w. L.Waronker	Doobie Brothers	*The Doobie Brothers*	WB	1971
	Doobie Brothers	*Toulouse Street*	WB	1972
	Doobie Brothers	*The Captain And Me*	WB	1973
	Doobie Brothers	*What Were Once Vices Are Now Habits*	WB	1974
	Doobie Brothers	*Stampede*	WB	1975
	Doobie Brothers	*Taking It To The Streets*	WB	1976
	Doobie Brothers	*Living On The Fault Line*	WB	1977
	Doobie Brothers	*Minute By Minute*	WB	1978
	Doobie Brothers	*One Step Closer*	WB	1980
	Doobie Brothers	*Farewell Tour*	WB	1983
	Lorraine Ellison	*Lorraine Ellison*	WB	1974
	Tom Johnston	*Everything You've Heard Is True*	WB	1979

	Nicolette Larson	*Nicolette Larson*	WB	1978
	Nicolette Larson	*In The Nick Of Time*	WB	1979
	Nicolette Larson	*Radioland*	WB	1980
	Little Feat	*Sailin' Shoes*	WB	1972
	Little Feat	*Time Loves A Hero*	WB	1977
	Montrose	*Montrose*	WB	1973
	Montrose	*Paper Money*	WB	1975
w. L.Waronker	Michael McDonald	*If That's What It Takes*	WB	1982
	Van Morrison	*Tupelo Honey*	WB	1971
	Van Morrison	*St.Dominic's Preview*	WB	1972
	Van Morrison	*It's Too Late To Stop Now*	WB	1974
w. John Ryan	Patrick Simmons	*Arcade (4 tracks)*	WB	1983
	Carly Simon	*Another Passenger*	Elektra	1976
	Van Halen	*Van Halen*	WB	1978
	Van Halen	*Van Halen 2*	WB	1979
	Van Halen	*Women And Children First*	WB	1980
	Van Halen	*Fair Warning*	WB	1981
	Van Halen	*Diver Down*	WB	1982
	Van Halen	*1984*	WB	1983
	Lauren Wood	*Lauren Wood*	WB	1979

T013 Brian Tench

	OMD	*Junk Culture*	Virgin	1984

T014 Ed Thacker

	Peter Allen	*It's Time For Peter Allen*	A&M	1977
	Great Buildings	*Great Buildings*	CBS	1981
	Group 87	*Group 87*	CBS	1980
	Red Rider	*Neruda*	Capitol	1983
	Tommy Tutone	*Tommy Tutone*	CBS	1980
	Tommy Tutone	*National Emotion*	CBS	1983
	Bill Wray	*Fire And Ice*	Liberty	1981

T015 Bob Thiele

Don Adams/ Airto/ Henry 'Red' Allen/ Peter Allen/ Steve Allen/ Laurindo Almeida/ Don Ameche/ Louis Armstrong/ Albert Ayler/ Pearl Bailey/ Gato Barbieri/ Count Basie/ Louis Belson/ Art Blakey/ Arthur Blythe/ Pat Boone/ Johnny Bothwell/ Bobby Bradford/ Ruby Braff/ Teresa Brewer/ Les Brown/ Dorsey Burnette Ralph Burns/ Artie Butler/ Don Byas/ Cab Calloway/ Larry Carlton/ Benny Carter/ Ron Carter/ George Cates/ Carol Channing/ Stanley Clarke/ Myron Cohen/ Al Cohn/ Al "Jazzbo" Collins/ John Coltrane/ Eddie Condon/ Jackie Cooper/ J. Fred Coots/ Don Cornwell/ Bob Crewe/ Bob Crosby/ Billy Dana/ Johnny Desmond/ Billy DeWolfe/ Vic Dickenson/ Sacha Distel/ Eric Dolphy/ Cornell Dupree/ Duke Ellington/ Jon Faddis/ Sid Feller/ Jerry Fielding/ Tommy Flanagan/ Rhonda Fleming/ Fontaine Sisters/ Pete Fountain/ Peter Frampton/ Alan Freed/ Bud Freeman/Slim Gaillard/ Judy Garland/ Erroll Garner/ Eric Gayles/ Dizzy Gillespie/ Hermione Gingold/ Arthur Godfrey/ Eydie Gorme/ Stephane Grappelli/ Buddy Greco/ Joe Guercio/ Bobby Hackett/ Buddy Hackett/ Connie Haines/ Chico Hamilton/ Lionel Hampton/ Pat Harrington, Jnr/ Coleman Hawkins/ Peter Lind Hayes/ Roy Haynes/ Neal Hefti/ Earl 'Fatha' Hines/ Art Hodes/ Chas Hodges/ Johnny Hodges/

Buddy Holly and The Crickets/ Richard 'Groove' Holmes/ Freddie Hubbard/ Bud Jackson/ James P Johnson/ Elvin Jones/ Hank Jones/ Quincy Jones/ Thad Jones/ Dick Jurgens/ Steve Kahn/ Jack Kerouac/ B.B.King/ Roland Kirk/ Frankie Laine/ Arnie Lawrence/ Steve Lawrence/ Yank Lawson/ Lennon Sisters/ Mel Lewis/ Liberace/ Abby Lincoln/ Charles Lloyd/ Dorothy Loudon/ McGuire Sisters/ Barbara McNair/ Jimmy McPartland/ Marion McPartland/ Henry Mancini/ Shelley Manne/ Mickey Mantle/ Bob Merrill/ Mills Brothers/ Charles Mingus/ Liza Minnelli/ Benny Morton/ Carlos Montoya/ Oliver Nelson/ Louis Nye/ Anita O' Day/ Sy Oliver/ Gene Page/ Hot Lips Page/ Jackie Paris/ Dave Peacock/ Bernard/ 'Pretty' Purdie/ Don Redman/ Della Reese/ Debbie Reynolds/ Max Roach/ Sonny Rollins/ Jane Russell/ Pee Wee Russell/ Sabicas/ Pharoah Sanders/ Tom Scott/ Gil Scott-Heron/ George Segal/ Archie Shepp/ Zoot Sims/ George 'Harmonica' Smith/ Lonnie Liston Smith/ Otis Spann/ Kay Starr/ Sonny Stitt/ Ralph Sutton/ Gabor Szabo/ Grady Tate/ Clark Terry/ Toots Thielemans/ Leon Thomas/ Dimitri Tiomkin/ Joe Turner/ Stanley Turrentine/ McCoy Tyner/ Joe Venuti/ Eddie 'Cleanhead' Vinson/ T-Bone Walker/ Clara Ward/ Muddy Waters/ Ben Webster/ Lawrence Welk/ Bob Wilbur/ Billy Williams/ Cootie Williams/ Jackie Wilson/ Phil Woods/ Lester Young/ Henny Youngman.

This is just a sample of the list of people produced by Bob Thiele over the years. Obviously many of these acts fall outwith the scope of this listing. However if demand warrants the inclusion of these and thousands of similar groups and individuals then they could be included in future editions of The Record Producer's File.

T016 Chris Thomas

	Badfinger	*Ass*	Apple	1973
	Badfinger	*Badfinger*	WB	1973
	Badfinger	*Wish You Were Here*	WB	1974
	John Cale	*Paris 1919*	Reprise	1973
	Climax Blues Band	*Climax Chicago Blues Band*	Parl/Sire	1968
	Climax Blues Band	*The Climax Blues Band Plays On*	Parl/Sire	1969
	Climax Blues Band	*A Lot Of Bottle*	Harv/Sire	1969
	Climax Blues Band	*Tightly Knit*	Harv/Sire	1970
	Bryan Ferry	*Let's Stick Together*	Poly/Atl	1976
w. Hugh Padgham	Human League	*Hysteria*	Virg/A&M	1984
& Clive Franks	Elton John	*The Fox*	Rocket	1981
	Elton John	*Jump Up*	Rocket	1982
	Elton John	*Too Low For Zero*	Rock/Geff	1983
	Elton John	*Breaking Hearts*	Rock/Geff	1984
	Kokomo	*Kokomo*	CBS	1975
	Krazy Kat	*China Seas*	Mountain	1077
	Christopher Milk	*Some People Will Drink Anything*	Reprise	1972
	Sadistic Mika Band	*Black Ship*	Harvest	1974
	Sadistic Mika Band	*Hot! Menu*	Harvest	1975
	Frankie Miller	*Full House*	Chrysalis	1977
	Nirvana	*Dedicated To Markos Three*	Pye	1970
	Pink Floyd	*Dark Side Of The Moon*	Harv/CBS	1973

(Not produced by Thomas, although he did mix the album.)

	Pretenders	*The Pretenders*	Real/Sire	1979
	Pretenders	*Pretenders 2*	Real/Sire	1981
	Pretenders	*Learning To Crawl*	Real/Sire	1984
	Procol Harum	*Home*	RZ/A&M	1970
	Procol Harum	*Broken Barricades*	Chrysalis	1971
	Procol Harum	*Live In Concert With The Edmonton Symphony*	Chrysalis	1971
	Procol Harum	*Grand Hotel*	Chrysalis	1973
	Procol Harum	*Exotic Birds And Fruit*	Chrysalis	1974
	Quiver	*Gone In The Morning*	WB	1972
	Philip Rambow	*Jungle Law (2 tracks)*	EMI	1981
	Tom Robinson Band	*Power In The Darkness*	EMI	1978
	Roxy Music	*For Your Pleasure*	Isl/Atl	1973
	Roxy Music	*Stranded*	Isl/Atl	1973
	Roxy Music	*Country Life*	Isl/Atl	1974
	Roxy Music	*Siren*	Isl/Atl	1974
	Roxy Music	*Viva*	Isl/Atl	1975
w. Bill Price	Sex Pistols	*Never Mind The Bollocks Here's The Sex Pistols*	Virg/WB	1977
	Chris Spedding	*Hurt*	Rak	1977
	Chris Spedding	*Guitar Graffiti (1 tr.)*	Rak	1978
	Pete Townshend	*Empty Glass*	Atco	1980
	Pete Townshend	*All The Best Cowboys Have Chinese Eyes*	Atco	1982
	various artists	*Concerts For The People Of Kampuchea*	Atlantic	1981
w. P.McCartney	Wings	*Back To The Egg*	MPL/CBS	1979

T017 Ken Thomas

	Bongos	*Time And The River*	Fetish	1982
	Clock DVA	*Thirst*	Fetish	1981

T018 Nigel Thomas

w. D.Cordell	Joe Cocker	*Something To Say*	Cube/A&M	1972
	Joe Cocker	*Live In L.A.*	Cube	1976
	Girl	*Wasted Youth*	Jet	1982
	Grease Band	*The Grease Band*	Harv/Shel	1971
w. Gerry Bron	Juicy Lucy	*Lie Back And Enjoy It*	Vertigo	1970
	Morty	*Love Blind*	Ariola	1980

(Morty was formerly the singer with Racing Cars.)

	Saxon	*Denim And Leather*	Carrere	1981
	Paul Williams and Friends	*In Memory Of Robert Johnson*	Sonet	1973

T019 Mayo Thompson

w. Geoff Travis	Red Crayola	*Soldier Talk*	Radar	1979
w. Adam Kidron	Red Crayola	*Kangaroo*	R.Trade	1981
w. Geoff Travis	Stiff Little Fingers	*Inflammable Material*	R.Trade	1979

T020 Mike Thorne

	Berlin Blondes	*Berlin Blondes*	EMI	1980
	John Cale	*Honi Soit*	A&M	1981
	Carmel	*The Drum Is Everything*	London	1984

Roger Daltrey	Parting Should Be Painless	WEA	1984
Kit Hain	Spirits Walking Out	Mercury	1981
Kit Hain	Looking For You	Mercury	1982
Kit Hain	School For Spies	Mercury	1983
Human Sexual Response	In A Roman Mood	DFOTM/Pass	1981
Nina Hagen	Nunsex Monkrock	CBS	1982
Metro	New Love	EMI	1979
Colin Newman	A-Z	B.Banquet	1980
Rockats	Make That Move (12" EP)	RCA	1983
Shirts	The Shirts	Harv/Cap	1978
Shirts	Street Light Shine	Harv/Cap	1979
Soft Cell	Non-Stop Erotic Cabaret	S.B./Sire	1981
Soft Cell	Non-Stop Ecstatic Dancing	SB/Sire	1982
Soft Machine	Alive And Well In Paris	Harvest	1978
Soft Machine	Land Of Cockayne	EMI	1981
Urban Verbs	The Urban Verbs	WB	1980
Holly Beth Vincent	Holly and The Italians	Virgin	1982
Wire	Pink Flag	Harvest	1977
Wire	Chairs Missing	Harvest	1978
Wire	154	Harv/WB	1979

T021 Colin Thurston

	Books	Expertise	Logo	1980
	Bow Wow Wow	See Jungle	RCA	1981
	Carpettes	Fight Amongst Yourselves	B.Banquet	1980
	Duran Duran	Duran Duran	EMI/Cap	1981
	Duran Duran	Rio	EMI/Cap	1982
	Human League	Reproduction	Virgin	1979
	Interview	Big Oceans	Virgin	1979
	Philip Jap	Philip Jap (4 tracks)	A&M	1983
	Nick Jones	Human's Lib (1 track only.)	WEA/Elek	1984
w. Nick Rhodes	Kajagoogoo	White Feathers	EMI	1983
	Kajagoogoo	Islands	EMI	1984
	Magazine	Secondhand Daylight	Virgin	1979
	Eve Moon	Eve Moon	Capitol	1981
	Loz Netto	Bzar	21 Records	1983
	Only Ones	Baby's Got A Gun	CBS	1980
	Our Daughters's Wedding	Digital Cowboy (12"EP)	EMI-Amer	1981
w. Tony Visconti	Alan Ross	Are You Free This Saturday	Ebony	1977
	Secret Affair	Business As Usual (2 tracks only.)	I-Spy	1982
	Talk Talk	The Party's Over	EMI/EMI-Am	1982

T022 David Tickle

	Red Rider	Neruda	Capitol	1983
	Red Rider	Breaking Curfew	Capitol	1984

	Ellen Shipley	Breaking Through The Ice Age	RCA	1980
	Split Enz	True Colours	A&M	1980
	Split Enz	Waiata	A&M	1981
	Vapors	Magnets	UA	1981

T023 Bob Tischler

	Blues Brothers	A Briefcase Full Of Blues	Atlantic	1978
	Blues Brothers	Blues Brothers original soundtrack album	Atlantic	1980
w. Paul Shaffer	Blues Brothers	Made In America	Atlantic	1980
w. W.Craig	David Frye	Richard Nixon:A Fantasy	Buddah	1973
	National Lampoon	Radio Dinner	B.Thumb	1972
	National Lampoon	Gold Turkey	Epic	1975
	National Lampoon	That's Not Funny, That's Sick	Rad/N.Lamp	1977
	National Lampoon	Goodbye Pop	Epic	1975
	Lily Tomlin	On Stage	Arista	1977

T024 Russ Titelman

w. L.Waronker	Gregg Allman	Playin' Up A Storm	Capricorn	1977
w. L.Waronker	Ry Cooder	Paradise And Lunch	Reprise	1974
	Credibility Gap	A Great Gift Idea	Reprise	1973
	James Dean	James Dean: Original Soundtrack Excerpts	WB	1975
	George Harrison	George Harrison	WB	1979
w. L.Waronker	Rickie Lee Jones	Rickie Lee Jones	WB	1979
w. L.Waronker	Rickie Lee Jones	Pirates	WB	1981
	Bill LaBounty	Bill LaBounty	WB	1981
w. L.Waronker	Gordon Lightfoot	Dream Street Rosie	WB	1980
	Little Feat	Little Feat	WB	1970
	Christine McVie	Christine McVie	WB	1984
	Adam Mitchell	Redhead In trouble	WB	1979
	Randy Newman	Live	Reprise	1971
	Randy Newman	Sail Away	Reprise	1972
	Randy Newman	Good Old Boys	WB	1974
	Randy Newman	Little Criminals	WB	1977
	Randy Newman	Born Again	WB	1979
	Randy Newman	Ragtime	Elektra	1981
	Randy Newman	Trouble In Paradise	WB	1983
	(All the Newman albums were co-produced by Lenny Waronker.)			
	Gene Parsons	Kindling	WB	1974
	Rufus and Chaka Khan	Live – Stompin' At The Savoy	WB	1983
w. Roy Halee	Paul Simon	Hearts And Bones	WB	1983
w. L.Waronker	James Taylor	Gorilla	WB	1975
w. L.Waronker	James Taylor	In The Pocket	WB	1976

T025 John Tiven

w. Doug Snyder	Bionic Gold	(Phil Spector songs done Seventies style.)	Big Sound	1977
	Alex Chilton	One Day In New York	Trio	1980
	Alex Chilton	Bach's Bottom	Line	1981
w. Doug Snyder	Van Duren	Are You Serious	Big Sound	1977

T026 George Tobin

Kim Carnes	*Romance Dance*	EMI-Amer	1980
Chocolate Milk	*Hipnotism*	RCA	1980
Natalie Cole	*Happy Love*	Capitol	1981
Robert John	*Robert John*	EMI-Amer	1979
Robert John	*Back On The Street*	EMI-Amer	1980
Smokey Robinson	*Being With You*	Motown	1981

T027 Allen R. Toussaint

	Badger	*White Lady and Badger*	CBS	1974
	Browning Bryant	*Browning Bryant*	WB	1974
	Chocolate Milk	*Chocolate Milk*	RCA	1976
	Chocolate Milk	*Comin'*	RCA	1976
	Chocolate Milk	*We're All In This Together*	RCA	1976
	Joe Cocker	*Luxury You Can Afford*	Asylum	1978
	Lee Dorsey	*Yes We Can*	Polydor	1970
	Dr. John	*In The Right Place*	Atco	1973
	Dr. John	*Desitively Bonnaroo*	Atco	1974
	Eric Gale	*Touch Of Silk*	CBS	1980
	High Cotton	*High Cotton*	Island	1975
	Etta James	*Changes*	T-Electric	1980
	Albert King	*New Orleans Heat*	Tomato	1979
	King Biscuit Boy	*King Biscuit Boy*	Epic	1974
	Labelle	*Nightbirds*	Epic	1974
	Labelle	*Phoenix*	Epic	1975
	Patti Labelle	*Released*	Epic	1980
	Mylon Lefevre	*Rock And Roll Resurection*	Mercury	1979
	Ramsey Lewis	*Routes (side 2)*	CBS	1980
	John Mayall	*Notice To Appear*	ABC	1976
	Meters	*Cabbage Alley*	Reprise	1972
	Meters	*Rejuvenation*	Reprise	1974
	Meters	*Fire On The Bayou*	Reprise	1975
	Meters	*Trick Bag*	Reprise	1976
	Frankie Miller	*High Life*	Chrysalis	1974
	James Montgomery Band	*The James Montgomery Band*	Island	1976
w. C.Blackwell	Jess Roden	*Jess Roden*	Island	1974
w. C.Greene	Allen Toussaint	*Toussaint*	DJM	1970
	Allen Toussaint	*Life, Love and Faith*	WB	1972
w. M.Sehorn	Allen Toussaint	*Southern Nights*	WB	1975

T028 Pete Townshend

Thunderclap Newman	*Hollywood Dream*	Track/MCA	1970
Simon Townshend	*Sweet Sound*	Polydor	1983

T029 Bill Traut

American Breed	*Pumpkin, Powder, Scarlet and Green*	Dot	1967
American Breed	*Bend Me Shape Me*	Dot	1968
Exile	*Exile*	RCA	1977
Exile	*Stage Pass*	RCA	1978
Lovecraft	*We Love You Whoever You Are*	Mercury	1975

	Mason Proffit	*Wanted*	H.Tiger	1969
	Mason Profitt	*Last Night I Had The Strangest Dream*	Ampex	1971
	Mason Proffit	*Come And Gone*	WB	1973
w. G.Badonsky	The Mauds	*Hold On*	Mercury	1967

T030 Chris Tsangarides

	Anvil	*Forged In Fire*	Attic	1983
	Fortnox	*Fortnox*	Epic	1982
	Girl	*Sheer Greed*	Jet	1980
	Money	*First Investment*	Gull	1979
	Gary Moore	*Back On The Streets*	MCA	1978
	Rock Goddess	*Hell Hath No Fury*	A&M	1983
	Spider	*Rough Justice*	A&M	1984
	Thin Lizzy	*Renegade*	Vert/WB	1980
	Thin Lizzy	*Thunder And Lightning*	Vert/WB	1983
	Tygers Of Pan Tang	*Wild Cat*	MCA	1980
	Tygers Of Pan Tang	*Spellbound*	MCA	1981
	Y&T	*Mean Streak*	A&M	1983

T031 Marcus Tybalt

	The Seeds	*The Seeds*	GNP	1966
	The Seeds	*Web Of Sound*	GNP	1966
	The Seeds	*Future*	GNP	1967
	The Seeds	*Fallin' Off The Edge*	GNP	1968
	Sky Saxon Blues Band	*Spoonful Of Seedy Blues*	GNP	1967

T032 Sean Tyla

	Little Bob Story	*Off The Rails*	Chiswick	1977

T033 Steve Tyrell

	Woody Allen	*Standup Comic*	Casab	1979
	Blood Sweat And Tears	*No Sweat*	CBS	1973
	Randall Bramlett	*That Other Mile*	Polydor	1975
	Merry Clayton	*Emotion*	MCA	1980
	Odyssey	*I've Got The Melody*	RCA	1981
	Michael Wycoff	*Come To My World*	RCA	1980

U001 Midge Ure

	Modern Man	*Concrete Scheme*	MAM	1980
	Visage	*Visage*	Polydor	1980
	Visage	*The Anvil*	Polydor	1982

U002 Gary Usher

	Keith Allison	*In Action*	CBS	1967
	The Byrds	*Younger Than Yesterday*	CBS	1967
	The Byrds	*Notorious Byrd Brothers*	CBS	1968
	The Byrds	*Sweetheart Of The Rodeo*	CBS	1968
	Danny Cox	*Birth Announcement*	Together	1969
	Firesign Theatre	*Waiting For The Electrician Or Someone Just Like Him*	CBS	1968

Andy Goldmark	*Andy Goldmark*	WB	1973
Bruce Johnston	*Going Public*	CBS	1977
Peanut Butter Conspiracy	*The Peanut Butter Conspiracy Is Spreading*	*CBS*	1967
Peanut Butter Conspiracy	*The Great Conspiracy*	CBS	1967
Sagittarius	*Present Tense*	CBS	1968
Sagittarius	*The Blue Marble*	Together	1969
The Ship	*The Ship*	Elektra	1972
("A contemporary folk music journey.")			
Chad Stuart and Jeremy Clyde	*Of Cabbages And Kings*	CBS	1967
Chad Stuart and Jeremy Clyde	*The Ark*	CBS	1968
Wackers	*Wackering Heights*	Elektra	1971
Wackers	*Hot Wacks*	Elektra	1972

V001 Kenny Vance

Donald Fagen and Walter Becker	*You Gotta Walk It Like You Talk It*	Visa	1978
Danny O'Keefe	*American Roulette*	WB	1977
Rockats	*Live At The Ritz*	Island	1981
soundtrack	*American Hot Wax*	A&M	1978
soundtrack	*Eddie and The Cruisers*	Scotti	1983
soundtrack	*The Hollywood Knights*	Casab	1980
soundtrack	*The Warriors*	A&M	1979

V002 Harry Vanda and George Young

AC/DC	*Dirty Deeds Done Dirt Cheap*	Atlantic	1976
AC/DC	*High Voltage*	Atlantic	1976
AC/DC	*Let There Be Rock*	Atlantic	1977
AC/DC	*If You Want Blood*	Atlantic	1978
AC/DC	*Powerage*	Atlantic	1978
Cheetah	*Rock And Roll Women*	Epic	1981
Easybeats	*Falling Of The Edge Of The World*	UA	1968
Easybeats	*Friends*	Polydor	1970
Flash and The Pan	*Flash and The Pan*	Epic	1979
Flash and The Pan	*Lights In The Night*	Epic	1980
Flash and The Pan	*Headlines*	Ensign	1982
Flash and The Pan	*Pan-O-Rama*	Ensign	1983
Marcus Hook Roll Band	*The Marcus Hook Roll Band*	Capitol	1983
Rose Tattoo	*Rock 'n' Roll Outlaws*	Carr/Mir	1981
Rose Tattoo	*Assault And Battery*	Carr/Mir	1981
Rose Tattoo	*Scarred For Life*	Carrere	1982
Steve Wright	*Hard Road*	Polydor	1974
John Paul Young	*Love Is In The Air*	Ariola/Sco	1978
John Paul Young	*Heaven Sent*	Ariola/Mid	1980

V003 Nick Venet (a.k.a. Nikolas Kostantinos Venetoulis.)

Beach Boys	*Surfin' Safari*	Capitol	1962
Beach Boys	*Surfin' USA*	Capitol	1963
King Curtis	*Soul Serenade*	Capitol	1964
Dinsmore Payne	*Dinsmore Payne*	UA	1973

	George Gerdes	Son Of Obituary	UA	1972
	Lothar and The Hand People	Space Hymn	Capitol	1969
	Mad River	Mad River	Capitol	1969
	Maffitt-Davies	The Rise And Fall Of Honesty	Capitol	1969
	Ian Matthews	Hit And Run	CBS	1977
	Fred Neil	Everybody's Talkin'	Capitol	1969
	Fred Neil	Sessions	Capitol	1971
	Dory Previn	On My Way To Where	UA	1970
	Dory Previn	Mythical Kings And Iguanas	UA	1971
	Dory Previn	Reflections In A Mud Puddle	UA	1971
	Dory Previn	Mary C. Brown and The Hollywood Sign	UA	1972
	Dory Previn	Dory Previn	WB	1974
w. David Briggs	Murray Roman	Busted	UA	1972
	Stone Poneys (Featuring Linda Ronstadt.)	The Stone Poneys		
	John Stewart	California Bloodlines	Capitol	1969
	John Stewart	Phoenix Concerts Live	RCA	1974
	John Stewart	Wingless Angels	RCA	1975
	Guthrie Thomas	Guthrie Thomas 1	Capitol	1975
	Wendy Waldman	Wendy Waldman	WB	1975
	Sammy Walker	Sammy Walker	WB	1976
	Sammy Walker	Blue Ridge Mountain Skyline	WB	1977

V004 Michael Verdick

	Breathless	Nobody Leaves This Song Alive	EMI-Amer	1980
	Jay Ferguson	Terms And Conditions	Capitol	1980
	Jay Ferguson	White Noise	Capitol	1982
	Bob Welch	Bob Welch	RCA	1981

V005 Mike Vernon

	Artwoods	The Artwoods	Spark	1966
	Duster Bennett	Smiling Like I'm Happy	B.Horizon	1968
	Duster Bennett	Bright Lights	B.Horizon	1969
	Duster Bennett	12 DB's	B.Horizon	1970
	Bloodstone	Unreal	London	1974
	David Bowie	Images	Deram	1967
	Chicken Shack	40 Blue Fingers Freshly Packed And Ready To Serve	B.Horizon	1968
	Chicken Shack	O.K. Ken	B.Horizon	1968
	Chicken Shack	The 100 Ton Chicken	B.Horizon	1969
	Chicken Shack	Accept	B.Horizon	1970
	Climax Blues Band	Gold Plated	Sire	1976
	Dr. Feelgood	Let It Roll	UA	1979
	Champion Jack Dupree	When You Feel The Feeling You Was Feeling	B.Horizon	1968
	Ellis	Why Not	Epic	1973
	Fleetwood Mac	Fleetwood Mac	B.Horizon	1968
	Fleetwood Mac	Mr. Wonderful	B.Horizon	1968

Focus	*Moving Waves*	B.Horizon	1971
Focus	*Focus*	Poly/Sire	1972
Focus	*Focus 3*	Poly/Sire	1972
Focus	*At The Rainbow*	Poly/Sire	1973
Focus	*Hamburger Concerto*	Poly/Atco	1974
Foster Brothers	*On The Line*	Rocket	1977
Rick Hayward	*Rick Hayward*	B.Horizon	1971
Mickey Jupp	*Some People Can't Dance*	A&M	1982
Freddie King	*Larger Than Life*	RSO	1975
Freddie King	*Burglar*	RSO	1974
Level 42	*Level 42*	Polydor	1981
Level 42	*The Pursuit Of Accidents*	Polydor	1982
Lightnin' Slim	*London Gumbo*	B.Horizon	1972
John Mayall and Eric Clapton	*Bluesbreakers*	Decca/Lon	1966
John Mayall and The Bluesbreakers	*A Hard Road*	Decca/Lon	1967
John Mayall and The Bluesbreakers	*Crusade*	Decca/Lon	1967
John Mayall	*The Blues Alone*	AOC/Lon	1967
John Mayall	*Diary Of A Band Vol.1*	Decca	1968
John Mayall	*Diary Of A Band Vol.2*	Decca	1968

(Issued in the USA as a double album on London in 1970.)

John Mayall and The Bluesbreakers	*Bare Wires*	Decca/Lon	1968
John Mayall	*Blues From Laurel Canyon*	Decca/Lon	1968
John Mayall	*Looking Back*	Decca/Lon	1969
John Mayall	*Thru' The Years*	Decca	1971
Olympic Runners	*Out In Front*	London	1975
Olympic Runners	*Keepin' It Up*	RCA	1978
Olympic Runners	*Hot To Trot*	C.Norton	1977
Olympic Runners	*Puttin' It On You*	Polydor	1978
Olympic Runners	*Dancealot*	Polydor	1979
Olympic Runners	*Out Of The Ground*	RCA	1979
Christine Perfect	*Christine Perfect*	B.Horizon	1970

(Issued in the USA as "The Legendary Christine Perfect Album" on Sire 1970.)

Rocky Sharpe and The Replays	*Rock It To Mars*	Chiswick	1980
Rocky Sharpe and The Replays	*Rama Lama*	Chiswick	1981
Rocky Sharpe and The Replays	*Come On Let's Go*	Chiswick	1981
Rocky Sharpe and The Replays	*Shout Shout*	Chiswick	1981
Rocky Sharpe and The Replays	*Stop Please Stop*	Polydor	1983
Savoy Brown	*Shake Down*	Decca	1967
Savoy Brown	*Getting To The Point*	Dec/Parr	1968
Savoy Brown	*Blue Matter*	Dec/Parr	1969
Gordon Smith	*Long Overdue*	B.Horizon	1968
Sunnyland Slim	*Midnight Jump*	B.Horizon	1969
w. Gus Dudgeon Ten Years After	*Ten Years After*	Deram	1967

Ten Years After	*Undead*	Deram	1968
Ten Years After	*Stonedhenge*	Deram	1968
Top Topham	*Ascension Heights*	B.Horizon	1970
Jimmy Witherspoon and Robben Ford	*Live*	LAX	1977
Martha Velez	*Hypnotized*	Polydor	1972

V006 Peter Vernon-Kell

Duffo	*Disappearing Boy*	PVK	1980
Peter Green	*In The Skies*	PVK	1979
Peter Green	*Little Dreamer*	PVK	1980
Peter Green	*Watcha Gonna Do ?*	PVK	1981
Peter Green	*Blue Guitar*	Creole	1981

V007 Steve Verocca

Kevin Coyne	*Marjory Razor Blade*	Virgin	1973
Kevin Coyne	*Blame It On The Night*	Virgin	1974
Johnny Destry and Destiny	*Girls, Rock And Roll And Cars*	Millenium	1980
Franke and The Knockouts	*Franke and The Knockouts*	Millenium	1981
Mordicai Jones	*Mordicai Jones*	Polydor	1972
Macko Palmer	*Passing Clouds*	RSO	1975
Link Wray	*Link Wray*	Polydor	1971
Link Wray	*Beans And Fatback*	Virgin	1973

V008 Tony Visconti

Afraid Of Mice	*Afraid Of Mice*	Charisma	1981
Altered Images	*Bite*	Epic/Port	1983
Argent	*Counterpoints*	RCA	1975
Badfinger	*Magic Christian Music*	Apple	1970
Boomtown Rats	*Mondo Bongo*	Merc/CBS	1980
Boomtown Rats	*V Deep*	Merc/CBS	1982
David Bowie	*Space Oddity*	RCA	1969
David Bowie	*The Man Who Sold The World*	RCA	1970
David Bowie	*David Live*	RCA	1974
David Bowie	*Young Americans*	RCA	1975
David Bowie	*Low*	RCA	1977
David Bowie	*Heroes*	RCA	1977
David Bowie	*Stage*	RCA	1978
David Bowie	*Lodger*	RCA	1979
David Bowie	*Scary Monsters And Super Creeps*	RCA	1980
Caravan	*Better By Far*	Arista	1977
Carmen	*Fandangos In Space*	RZ/Dunh	1973
Carmen	*Dancing On A Cold Wind*	R.Z.	1974
Dirty Tricks	*Hit And Run*	Polydor	1976
Dirty tricks	*Night Man*	Polydor	1977
Gasworks	*Gasworks*	Regal	1972
Gentle Giant	*Gentle Giant*	Vertigo	1971
Gentle Giant	*Acquiring The Taste*	Vertigo	1972
Steve Gibbons	*Down In The Bunker*	Polydor	1978
Zaine Griff	*Ashes And Diamonds*	Auto/WB	1980
Haysi Fantayzee	*Battle Hymns For Children (2 tracks)*	Regard	1983

John Hiatt	*All Of A Sudden*	Geffen	1982
Marsha Hunt	*Woman Child*	Track	1971
Mary Hopkin	*Earth Song, Ocean Song*	Apple	1971
Mary Hopkin	*Those Were The Days (1 track)*	Apple	1972
Legend	*Legend*	Vertigo	1970
Ralph McTell	*Not Till Tomorrow*	Reprise	1972
Ralph McTell	*Easy*	Reprise	1973
Modern Romance	*Trick Of The Light*	WEA	1983
Hazel O' Connor	*Breaking Glass*	A&M	1980
Hazel O' Connor	*Cover Plus*	Albion	1981
Omaha Sherriff	*Come Hell or High Water*	RCA	1977
Osibisa	*Osibisa*	MCA	1971
Osibisa	*Woyaya*	MCA	1972
Elaine Page	*Stages*	K-Tel	1983
Tom Paxton	*Peace Will Come*	Reprise	1972
Tom Paxton	*New Songs For Old Friends*	Reprise	1973
Iggy Pop	*The Idiot*	RCA	1977
Radiators	*Ghost Town*	Chiswick	1978
Alan Ross	*Are You Free This Saturday*	RCA	1977
Sparks	*Indiscreet*	Island	1975
Stranglers	*La Folie*	UA	1981
Strawbs	*Dragonfly*	A&M	1970
Strawbs	*Antiques And Curios*	A&M	1970
Strawbs	*From The Witchwood*	A&M	1971
Strawbs	*Grave New World*	A&M	1972
Surprise Sisters	*The Surprise Sisters*	Good Earth	1976
Thin Lizzy	*Bad Reputation*	Vert/Mer	1977
Thin Lizzy	*Live And Dangerous*	Vert/WB	1978
Thin Lizzy	*Black Rose*	Vert/WB	1979
Tyrannosaurus Rex	*My People Were Fair And Had Sky In Their Hair*	RZ	1968
Tyrannosaurus Rex	*Prophets, Seers and Sages, The Angels Of The Ages*	RZ	1969
Tyrannosaurus Rex	*Unicorn*	RZ/B.Thumb	1969
Tyrannosaurus Rex	*A Beard Of Stars*	RZ/B.Thumb	1970
T.Rex	*T.Rex*	Fly/Rep	1970
T.Rex	*Electric Warrior*	Fly/Rep	1971
T.Rex	*The Slider*	EMI	1972
T.Rex	*Bolan Boogie*	Fly	1972
T.Rex	*Tanx*	EMI/Rep	1973
T.Rex	*Zinc Alloy*	EMI	1974
T.Rex	*Marc (Words And Music)*	Pye	1978
T.Rex	*T.Rex In Concert*	Marc	1981
Rick Wakeman	*Rhapsodies*	A&M	1979

V009 Klaus Voorman

Lon and Derek Van Eaton	*Brother*	Apple	1973

W001 Dick Wagner

w. M.Kamen	Tim Curry	*Fearless*	A&M	1979

w. A.Cooper	Mark Farner	*Mark Farner*	Atlantic	1977
	Gentlemen After Dark	*Gentlemen After Dark*	GAD	1983

W002 Phil Wainman

	Bay City Rollers	*Bay City Rollers*	Bell	1975
	Bay City Rollers	*Wouldn't You Like It*	Bell	1975
	Bay City Rollers	*Once Upon A Star*	Bell	1975
	Boomtown Rats	*Fine Art Of Surfacing*	Ens/CBS	1979
	Mud	*Use Your Imagination*	P.Stock	1975
	Mud	*Mudpack*	P.Stock	1977
	Sensational Alex Harvey Band	*Next*	Vertigo	1974
	Scooters	*Young Girls*	EMI-Amer	1980
	Scooters	*Blue Eyes*	EMI-Amer	1981
	(Known in the UK as The US Scooters.)			
	Sweet	*Sweet Fanny Adams*	RCA	1974
	Sweet	*Strung Up*	RCA	1975

W003 Greg Walsh

	Dollar	*The Paris Collection*	WEA	1980
	Howard Devoto	*Jerky Versions Of The Dream*	Virgin	1983
	Grand Prix	*There For None To See*	RCA	1982
	Heaven 17	*The Luxury Gap*	Virg/Aris	1983
	Landscape	*Landscape*	RCA	1979
	Villa De Ville	*For The Time Being*	RCA	1981

W004 Joe Walsh

	Dan Fogelberg	*Souvenirs*	CBS	1975
	Fools Gold	*Fools Gold*	Arista	1976
	Ringo Starr	*Old Wave*	Boardwalk	1983
	Joe Walsh	*There Goes The Neighborhood*	Asylum	1981

W005 Peter Walsh

	China Crisis	*Difficult Shapes and Passive Rhythms (two tracks only)*	Virgin	1982
	Peter Gabriel	*Plays Live*	Char/Geff	1983
	Passion Puppets	*Beyond The Pale*	Stiff	1984
	Simple Minds	*New Gold Dream (81,82,83,84)*	Virg/A&M	1982
	Scott Walker	*Climate Of Hunter*	Virgin	1984

W006 Bob Ward

	Kevin Coyne	*Dynamite Daze*	Virgin	1977
	Kevin Coyne	*Millionaires and Teddy Bears*	Virgin	1978
	Kevin Coyne and Dagmar Krause	*Babble*	Virgin	1973

W007 Kingsley Ward

w.Dave Robinson	Brinsley Schwarz	*Nervous On The Road*	UA	1972
w. Malcolm Jones	Love Sculpture	*Blues Helping*	Parlophone	1968

W008 Martin Ware

	Allez Allez	*Promises*	Virgin	1982
w. Ian Craig Marsh	B.E.F.	*Music Of Quality And Distinction*	Virgin	1982

W009 Don Was

w. David Was & Jack Tann	Sweet Pea Atkinson	*Don't Walk Away*	ZE	1982
	Cristina	*Sleep It Off*	Mercury	1984
w. T.Rundgren & John Robie	Jules Shear	*Jules*	EMI-Amer	1984

W010 Andy Warhol

	Velvet Underground and Nico	*The Velvet Underground and Nico*	MGM	1967

W011 Lenny Waronker

w. Russ Titelman	Greg Allman	*Playing Up A Storm*	Capricorn	1977
	Beau Brummels	*Triangle*	WB	1967
	Beau Brummels	*Bradleys Barn*	WB	1968
w. Ted Templeman	Beau Brummels	*The Beau Brummels*	WB	1975
w. V.D.Parks	Ry Cooder	*Ry Cooder*	Reprise	1970
w. Jim Dickinson	Ry Cooder	*Into The Purple Valley*	Reprise	1972
w. Jim Dickinson	Ry Cooder	*Boomer's Story*	Reprise	1972
w. Russ Titelman	Ry Cooder	*Paradise And Lunch*	Reprise	1974
w. Ted Templeman	Doobie Brothers	*The Doobie Brothers*	WB	1971
	Everly Brothers	*Roots*	WB	1968
w. John Pilla	Arlo Guthrie	*Hobo's Lullaby*	Reprise	1972
	Arlo Guthrie	*The Last Of The Brooklyn Cowboys*	Reprise	1973
	Arlo Guthrie	*Arlo Guthrie*	Reprise	1974
	Harpers Bizarre	*Feelin' Groovy*	WB	1967
	Harpers Bizarre	*Anything Goes*	WB	1967
	Harpers Bizzare	*The Secret Life Of Harpers Bizarre*	WB	1968
	Harpers Bizarre	*4*	WB	1969
w. Andy Wickham	Goldie Hawn	*Goldie*	WB	1972
w. Russ Titelman	Rickie Lee Jones	*Rickie Lee Jones*	WB	1974
w. Russ Titelman	Rickie Lee Jones	*Pirates*	WB	1981
	Gordon Lightfoot	*Sundown*	Reprise	1974
	Gordon Lightfoot	*Cold On The Shoulder*	Reprise	1975
w. Joe Wissert	Gordon Lightfoot	*Gord's Gold*	Reprise	1975
	Gordon Lightfoot	*Summertime Dream*	Reprise	1976
	Gordon Lightfoot	*Endless Wire*	Reprise	1978
w. Russ Titelman	Gordon Lightfoot	*Dream Street Rosie*	Reprise	1980
w. Ted Templeman	Michael McDonald	*If That's What It Takes*	WB	1982
w. Joe Boyd	Maria Muldaur	*Maria Muldaur*	Reprise	1974
w. Joe Boyd	Maria Muldaur	*Waitress In A Donut Shop*	Reprise	1974
w. Joe Boyd	Maria Muldaur	*Sweet Harmony*	Reprise	1976
w. V.D.Parks	Randy Newman	*Randy Newman*	Reprise	1968

Randy Newman	*12 Songs*	Reprise	1970
Randy Newman	*Live*	Reprise	1971
Randy Newman	*Sail Away*	Reprise	1972
Randy Newman	*Good Old Boys*	WB	1974
Randy Newman	*Little Criminals*	WB	1977
Randy Newman	*Born Again*	WB	1979
Randy Newman	*Ragtime (soundtrack)*	Elektra	1981
Randy Newman	*Trouble In Paradise*	WB	1983

(All Newman albums from "Live" to "Trouble In Paradise" inclusive co-produced by Russ Titelman.)

	Van Dyke Parks	*Song Cycle*	WB	1968
	Paul Simon	*Hearts And Bones (3 tracks only)*	WB	1983
w. Russ Titelman	James Taylor	*Gorilla*	WB	1975
w. Russ Titelman	James Taylor	*In The Pocket*	WB	1976

W012 Charlie Watts

People Band	*The People Band*	Tra	1970

W013 Jeff Wayne

David Essex	*Rock On*	CBS	1973
David Essex	*David Essex*	CBS	1974
David Essex	*All The Fun Of The Fair*	CBS	1975
David Essex	*Out On The Street*	CBS	1976
David Essex	*Live On Tour*	CBS	1976
David Essex	*Gold And Ivory*	CBS	1977
Justin Hayward	*Night Flight*	Decca	1980
soundtrack	*McVicar*	Polydor	1980
various	*War Of The Worlds*	CBS	1978
Vigrass and Osborne	*Queues*	MCA	1972
Vigrass and Osborne	*Steppin' Out*	Epic	1974
Winds Of Change	*Illusions*	EMI	1979

W014 Jim Webb

Cher	*Cher*	WB	1975
Fifth Dimension	*Earthbound*	ABC	1975
Richard Harris	*The Love Album*	ABC	1969
Supremes	*The Supremes*	Motown	1972
Susan Webb	*Bye Bye Pretty Baby*	ABC	1969

W015 Jeffrey Weber

Toni Tenille	*More Than You Know*	Mirage	1984

W016 Bob Weir

David Rea	*Slewfoot*	CBS	1973

W017 Ronny Weiser

Blasters	*American Music*	Rollin'	1980
Ray Campi	*Rockabilly Rebel*	Rollin'	1977
Ray Campi	*Born To Rock*	Rollin'	1977
Ray Campi	*Rockabilly Rocket*	Rollin'	1977
Ray Campi	*Wildcat Shakeout*	Rollin'	1978
Ray Campi	*Rockabilly Music*	Rollin'	1980
Ray Campi	*Rockin' At The Ritz*	Rounder	1980
Ray Campi	*Rockabilly Man*	Rollin'	1981

Ray Campi	*Hollywood Cats*	Rollin'	1983
Johnny Carroll	*Texabilly*	Rollin'	1977
Jackie Lee Waukeen Cochran	*Swamp Fox*	Rollin'	1977
Jackie Lee Waukeen Cochran	*Rockabilly Legend*	Rollin'	1977
Mac Curtis	*Good Rockin' Tomorrow*	Rollin'	1975
Mac Curtis	*Ruffabilly*	Rollin'	1977
Mac Curtis	*Rock Me*	Rollin'	1978
Mac Curtis	*Rockin' Mother*	Rollin'	1979
Chuck Higgins	*Ph.D (Pretty Heavy Dude)*	Rollin'	1979
Jimmie Lee Maslon	*Salacious Rockabilly Cat*	R.R./Bomp	1980
Jimmie Lee Maslon	*Your Wildcat Ways*	Rollin'	1981
soundtrack	*Teenage Cruisers*	Rhino	1980
various artists	*California Rockabilly Volume 1*	Rollin'	1977
various artists	*California Rockabilly Volume 2*	Rollin'	1978
various artists	*California Rockabilly Volume 3*	Rollin'	1978
Gene Vincent	*Forever*	Rollin'	1980

W018 Bruce Welch

Alan David	*Alan David*	EMI	1981
Sutherland Brothers and Quiver	*Reach For The Sky*	CBS	1977

W019 Jann Wenner
w. M.Greene

Boz Scaggs	*Boz Scaggs*	Atlantic	1972

W020 Tom Werman

Brownsville	*Air Special*	CBS	1978
Cheap Trick	*In Color*	Epic	1977
Cheap Trick	*Heaven Tonight*	Epic	1978
Cheap Trick	*Dream Police*	Epic	1979
Blue Oyster Cult	*Mirrors*	CBS	1979
The B'zz	*Get Up*	Epic	1983
Hawks	*The Hawks*	CBS	1981
Molly Hatchet	*Molly Hatchet*	Epic	1978
Molly Hatchet	*Flirtin' With Disaster*	Epic	1979
Molly Hatchet	*Beatin' The Odds*	Epic	1980
Molly Hatchet	*Take No Prisoners*	Epic	1981
Molly Hatchet	*No Guts...No Glory*	Epic	1983
Gary Myrick and The Figures	*Gary Myrick and The Figures*	Epic	1980
Mothers Finest	*Mothers Finest*	Epic	1976
Mothers Finest	*Another Mother Further*	Epic	1977
Motley Crue	*Shout At The Devil*	Elektra	1983
Ted Nugent	*Ted Nugent*	Epic	1975
Ted Nugent	*Free For All*	Epic	1976
Ted Nugent	*Cat Scratch Fever*	Epic	1977
Ted Nugent	*Double Live Gonzo*	Epic	1978
Ted Nugent	*Weekend Warriors*	Epic	1978

	Ted Nugent	State Of Shock	Epic	1979
	(all the Nugent albums here co-produced with Lew Futterman.)			
	Off Broadway	On	Atlantic	1980
	The Producers	You Make The Heat	Portrait	1982
	Robey, Falk and Bod	Kentucky Gambler	CBS	1973
	Twisted Silver	Stay Hungry	Atlantic	1984

W021 Tommy West (see also: Cashman and West)

	Ed Bruce	Ed Bruce	MCA	1980
	Ed Bruce	One To One	MCA	1981
	Ed Bruce	I Write It Down	MCA	1982
	Ed Bruce	You're Not Leaving Here Tonight	MCA	1983
	Corbin/Hanner Band	For The Sake Of The Song	Alfa	1981
	Gail Davies	Gail Davies	Lifesong	1978

W022 John Wetton

	Jack Knife	I Wish You Would	Polydor	1979
	Duncan Mackay	Score	EMI	1977

W023 Jerry Wexler

w. Glenn Frey	Lou Ann Barton	Old Enough	Asylum	1982
w. Barry Beckett	Steve Bassett	Steve Bassett	CBS	1984
	Maggie Bell	Queen Of The Night	Poly/Atl	1974
	Ronne Blakeley	Welcome	WB	1975
	Solomon Burke	King Of Rock And Soul	Atlantic	1966
w. Barry Beckett	Bob Crewe	Motivation	Elektra	1977
w. Barry Beckett	Kim Carnes	Sailin'	A&M	1976
w. Arif Mardin and Tom Dowd	Cher	3614 Jackson Highway	Atlantic	1969
w. Tom Dowd	Delaney and Bonnie	To Bonnie From Delaney	Atco	1970
	Jackie De Shannon	Jackie	Atlantic	1972
w. Barry Beckett	Dire Straits	Communique	Vert/WB	1979
w. Bruce Robb	Donovan	Lady Of The Stars	Allegiance	1983
w. Bert Berns	Drifters	Take You Where The Music's Playing	Atlantic	1965
w. H.Battiste	Dr.John	Gumbo	Atco	1972
w. Barry Beckett	Bob Dylan	Slow Train Coming	CBS	1979
w. Barry Beckett	Bob Dylan	Saved	CBS	1980
	Electric Flag	The Band Kept Playing	Atlantic	1974
w. Barry Beckett	Jose Feliciano	Sweet Soul Music	P.Stock	1976
	Mike Finnigan	Mike Finnigan	WB	1976
	Aretha Franklin	Aretha Arrives	Atlantic	1967
	Aretha Franklin	I Never Loved A Man	Atlantic	1967
	Aretha Franklin	Lady Soul	Atlantic	1968
w. Tom Dowd	Aretha Franklin	Soul 69	Atlantic	1969
	Aretha Franklin	Young Gifted And Black	Atlantic	1972
	Aretha Franklin	Amazing Grace	Atlantic	1972
	Aretha Franklin	With Everything I Feel In Me	Atlantic	1974
	Aretha Franklin	You	Atlantic	1975
w.Kris Kristofferson	Donnie Fritts	Prone To Lean	Atlantic	1974
w. Bob Dylan	Barry Goldberg	Barry Goldberg	Atlantic	1974
w. Arif Mardin	Donny Hathaway	In Performance	Atlantic	1980

w. Tom Dowd	Ronnie Hawkins	*The Hawk*	Atlantic	1971
	Etta James	*Deep In The Night*	WB	1978
	King Curtis	*That Lovin' Feelin'*	Atlantic	1966
	King Curtis	*Plays The Great Memphis Hits*	Atlantic	1967
w. Arif Mardin and Tom Dowd	Lulu	*Melody Fair*	Atco	1970
w. Barry Beckett	McGuinn-Hillman	*McGuinn-Hillman*	Capitol	1980
	Willie Nelson	*Phases and Stages*	Atlantic	1974
w. Barry Beckett	Tony Orlando	*Tony Orlando*	Elektra	1978
	Gilda Radner	*Live From New York*	WB	1979
	Doug Sahm and Band	*Doug Sahm and Band*	Atlantic	1973
	Doug Sahm	*Texas Tornado*	Atlantic	1973
w. Barry Beckett	Sanford/Townsend Band	*The Sanford Townsend Band*	WB	1976
w. Barry Beckett	Santana	*Havana Moon*	CBS	1983
w. Arif Mardin and Tom Dowd	Dusty Springfield	*In Memphis*	Atlantic	1968
w. Barry Beckett	Mavis Staples	*Oh What A Feeling*	WB	1979
w. Barry Beckett	Staples Singers	*Unlock Your Mind*	WB	1978
w. Tom Dowd	Ira Sullivan	*Horizons*	Discovery	1983
	Allen Toussaint	*Motion*	WB	1978

W024 Paul A. Wexler

	Fleshtones	*Upfront (12" EP)*	IRS	1980
	Tin Huey	*Contents Dislodged*	WB	1979
	Weirdos	*Action Design (12" EP)*	Rhino	1980

W025 Chris White

	Colin Blunstone	*Journey*	Epic	1974
	Michael Fennelly	*Lane Changer*	Epic	1974

W026 Jack White

w. Greg Mathieson	Laura Branigan	*Branigan*	Atlantic	1982
	Laura Branigan	*Branigan 2*	Atlantic	1983
w. R. Buchanan	Laura Branigan	*Self Control*	Atlantic	1984

W027 James White

	James Chance	*Live Aux Bains Douches*	Invisible	1980
	Contortions	*Buy*	Ze	1979

W028 Sam Whiteside

	Cowboy	*Cowboy*	Capricorn	1972
	Sea Level	*A Long Walk Off A Short Pier*	Capricorn	1979
	Sea Level	*Ball Room*	Arista	1980
	Winter Brothers	*The Winter Brothers Band*	Atco	1976

W029 Neil Wilburn

	Guy Clark	*Old Number One*	RCA	1975
	Guy Clark	*Texas Cooking*	RCA	1976
	Guy Clark	*Cuy Clark*	WB	1978
	Lee Clayton	*Border Affair*	Capitol	1978
	Lee Clayton	*Naked Child*	Capitol	1979
	Vassar Clements Band	*The Vassar Clements Band*	MCA	1977

w. Charlie Daniels	Ramblin' Jack Elliot	*Bull Durham Sacks and Railroad Tracks*	Reprise	1970
	Earl Scruggs	*His Family And Friends*	CBS	1972
	Buck White	*Poor Folks Pleasure*	Sugar Hill	1979

W030 Ricky Wilde

	Kim Wilde	*Kim Wilde*	Rak	1981
	Kim Wilde	*Select*	Rak	1982
	Kim Wilde	*Catch As Catch Can*	Rak	1983

W031 John "Bucky" Wilkin

	Ronny and The Daytonas	*Sandy*	MGM	1964

W032 Mentor Williams

	Kim Carnes	*Kim Carnes*	A&M	1975
	Barbara Dickson	*Morning Comes Quickly*	RSO	1977
	Dobie Gray	*Drift Away*	MCA	1972
	Dobie Gray	*Loving Arms*	MCA	1974
	Dobie Gray	*Hey Dixie*	MCA	1974
	Tom Jans	*Tom Jans*	A&M	1974
	Stealers Wheel	*Right Or Wrong*	A&M	1975
	John Stewart	*Fire In The wind*	RSO	1977
	Mentor Williams	*Feelings*	MCA	1974
	Paul Williams	*A Little On The Windy Side*	Portrait	1979

W033 Pip Williams

	Bardot	*Rocking In Rhythm*	RCA	1978
	Barclay James Harvest	*Ring Of Changes*	Polydor	1983
	Barclay James Harvest	*Victim Of Circumstance*	Polydor	1984
	Graham Bonnet	*Graham Bonnet*	Ring-O	1977
	Kiki Dee	*Perfect Timing*	Ario/RCA	1981
	Geordie	*Save The World (7 tracks)*	EMI	1976
	Catherine Howe	*Silent Mother Nature*	RCA	1976
	Heroes	*Border Raiders*	Polydor	1980
	Moody Blues	*Long Distance Voyager*	Threshold	1981
	Moody Blues	*The Present*	Threshold	1983
	Mud	*It's Better Than Working*	P.Stock	1976
	Samson	*Don't Get Mad, Get Even*	Polydor	1984
	Starjets	*God Bless*	Epic	1979
	Status Quo	*Rockin' All Over The World*	Vert/Cap	1970
	Status Quo	*If You Can't Stand The Heat*	Vertigo	1978
	Status Quo	*Whatever You Want*	Vertigo	1979
	Status Quo	*Now Hear This*	Riva	1980

W034 James Williamson

	Iggy Pop	*New Values*	Arista	1979

W035 Brian Wilson

	American Spring	*American Spring*	UA	1972
	Beach Boys	*Surfer Girl*	Capitol	1963
	Beach Boys	*Little Deuce Coupe*	Capitol	1963
	Beach Boys	*Shut Down Volume 2*	Capitol	1964
	Beach Boys	*All Summer Long*	Capitol	1964
	Beach Boys	*Beach Boys Concert*	Capitol	1964
	Beach Boys	*Today*	Capitol	1965
	Beach Boys	*Party*	Capitol	1965
	Beach Boys	*Christmas Album*	Capitol	1964
	Beach Boys	*Summer Days Summer Nights*	Capitol	1965
	Beach Boys	*Pet Sounds*	Capitol	1966
	Beach Boys	*15 Big Ones*	Reprise	1976
	Beach Boys	*Love You*	Reprise	1978
	Beach Boys	*M.I.U. Album*	Reprise	1978

W036 Carl Wilson

	Flame	*The Flame*	Stateside	1971
w. Billy Hinsche	Ricci Martin	*Beached*	CBS	1977

W037 Norro Wilson

	Rex Allen	*Brand New*	WB	1978
	Rex Allen	*Oklahoma Rose*	WB	1980
	John Anderson	*John Anderson*	WB	1980
	John Anderson	*2*	WB	1981
	Asleep At The Wheel	*Asleep At The Wheel*	CBS	1974
	Razzy Bailey	*The Midnight Hour*	RCA	1984
	Mickey Gilley and Charly McLain	*Surround Me With Love*	Epic	1981
	Reba McEntire	*Just A Little Love*	MCA	1984
	Buck Owens	*Buck Owens*	WB	1976
	Buck Owens	*Our Old Mansion*	WB	1977
	Charley Pride	*Night Games*	RCA	1983
	Margo Smith	*A Woman*	WB	1979
	Margo Smith	*Just Margo*	WB	1979
	Steve Warner	*Midnight Fire*	RCA	1983

W038 Peter Wilson

	Angelic Upstarts	*We Gotta Get Out Of This Place*	WB	1980
	Angelic Upstarts	*2,000,000 voices*	EMI	1981
w. J.Pursey	Cockney Rejects	*Greatest Hits Vol.1*	EMI	1980
w. Chris Briggs	Cockney Rejects	*Greatest Hits Vol.2*	EMI	1980
	Comsat Angels	*Waiting For A Miracle*	Polydor	1980
	Comsat Angels	*Sleep No More*	Polydor	1981
	Comsat Angels	*Fiction*	Polydor	1982
	Patrick Fitzgerald	*Grubby Stories*	Polydor	1979
	The Jam	*The Gift*	Polydor	1982
	The Jam	*Dig The New Breed*	Polydor	1982
	Passions	*30,000 Feet Over China (2 tracks)*	Polydor	1981
	Sham 69	*Tell Us The Truth*	Poly/Sire	1978

	Sham 69	*That's Life*	Polydor	1979
	Sham 69	*Hersham Boys*	Polydor	1979
	Sham 69	*The Game*	Polydor	1980
w. Paul Weller	Style Council	*Introducing The Style Council*	Polydor	1983
w. Paul Weller	Style Council	*Cafe Bleu*	Poly/Geff	1984
	Wall	*Anthems And Dirges*	Polydor	1982

W039 Tom Wilson

	Animals	*Animalization*	MGM	1966
	Bagatelle	*11PM Saturday*	ABC	1966
	Blues Project	*Projections*	MGM	1966
	Eric Burdon and The Animals	*Winds Of Change*	MGM	1967
	Eric Burdon and The Animals	*Eric Is Here*	MGM	1968
	Eric Burdon and The Animals	*The Twain Shall Meet*	MGM	1968
	Country Joe and The Fish	*C.J. Fish*	Vanguard	1970
	Bob Dylan	*The Times They Are-A Changin'*	CBS	1964
	Bob Dylan	*Another Side Of*	CBS	1964
	Bob Dylan	*Bringing It All Back Home*	CBS	1965
	Fraternity Of Man	*The Fraternity Of Man*	ABC	1966
	Fraternity Of Man	*Get It On*	Dot	1967

(Featured Richie Hayward, later with Little Feat and Elliot Ingber, later with The Mothers Of Invention and Captain Beefheart.)

	Mothers Of Invention	*Freak Out*	MGM	1966
	Mothers Of Invention	*Absolutely Free*	MGM	1967
	Nico	*Chelsea Girl*	MGM	1971
	Two Friends	*Two Friends*	Nat. Res	1972
	Velvet Underground and Nico	*The Velvet Underground and Nico (1 track)*	MGM	1967
	Velvet Underground	*White Light/White Heat*	MGM	1968

W040 Thom Wilson

	Stiv Bators	*The Church And The New Creatures*	Lolita	1983
	Stiv Bators	*Disconnected*	Bomp	1980
	Christian Death	*Only Theatre Of Pain*	Future	1983
	Dead Kennedys	*Plastic Surgery Disasters*	Alt Tents	1982
w. John Blair	Jon and The Niteriders	*Live At The Whiskey*	Bomp	1981
	Red Wedding	*Up And Down The Aisle (12" EP)*	Bemis	1982
	T.S.O.L.	*Dance With Me*	Frontier	1981
	Youth Brigade	*Sound And Fury*	BYO	1983

W041 Jai Winding

	Marie and Cherie Curry	*Messing Around With The Boys*	Capitol	1980
	Le Roux	*Up*	Capitol	1980

W042 Pete Wingfield

Blue Rondo A La Turk	*Chewing The Fat*	Virgin	1982
Dexys Midnight Runners	*Searching For The Young Soul Rebels*	EMI	1980
L.G.T.	*Too Long*	Imp	1982
Second Image	*Second Image*	Polydor	1983
Pete Wingfield	*Breakfast Special*	Island	1975

W043 Alan Winstanley (see also: Clive Langer and Alan Winstanley)

	J.J.Burnel	*Euroman Cometh*	UA	1979
	Face Dance	*About Face*	Capitol	1980
	Four Out Of Five Doctors	*Four Out Of Five Doctors*	Nemperor	1980
	Lene Lovich	*Flex*	Stiff	1979
	Original Mirrors	*Original Mirrors*	Mercury	1980
	Rumour	*Purity Of Essence*	Stiff	1980
	Stranglers	*The Raven*	UA	1979
w. M.Rushent	Rachel Sweet	*Protect The Innocent*	Stiff	1980
w. Bob Andrews	Tenpole Tudor	*Eddie, Old Bob, Dick And Gary*	Stiff	1981
	Tenpole Tudor	*Let The Four Winds Blow*	Stiff	1981

W044 Edgar Winter

Montrose	*Open Fire*	WB	1978

W045 Johnny Winter

Muddy Waters	*Hard Again*	Blue Sky	1977
Muddy Waters	*I'm Ready*	Blue Sky	1978
Muddy Waters	*King Bee*	Blue Sky	1981
Muddy Waters	*Hoochie Coochie Man*	Blue Sky	1983

W046 Muff Winwood

w. Rhett Davies	After The Fire	*Laser Love*	CBS	1979
	Kevin Ayers	*Yes We Have No Mananas*	Harvest	1976
w. Rhett Davies	Russ Ballard	*Winning*	Epic	1976
	Dire Straits	*Dire Straits*	Vert/WB	1978
	Fabulous Poodles	*Think Pink*	Blue/Epic	1979
	Philip Goodhand-Tait	*Teach An Old Dog New Tricks*	Chrysalis	1977
	Milk 'n' Cookies	*Milk 'n' Cookies*	Island	1975
	Noel Redding Band	*Clonakilty Cowboys*	RCA	1975
	Sparks	*Kimono My House*	Island	1974
	Sparks	*Propaganda*	Island	1974
	Sutherland Brothers	*The Sutherland Brothers Band*	Island	1970
	Sutherland Brothers and Quiver	*Lifeboat*	Island	1972
	Sutherland Brothers and Quiver	*Dream Kid*	Island	1973
	Sutherland Brothers and Quiver	*Beat Of The Street*	Island	1974

W047 Steve Winwood

Jim Capaldi	*Fierce Heart*	WEA	1983
Third World	*Aiye-Keta*	Island	1973

(Steve Winwood also produced much of Traffic's post Jimmy Miller albums as well as his own three solo albums.)

W048 Richie Wise

Tim Bogert	*Progressions*	Accord	1981
Tim Bogert	*Master's Brew*	Allegiance	1983
Face Dancer	*This World*	Capitol	1979
Savoy Brown	*Live In Concert*	Accord	1981
Savoy Brown	*Destined To Conquer*	Accord	1981
The following albums all co-produced with Kenny Kerner			
Elkie Brooks	*Rich Man's Woman*	A&M	1975
Danny Cox	*Feels So Good*	Casab	1971
Dust	*Dust*	KS	1971
Emperor	*Emperor*	P.Stock	1977
Faragher Brothers	*Family Ties*	ABC	1977
Jose Feliciano	*And The Feeling's Good*	RCA	1974
KGB	*Motion*	MCA	1976
Kiss	*Kiss*	Casab	1974
Gladys Knight and The Pips	*Imagination (4 tracks)*	Buddah	1973
Gladys Knight and The Pips	*2nd Anniversary (4 tr)*	Buddah	1975
Pets	*Wet Behind The Ears*	Arista	1978
Steve Marriott	*Marriott*	A&M	1976
Stories	*About Us (1 track only; US hit version of "Brother Louie".)*		
Stories	*Travelling Underground*	KS	1973

W049 Jimmy "The Wiz" Wisner

Buckinghams	*In One Ear And Gone Tomorrow*	CBS	1968
Dion	*Wonder Where I'm Bound*	CBS	1966
Paul Evans	*Hello This Is Paul Evans*	Spring	1979
Scarlet Rivera	*Scarlet*	WB	1977
Scarlet Rivera	*Scarlet Fever*	WB	1978
soundtrack	*Scrambled Feet*	DRG	1980

W050 Joel "Joe" Wissert

	Jackie De Shannon	*This Is Jackie De Shannon*	Liberty	1966
w. J.Nitzsche	Jackie De Shannon	*Me About You*	Liberty	1968
	Flo and Eddie	*Illegal, Immoral and Fattening*	CBS	1975
	Ruthann Friedman	*Constant Companion*	WB	1970
	J.Geils Band	*Sanctuary*	EMI-Amer	1978
	Murray Head	*Nigel Lived*	CBS	1972
	Heaters	*Energy Transfer*	CBS	1980
	Janis Ian	*Janis Ian*	CBS	1978
	Tom Jans	*Dark Blonde*	CBS	1976
	Robin Lane and The Chartbusters	*Robin Lane and The Chartbusters*	WB	1980
	Gordon Lightfoot	*Summer Side Of Life*	WB	1971
w. L.Waronker	Gordon Lightfoot	*Gord's Gold*	WB	1975
	Lovin' Spoonful	*Everything Playing*	KS	1968

	Dave Mason	*Old Crest On A New Wave*	CBS	1980
	Helen Reddy	*Free And Easy*	Capitol	1974
	Helen Reddy	*No Way To Treat A Lady*	Capitol	1975
	Helen Reddy	*Music Music*	Capitol	1976
	Helen Reddy	*Imagination*	MCA	1983
	Boz Scaggs	*Silk Degrees*	CBS	1976
	Boz Scaggs	*Down Two, Then Left*	CBS	1977
	Sinceros	*The Sound Of Sunbathing*	CBS	1979
	Small Wonder	*Small Wonder*	CBS	1976
	Turtles	*Happy Together*	Lon/WW	1967

W051 Ed Wodenjak

	Dillards	*Mountain Rock*	Crystal	1979
	Taj Mahal	*Live*	Crystal/Ma	1980

W052 Bill Wolf

w. Doc Storch	Bodacious D.F.	*Bodacious D.F.*	RCA	1973
	Martin Mull	*Sex And Violins*	ABC	1978
w. D.Diadem	Rowan Brothers	*The Rowan Brothers*	CBS	1972
	Rowans	*Sibling Rivalry*	Asylum	1976

W053 David Wolfert

	Lyn Anderson	*Outlaw Is Just A State Of Mind*	CBS	1979
	Paul Anka	*Listen To Your Heart*	RCA	1978
	Cher	*I Paralyze*	CBS	1982
	Peter Criss	*Out Of Control*	Mercury	1980
	Sarah Dash	*Close Enough*	Kirshner	1981
	Dr.Buzzard	*Dr.Buzzard Goes To Washington*	Elektra	1979
	Four Tops	*Tonight!*	Casab	1981
	Four Tops	*One More Mountain*	Casab	1982
	Heat	*Heat*	MCA	1980
	Marilyn McCoo	*Solid Gold*	RCA	1983
	Stephanie Mills	*Merciless*	Casab	1983
	Peaches And Herb	*Remember*	CBS	1983
	Gary Portnoy	*Gary Portnoy*	CBS	1980
	Dusty Springfield	*Living Without Your Love*	Merc/UA	1979

W054 John Wood

w. Joe Boyd	The Act	*Too Late At 20*	Hannibal	1981
	Any Trouble	*Where Are All The Nice Girls*	Stiff	1980
w. Will Birch	Any Trouble	*Wrong End Of The Race*	EMI-Amer	1984
w. Joe Boyd	James Booker	*Junco Partner*	Island	1976
	Cajun Moon	*Cajun Moon*	Chrysalis	1976
w. Joe Boyd	Julie Covington	*Julie Covington*	Virgin	1978
w. Trevor Lucas	Sandy Denny	*Like An Old Fashioned Waltz*	Island	1973
w. R.Thompson	Sandy Denny	*The North Sea Grassman And The Raven*	Island	1971
	Fairport Convention	*Angel Delight*	Island	1971
w. Simon Nicol	Fairport Convention	*Babbacombe Lee*	Island	1971

w. Trevor Lucas	Fairport Convention	*9*	Island	1973
w. Trevor Lucas	Fairport Convention	*Live Convention*	Island	1974
	John Martyn	*Bless The Weather*	Island	1971
	John Martyn	*Solid Air*	Island	1973
	John Martyn	*Sunday's Child*	Island	1975
	Pierre Moerlen's Gong	*Expresso 2*	Arista	1978
	Pentangle	*Solomon's Seal*	Reprise	1972
	Squeeze	*Cool For Cats*	A&M	1979
	Squeeze	*Argy Bargy*	A&M	1980
	David Swarbrick	*Smiddyburn*	Logo	1981
	Richard Thompson	*Henry The Human Fly*	Island	1972
	Richard and Linda Thompson	*I Want To See The Bright Lights*	Island	1974
w. Simon Nicol	Richard and Linda Thompson	*Hokey Pokey*	Island	1974
	Richard and Linda Thompson	*Pour Down Like Silver*	Island	1975
	Richard and Linda Thompson	*First Light*	Chrysalis	1978
	Richard and Linda Thompson	*Sunny Vista*	Chrysalis	1979
	various artists	*Morris On*	Island	1972
	Loudon Wainwright III	*A Live One*	Rad/Round	1979

W055 Roy Wood

	Darts	*Dart Attack*	Magnet	1979
	Annie Haslam	*Annie In Wonderland*	WB	1978

W056 Kit Woolven

	Philip Lynott	*Solo In Soho*	Vert/WB	1980
	Philip Lynott	*The Philip Lynott Album*	Vert/WB	1982
	Thin Lizzy	*Chinatown*	Vert/WB	1980
	Wild Horses	*Stand Your Ground*	EMI	1981

W057 Geoff Workman

	Sammy Hagar	*Danger Zone*	Capitol	1980
w. Kevin Elson	Journey	*Departure*	CBS	1980
	Ian McLagan	*Troublemaker*	Mercury	1980
	Gary Myrick	*Living In A Movie*	Epic	1981
	Toto	*Turn Back*	CBS	1980
	Tommy Tutone	*Tommy Tutone 2 (side 2 only)*	CBS	1981
	Dwight Twilley	*Scuba Divers (2 tr.)*	EMI-Amer	1982

W058 Link Wray

	Eggs Over Easy	*Good 'n' Cheap*	A&M	1972

W059 Bob Wyld

w. Art Polhemus	Blues Magoos	*Psychedelic Lollipop*	Mercury	1966
	Blues Magoos	*Never Going Back To Georgia*	ABC	1969
	Blues Magoos	*Gulf Coast Bound*	ABC	1970
w. Art Polhemus	Bunky and Jake	*Bunky and Jake*	Mercury	1967
	Kangaroo	*Kangaroo*	MGM	1968

W060 Bill Wyman

	Buddy Guy and	*Drinkin' TNT,*		
	Junior Wells	*Smokin' Dynamite*	Red L	1980
	Sons Of Heroes	*Sons Of Heroes*	Ripp/MCA	1983
	Tucky Buzzard	*Warm Slash*	Capitol	1969
	Tucky Buzzard	*Coming On Again*	Capitol	1971
	Tucky Buzzard	*Alright On The Night*	Purple	1973
	Tucky Buzzard	*Buzzard*	Purple	1973
	Bill Wyman	*Monkey Grip*	RSR	1974
	Bill Wyman	*Stone Alone*	RSR	1976
w. Chris Kimsey	Bill Wyman	*Bill Wyman*	A&M	1982

Y001 Jerry Yester

	Association	*Renaissance*	Valiant	1967
	Aztec Two-Step	*Aztec Two-Step*	Elektra	1972
	Tim Buckley	*Goodbye and Hello*	Elektra	1967
w. Zal Yanovsky	Tim Buckley	*Happy Sad*	Elektra	1968
	Tim Dawe	*Penrod*	Straight	1969
w. Zal Yanovsky	Judy Henske and			
	Jerry Yester	*Farewell Aldebaran*	Straight	1969
	Billy Mernit	*Special Delivery*	Elektra	1973
	Rosebud	*Rosebud*	Straight	1971
	(Group comprised Judy Henske, Jerry Yester, Craig Doerge and John Seiter.)			
	Tom Waits	*Closing Time*	Asylum	1973
	Zal Yanovsky	*Alive And Well In Argentina*	KS	1971

Y002 Chip Young

	Toni Brown	*Good For You Too*	MCA	1974
	Lee Clayton	*Lee Clayton*	MCA	1973
	Lee Clayton	*The Dream Goes On*	Capitol	1981
	Joe Ely	*Joe Ely*	MCA	1977
	Joe Ely	*Honktonk Masquerade*	MCA	1978
	Lloyd Green	*Steel Rides*	Monument	1975
	Mickey Newbury	*I Came To Hear The Music*	Elektra	1974
	Mickey Newbury	*Lovers*	Elektra	1975
	Delbert McClinton	*Victim Of Life's Circumstances*	ABC	1975
	Delbert McClinton	*Genuine Cowhide*	ABC	1976
	Delbert McClinton	*Love Rustler*	ABC	1977
	Jerry Reed	*Half and Half*	RCA	1979
	Jerry Reed	*Live*	RCA	1979
	Jerry Reed	*Jerry Reed Sings Jim Croce*	RCA	1980
	Ronnie Sessions	*Ronnie Sessions*	MCA	1977
	Spanky and Our Gang	*Change*	CBS	1975
	Billy Swan	*I Can Help*	Monument	1975
	Billy Swan	*Rock 'n' Roll Moon*	Monument	1975
	Billy Swan	*Billy Swan*	Monument	1976

Y003 Jesse Colin Young

	Michael Hurley	*Armchair Boogie*	Raccoon	1971

Y004 Kenny Young

	Fox	Fox	GTO	1975
	Fox	Tales Of Illusion	GTO	1975
	Fox	Blue Hotel	GTO	1975
	Methuselah	Matthew, Mark, Luke and John	Elektra	1968
	Yellow Dog	Yellow Dog	Virgin	1977
	Yellow Dog	Beware Of The Dog	Virgin	1978
w. R.Appere	Kenny Young	Last Stage To Silverwood	WB	1973

Z001 Robert W. Zachary, Jnr.

	Ronee Blakeley	Ronee Blakeley	Elektra	1972
	Crabby Appleton	Rotten To The Core	Elektra	1971
	Rainbow Band	The Rainbow Band	Elektra	1970
	Paul Siebel	Jack-Knife Gypsy	Elektra	1971

Z002 Joe Zagarino

	Henry Gross	Henry Gross	ABC	1972
	B.B.King	In London	ABC	1971
	B.B.King	Guess Who	ABC	1972
w. Jimmy Miller	Bobby Whitlock	Raw Velvet	CBS	1972

Z003 Frank Zappa

Captain Beefheart	Trout Mask Replica	Straight	1969
Lenny Bruce	The Berkeley Concert	Bizarre	1968
Wild Man Fischer	An Evening With Wildman Fischer	Bizarre	1968
GTO's	Permanent Damage	Straight	1969
Grand Funk Railroad	Good Singing Good Playing	MCA	1976
Mothers Of Invention	We're Only In It For The Money	Verve	1968
Mothers Of Invention	Ruben and The Jets	Verve	1968
Mothers Of Invention	Uncle Meat	Bizarre	1969
Mothers Of Invention	Burnt Weeny Sandwich	Bizarre	1969
Mothers Of Invention	Weasels Ripped My Flesh	Bizarre	1970
Mothers Of Invention	Chunga's Revenge	Bizarre	1970
Mothers Of Invention	Fillmore East - June 1971	Bizarre	1971
Mothers Of Invention	200 Motels	UA	1971
Mothers Of Invention	Just Another Band From LA	Bizarre	1972
Mothers Of Invention	Grand Wazoo	Bizarre	1972
Mothers Of Invention	Overnite Sensation	DiscReet	1973
Mothers Of Invention	Roxy And Elsewhere	Discreet	1974
Mothers Of Invention	One Size Fits All	Discreet	1975
Ruben and The Jets	For Real	Mercury	1973
L.Shankar	Touch Me There	Zappa	1979
Jeff Simmons	Lucille Has Messed Up My Mind	Straight	1969
Frank Zappa	Lumpy Gravy	Verve	1968
Frank Zappa	Hot Rats	Bizarre	1969
Frank Zappa	Waka Jawaka	Bizarre	1972
Frank Zappa	Apostrophe	DiscReet	1974

	Frank Zappa	*Zoot Allures*	WB	1976
	Frank Zappa	*Zappa In New York*	Discreet	1977
	Frank Zappa	*Studio Tan*	Discreet	1978
	Frank Zappa	*Sleep Dirt*	DiscReet	1979
	Frank Zappa	*Sheik Yerbouti*	Zappa	1979
	Frank Zappa	*Orchestral Favourites*	Discreet	1979
	Frank Zappa	*Joe's Garage*	Zappa	1979
	Frank Zappa	*Joe's Garage Acts 2 and 3*	Zappa	1979
	Frank Zappa	*Tinseltown Rebellion*	B.Pumpkin	1981
	Frank Zappa	*You Are What You Is*	B.Pumpkin	1981
	Frank Zappa	*Shut Up 'n' Play Yer Guitar*	B.Pumpkin	1981
	Frank Zappa	*Ship Arriving Too Late To Save A Drowning Witch*	B.Pumpkin	1982
	Frank Zappa	*Man From Utopia*	B.Pumpkin	1983
	Frank Zappa and Captain Beefheart	*Bongo Fury*	DiscReet	1975

Z004 Ritchie Zito

		Tony Basil	*Tony Basil*	Virgin	1984
w. Mike Howlett & G.Moroder	Berlin	*Love Life*	Geffen	1984
w. Marty Cohn	Dukes	*The Dukes*	WB	1979
w. Joey Carbone	John O'Bannion	*John O'Bannion*	Elektra	1981

League Tables of Producers' Chart Successes

Cumulative points total based on averaging out all available charts, 100 points for number 1, 99 points for number 2 and so on down to one point for number 100. Airplay and retail figures are also taken into consideration when determining the lower positions. All 4 lists cover the same time span; 1st January, 1984 – 1st June, 1984 inclusive.

PART ONE: US singles producers

Alex Sadkin 3439
Hugh Padgham 2925
Steve Levine 2912
Richard Perry 2767
James Anthony Carmichael
  and Lionel Richie 2683
Chris Thomas 2302
Quincy Jones 2225
Huey Lewis and The News 2215
Giorgio Moroder 2192
Ted Templeman 2186
Rick Chertoff 2150
Ronald Bell/Jim Bonnefond/
  Kool and The Gang 2148
Phil Ramone 2127
Trevor Horn 1964
Ian Little/Duran Duran 1946
John Cougar Mellencamp/
  and Don Gehman 1733
Martyn Ware/Greg Walsh 1705
David A. Stewart 1661
Peter Collins 1651
George Duke 1646
Daryl Hall and John Oates 1636
Kenny Loggins/Lee De Carlo 1604
Russ Titelman 1594
Mark Liggett/Chris Barbosa 1573
Pete Solley 1533
Curtis Anthony Nolen 1505
Tom Bailey 1493
John "Jellybean" Benitez 1414
John Punter 1394
David Foster 1384
Bill Drescher and Rick Springfield 1346
George Martin 1338
Pete Bunetta/Rick
  Chudacoff/Bill Elliott 1318
Genesis 1276
Police 1275
Arif Mardin 1261

Jim Steinman 1240
Robert John "Mutt"
  Lange 1206
Rodney Mills 1173
Howie Casey/R.Finch 1144
Bob Clearmountain 1129
Pat Glasser 1086
John Lennon/Yoko Ono 1080
Alan Parsons 1052
Mack 982
Rick Derringer 973
Michael Omartian 967
Barry Gibb/Karl Richardson
  Albhy Gaulten 961
Mark Smith/Noah Shark 960
Marty Lewis/Dan Fogelberg 950
Martin Rushent 923
Greg Mathieson 905
John Hug 896
Richie Zito 862
Laurie Latham 855
Keith Forsey 852
Peter Hauke 813
Manfred Mann 810
Reggie Lucas 807
Bill Wolfer/D.Pitchford 773
Eldra and Bobby
  DeBarge 763
Jimmy Iovine 743
Val Garay 732
Colin Thurston 730
Chris Hughes/Ross Cullum 721
Spencer Proffer 718
Laid Back 711
Queen 711
Robbie Buchanan 703
Rupert Hine 647
Ray Parker,Jnr 643
Steve Perry 639
Chris Kimsey/Glimmer Twins 620
Tim Friese-Green 616
Ray "Pablo" Falconer 615

Dieter Dierks 613
Lance Quinn 573
Tony Bongiovi 544
Jack White 540
R.Cockle/G.Wheatley 536
Keith Olsen 511
Richard Landis 473
Bruce Botnick 469
Steve Hillage 468
Charlie Calello 464
David Kershenbaum/Joe Jackson 456
Paul Weller/Peter Wilson 443
John Ryan 404
Reggie Calloway 400
Dexter Wansel/Kenny Gamble/
    C.Biggs 382
Phil Collins 374
Larry Blackmon 369
Neil Geraldo/Peter Coleman 356
Steve Lillywhite 354
Hugh Jones 348
Rick James 326
Greg Ladanyi/Jackson Browne 298
Tom Dowd/Eddie Money 292
Prince 287
Nile Rodgers 287
J.Ellis 277
R.Andrews 273
Chuck Plotkin 271
Styx 256
Norman Whitfield 252
Tom Werman 248
Robert Plant/Benji Lefevre/ Pat Moran 247
Sergio Mendes 240
Mike Thorne 240
Peter Mclan 236
Barry Mann 212
Bob Gaudio/Bob Crewe 201
Ron Nevison 193
Bob Dylan 187
Thomas Dolby 177
Bob Ezrin/David Gilmour 175
Dave Edmunds 172
Dan Hartman 166
Chris Neil 158
Joe Macre/Rick Witkowski 157
Jim Ed Norman 153
Bill Ham 153
Narada Michael Walden 150
Bruce Springsteen/Jon
    Landau/Miami Steve 148
Michael Masser 146
Cheryl Lynn/T.Lewis/
    J.Harris 141
Terry Bozio/Bruce Swedien 137
Mike Stone 131

Brian MacLeod 125
Myles Goodwyn 124
Amir Bayyan 124
Leon F.Sylvers III/ D.Meyers 114
Peter Asher 113
Dennis Lambert 112
Bob Rivers 102
Glen Kolotkin 100
John Robie 97
Clive Langer/Alan Winstanley 96
David Bowie 91
Dave Grusin 90
Tony Mansfield 81
Michael Gore 80
Paul Cotton/Rusty Young 75
Eddy Grant 68
Andy Fraser 63
Tony Peluso/Michael Lovesmith/Steve Barri 63
Terry Britten 63
Jon Astley/Phil Chapman 62
Frank Stallone 59
Paul Rothchild 58
Gary Katz 51
Bobby Womack/Andrew Oldham/
    James Gadson 50
Luther Vandross 45
Michael James Jackson/ Gene Simmons 42
Bruce Fairbairn 41
Ollie E. Brown 39
A.A.Jones 39
Bobby and Larson Paine 28
Maurice and Robin Gibb 28
Harold Shedd/Alabama 27
ABC/Gary Langan 27
Athur Baker 21
Barry Goudreau/Lenny Petzke 13
Sammy Hagar/Neil Schon 6
J. Webb/J. Fair 4

PART 2: US Albums

Quincy Jones 4602
Alex Sadkin 3676
Hugh Padgham 3461
Steve Levine 3002
James Anthony Carmichael and
    Lionel Richie 2747
Chris Thomas 2286
Robert John "Mutt" Lange 2028
Phil Ramone 2007
Huey Lewis 1973
John Cougar Mellencamp and
    Don Gehman 1943
Police 1847
Ted Templeman 1844

Bill Ham 1817
David A. Stewart 1755
Tom Werman 1737
Trevor Horn 1617
Genesis 1614
Rick Chertoff 1584
Harold Shedd/Alabama 1529
Keith Forsey 1495
Rodney Mills 1474
Peter Asher 1386
Jimmy Iovine 1349
George Duke 1326
Kool and The Gang 1321
Mark Knopfler 1310
Russ Titelman 1279
Luther Vandross/Marcus
Miller 1179
Pete Solley 1178
Spencer Proffer 1167
Steve Lillywhite 1160
Curtis Anthony Nolen 1035
John Lennon/Yoko Ono 1022
Dieter Dierks 1021
Reggie Calloway 995
Barry Gibb/Karl Richardson/Albhy
  Galuten 987
Marty Lewis/Dan Fogelberg 970
Bill Drescher/Rick
  Springfield 932
Tom Bailey 917
Alan Parsons 880
Max Norman/Ozzy Osbourne/
  Bob Daisley 858
Ray "Pablo" Falconer/UB 40 828
Material/Herbie Hancock 815
Mark Liggett/Chris Barbosa 814
Rick Derringer 808
Queen/Mack 792
Giorgio Moroder 788
Eldra DeBarge 782
Reggie Lucas 769
Barbra Streisand/Alan and
  Marilyn Bergman 727
George Martin 712
Bob Ezrin/David Gilmour 693
Mike Stone 685
Larry Blackmon 672
Glimmer Twins/Chris Kimsey 657
Prince 654
Lance Quinn/Tony Bongiovi 629
Thomas Dolby 628
Peter Collins 627
Martin Rushent 623
Rupert Hine 620
Mark Smith/Noah Shark 595
David Kershenbaum/Joe Jackson 579

Kenny Gamble/Dexter Wansel 573
Kevin Elson 561
Neil Geraldo 551
Ray Parker, Jnr. 545
Nile Rodgers/David Bowie 532
Mike Howlett 530
Richie Zito 530
Alan Shacklock 528
Terry Bozio 518
Bob Dylan 511
Steve Perry 501
Styx 475
Michael James Jackson/
  Gene Simmons/Paul Stanley 446
John Punter 445
Sammy Hagar/Neil Schon 426
Peter Henderson 425
Dennis Lambert 422
Manfred Mann 418
Pete Bunetta/Rick Chudacoff 367
Ashley Howe 336
R.Wilson 300
Laurie Anderson 300
Robert Plant 299
Paul Simon 298
Lenny Waronker 298
Val Garay 296
Peter Hauke 290
Paul Rothchild 289
Ross Cullum/Chris Hughes 289
Wayne Braithwaite 284
Maurice White 267
David Byrne/Talking Heads 259
Bobby Womack/Andrew Oldham/
  James Gadson 258
King Crimson 240
Reggie Andrews 235
Mitch Easter 220
Jim Steinman 209
Richard James Burgess 200
Booker T. Jones 185
A A Jones 176
Laid Back 176
Richard Carpenter 174
Bruce Fairbairn 160
Tim Friese-Green 156
Jermaine Jackson 155
ABC/Gary Langan 155
Jack White/Robbie Buchanan 140
Jim Lea 139
Todd Rundgren 136
David Sanborn 124
Myles Goodwyn 124
Michael Omartion 123
Peter Wilson/Paul Weller 120
Michael Kamen/Roger Waters 119

Roger Glover 100
Hugh Jones 100
Joe Sample/Wilton Felder
  Ndugu Chancler 96
Laurie Latham 90
Bob Gaudio/Bob Crewe 87
Greg Ladanyi/Jackson
  Browne 87
Earl Klugh 84
Narada Michael Walden 82
Dave Edmunds 79
Gordon Fordyce 74
Tom Dowd 72
Peter Mclan 67
Greg Mathieson 61
Bob Sargeant 56
Rick James 44
David Foster 10
Howie Casey/R.Finch 10
Nick Launay 9

PART 3: UK Singles

Peter Collins 4137
Alex Sadkin 3324
Trevor Horn 2740
Tom Bailey 2329
Steve Levine 2212
Phil Ramone 1896
Kool and The Gang 1892
James Anthony Carmichael
  and Lionel Richie 1801
Jacques Morali 1788
Arif Mardin 1750
Rupert Hine 1655
Peter Wilson 1655
Quincy Jones 1643
Clive Langer/Alan
Winstanley 1620
Mack/Queen 1596
John Punter 1553
Paul Jabara/Bob Esty 1515
Richard Perry 1392
Steve Lillywhite 1329
John Porter 1318
Chris Liggett/Mark Barbosa 1300
Hugh Padgham 1138
Rick Chertoff 1104
Chris Hughes/Ross Cullum 1102
Robin Millar 1067
Tony Swain/Steve Jolley 1044
Colin Fairley 1040
Ian Little/Duran Duran 988
Ted Templeman 984
Christopher Neil 974

George Martin 968
Dave Mackay 952
John Sherry/Flying Pickets 937
Pete Bunetta/Rick Chudacoff 929
David Lord 923
Thomas Dolby 915
Chris Thomas 913
Paul Weller 858
John "Jellybean" Benitez 851
George Duke 840
Richard Hewson/Shakin'
Stevens 830
Brian Tench 822
Mike Batt 793
Joel Diamond 793
Robert Andrews 790
Nick Martinelli 781
Pete Wingfield 778
Status Quo 773
Russ Titelman 772
John Lennon/Yoko Ono 757
Nick Tauber 754
Phil Fearon 753
Curtis Anthony Nolen 751
Colin Thurston 741
Daniel Miller 717
Elvis Costello 716
Tony Mansfield 716
Zeus B. Held 714
Hugh Jones 660
Reggie Lucas 646
Mickie Most 636
Mike Thorne 625
Ultravox 625
Kuma Harada/Snowy White 623
Chris Parry 573
Bruce Welch 564
Ian Levine 559
Ray "Pablo" Falconer/UB 40 552
Alan Shacklock 545
Barry Gibb/Karl Richardson
  Albhy Galuten 536
D.Ylvisaker 511
August Darnell 509
Tim Friese-Green 504
John L.Walters 501
Phil Thornally 493
Kenny Loggins/Lee De Carlo 487
Louis Clark/Juan Martin 480
Richard Rudolph 472
Ian Anthony Stephens 470
Bob Marley 469
Laurie Latham 448
Bill Drescher/Rick
  Springfield 443
Chris Kimsey 442

Keith Forsey 442
Fiachra French 431
Joe Sample/Wilton Felder/
   Ndugu Chancler 418
Paul Curtis 413
Cocteau Twins 410
Stewart Levine 403
Martyn Ware/Greg Walsh 401
Stephen Hague 398
Keith Olsen 382
George Michael 377
Genesis 375
Mike Hedges 369
S.Jeffries/M.Rye 364
Martin Birch 355
Steve Brown 349
Human League 315
Tom Dowd 312
Nigel Wright 271
Was Brothers/Jack Tann 269
Neil Geraldo/Peter Coleman 269
Rick Derringer 249
Arthur Baker 249
Glimmer Twins 247
Butch Ingram 241
Stephen Lovell 239
Gary Langan/ABC 228
Jim Steinman 219
Michael Omartian 213
Tony Clarke 203
Jeremy Green 198
Chris Tsangarides 191
Nile Rodgers 187
Dennis Lambert 185
Alan Parsons 177
Talking Heads 168
Peter Walsh 162
Rod Stewart 159
Bernard Edwards 158
Giorgio Moroder 153
Ozzy Osbourne/Bob Daisley/
   Max Norman 150
Tom Allom 147
Alan Barton 147
Mark Knopfler 146
Jeff Glixman 146
Eddie Grant 144
Jermaine Jackson 143
Bruce Springsteen/Jon
   Landau/Miami Steve/Chuck
   Plotkin 140
David Kershenbaum 140
Jerry Crutchfield 139
Andy Hill 138
Material/Herbie Hancock 126
Michael Campbell 126

Wayne Braithwaite 125
J.Barnes 124
Nick Lowe 115
Paul Bass 115
Godwin Logie 113
Brad Shapiro 113
Dave Brewis 112
Pete Bellotte 110
John Fryer 110
Phil Collins 108
Mike Oldfield 107
Bill Wolfer 103
Assembly 102
Bob Clearmountain 101
John Brand/Bernie Clarke 100
Chas Chandler 99
Dennis Bovell 99
Gary Klein 95
Dennis Weinrich 87
Peter Henderson 86
Dave Richards/Chris Rea 84
David Sylvain/Steve Nye 82
Bob Carter 78
Michael Kamen 74
Jonathan King 73
John Luongo 72
John Brand 66
Martin Rushent 62
Leon F.Sylvers 62
Kevin Beamish 62
Brian May 61
Bob Lamb 60
Bill Ham 58
John Lydon/Martin Atkins 58
Robin Gibb/Maurice Gibb/
   Dennis Byron 52
Lamont Dozier 46
Eddie Offord 44
James Guthrie 43
Peter Mclan 42
Eric Matthew 59
Chas and Dave 40
McFadden and Whitehead 36
Simon Boswell 36
Pat Collier 36
Tim Palmer/Dave Harris 33
Richard James Burgess 32
Dieter Dierks 32
Brian Robson 31
Tom Werman 30
Geoff Emerick/Nick Heyward 30
Steve Barri/Brian Potter 30
Peter Gabriel 29
Martin Hannett 29
Tony Visconti 29
P.Gosling 29

Stuart Colman 26
Bob Sargeant 23
Spencer Proffer 22
Marc Durand 22
Wally Brill 17
Al Kooper 14
Neville Staples/
    Lynval Golding 10
Pip Williams 9
Lance Quinn 6
Bruce Fairbairn 4
Kenny Gamble/Leon Huff 2
Nigel Gray 2

PART 4: UK Albums

Quincy Jones 4244
Alex Sadkin 4221
Steve Lillywhite 3574
Hugh Padgham 3160
Chris Thomas 2800
Anthony James Carmichael
    and Lionel Richie 2603
David A.Stewart 2375
Jimmy Iovine 2342
Mark Knopfler 2235
Steve Levine 2049
Phil Ramone 1990
Laurie Latham 1810
Ray "Pablo" Falconer/UB 40 1693
Christopher Neil 1473
Ian Little/Duran Duran 1472
Tom Bailey 1438
Tony Visconti 1355
Genesis 1351
Rupert Hine 1290
Mack/Queen 1217
Barbra Streisand/Alan and
    Marilyn Bergman 1215
John Porter 1183
Ted Templeman 1146
Richard Hewson
    Shakin' Stevens 11119
Nick Tauber 1109
Tony Swain/Steve Jolley 1107
Steve Brown/George Michael 1066
George Martin 1044
Peter Collins 970
Clive Langer/Alan
    Winstanley 946
Paul Weller 920
Peter Wilson 920
David Bowie 903
Todd Rundgren 885

Arif Mardin 864
Police 841
Tony Clark 810
Kool and The Gang 800
John Lennon/Yoko Ono 768
Spandau Ballet 742
Thomas Dolby 725
Nile Rodgers 694
Mike Howlett 683
Phil Collins 677
Status Quo 663
Alan Shacklock 659
David Kershenbaum/Joe
    Jackson 654
Ultravox 652
Oliver Hitch 630
Tony Clarke 526
Alan Parsons 486
Crash/A.Williams 474
Peter Henderson 465
Martin Birch 464
Mike Thorne 461
Kevin Beamish 457
Andy Hill 430
Bob Ezrin/David Gilmour 428
Trevor Horn 427
Colin Thurston 422
Juan Martin/Louis Clark 418
Reggie Lucas 397
Jeff Glixman 384
Roxy Music 383
Rhett Davies 382
Chris Kimsey/Glimmer Twins 368
Dave Brewis 356
Bobby Womack/Andrew Oldham/
    James Gadson 336
Brian Tench 329
Hugh Jones 328
David Lord 328
M.Liggett/Chris Barbosa 327
Gary Langan/ABC 322
Dave Richards/Chris Rea 320
Michael Kamen/Roger Waters 318
Chris Parry 317
Chas and Dave 310
Yes 298
Peter Walsh 296
Luther Vandross 292
Marcus Miller 292
Bill Ham 287
Dieter Dierks 278
John Punter 272
Jim Lea 272
Nick Martinelli 271
Michael Campbell 271
Tom Newman/Kume Harada 269

Richard Perry 266
Tom Allom 265
Stewart Levine 258
Pip Williams 254
Russ Titelman 249
Tim Friese-Green 237
Keith Forsey 230
Dennis Bovell 223
Barry Gibb/Karl Richardson/
    Albhy Galuten 218
Peter Asher 216
Flying Pickets/John Sherry 211
Richard Carpenter 209
Chris Hughes/Ross Cullum 199
John Fryer 198
Cocteau Twins 196
Nigel Gray 196
Bill Drescher/Rick
    Springfield 196
Martin Hayles 196
John Luongo 187
Siousxie and The Banshees 174
Zeus B. Held 170
George Duke 164
Brad Shapiro 158
Mike Hedges 145
David Mackay 141
Greg Walsh 140
Jim Steinman 139
Van Morrison 136
Simon Phillips 134
Stephen Lovell 133
D.Stafford 128
British Electric
    Foundation 126
Phil Spector 125
Mike Oldfield 124
Ken Scott 114
Nick Heyward/Geoff
    Emerick 107
Joe Sample/Wilton Felder/
    Ndugu Chancler 107
Richard Rudolph 95
Rick Chertoff 94
Stan Shaw 92
Roy Halee/Simon and
    Garfunkel 91
Styx 91

Eddie Offord 84
Wayne Braithwaite 82
Andy Latimer 81
Curtis Anthony Nolen 79
Max Norman/Ozzy Osbourne/
    Bob Daisley 79
Richard Dashut/Ken Caillatt
    Fleetwood Mac 77
David Essex 76
Mike Batt 76
Adam Kidron 72
Vangelis 72
Bob Dylan 72
Garth Fundis 71
Nick Sykes 68
John Farrar 62
Nick Cave 61
D.Reedman/J.Jarrett 57
E.C.Radcliffe/Yazoo 51
Tony Bongiovi/Lance Quinn 51
Neil Geraldo/ 50
Joe Zawinul 47
Midge Ure 46
Visage 46
Jack Douglas 46
Rod Stewart/Tom Dowd 45
Thin Lizzy/Phil Lynott 44
John Hudson 44
John Anthony 33
Mond Cowie 29
John G. Perry 28
Dick Taylor/Hawkwind 26
John Starkey 26
Howard Gray 26
Jack Richardson 24
Wally Brill/David Anderle 17
Robert John "Mutt" Lange 15
Alan Barson 14
Adam Ant/Richard James
    Burgess/Marco Pironi 13
Larry Dunn/Verdine White 12
Mitch Easter/Don Dixon 12
Vincent Davies 11
Dennis Lambert 10
John Cougar/Don Gehman 9
Hagar and Schon 9
Artie Ripp 6
Peter Mclan 4

Index of Groups, Artists and Soundtracks

The singers and bands are indexed according to their code letter and number in the main directory section. Also, the alphabetical listing of the artistes cannot handle those bands whose names consist of numbers – so here they are first of all.

3-D S13
38 Special H22, M71
805 M18
100% Whole Wheat C42
101-ers A23, M21
1910 Fruitgum Co K6
1994 D44
20/20 M28, P25

A
A's C30, G16
ABC H56, L11
A.B.Skhy D24, F22
AC/DC L12, P23, V2
Abrahams, Mick T12
Ace A19, L19
A Child's Garden Of Grass J3
Acid Casualties B74
Ackles, David A15, M68, T8
Act B59, W54
Action M40
Adams, Arthur L36
Adams, Bryan C38
Adams, Don T15
Adams, Greg B22
Adams, Jay Boy H11
Addis and Crofut H13
Addrisi Brothers P42
Advertising A25, L4
Adverts L24, N11
Aerosmith B7, B50, D44, L61
A Flock Of Seagulls H64
Afraid Of Mice V8
After The Fire D9, H45, L24, M16, W46
Aim H72
Ainley, Charlie P28
Airborne O10
Aire, Jane S62
Airplay F21, G56
Air Raid K34
Air Supply H58, M44, P29
Airto T15
Airwaves M82
Akkerman, Jan D17, H23
Alarm S21
Alabama State Troopers N16

Albania A26
Alberto Y Los Trios Paranoias J9, J15
Alda Reserve S58
Alessi Brothers C72, G18, H62, L58, S25
Alexander, Arthur C44
Alexander, Gordon B18
Alexander, Karen P24
Alexander, Willie L31
Alibi R7
Alkatraz M50
Allen, David D41
Allen, Henry "Red" T15
Allen, Laura P24
Allen, Peter A24, F21, L10, P30, T14, T15
Allen, Rex W37
Allen, Steve T15
Allen, Terry H63
Allen, Woody T33
Allez Allez W8
Allison, Keith U2
Allison, Mose D41, E5
Allman, Greg G8, S5, T24, W11
Allman Brothers B7, D46, R50, S5
Almeida, Laurindo B44, T15
All This And World War 2 s/t R11
Alpha Band H47, S44
Alquin B1
Altered Images C24, R48, S20, S59, V8
Alternative TV M52, O13
All The Right Moves s/t A24
Amazing Blondel G34
Amazing Rhythm Aces J19
Ambergris C70
Amboy Dukes K34
Ambrosia G68
Ameche, Don T15
Amen Corner T3
America B6, D31, M3, M40, M75, S2
American Breed T29
American Dream R46
American Flyer F38, M40
American Gigolo s/t M84
American Hot Wax s/t V1

American Noise L3
American Patrol G7
American Spring W35
American Standard Band C6
An American Werewolf In
London s/t Q1
Ancient Grease R11
Anders and Poncia P18
Andersen, Eric G44, G49, L55, P42,
S18, T5
Anderson, Al S46
Anderson, James D13
Anderson, John (UK) K16
Anderson.John (US) W37
Anderson, Lynn W53
Anderson Tapes s/t J27
Andrews, Harvey G38
Andrews, Mark B51
Angel K34, L18, L32
Angelic Upstarts L35, P41, W38
Angelo S69
Animals C23, M87, W39
Anka, Paul W53
Ant, Adam B91, H68
Anvil T30
Any Trouble B16, B33, H64, K17, W54
Apache E16, G60
Apocalypse Now s/t R44
A Poke In The Eye G38
Appaloosa K30
Appice, Carmine P25
Applejacks S40
Appletree Theatre S48
April Wine B35, G48, K34, M94, S71
A.Raincoat A25
Aranbee Symphony Orchestra R17
Archies B10
Area Code 615 B100, M53
Argent A22
Argent, Rod L59
Armatrading, Joan D49, G1, G13, G52,
J18, L41, L43
Armstrong, Louis T15
Arnold, Eddy M78
Arnold, P.P. H71, J4, O9
Arrogance G22
Arrows M39
Ars Nova G51, R42
Artful Dodger D15, D44, L32
Arthur, Hurley and Gottlieb S52
Art In America O6
Art Of Noise H56
Artwoods V5
Ashra G32
Ashton, Tony A29
Ashworth-Jones, Alan R30

Asia S71
Asleep At The Wheel A11, D41, W37
Assembled Multitude S18
Associates H28
Association B18, B60, H62, M63
P26, Y1
Asylum Choir R49
Atkin, Pete P12
Atkinson, Sweet Pea T4, W9
Atlanta Rhythm Section B88
Atlantics S74
Atomic Rooster N11
Attitudes L38
Attractions B19
Audience D49
Auldridge,Mike M12
Aum G52,R44
Auracle M15
Aural Exciters B38
Australian Crawl C24
Automatic Man L48
Autopilot B13
Average White Band F21,H22,M35
Aviary L61
Aviator M26
Axe L48,N3
Axelrod,D. A33
Axis J17
Axton,Hoyt H24,J20,K17,L41,M8,M60
Ayers,Kevin H45,J15,W46
Ayler,Albert T15
Aztec Camera B81
Aztec Two-Step L29,P27,Y1

B
B-52's A26,B34,B101,D9,S56
Babe Ruth R43,S21
Baby P19
Baby Grand C30
Babys E21,N9,O10
Back Door P6
Bad Brains O2
Bade,Lisa K17
Badfinger E12,E19,H20,M25,
R21,R46,T16,V8
Badger H23,T29
Bad Manners L52
Badowski,Henry B69
Baez,Joan B22,K17,L28,P42
Bagatelle D49,W39
Bailey,Pearl T15
Bailey,Razzy W37
Baio,Scott L48
Baker,Chet B44
Baker,Duck D27,G65

Baker,Ginger M67
Baker,Mickey B50
Baker Gurvitz Army O6
Baldry,Long John H58
Balin,Marty G13,H66
Ball,Marcia B86
Ballard,Larry D48
Ballard,Russ D9,O10,W46
Bananarama B43,S77
Band R31,R46,S32
Bandit A8,F9
Banks,Tony H36
Bannon,R.C. T1
Barbata,Johnny R42
Barbieri,Gato M15,R44,T15
Barclay,Bill K14
Barclay,Nickey O10
Barclay James Harvest B1,M53,W33
Bardot W33
Bare,Bobby C73,L24
Barefoot Jerry M86
Barnaby Bye E16
Barne,Richard E1
Barooga Bandit P38
Barraclough,Elizabeth M73,S32
Barracudas G1,M82
Barrere,Paul G31
Barrett,Syd G25
Barrish,Jesse B4,H66
Barron,Kenny D41
Barron,Ronnie S29
Barrow,Barbara K32
Barton,Lou Ann F32,W23
Basement Five H15
Basho,Robbie D27
Basie,Count T15
Basil,Toni Z4
Bassett,Steve B22
Batdorf and Rodney E16,H10,S15
Batt,Mike B13
Batteau,David S13
Batteaux L41
Battin,Skip M23
Bators,Stiv W40
Baumann,Peter P4
Bay City Rollers I1,M39,M44,W2
B.B.Blunder C31
Beach Boys G66,J21,V2,W35
Bear B60
Bear,Richard T.
Bearfoot S53
Beat S7
Beatlemania s/t L4
Beatles B2,M40,S51
Beau Brummels D39,S72,T12,W11
Be Bop Deluxe B3,L24,M14

Bechirian,Roger B19
Beck,Jeff C70,M40,M87,N11,S13
Beck,Joe R21
Beck,Bogert and Appice N16
Becker,Walter V1
Beckies F26
Bedford,David O8
Beds M55
Bee Gees B102,M35,R20,S70
Bees Make Honey R32
BEF W8
Beggars Opera M39
Bell,Delia H18
Bell,Graham J20
Bell,Maggie M35,R2,W23
Bell,William J23
Bellamy Brothers B54,G22,L48
Bell and Arc J20
Belle Stars C51
Belson,Louis T15
Benatar,Pat C24,C47,G21,O10
Bengali Bauls H65
Bennett,Cliff D10
Bennett,Duster V5
Benno,Marc A15,J18
Benson,George J27,L45,M35
Benton,Brook M35
Berlin H64,M84,Z4
Berlin Blondes T20
Berry,Chuck E45
Berry,Mike B16
Best Little Whorehouse
    In Texas s/t S32
Beth,Karen S32
Bethnal A30,C27,L4
Betjeman,Sir John M93
Betrayal s/t M15
Better Days J8
Betts,Dickey R21,S5
Bezerk Times K9
Big Brother G54,S17
Big Country L43
Big Star D33,F40
Bikel,Theodore P18
Billy & The Beaters B15
Bim R15
Bionic Gold T25
Birtha M57
Bishop,Elvin B39,B63,R44,S5,S79
Bishop,Randy M1,P37
Bishop,Stephen L41,L45,M22
Bishops R22
Black,Cilla M40
Blackfoot B22,H55,J19,N3
Blackjack D46,O6
Blackmore,Richie L18

Black Oak Arkansas C8,D46,P25,R18,R50
Black Rose H60
Black Sabbath B1,B32,B96,M56
Blake,Ran C76
Blakey,Art T15
Blakeley,Ronee W23,Z1
Blancmange H64,L60
Bland,Bobby B9,E5,G9
Blanket Of Secrecy B19
Blasters W17
Blegvad,Peter P11
Blind Date G31
Blind Faith M67
Bliss Band B15
Block,Rory K8
Blondie C24,G52
Blood,Sweat & Tears C55, C64, G44, G66, H5,
   I1, J6, S32, T33
Bloodstone V5
Bloomfield,Mike D16,G54,K11, K30, P28
Blossom Toes G45
Blow Up S/t S48
Blue F27,J16,M53
Blue,David G40,G51,G67,L41, M57, N5, T5
Blue,Peggy R1
Blue Angel H5
Blue Ash F36,G57
Blue Cheer K18
Blue Collar s/t N15
Bluejays C37
Blue Mink M17
Blue Mountain Eagle H10
Blue Oyster Cult B32,F1,K36, L58, P15, W20
Blue Ridge Rangers F15
Blue Rondo A La Turk C24,G36, L14, W42
Blue Steel C8,S23
Blue Velvet Band J5
Blue Zoo F37
Blues Band B19,D38
Blues Brothers T23
Blues Guitar Workshop G65
Blues Image H10,P25
Blues Magoos W59
Blues Project K30,M57,T3,W39
Blunstone,Colin A22,D49,S10,W25
Blythe,Arthur T15
Bob & Carol & Ted & Alice s/t J27
Bodacious DF W52
Bobb.B.Soxx S51
Boettcher,Curt B18
(aka Curt Becher)
Bogert,Tim N11,W48
Bogey Boys L62
Bo Grumpus P6
Bolan,Marc B64,N4
Bolin,Tommy M18

Bonds, Gary US M66,S54
Bones P18
Bonfire,Mars G28
Bongos T17
Bon Jovi B50,Q1
Bonnett,Graham E3,W33
Bonniwell,Sean B68,R39,
Bonoff,Karla E6,G37
Bonzo Dog Band B73,D49,I3
Booker,James B59,W54
Booker T. A15,J23
Books T21
Boom,Taka R50
Boomtown Rats L12,V8,W2
Boone,Debby A24
Boone,Pat T15
Boones Farm M65
Bootsys Rubber Band C41
Boston B60
Bothwell,Johnny T15
Boulder D1
Bowie,David B55,M44,R34,S13, V5, V8
Bown,Alan C50,H71
Bown,Andy A10,N6
Bow Wow Wow C24,L4,M13,T6,T21
Boxer D36,G31
Box Tops C44,M76,P17
Boyce and Hart B56
Boylan,Terence B61
Boys T7
Boys Brigade L25
Boys In The Bunkhouse G12
Boyzz A6
Braddock,Bobby G9
Braden,John L41
Bradford,Bobby T15
Brady,Paul M93
Braff,Ruby T15
Brains L43
Bramblett,Randall T33
Bramlett,Bonnie A15,R18,S5
Bramlett,Delaney B54,B63
Brand X K16,L59,M18
Branigan,Laura M49,W26
Bread G17
Breaks P27
Breakwater C30
Breathless V4
Brecker Brothers M22
Bremner,Billy B33
Bresh,Tom B54
Brett,Paul N11
Brewer,Michael F14
Brewer,Teresa T15
Brewer and Shipley B60,G54,P42,S57
Brick S10

Brides Of Funkenstein C41
Brigati R3
Bright,Bette L14
Briley,Martin B39,C47
Brinsley Schwarz E4,M21,R32,W7
Bristol,Johnny D49
Jo Broadberry and The Standouts H64
Broken Edge R50
Broken Home L12
Bromberg,David A5,M59,P35
Bronco D21
Bronco Billy s/t G12
Brood,Herman O1
Brooker,Gary M40
Brooklyn Dreams E18
Brooks,Denny M80
Brooks,Dianne A5
Brooks,Elkie D49,K14,K15,L28,W48
Brooks,Harvey S79
Brooks,Mel B59
Brothers Johnson J27
Broughton,Edgar J15
Brown,Arthur B1,M28
Brown,Danny Joe J18
Brown,James C22
Brown,Les T15
Brown,Toni M86,S69,Y2
Browne,Cooder H57
Browne,Duncan M87,O9
Browne,Jackson B85,L2,L9,O14,S9
Browne,Severin M95
Browns Home Brew C57
Brownsville Station K34,N3,P38, S63, W20
Bruce,Ed W21
Bruce,Jack H10,J17,P6
Bruce,Lenny D42,F34,Z3
Bruford,Bill L59
Brush Arbor F24
Bryant,Browning T27
Bubble Puppy R47
Buchanan,Roy C36,F29,R10,S30,S31
Buckacre J18
Buckingham,Lindsey D6
Buckingham Nicks O10
Buckinghams B48,G66,W49
Buckley,Lord B44
Buckley,Tim F3,G44,H54,K37,R5,R42,Y1
Bucks Fizz H41
Buckwheat D37/M36
Buda,Max D5
Budd,Harold E13
Budgie B1,M33
Buell,Bebe O2
Buffalo Springfield G60,M65
Buffett,Jimmy G9,P42
Bugatti and Musker M35

Buggles H56
Bull,Ritchie B58
Bullseye S65
Bullens,Cindy B50,Q1
Bullet D35
Bunky and Jake W59
Bunyan,Vashti B59
Burdon,Eric C23,G44,W39
Burke,Solomon B29,W23
Burlesque H23
Burnel,Jean-Jacques R48,W43
Burnett,T-Bone E20,F11
Burnette,Billy B22,M76,S16
Burnette,Dorsey T15
Burnette,Rocky H59
Burnin' Red Ivanhoe P16
Burning Rome S58,S62
Burns,Jack R44
Burns,Lisa L31
Burns,Panther K20
Burns,Ralph T15
Burns,Randy A2,S16
Burrell,Kenny H13
Burrito Brothers L48
Burton,James J12
Burton,Pat M59
Burton & Cunico R24
Bus Boys S45
Bush,Kate K13,P33
Bush,Stan B17
Buskin,David P42,S53
John Butcher Axis M82
Butler,Artie T15
Butler,Jerry L28
Butterfield,Paul A2,C66,G33
        M73,R1,R42,R46
Butts Band B52,F42
Buzzards C23,L43,S7
Buzzcocks R48
Byard,Jackie E5
Byas,Don T15
Byrds C71,D34,J20,M58,S57,U2
Byrne,David B101,E13
Byrne,Robert I6
Byron D.L. I5
B'zz W20

C
Cactus H23
Cactus Flower s/t J27
Cadd,Brian A21
Caddyshack s/t B52
Cado Belle O10
Cafe Jacques H45
Cafe Society D7
Cain,Tane O10

Cajun Moon W54
Caldara M36
Cale J.J. A31
Cale,John C4,M4,M63,T16,T20
Calico B99
California Jam B52
Call,Alex N9
Call P1
Calliope M63
Calloway,Cab T15
Calvert,Bob B3
Camel D9,G32,H45,H48
Camp,Hamilton D34
Campbell,Dick R11
Campbell,Glen B54,G12,K24,L7
Campbell,Jimmy H8
Campi,Ray W17
Canned Heat B22,S37,T11
Capability Brown R43
Capaldi,Jim B34,M67,S42,W47
Captain Beefheart D37,K35,P13,T12,Z3
Captain Sensible M32
Cara,Irene M84
Carasco,Joe "King" A14,G52
Caravan H48,V8
Caravans s/t B13
Carawan,Guy D5
Cargoe M30
Carillo K21
Carlton,Larry C9,T15
Carlos,Roberto D18
Carmel T20
Carmen,Eric I/1,M44
Carnes,Kim B22,G13,M80,O10,T26,
    W23,W32
Carnival H62
Carny s/t R31
Carp M80
Carpettes S7,T21
Carr,Pete C10
Carrack,Paul L59
Carradine,Keith A24,G67
Carrera T12
Caroll,Jim M11
Cars L12
Carter,Benny T15
Carter,Carlene A18,B19,B50,L57,Q1,
    S11,S39
Carter,Clarence H6
Carter,Lynda P27
Carter,Ron T15
Carter,Valerie H60,M48
Cartwright,Dave M93
Casey's Shadow s/t L36
Cash,Johnny A5,C73,S26
Cash,Roseanne C73

Cashman and West B9,C15
Casino Lights L45
Casino Music S59
Cason,Buzz C16
Cassidy,David J11,J21
Cassidy,Shaun L48,R46
Cate Brothers A26,C70,D46,M46,M39
Cates,George T15
Cates Gang A28,M53
Catfish Hodge Band F28
Cat Mother H34
Cat People s/t M84
Cavaliere,Felix R46
CCS M87
Cecilio and Kapono S69
Celebration A12
Certain Ratio H15
Chad and Jeremy U2
Challengers D24
Champion L61
Champlin,Bill F21
Chance,James W27
Channing,Carol T15
Chanter Sisters C57
Chapin,Harry A6,H54,L29,P24
Chaplin,Blondie F25
Chapman,Beth Nielsen B22
Chapman,Marshall D48,K30,T1
Chapman,Michael A10,D44
Chapman,Roger C67
Charlatans H27
Charles,Bobby D3,S32
Charles River valley Boys R42,S30
Charlie B17,S71
Charlie & The Pep Boys L50
Charo M88
Chas & Dave A29
Chase,Carol G12,P42
Chater,Kerry B9,O12
Cheap Trick B3,D44,M40,R46,W20
Checkmates,Ltd S51
Cheech & Chong A4
Cheetah V2
Cher B9,D46,E18,G12,M35,O12,W14,
    W23,W53
Cherokee B9
Cherry,Ava E18
Chic R35
Chicago D46,F21,G66,R3
Chicago original cast album R3
Chicago Breakdown D16
Chicken Shack B16,V5
Child,Desmond L10
Chilliwack B8,F12,G52,L31,T24
Chilli Willi N9,R23
Chilton,Alex D33,T25

China J20
China Crisis H64,L35,W5
Chocolate Milk T26,T27
Chocolate Watch Band C42
Chopper B10
Chorale N6
Chords A25
Chowning,Randle L29
Christ Child J26
Christian M39
Christian Death W40
Christian,Chris G18
Christlieb,Pete and Marsh, Warne B21
Church C38
Cipollina,John G54
Circle Jerks A15,G44
City A4,L8
City Boy L12
City Lights L31
City Streets H2
Clancy S42
Clannad C37
Clapton,Eric A30,B63,D30,F25,J18, P36,V5
Clark,Gene D12,K11,M38
Clark,Guy C73,W29
Clark-Hutchinson S27
Clark,Michael S19
Clark,Roy B99
Clarke,Allan P37
Clarke,John Cooper H15
Clarke,Stanley S13,Ti5
Clash F18,J18,P15,S64
Classics IV B88
Classix Nouveau S1
Clayton,Lee W29,Y2
Clayton,Merry A4,T33
Clayton-Thomas,David H71,M57,R21
Clean Living S46
Clear Light R42
Clements,Vassar M59,W29
Clemmons,Gregg S45
Clemmons,Clarence S28
Cliff,Jimmy J20,K21,L19,O9
Clifford,Doug G14
Climax Blues Band E3,H33,R50,T16,V5
Climax Chicago G52
Clinton,George C41
Clock DVA J24,T17
Clocks F12
Clouds E10
Clover B46,L12,R32
CMU F41
Coasters L28
Coast Road Drive J10
Coati Mundi H37
Cobble Mountain Band P21

Cobham,Billy S13
Cocciante,Richard H60
Cochise S43
Cochran,Jackie Lee Waukeen W17
Cocker,Joe B34,C62,F25,K5,L36,P35,R49,
     S1,T18,T27
Cockney Rebel P10
Cockney Rejects C32,W38
Cockrell and Santos M77
Coconuts D4
Code Blue G55
Cody,Phil A24
Coe,David Allan B40,S26
Cogic's C42
Cohen,David G65
Cohen,Leonard J20,L41,L46,S32,S51
Cohen,Linda A17
Cohen,Myron T15
Cohn,Al T15
Cole,Tony M17
Cole,Natalie T26
Coley,John Ford L27,S25
Collage D45
Collins,Albert S79
Collins,Judy A2,A15,H4,H54,K24,M35
Collins,Paul B52
Collins,Phil C52,P1
Collins,Shirley R30
Color Me Gone M89,S62
Colosseum B73
Colours D24,M80
Colter,Jessi A7,M31,M76
Coltrane,Chi F31
Coltrane,John C76,T15
Comanor,Jeffrey B60
Commander Cody A8,Al6,A34,B60,C45,H66,
     J13, M19, S74
Comsat Angels H64,W38
Conaway,Jeff A20
Concerts For The People of Kampuchea T16
Condon,Eddie T15
Coney Hatch N18
Contortions W27
Cooder,Ry D33,P8,T20,W11
Cook,Roger B90
Coolidge,Rita A15,G37,J23
Coolidge-Jones,Priscilla J23
Cooper,Alice B3,B67,D44,E21,F21,P25,R21
Cooper D.B. G7
Cooper,Jackie T15
Cooper,Marty M31
Copeland,Greg B85
Copperhead B80
Corbett,Mike and Hirsch,Jay E16
Corbetta,Jerry B9
Corbin/Hanner Band W21

Corbitt,Jerry D2
Corea,Chick R44
Cortez,Dave "Baby" G33
Cortinas B32
Coryell,Larry C76
Cosby,Bill B59
Cosmic Sounds H24
Costello,Elvis B19,E12,L14,L57 S26
Cotton,Gene G23,T2
Cotton,James R46
Cottonwood South R42
Couchois B9
Cougar,John A6,C70,G19,P39
Country E16
Country Gazette D34,S39
Country Gentlemen L55
Country Joe B25,C29,L19,M62,
   S46,S61,W34
Country Joe & The Fish C29,W22
Countryman s/t B34
Coup L33
Cousins,Dave A10
Coven T3
Coverdale,David G35
Covington,Joey I2
Covington,Julie B59,W54
Cowboy S5,W28
Cowboys International M18
Cox,Billy R37
Cox,Danny G54,K15,U2,W48
Coyne,Kevin H23,L12,S41,V7,W6
Crabby Appleton G5,Z1
Crackin' O12
Crack The Sky M72,S65
Craddock,Billy "Crash" J19
Cramps C25
Crawford,Randy L36,L45,M78
Crawler L61
Crazy Elephant K6
Crazy Horse B52,C19,H29,N15
Creach,Papa John J26,M42,R21
Cream P6,S70
Creation T3
Creative source S22
Creatures H20
Credibility Gap T24
Creed M25
Creedence Clearwater F15
Crenshaw,Marshall G52,L43
Cretones B30
Crewe,Bob B22,T15,W23
Crimson Tide C13,C70,D51,L10
Crickets C16,G12,M78
Criss,Peter P27,W33
Cristina D4,W9
Critters K31,R24,

Croce,Jim C15
Crooks B51
Cropper,Steve C70,R28
Crosby,Bob T15
Crosby,David C71,H10
Crosby,Stills & Nash A6,J22
Cross,Christopher O12
Cross Country M55
Crow M77
Crow,Alvin A11
Crowbar D44
Crow Dog's Paradise S30
Crowell,Rodney A5,C73,L31
Crowfoot G14
Cruisin' s/t N15
Crusaders L36
Cryan' Shames G41,M77
Crystal Mansion A24
Crystals S51
Cuban Heels L24
Culture Club L35
Cumberland Three K4
Cummings,Burton P18,R28
Cunha,Rick M31
Cunico,Gino P27
Cupid's Inspiration D50
Cure H28,P9
Currie,Cherie F22,W41
Curry,Tim E14,K3,W1
Curtis,Mac W17
Curtis,Sonny H49
Curved Air A6,H48,M18,R48
Cutler,Jesse R13
C.Y.Walkin' Band N17

D
D'Abo,Mike M53
Daddy Cool P29
DAF P22
Dal Ballo,Lisa E18,M77
Dale,Kenny M78
Dalton,Karen B76
Dalton,Kathy D25
Dalton,Lacy J. S26
Dalton & Dubarri L48
Daltrey,Roger B6,C67,F2,T20
Damnation S63
Damned A23,J24,L57,M47
Dana B43
Dance Band A18
Danceclass C24
Dance People L35
Daniels,Charlie B60,C61,H57,K24
Danko,Rick
Danse Society G55
Darien Spirit R43

Darin,Bobby E16
Darling G52
Darling,Erik H54
Darrell,Johnny M95
Darrow,Chris B86,D5,O4
D'Arrow,Philip G3,L37
Darts B57,W55
Dash,Sarah W53
Daughters Of Albion R49
David,Alan W18
David And Jonathan M40
Davidson,Dianne A31,T2
Davies,Dave D8
Davies,Gail W21
Davies,Ray D9
Davies,Ron S75
Davis,Betty E15
Davis,Eddie "Lockjaw" C76
Davis,Jess "Ed" D12,G6
Davis,Mac B99,D18,H2,H6,K24
Davis,Miles M15
Davis,Paul B10,M76
Davis,Spencer B34,M8
Davis,Tim J18
Dawe,Tim Y1
Dawn M55
Daye,Cory L44
Dayton,Peter O2
DB's B19,L47
Dead Boys P6,R6
Dead End Kids B43
Dead Fingers Talk R38
Dead Kennedys W40
Dead Or Alive H30
Deaf School D32,L12
Deardrof and Joseph S25
James Dean s/t T24
De Burgh,Chris A15,C1,H45,P33,S3
Decameron A10
De Caro,Nick L45
De Coteaux,Bert D20
Dedringer H64
Dee,Joey G43
Dee,Kiki D49,F27,J16,S10,W33
Deep Purple B32,L18,T7
Dees,Stephen H7
Def Leppard G63,L12
Defunkt B59
Dekker,Desmond P4
Delaney,Sean S71
Delaney & Bonnie B63,D46
    D51,M67,N16,W23
Delbert & Glen H23,M80
Delgado,Gabi P22
Dells C41,D11
Delta 5 K20

Denny,Sandy W54
Denver,John O7
Deodato L45
De Paul,Lindsey H53
Depressions B27,K11
Derek and Clive B34
Derek & The Dominoes D30
Derringer,Rick C24,R46,S79
De Sario,Terri A6,R20
Des Barres,Michael C24
Descloux,Lizzy Mercier S56
Deserters C13
De Shannon,Jackie D46,M23,M35,N15,N17,
    P3, S69, W23,W50
Desmond,Andy D8,H62
Destri,Jimmy K3
Destry,Johnny & Destiny V7
Detective J17,S42
Detroit (feat. Mitch Ryder) E21
Devo B3,E13,M36,S13
Devoto,Howard W3
Dexys Midnight Runners L14,W42
DFK Band H60,J17
Diamond,Barry C60
Diamond,Dyan F22
Diamond, Legs I 20
Diamond,Neil C18,G18,R31
Diamond Head H28
Dice K21
Dickie,Tom & The Desires R48
Dickies C1,H38
Dickinson,Jim D30,D46
Dickson,Barbara C7,H62,T6,W32
Dictators K36,P15
Difference D36
Digance,Richard B103,M93
Diga Rhythm Band H21
Dillard,Doug D34
Dillard and Clark M38
Dillard,Hartford,Dillard M59
Dillards B60,D34,P25,W51
Dinner,Michael B60
Di Meola,Al M18
Dingoes M53
Dinner,Michael O10
Dino and Sembello L28
Dinsmore Payne V3
Dion B9,C15,G22,O12,S1,T24,W49
Dire Straits B22,I5,W23,W46
Dirt Band H14
Dirty Angels F43,G52
Dirty Looks F37,G16
Dirty Tricks B1,V8
Distractions A30,C27
Divine,Sweet Linda K30
Dixie Cups L28

Dixie Dregs L36,S13
Dixon,Jessy S15
Dixon House F12
Dixon House Band F12
DMZ F13
DNA P37
Doc Holliday A10,A15,K21,M16
Doctors Of Madness L24,P39
Dodgers M82
Doerge,Craig M38
Doheny,Ned C70,H1
Doherty,Denny S79
Dokken D35
Dolby,Thomas F37
Dolenz,Jones,Boyce and Hart B56
Doll L24
Dollar N6,W3
Doll By Doll N11,P34
Dolphy,Eric E5,T15
Domino,Fats D21,P18,R48
Donaldson,Bo & The Heywoods B9
Donnegan,Lonnie F2
Donohue,Dane B60
Donovan M87,O9,P42,W23
Doobie Brothers T12,W11
Dooleys B43
Doors B52,H1,R42
Dore,Charlie A31,L36,T6
Dorsey,Lee T27
Dorsey,Tommy D41
Doss,Kenny M73
Doucette R50
Doug & The Slugs C63,K29
Downliner Sect C48
Doyle,Bobby P30
Doyle,Peter T6
DP's K14
Dragonfly L18
Drake,Nick B59
Dramatics D11
Dream 6 M28
Dream Syndicate P15
Dregs M64,O6
Dresser,Lee B54
Drifters B29
Driscoll,G45
Drivers B84
Drones H69
Druid H17
Dr.Buzzard B79,K24,L44,W53
Dr.Demento B74,G7
Dr.Feelgood D20,G52,L57,M21,V5
Dr.Hook H2
Dr.John B14,D46,G60,K11,L45,T27,W43
Ducks S32
Ducks De Luxe B42,E4

Dudek,Les B52,J17,S8
Dudes S50
Dufay,Rick D44
Duffo V6
Dugites A18
Duke & The Drivers K34,R18
Duke Jupiter H61,K29,L23
Dukes M35,Z4
Duncan,Johnny S26
Duncan,Lesley H58
Dunn & McCashen F31
Dupree,Cornell C76,T15
Dupree,Jack D41,V5
Dupree,Robbie B89
Duran Duran S1,T21
Durocs M53,N1
Durutti column H15
Dury,Ian K20,S56
Dust,K15,W48
Dylan,Bob B22,D30,F25,H13,J20,K27, P24,
    R31, W23,W39

E
Earth Opera S30
Earthquake K9,L4
East Of Eden H48
Easton,Sheena G56,M49,N6
East Side Kids M80
Easybeats T3,V2
Eater G46
Echo & The Bunnymen B77,J24
Eddie & The Cruisers V1
Eddie & The Hot Rods H51,K30,L43,M21
Edelman,Randy B83,M3,M75,S10
Edge M88
Edison Electric Band D41
Edmunds,Dave E4
Edward Bear B84
Edwards,Dennis L6
Edwards,Jonathan A5,C17
Edwards,Stoney T9
Edwards and Ralph B22
Egan,Joe C67
Egan,Walter B87,D6,M28,S12,
Egg S36
Eggs Over Easy W58
Eight Eyed Spy B38
Eire Apparent H34
Elbow Bones & The Racketeers D4
Electric Chairs B32
Electric Flag B76,C66,S32,W23
Electric Prunes H25
Elektra Glide In Blue G46
Elektriks B50,K14,Q1
Elephant's Memory L30,S42
Elevators M28

Elf G35
Elijah K30
Elliman, Yvonne A21,B9,C70,H45
Ellington,Duke T15,J27
Elliott,Brian J5
Elliott,Cass B9,M63
Elliott,Ramblin' Jack D2,W29
Elliott,Ken R22
Elliott,Ron D47
Ellis V5
Ellis, Shirley C6
Ellison,Lorraine R1,T12
Ely,Joe B78,J20,Y2
Emmons,Buddy M59
Emperor K15,W48
Engelhardt,Tolouse D5
England,Dan L27,S25
English,Scott P37
Enid S35
Eno,Brian B101,D9,E13
Entwistle,John A8
Equators A18
Erikson,Roky & The Aliens C58
Esperanto C1,S13,S33
Espionage B3
Essential Logic J24
Essex,David B13,K30,N6,W13
ET s/t B52
Etheridge,Chris R42
Europeans S43
Eurythmics P22
Evans,Bill L45
Evans,Gil S32
Evans,Paul W49
Everage,Dame Edna M17
Evergreen Blueshoes B54
Everly,Phil C54,C56,E2,G12
Everly Brothers G27,H43,R42,W11
Everyone R30
Every Which Way But Loose G12
Exciters L28
Exile (1) C24
Exile (2) T29
Exploited S49
Explosives C58
Eye To Eye K5

F
Fabulous Farquahr T9
Fabulous Poodles E14,W46
Fabulous Rhinestones S79
Fabulous Thunderbirds B86,L57
Face Dancer W43,W48
Faces J18
Fagan,Richard G18

Fagen,Donald K5,V1
Fahey,John B86,C29,D19,D16,
Fairchild,Barbara S26
Fairport Convention B59,J18,W54
Fairweather-Low,Andy C28,J18,M53
Faith K26
Faith,Adam B90,C67
Faithfull,Marianne C3,M92
Falcon,Billy M67,M70
Falconer,Roderick F9
Falkstog,Agnetha C24
Fall M52,S7
Fallen Angels S16
Fame,Georgie J18,S2
Family J18,M45
Family Dogg R43
Family Tree J11
Family Way s/t M2
Fancy H71
Fandango B39
Fanny P18,R46
Fargaher Brothers K15,P27,W48
Fardon,Lee F41
Farina,Mimi J2
Farina,Mimi K24
Farlowe,Chris J4
Farlow,Tal M15
Farmers Boys C51
Farner,Mark I5,W1
Farquahr R1
Farrell,Joe L19
Faryar,Cyrus S32
Fashion H30
Fast Fontaine R42
Fastway K34
Fat City O7
FCC I6
Feiten,Buzz L31
Feliciano,Jose B22,C70,J11,K15, W23,W48
Felix,Julie M87
Fellini,Suzanne B92
Fender,Freddy M54
Fennelly,Michael B86,W25
Ferguson,Jay S79,V4
Ferguson,Steve P24
Ferron G15
Ferry,Brian N19,P28,P39,T16
Fifth Dimension H62,W14
Finders Keepers K6
Finger,Peter G65
Fingerprintz G16,K21
Finn,Tim F6
Finnigan,Mike N9,W23
Fire Engines L15
Fireball M5
Fireballs P19

Firefall A6,D46,M46,
Firesign Theatre F4
Fischer,Wild Man B74,Z3
Fine Wine O4
Fischer-Z H64,M33
Fist L18
Fitzgerald,Ella P18
Fitzgerald,Patrick W38
Five Man Electrical Band S37
Five Stairsteps K6
Fixx H45
Flack,Roberta D41,M35
Flame I5,W36
Flamin' Groovies B19,E4,G42,R33
Flash L18
Flashbeagle B46
Flash Cadillac F32,F31
Flash & The Pan V2
Flash Fearless A8
Flat Picking Guitar Festival D23,D27
Flatt & Scruggs J20
Fleetwood,Mick D6
Fleetwood Mac B32,B87,C2,H67,O10,V5
Fleischmann,Robert I5
Fleming,Joy B24
Fleshtones M52,W24
Flicks K16
Floating Bridge M69
Flo & Eddie E21,F13,N9,T11,W50
Flock M4
Flower,Robin G62
Flower L56
Flying Bear Medicine Show M83
Flying Burritos B47,D34,F8,H67,L41,M38, P42,S53
Flying Lizards C75
Flying Squad R41
Flys F7
Focus V5
Fogelberg,Dan L39,P42,W4
Fogerty,John F15
Fogerty,Tom G11,G14
Foghat J8,K34,O16
Foley,Ellen H70,J25,P27,
Fools P27,S45
Fools Gold F32,J18,O10,S74,W4
Forbert,Steve B92,S32,S45
Force Ten S74
Ford,Dean P10
Ford,Lita M64,Q1
Ford,Robben C70,H72,V5
Ford Theatre S79
Foreigner B3,L12,L61,O10,S35
Forever More N4,S34
Forman,David D41
Forsey,Keith F23
Fortnox T30

Foster Brothers V5
Fotheringay B59
Fotomaker A6,K34,L3,M89
Fourmost M40
Four On The Floor K30
Four Out Of Five Doctors W43
Four Seasons C6,C69,G18
Four Tops B9,C37,L7,W53
Fowley,Kim F22,L48
Fox Y4
Foxes s/t M84
Foxton,Bruce L43,S24
Foxx C16
Foxx,John H30
Frady,Garland N8
Frampton,Peter K17,K21,K34,T15
Frank,Stanley C1
Franke & The Knockouts S10,S45,V7
Franklin,Aretha D46,J27,M35,W23
Franks,Michael L45,S32
Fraser,Andy S22,E3
Fraternity Of Man W39
Fred,John & His Playboys L40
Freddie & The Dreamers B90
Frederick,Jeffrey N2
Frederick,Jesse F35
Free B34,J17,S64
Free Beer L53
Freed,Alan T15
Freedom B1
Free Flight H62
Freeman,Bud T15
Freeway M58
Frehley,Ace K34
Fresh N4,S34
Fresh (US) N8
Frey,Glenn B39,F32,N17
Fricke,Janie M78,N17,S26
Frida (of Abba) C52
Friedman,Dean S65
Friedman,Kinky B9,G26,M54
Friedman,Ruthann W50
Friends & Lovers B88
Fripp & Eno E13,F39
Fripp,Robert F39
Fritts,Donnie W23
Frizell,David G12
Frizell,David & West,Shelly G12
Froggatt,Raymond B99
Fromholz,Steve H19,L20,R13
Frost C29
Frye,David A2,T23
Fugs S4
Fuller,Craig G13
Full Moon L45
Full Swing P18

Fumble T3
Fun Boy Three B101,J29
Funkadelic C41,E15
Funkapolitan D4
Funky Kings F25,R42
Funny Game Politics M40
Furay,Richie G13,M46,O12,S10
Fure,Tret G20
Furey,Lewis G20,L46
Fury,Billy C54,L32
Fuse M69

G
Gabor,B.B. B84
Gabriel S37
Gabriel,Peter E21,F39,L43,L54,W5
Galdston & Thom S32
Gale,Arlyn A20
Gale,Eric J6,T27
Gale Force S69
Gallagher & Lyle J18,K17,S10
Gambler G31
Gamma L61,S13
Gang Of 4 A6
Garcia,Jerry D42,K1,M53
Garfeel Ruff L31
Garfunkel,Art H5,P18,S25
Garland,Judy T15
Garner,Erroll T15
Garrett,Amos M59
Garrett,Leif L48
Garrett,Snuff G12
Garthwaite,Terry G67,R44,S69
Garvey,Nick G16
Gas G55
Gasolin B3
Gasworks V8
Gates,David G17
Gatlin,Larry F24
Gayden,Mac C16,J20
Gayle,Crystal B54
Geils,J B39,H23,S22,S79,W50
Gene Loves Jezebel B65
General Johnson C30
Generation X F23,H70,R48
Genesis A19,B95,H36,H48,K21,P1
Gentle Giant V8
Gentlehood G28,S6
Gentleman Afterdark C59,W1
Gentle Soul M58
Gentrys M76
Geordie W33
George,Lowell G20
Gerard G66
Gerber,Alan C62

Gerdes,George V3
Geremia,Paul G52
Geronimo Black O10
Gerry & The Pacemakers M40
Get Wet R3
Geyer,Renee F25
Ghent,Tom P42
Ghost Rides M61
Giants E15
Giants N2
Gibb,Steve C16
Gibbons,Steve L4,P36,S21,V8
Gichy Dan D4
Giguere,Russ B60
Gilder,Nick C24,C47,L56,M31
Gillan G32,S42
Gillespie,Dana B55,C1,P28,R38
Gillespie,Dizzy T15
Gillette,Steve N5
Gilley,Mickey N17,W37
Gilmour,David E21
Ginsberg,Allen H13
Giorgio M84
Giorgio & Chris B24,M84
Girl T18,T30
Girlschool G55,L21,M21,
Glaser,Tompall B54,M31
Glass,Dick G44
Glass Family P25
Gleaming Spires H3
Glitter,Gary D20,L22
Glitter Band L22
Global Village Trucking Co F41
Gloria Mundi P39
Glover,Roger B32,G35
Godard,Vic R14,S1,
Godfrey,Robert John S36
Godmoma C53
Godspell L22
Godz B66
Goffin,Louise K33
Go Go's F30,G52,R48
Gold,Andrew A27,P24
Gold,Frannie R20
Goldberg,Barry A9,D52,M63,P35,W23
Golden Earring I5
Goldmark,Andy U2
Gomm.Ian G29,R48
Gong G45,H39,H64,M18,M47,W54
Gonzalez B24,F7,J28
Good,The Bad,The Ugly M54
Good Guys D24
Goodhand-Tait,Philip B90,C1,W46
Gooding,Cuba L7
Goodman,Steve B89,B92,D41,M35,P42
Goodman,Tim M10

Good Old Boys G10
Good Rats F13,G3,J10
Goodness And Mercy M37
Goodthunder R42
Gordon,Alan N15
Gordon,Dexter C76
Gordon,Robert G52,L47,Q1
Gore,Lesley J27
Gorgoni,Martin & Taylor T9
Gorl,Robert H28
Gorman,John J15
Gosdin,Vern P13
Goudreau,Barry B60
Graf K8
Gouldman,Graham G53
Gowan,Larry F30
Graham,Davey G65
Graham,Ernie R32
Grand Funk C20,I1,K26,L61
Grand Hotel D9
Grand Prix E3,W3
Grand Theft G35
Grant,David L35
Grassroots B9
Grateful Dead G20,H25,L61,M51, O10,S55
Gravenites,Nick G54
Gray,Dobie W32
Gray,Mark M78
Grease Band P31,T18
Great Buildings B60,T14
Greatest Show On Earth P16
Great Speckled Bird R46
Green,Al M73
Green,Danny N16
Green,Lloyd Y2
Green,Peter V6
Green,St.John F22,L48
Greenbaum,Norman J5
Greenslade,Dave H45,L59
Gregory,Michael R34
Griff,Zaine V8
Griffith,Glenda H35,N17
Grimes,Carol N16,P31
Grimms I3,J15
Grin B67
Grinderswitch H57
Gronenthal,Max F25,J2
Gross,Henry C15,C55,Z2
Group 87 T14
Group Therapy R11
GTO's Z3
Guess Who R21
Guidry,Greg R50
Guillory,Isaac D31,S2
Gulliver S18
Gun Club S59

Gus L32
Guthrie,Arlo H31,P21,W11
Guthrie,Gwen S56
Guthrie,Woody P21
Guy,Buddy D46,W59

H
Hackett,Steve A3
Hagar,Sammy C13,O10,W57
Hagen,Nina F23,M84,T20
Haggard,Merle B54,S26
Haig,Paul S1
Hain,Kit T20
Haircut 100 S7
Haley,Bill H23
Halfbreed A19
Halfnelson R46
Hall,Carol M68
Hall,Daryl F39
Hall,Jimmy P42
Hall,John B76,O14,P24
Hall,Lani K17
Hall,Tom T. S15
Hall & Oates B49,C38,F21,K16,M35, P1,R46
Hambi & The Dance G32
Hamilton,Chico T15
Hamilton,Dirk G42,K5
Hamilton,Joe Frank & Reynolds B9
Hamilton Streetcar D24
Hammill,Claire B34,S3
Hammill,Peter A19
Hammond,Albert A13,N17
Hammond,John B63,G61,H46,K11, M15,S46
Hamner,Lowry & The Cryers M46
Hampton,Lionel T15
Hancock,Herbie G56,R44
Hanoi Rocks G63
Hansen,Randy R44
Happy The Man S13
Hapshash & The Coloured Coat B13,S64
Hardin,Tim F29,H58,J5,K24,K31
Hard Meat R30
Hargrove,Linda D48
Harlequin D44
Harley,Steve H58,J2
Harper,Roy J15,L24,T3
Harpers Bizarre W11
Harris,Don "Sugarcane" O15
Harris,Eddie H23
Harris,Emmylou A5
Harris,Joey C38
Harris,Major R1
Harris,Richard M35,W14
Harrison,Don S13
Harrison,George H20,S51,T20

Harrison,Mike B34,K21
Harrold,Melanie M93
Harry,Debby R35
Hart,Mike P16
Hartford,John B72,J11,J12,M59,S32
Hartley,Keef B95,S36
Hartman,Dan H22
Hartman,Lisa L48
Harvey,Alex B12,W2
Harvey,Alex (USA) M63,R36,T1
Harvey,Tina K22
Haskell,Gordon D50,M35
Haslam,Annie W55
Hassell,John E13
Hassles K11
Hatcher,George A10
Hatfield & The North N11
Hathaway,Donny M35,W23
Havens,Richie B49,C6,C66,K17
Hawkins,Coleman T15
Hawkins,Ronnie D46,M75,W23
Hawks R50,W20
Hawkwind B26,C31,H61,M82
Hawn,Goldie W11
Haworth,Bryn A30,A31,D36,P28
Hayes,Isaac D51
Haysi Fantayzee B83,L9,V8
Hayward,Rick V5
Hayward,Justin C37,W13
Hazard,Robert K17
Hazel,Eddie C41
Head,Murray N19,S3,W50
Head,Roy B54
Headboys K14
Head East G31,L33,P25
Headpins H32
Headstone A19
Heart F12 O10
Heartbreakers C74,K12
Heartsfield R44
Heat W53
Heaters W50
Heatwave B43,G68,R3
Heaven 17 W3
Heavy Metal Kids D21,M87
Heavy Pettin' M16
Heist J27
Hell,Richard B31,G52,
Hello L22
Hello People R46
Helm,Levon B22,C11,D51
Helmet Boy S19
Help Yourself C28,R32
Hendricks,James R25
Hendrix,Jimi A4,B50,B59,C23,
D42,J10,K34

Henley,Don L2,K33
Henry,Freddy K30
Henry Cow N11
Henske,Judy Y1
Hentschel,David H36
Herd R43
Hermans Hermits M87
Hero L48
Heroes W33
Heron,Mike B59,M93
Hewitt,Garth R16
Hey Elastica! R48
Heyward,Nick E12
Hiatt,John B86,L57,N1,S53,V8
Hibbert,Jimmy L16
Hicks,Dan J20,L45
Higgins,Chuck W17
High Cotton T27
Highway L38
Highway Robbery K10
High Wind H10
Hildebrand,Diane A15
Hill,Dan B60,H5,M3,M75
Hill,Joel Scott R42
Hill,Roy D49
Hillage,Steve C22,H39,M47,R46
Hillman,Chris A6,D34,M40
Hillmen D34
Hine,Rupert H45
Hinton,Eddie B22
Hitchcock,Robyn C49,H42
Hi-Tension S1
Hitmen D9,H59
Hobo M82
Hobbs/Adams/Bryars E13
Holien,Danny S79
Holland,Amy M6
Holland,Jools J18
Hollies J22,N5,R19
Holly & The Italians G52
Hollywood Knights s/t V1
Hollywood Stars M44
Holy Mackerel P18
Holmes,Rupert H53,L33
Holster,David James E6,L2
Holy Modal Rounders M74
Honeys A32,B74
Honk L41
Honky Tonk Freeway M40
Hoodoo Rhythm Devils I6,R44
Hook,Marcus V2
Hooker,John Lee E7
Hopkin,Mary M2,M87,V8,
Hopkins,Sam "Lightnin'" R37
Hopkins,Nicky B67,J18
Horn,Jim C62,R49

Horn,Paul S9
Horslips F41,K8,O5
Hot Chocolate M87
Hot Dogs M30
Hot Tuna I2,M44,P6,S9
Hounds L33
House,Bill H59
House,James K5
Houston,Thelma I6,S69
Howard,Randy H57
Howdy Moon G20
Howe,Catherine N10,W33
Howe,Steve O6
Howell,Eddie L59,M18
Howlin' Wolf D16
Huang Chung B19,D9
Hubbard,Freddie R42 T15
Hubbard,Ray Wyllie B78
Hudson L48
Hudson-Ford A10,C1
Hues Corporation K17
Hughes/Thrall F25,J18
Human League M33,P1,R48,T16,T21
Humans K2
Human Sexual Response T20
Humble Pie J18,L61,O9
Hummingbird S2
Humphrey,Paul L45
Hunley,Con W37
Hunt,Marsha V8
Hunter,Alberta H13
Hunter,Ian B3,H70,J25,N18,R38
Hunter,Robert G10
Hunter,Steve E21
Hunters & Collectors H64,P22
Hurley,John J11
Hurley,Michael N2,Y3
Hustler B3,G1
Hybrid Kids F10
Hydra S5
Hyland,Brian G12

I
Ian & Sylvia C66
Ian,Janis A24,C6,F26,K24,M84,
  M85,W50
Ice Castles s/t P10
Icehouse F23
Icicle Works J24
Ideal P22
Idle Race O6
Idol,Billy F23
Idolmaker B10
If F43
Illinois Speed Press G66
Illusion S3

Imagination S77
Incantation O5
Incredible String Band B59
Industrials F22
Ingram,James J27
Inman,Jerry G12
Inmates C54,M21
Inner Circle M36
Inner City Unit R23
Innes,Neil I3,N11
Innocence P27
Innocents M36
In The Heat Of The Night s/t J27
Intergalactic Touring Band G3
International Elvis
Impersonators Convention B74
International Submarine Band H50
Interview G32,T21
Invisible Zoo L33
Inxs L17,R34
Iron Butterfly P25,R5
Iron City Houserockers C70,R38
Iron Horse M18
Iron Maiden B32,M26
Ironside J27
Italian Job s/t J27
I-Ten O10

J
Jabara,Paul E18
Jack-Knife W22
Jackson,Gordon M45
Jackson,Joe K17
Jackson,Michael J27,M93
Jackson,Millie S22
Jackson,Ray M72
Jackson Highway H55,J19
Jack The Lad A10,M93
Jagger,Chris S42
Jags H69,S1
Jam P9,S43,W38
Jamal,Ahmad H62,S69
James,Etta M57,T27,W23
James,Jamie M36
James,Tommy B10,C63,D48,G33,L4
James Gang D46,S79
Jameson B18
Jankovic,"Weird Al" D28
Jans,Tom H1,J2,W32,W50
Jansch,Bert N8
Janus,Noel D10
Jap,Philip H56,M32,S26,T21
Japan N19,P39,S34
Jarreau,Al G56,L45,S9
Jarrett,Keith E5
Javaroo B43

Jay & The Americans B10,K11,L28
Jazz At The Opera House R44
JC & The Brown Bag Blues Band B74
Jefferson,Eddie C76
Jefferson Airplane J11,K7,S9
Jefferson Starship B17,C68,N9
Jeffreys,Garland C33,C38,C76,S52
Jelly P24
Jellyroll P25
Jenkins,Johnny S5
Jennings,Waylon A7,C39,M31,M76,S15
Jesse,Wolff & Whings C62
Jet B3
Jethro Tull E10,S3
Jett,Joan C63,L4
Jim & Jesse S26
Jimmy & The Mustangs L48
Jiva B8,L36,L56
JoBoxers S21
Jocko,J R4
Joel,Billy R3,R24,S69
Johansen,David M89,R33,R38
John,Elton B24,B83,D49,F27,T12
John,Robert T26
Johnny G A18,H51,K17
Johnny's Dance Band B50,Q1
Johnson,Linton Kwesi B53
Johnson,Michael M20,R3
Johnston,Bruce U2
Johnston,Tom O12,T12
Johnstone,Davy D49
Jo Jo Gunne D46,S74,S79
Jo Jo Zep S45
Jolliver Arkansaw P6
Jolt P9,S43
Jo Mama A27,D46,G6
Jon & The Niteriders B36,T3,W40
Jones,Davy L34
Jones,George S26
Jones,Gloria J28
Jones,Grace B34,M88,R2,S1
Jones,Howard H45,T21
Jones,Mordicai V7
Jones,Mose K30
Jones,Quincy J27,R3
Jones,Rickie Lee T24,W11
Jonesey H45
Joplin,Janis M53,M57,R42,S32
Jordan,Kent C36
Jordan,Marc G56,K5
Joseph,Margie M35
Journey,B17,E11,H5,S71,W57
Joy Division H15
Joy Of Cooking P3
Judd,Phil K30
Judas Priest A10,B1,G35,G68,M18

Juicy Lucy B73,T18
Jules & The Polar Bears H47
Junior C12
Junko Yagami A24
Jupp,Mickey B75,G36,L57,R41,V5

K
Kahn,Steve J6
Kajagoogoo T21
Kaleidoscope D5,F33,M69
Kane,Madleen M84
Kangaroo W59
Kansas G31,G39,K16,S13
Kantner,Amy M11
Kantner,Paul N1
Karloff,Billy S5
Kasenetz-Katz K6
Katzman,Nick D27
Kaukonen,Jorma C14,K2
Kay,John I6,P25
Kayak M18
Kaye,Thomas Jefferson K5
Kaz,Eric C76,G13
Kazoos Brothers B74
Keen,Speedy K12
Kelley,Peter G52
Kelly,Roberta B24,E18,M84
Kendricks,Eddie S5
Kennedy,Ray F21
Kenny M39
Kenny,Gerard N6,S53
Kenny & The Kasuals L26
Kensington Market P6
Kent,David A19
Kentucky Colonels B44,D23
Kerouac,Jack T15
Kerr,Richard B49,P42
Kershaw,Doug J20
Kershaw,Nik C51
Kessell,Barney S51
Keys J1
Keys,Bobby J17
KGB K15,P35,W48
Khan,Chaka H5,M35,T24
Kick Axe P37
Kicking Mule's Flat Picking
   Guitar Festival G65
Kids J17
Kids From Fame F5
Kid Creole D4
Kidd Glove B9
Kihn,Greg K9,L4
Kilburn & The High Roads A29,M72
Killing Joke P22
Killough & Eckley G9
Kilroy,Pat S30

Kim,Andy B10
Kind L31
King,Albert D20,D51,N16,T27
King,B.B. B9,E5,L36,S79,Z2
King Ben E. D20,L17,M35
King,Bobby B9,P32
King,Carole A4 F8
King,Don L13
King,Freddie C62,N16,R49,V5
King,Marva P18
King Biscuit Boy T27
King Crimson D9,F39,S33
King Curtis B63,D41,D46,E5,
    E17,M35,V3,W23
Kingfish H27,S5
King Harvest B10
King Kurt E4
King Of Comedy s/t R31
King Of Hearts L10
Kingpins K10
Kings E21
Kingsmen D26,T5
Kinks D7,T3
Kipner,Steve G40
Kirk,Roland D41
Kirwin,Danny D10,R48
Kiss D22,E21,J2,K15,K34,P27,W48
Kitchen Cinq H50
Kittyhawk L41
Kix A10,S45
Klaatu B49,B84
Kleinow,Sneaky Pete M80
Klondike Pete B16
Klugh,Earl J23
Knack C24,D44
Knickerbockers F42
Knight,Gladys K15,K24,W48
Knight,Jerry K17
Knighton,Reggie B3
Knopfler,David S49
Knox,Ohio H1
Koerner, John M74
Koerner,Ray & Glover H54,R42
Koinonia S10
Koklin,Tony B19
Kokomo M16,S22,T12
Koloc,Bonnie D41
Kooper,Al K30,S32,S79
Korda,Paul D14
Kortchmar,Danny K33
Kosinec,Tony A27
Kossoff,Paul P31
Kottke,Leo B86,B94,B100
Kowalski P22
Kracker M67
Kramer,Billy J. M40

Kraft,Robert C9
Krause,Dagmar W6
Krazy Kat C1,T16
Kreuger,Jim O12
Kris & Rita A15
Kristina,Sonja G55
Kristine T3
Kristofferson,Kris A15,P42,R3
Krokus A10,P23
Kubinec,Dave C4
Kunkel,Leah G13,L41
Kursaal Flyers B13,M21,M93
Kurtz,John Henry B9
Kweskin,Jim C66
Kyle R24

L
La Bounty,Bill S19,T24
La Costa M31
La Dusseldorf P22
L.A. Gospel Choir A4
L.A. Jets J20
Labelle,Patti R44,T27
Labelle L8,R44,T27
Lacy,Steve C76
Ladd,Cheryl K24
Lagrene,Birelli S32
Laing,Corky S5
Lake G66
Lamb C19
Lamb,Annabel A15,B69
Lamb,Kevin L61
Lambert,Dave P37
Lambert,Dennis B9,J18
Lambert & Nuttycombe A15,B5,J18
Lambrettas C51
Lampe,Nicholas E16
Lancaster,Jack L59
Landscape W3
Lane,Robin & The Chartbusters L61,W50
Lane,Ronnie J18
Langer.Clive B11,C65,L14
Larsen,Neil L45
Larsen-Feiten Band L45
Larson,Nicolette T12,G37
LaRue D.C. E18
Late Show B57
Lateef,Yusef D41
Lauber,Ken M53
Laughing Dogs B52,K14
Lauper,Cyndi C30
Lavender Hill Mob S65
LaVerne Ware Singers C42
Lawrence,Karen D44
Lay,Sam G54
Lazarus R3

Lazy Racer J18
Leadon,Bernie
League Unlimited Orchestra R48
LeBlanc,Lenny B22,C10
LeBlanc and Carr C10
Lee,Adrian T7
Lee,Albert A5,C73
Lee,Alvin H10,J20,S74
Lee,Brenda G12
Lee,Johnny B54,N17
Lee,Larry R50
Lee,Peggy L28
Lefevre,Mylon T27
Left Banke L29
Legend R30,V8
Legend Of Jesse James J18
Legs Diamond L32
Leiber-Stoller Big Band L28
Lemon Pipers K6,L29
Lennear,Claudia S2
Lennon,John D44,L30,S51
Lenny & Squiggy M55
Leonard,Deke C28,R48
Le Roux W41
Lettermen C42
Level 42
Levitt & McClure E9
Levy,Marcy B60
Lewie,Jona A18,H45
Lewis,Gary G12,K24,K31
Lewis,Huey S10
Lewis,Jerry Lee C73,H62
Lewis,Lew B11
Lewis,Jimmy & The Checkers S29
Lewis,Linda B13,D20,S2
Lewis,Ramsey D20,M15,M16,T27, LGT,W42
Liar A8
Liberace C42
Lieberman,Lori L29
Liebman,David M22
Lightfoot,Gordon C66,F35,F38,P7,S32, T24, W11,W50
Lightnin' M63
Lightnin' Red D42
Lightnin' Slim V5
Lights Out San Francisco K18
Lindisfarne A19,B3,D49,J20,M93,O6
Lindley,David B85,L2
Liner M35
Linhart B22,R11
Linn County K18
Linx C12
Lion H33
Little Bo Bitch A22
Little Bob Story T32
Little Feat G20,M48,T12,T24

Little Heroes H45
Littlejohn H5
Little Richard S41
Little River Band B60,M40
Little Shop Of Horrors s/t R3
Little Steven M66
Live Wire B51,J18
Liverpool Scene R30
Lloyd,Charles M35
Lloyd,Ian F1
Loading Zone J11
Lobo G22,M78
Local Boys J18
Lockie,Ken H42,M33
Lodge,John C37
Lofgren,Nils B15,B50,E21,K30,N12
Logan,Johnny M17
Loggins,Dave M20,S53
Loggins,Kenny B52,D46,J6,M48,R3
Loggins & Messina M65
Lomax,Jackie H20,R18,S32
Lonely Boys A25
Lone Star B3,L61
Longdancer N10,R30
Longmire,Wilbert J6
Look (US) S5
Look (UK) S21
Loose Ends M41
Lopez,Trini B50
Lord,Jon A29,B32
Lords Of The New Church R46
Los Lobos B94
Los Illegals R38
Lost And Found R37
Lost Gonzo Band B78
Lothar And The Hand People M36,V3
Loudermilk,John D. G9
Lounge Lizards M15
Love A2,B52,H54,R42,S74,T11
Love,Brad H66
Love,Mike B18
Lovecraft T29
Loverboy F1
Love Sculpture E4,F7,K14,W5
Lovesmith,Michael B9
Lovich,Lene B19,W43
Lovin' Spoonful J5,W30
Lowe,Nick B19,L57
Low Numbers B74
Lt Garcia's Magic Music Box K6
Lulu D46,M35,M87,W23
Lunch,Lydia B38
Lurkers G32
Lux,Kaz D17
Lyall,William C1
Lyle,Bobby L19

Lynn,Cheryl B43
Lynott,Philip W56
Lynyrd Skynyrd D46,J19,K30

Mc
McBride,Bob R21
McCabe,Pete S79
McCann,Les D20,D41
McCartney,Paul M2,M40
McClinton,Delbert B22,Y2
MacColl,Kirsty B16
McCoo,Marilyn & Billy Davis C70,W53
McCorison,Dan H44
McCormick,Gayle L7
McCoys G44,G52
McCreary,Mary C62,R49
McCulloch,Danny B68
McDaniels,Eugene D41
McDonald,Kathi B67
McDonald,Michael T12,W11
McDowell,Ronnie J12
McDuff,Brother Jack F43
McEntire,Reba W37
McGarrigle,Kate & Anna B59,N13
McGee,Parker L27
McGear,Mike M2
McGough,Roger L24
McGovern,Maureen L48
McGrath,Bat M3,M75
McGregor,Mary B22,C18
McGuinn,Roger B60,D30,H10,R38
McGuinn,Clark & Hillman A6,B22,W23
McGuinness Flint A29,J18,M29
McGuire,Barry A4
MacIver/Hine G35
McKenna,Mae G38
MacKenna's Gold J27
McKenzie,Scott A4.A15
McLagan,Ian F25,W57
McLain,Charly W37
McLean,Don B99,C61,D41,F29
McLelland,Sandy A30,C22
MacLeod,Robert P16
MacNally,Mac I6
McRary's L19
McTell,Blind Willie E16
McTell,Ralph D49,V88
McVicar s/t W13
McVie,Christine T24,V5

M
Mace,Terry H71
Machine D4
Mack,Jack B39,F32
Mack,Lonnie M68
Mackay,Duncan W22

Mackell,Joanne F3
Madness L14
Mad River V3
Maelen,Jimmy L60
Maffitt/Davies V3
Magazine B65,H15,L24,T21
Magma G45
Magna Carta D49
Magnet G3
Magnum G31,L62
Mahan,Larry G12
Mahavishnu Orchestra K36,M18,S13
Mainland B32
Malo R44
Mamas & Papas A4
Mama's Pride M35,M46
Man B3,B26
Manchester,Melissa M35,M44,P27
Mandalaband A8
Mandel,Harvey A9,K18,T11
Mangione,Gap C9
Manhattan Transfer E16,G56,P18
Manhattans D20
Manning,Terry M30
Mankey,Earle M28
Mann,Barry A24,J21
Mann,Herbie D46,H23
Mann,Manfred B90,M79
Manowar R21
Manzarek,Ray B52
Marbles S70
Mardin,Arif D46,M35
Mardones,Benny M89,O9
Marillion T7
Mark-Almond L45,M93
Marketts S6
Marley,Bob B34,S1,S42
Marriott,Steve K15,W49
Marsden,Bernie B32
Marseille P39
Marshall Hain N6
Marshal Tucker D46,H57,L36
Martha & The Muffins H64
Martin,Benny M59
Martin,Dean B54
Martin,Eric E11
Martin,George & his Orchestra M40
Martin,Moon G37,H59,L31,P4
Martin,Ricci W36
Martin,Steve M9
Matinez,Hirth R31,S32
Martyn,John B34,C52,R30,S66,W54
Martyn,John & Beverley B59
Marvin,Hank N6
Marx,Groucho R3
Mas,Carolyn A30,B92,C27

Masekala,Hugh L36
Maslon,Jimmie Lee W17
Mason,Dave B52,L45,N9,W50
Mason Profitt H10,T29
Mastro,James E1
Matchbox C51
Matrix S32
Matthews,Ian N8,P42,R30,S53,V3
Mauds T29
Maxfield Parrish D5
Maxus O12
Mayall,John J20,N16,S74,T27,V5
Mbulu,Letta L36
MC5 B52,H23,H54,L9
Meal Ticket G38,M17
Meatloaf D46,G3,R46
Meco B50,Q1
Medicine Head A29,P16,R12
Medley,Bill L48,M20,P18
Meighan,Bob P3
Meisner,Randy B62,F12,G13
Mekons L15
Melcher,Terry J21,M58
Melly,George H23
Melting Pot G5
Melton,Barry B41,C28,C29,D16,
Meltzer,Tina & David C29
Members H45,L43
Memphis Horns A1,J23
Mental As Anything C65
Mernit,Billy Y1
Merritt,Max N10,R13
Merry-Go-Round M38
Messina M65
Meters T27
Methuselah Y4
Metro T20
Micare,Franklin D41
Michaels,Hilly B3,L33
Michaels,Lee M38
Michalski & Costerveen S13
Midler,Bette A24,D41,K23,K25,
   M35,P24,R42
Midnight Express s/t M84
Midnight Flyer R2
Mighty Baby S64
Mighty Flyers L38
Mighty Sparrow P8
Miles,John D49,H53,L61,P10
Milk,Christopher T16
Milk 'n' Cookies M46
Millenium O10
Miller,Dale D27
Miller,Frankie B22,D44,H49,M17, M53, R17,
   T16,T27
Miller,Steve J18,M24

Mill Valley Jam session B41,G54
Mills,Stephanie K24,R3,W53
Mimms,Garnet L18
Minneli,Liza M38
Mink De Ville A6,D45,N15
Mirijian,Craig O14
Missing Persons S13
Mistress K11
Mitchell,Adam T24
Mitchell,Joni C71
Mitchell,Sam G65
Moby Grape J20,R44
Modern English J24
Modern Jazz Quartet M35
Modern Lovers K9,L4
Modern Man U1
Modern Romance V8
Mo-Dettes L52
Mohawk,Essra S18
Molly Hatchet W20
Mom's Apple Pie K26
Monda,Dick D24
Money T30
Money,Eddie B52,D46,N9
Monk,Thelonius M15
Monkees B10,B56,D43,N6
Monochrome Set S7
Monsoon J24
Montgomery,James D46,G6,T27
Montrose D44,T12,W44
Moody Blues C37,C62,W33
Moon (UK) B43,L36
Moon (USA) M81
Moon,Eve T21
Moon,Keith S74,T11
Moonlighters R21,L57
Moore,Daniel M80
Moore,Gary G31,I35,T30
Moore, G.T. B42
Moore,Jackie S22
Moore,Matthew A21
Moore,Melba B24
Moore,Scotty S26
Moore,Tim J2,J48,S13
Moped,Johnny A23
Morath,Max S48
More N3
Morning L38
Moroder,Giorgio M84
Morrill,Kent D37
Morris On W54
Morris,Gary N17
Morrison,Jim H1
Morrison,Tommy R27
Morrison,Van B29,L41,M63,R8,T12
Moses,Rick J11

Motels C13,G13
Mother Earth G40,R26
Mother Hen A15
Mothers Finest C55,G31,I5,W11
Mothers Of Invention W39,Z3
Mothmen J24
Motley Crue F20,W11
Motorhead F41,K12,M21,M67,P23
Motors G16,!5,K14,L12
Mott B55,K34,S64
Mountain P6
Mouskouri,Nana K24
Move C62
Movies G1,G68
Moxy R21
Mr. Big G13,P39
Mud C26,W2,W33
Muldaur Geoff B59,L19,M59
Muldaur,Geoff & Maria B59,W11
Muldaur,Maria B49,B59,N13,W6
Muleskinner B45
Mull,Martin H62,S5,W52
Mulligan,Gerry B44
Munich Machine M84
Murphey,Michael B60,J20,N17
Murphey,Willie M74
Murphy,Elliott C1,K8,P5,R42,S30
Murphy,J.F. & Salt I1,K34
Murphy's Law I1
Murray,Anne A5,C18,N17
Murray,Pauline H15
Muscle Shoals Horns B22
Music K34
Music Explosion K6
Musical Youth C51
Music For Pleasure H20
Music Machine R23,R39
Musselwhite,Charlie G40,G65
Myhill,Richard B3
Myrick,Gary M36,W20,W57

N
Nagle,Ron N15
Naked Eyes M32
Nantucket A10
Nash,Graham N5
Nashville West D23
Nasty Pop F19
Natasha N11
National Lampoon T23
Natural Gas P6
Navarro P3
Nazareth B3,B15,G35,H48,P39
Nazz R46
Necessaries B38
Neil,Fred R42,V3

Nelson,Bill L24
Nelson,Rick N15
Nelson,Tracy B54,J20,R26
Nelson,Willie B67,J23,M35,M76, R49,W23
Nervous Eaters M44
Nervus Rex C24
Nesmith,Mike J12,N8
Netto,Loz T21
Network L32,R20
Neu P22
Neutrons C28,M50
Neuwirth,Bob K11
Neville Brothers D41,N15
Newbury,Curt H8
Newbury,Mickey G9,J12,P42,Y2
New England R46,S71
Newman,Colin T20
Newman,Randy P8,T24,W11
New Musik M32
New Order H15
Newton,Juice A1,H62,L10,M53,P3
New World M87
New York City Band D42
New York Dolls M85,R46
New York Rock Ensemble M4
Nicholas,Paul N6
Nichols,Penny R24
Nichols,Roger L45
Nicks,Stevie I5
Nico C4,M74,W39
Nielsen/Pearson Band L10,S10
Night F37,P18
Nighthawk,Robert D16
Nighthawks N2
Nightingales S73
Nikki & The Corvettes J7
Nile,Willie H5,P5
Nilsson C1,C70,J11,L19,L30, P18,T10
Nine Below Zero B51,J18
Nine,Nine,Nine A25,M21,R48
Nirvana B34,H71,T16
Nitecaps L14
Nite City S19
Nitty Gritty Dirt Band L10,M9, P42,S37
Nitzsche,Jack B54,M53
Nix,Don N16
Noah R21
Noakes J20,M53
No Dice H45,H53,S42
Nonenga,Poppie B59
No New York E13
No Nukes B85,J22
Noonan,Steve R42
Noone,Peter P37
Norma Jean R35
Notes From The Underground C29

Nova H45,L59,R50
Novo Combo K21
NRBQ K34
NRPS B8,J20,M60,N17,P42
Nucleus F41
Nugent,Ted F43,H61,W20
Nuggets K10
Nuttycombe,Craig J18
Nutz A19,E3,L61,S35
Nyro,Laura C6,C21,H5,M35,O7

O
O'Bannion,John Z4
O'Connor,Gary L10
O'Connor,Hazel G55,V8
O'Day,Alan B9,S37
O'Keefe,Danny B60,C66,D26,E16, L38, M35,V1
O'Neal,Chief D27
O'Neill,Sharon B60
O'Sullivan,Gilbert D49,G53
O Band N10
Ocasek,Rick O2
Occasional Word P16
Ochs,Phil A2,H61,M78,P8,R42
Odyssey C6,T33
Off Broadway W20
Ogerman,Claus and Brecker,Michael L45
Ohio Express K6
Oingo Boingo M36,S45
Oklahoma – London Cast A18
Oldfield,Mike H36,N11
Oldfield,Sally H61,N11
Oldham,Andrew & Orchestra O9
Oliver S37
Olsson,Kai H36,M17,P24
Olsson,Nigel A21,D13
Olympic Runners V5
Omaha Sherriff V8
Omartian,Michael O12
Omartian,Stormie O12
O.M.I.T.D. D9,H64,M33,T13
One Flew Over The Cuckoo's Nest N15
Only Ones T21
Ono,Yoko D44,L30,S51
Orange Juice B53,K20
Orbison,Roy F24,I6
Orchestra Luna H53,L33
Orchestre Rouge K20
Orchids F22
Original Mirrors H64,W43
Original Modern Lovers F22
Orlando,Tony B22,M55,W23
Orleans B22,C33,L59,P24
Orphan B50,Q1
Orpheus L53

Orrall,Robert Ellis B19
Osbourne,Ozzy N18
Osibisa B73,P39,V8
Oskar,Lee E15,G44
Otis,Johnny O15
Otis,Shuggy K30,O15
Otway,John I3,S76
Our Daughter's Wedding T21
Outlaws B39,L12,L61,R42,S79
Outsets J14
Owens,Buck W37
O.X.O M31
Ozark Mountain Daredevils A15,B60,J18,K17

P
Pablo Cruise D46,G13,J2,S10
Pacesetters E13
Pacheco,Tom M85
Pacheco & Alexander H9
Pages C55
Page,Elaine V8
Pakalameredith S42
Palais Schaumberg H37
Paley,Tom G65
Paley Brothers M28
Pallon O6
Palmer,Macko V7
Palmer,Robert M88,P4,S42
Pan G13
Pappalardi,Felix P6,P40
Paris H67
Paris Pilot N16
Parker,Graham D44,I5,K17,L12, L57,N15
Parks,Van Dyke G42,L20,W11
Parlet C41
Parliament C41
Parrish,Paul S25
Parsons,Gene T24
Parsons,Gram D23
Parton,Dolly G13,K24,M25,P7,P30
Partridge,Andy L24
Pasadena Roof Orchestra G38
Pass,Joe B44
Passion C42
Passions G32,G35,P9,W38
Passion Puppets W5
Patton,Robbie C47
Paul,Henry A6,B17,S45
Paupers M53
Pavlov's Dog K36
Pawnbroker s/t J27
Paxton Brothers L41
Paxton,Tom O7,P13,R19,S46,V8
Paycheck,Johnny S26
Payne,Freda M77
Payne,Gordon A31

Payolas R38
Peaches & Herb W53
Peanut Butter Conspiracy U2
Pearl Harbor G4,K2
Peck,Danny F21,L38
Pedersen,Herb P30
Peebles,Anne M73
Peel,David L30,S30
Penetration H64,L43
Penfield,Holly C24,C47
People Band W12
Pentangle T3
Pere Ubu K20
Performance s/t N15
Performance,Gina X H30
Perkins,Carl C73
Perry,Joe B52,D44
Persuasions M23
Pet Clams K29
Peter & Gordon B90
Peter,Paul & Mary C66,R44
Peters,Bernadette A24
Pets K15,W48
Petty,Tom C62,I45
Pezband G3
Phillips,Anthony H45
Phillips,John A4
Phillips,Michelle N15
Phillips,Shawn A21
Phoenix L56
Phoenix,Willie A15
Photos B19
Pickett,Bobby "Boris" P13
Pickett,Courtland C10
Pickett,Wilson C44,D46,E17,S22
Pieces F5
Pierce Arrow A6,M55
Pilot (UK) B3,P10
Pilot (US) S13
Pinder,Michael M36
Pink Fairies H48,S36
Pink Lady L48
Pink Floyd E21,G68,K3,S41,T16
Pinpoint
Piranhas C51
Pirates H59,M21
Pirates Of Penzance (Broadway Cast) A27
Pitney,Gene B73,M17
Place,Mary Kay A5
Plain Sailing M17
Planets G55
Plain,John M82
Plainsong R30
Plant And See K24
Plasmatics M67
Plastics B34,S1

Player L7
Pleasure Fair G17
Plimsouls E20,H52
PM C32
Poco C70,F12,H16,M46,M65,
M70,O14,R21
Point Blank H11
Pointer,June P18
Pointer Sisters P18,R44
Polecats E4
Police G55,P1
Polland,Pamela D1
Pomeranz,David H5
Pookie(snackenburger) O5
Poole,Brian S40
Pop,Iggy B55,B57,P5,S59,V8,W34
Pop M20
Popeye s/t N14
Pop Group B53
Portsmouth Sinfonia E13
Portnoy,Gary W53
Post,Mike P30
Pousette Dart Band M55,P42
Powell,Cozy B32,G64
Powers,Tom L27
Pratt,Andy M35,N2,O6
Pratt & McClain B9,O12
Praying Mantis F37
Prelude F41,R19,S2
Presley,Elvis B67,J12
Preston,Billy C22,H20,M36
Preston,Don M80,S29
Pretenders L57,T16
Pretty Things A30,C27,S41
Preview O10
Previn,Dory D41,V3
Price,Alan H62,O5
Price,Bobby J17
Price,Ray G12
Pride,Charley W37
Principal Edwards P16
Prine,John B22,C70,G47,M35
Pringle,Peter A5
Priscilla J16
Prism C13,F1
Private Eye L32
Private Lightning C1
Procol Harum A6,C62,F9,L28,T16
Producers W20
Professionals G55
Professor Longhair E16
Proof L24
Prophet,Ronnie D48
Protheroe,Brian L62,N10
Psychedelic Furs F23,H15,L43,R46
Puckett,Gary G27

Pulte,Jim D12,T11
Punishment Of Luxury H64
Pure Prairie League A1,A6
B60,F25,R50
Purim,Flora M77
Purple Hearts P9

Q
Q-Tips S7
Quacky Duck G3
Quantum Jump H45
Quarterflash B60
Quatro,Charles John N5
Quartz I4
Quateman,Bill S74
Quatro,Michael A6,L56
Quatro,Suzi C24,C26,M87
Queen B3,M16,S71
? & The Mysterians B45
Quick F22,L60,M28
Quicksilver Messenger
    Service B76,G54,P3
Quiet Riot P37
Quincy F37
Quintet R44
Quiver T16

R
Racey M87
Racing Cars M46,P34
Radha Krsna Temple H20
Radiators A23,V8
Radner,Gilda W23
RAF K17
Rafferty,Gerry M93,N6
Rafferty,Jim S40
Rainbow B32,G35
Rainbow,Christopher C19,M36
Rainbow Band Z1
Raincoats K20
Raisins B23
Raitt,Bonnie A27,C76,F25,H9,M1,R42
Ramatam D46,H23
Rambow,Philip J15,L16,T16
Ram Jam K6
Ramones B50,C63,G53,L31,S58
Ramsey,Willis Alan C62
Random Hold H12
Rank And File E20,K2
Rankin,Billy R50
Rank Strangers D5
Rapp,Tom B99
Rare Earth R50
Raspberries I1
Raspberry,Larry M94,N16

Ratt S62
Raven,Eddy B54
Ravenscroft,Raphael M93
Ravyns C47
Rawls,Lou D41
Ray,Bob R25
Ray,Dave S30
Ray,Fay G55
Raybeats R48
Rea,Chris D49,K13
Rea,David P6,W16
Reading Festival 1973 N9
Records F37,L12,L31
Redbone,Leon D41
Red Crayola K20,R37,T19
Redding,Gene L7
Redding,Noel W46
Redding,Otis C70
Reddy,Helen C18,D18,F22,H2, M28, M38, P3,W50
Red Rider J2,L10,T11,T22
Red Rockers K2,L7
Reds K17
Reds s/t R3
Red Wedding W40
Red,White & Blue L20
Redwing G14
Reebop B34
Reed,Jerry Y2
Reed,Lou B55,E21,K8,R33,R38.J10
Reeves,Martha P18
Re-Flex P39
Refugee B95
Reid,John S53
Reid,Terry D46,K21,M87,N5,O6
Rejoice B9
Reluctant Stereotypes L52
Remains S26
Renaissance C60,G52,H36,S3
Renbourn,John G62
Renwick,Tim J18
REO Speedwagon B39,B60,H10,L29, S74,S79
Rescue M32
Rev,Martin O2
Revere,Paul M58,M76
Revillos H64
Reynolds,Barry S1
Rezillos B50,C38,P15
Rhinoceros A15
Rhinestones M46
Rhodes,Emitt M38
Rhodes,Red N8
Rhodes,Chalmers,Rhodes A6
Rhythm Devils H21
Rich,Charlie B99
Richard,Cliff B71,T6
Richards,Randy A21

Richards,Regina G52
Richards,Turley B40
Rich Kids R38
Richman,Jonathan K9,L4
Rico C77
Riggs J17
Righteous Brothers L7,S51
Riopelle,Jerry O10
Riot L49
Ripperton,Minnie L36,L41
Rip,Rig & Panic K20
Ritenour,Lee F21,M49
Rivera,Scarlet W49
Rivers,Johnny A4,H62,M78
Roadmaster F13,S74
Robbins,Marty S26
Roberts,Andy R30
Roberts,Bruce D46,M25
Roberts,David G56,M34,M49
Roberts,Rick A15,H44
Robertson,B.A. B71
Robey,Falk & Bod S53,W20
Robinson,Andy S18
Robinson,Carter M31
Robinson,Smokey T26
Robinson,Tom L43,M52,R46,T16
Roche,Maggie & Terre S2
Roches F39,H5
Rockats T20,V1
Rocket 88 S68
Rockets D44,G40,S5
Rock Goddess M21,T30
Rock Rose L7
Rock Workshop F41
Rocky Horror s/t A4
Roden,Jess B34,D41,H23,T27
Rodgers,Nile R34
Rodriguez,Johnny A7,S26
Roe,Tommy B9,C34,J12,M76
Rogers,Brian J18
Rogers,Jimmy C5
Rogers,Kenny B99,R20
Rollers G3,K14
Rolling Stones G30,J18,K21,M67,O9
Rollins,Sonny C76
Roman Holliday C51
Roman,Murray B67,V3
Romantics S45,S71
Romeo,Max R17
Romeo Void K2,O2
Ronettes S51
Ronin A27,G13
Ronnie & The Daytonas W31
Ronson,Mick R38
Ronstadt,Linda A27,B60,D43,M53,S47
Root Boy Slim K5

Roots s/t J27
Ro Ro A8
Rose,Biff M63
Rosebud Y1
Rose Garden G60
Rose Tattoo V2
Rosmini,Dick H24
Ross B32,F7,R20,T21,V8
Ross,Diana K5,P18,R35
Rossi,Steve L28
Rosslyn Mountain Boys D15
Rough Diamond S42
Roulette,Freddie M27
Roulettes B86
Roussos,Demis M17
Rovers R21
Rowans P25,W52
Roxy D9,P39,S33,T16
Roxy (US) H1
Royal,Billy Joe B88
Royal Guardsmen G22
Rozetta O6
RPM L11
Ruben & The Jets R5
Rubinoos K9,R46
Ruby F16
Ruffin,David D11
Rufus H5,J27,M77,S74,T24
Rumour B19,L12,W43
Rumplestiltskin T3
Runaways A8,F22,M28
Rundgren,Todd R46
Runner G68
Rush B84,H33
Rush,Chris C76
Rush,Tom A2,B67,C29,F29,G51,R42,S50
Rushing,Jimmy M15
Russell,Brenda L36,L45
Russell,Brian and Brenda A21
Russell,Leon A31,C5,C62,R49
Russell,Mary R31
Rutherford,Mike H36
Rutles I3
Ruts G32
Ruts DC B65
Ruzicka,Bob B67
Ryder,Maggie L29
Ryder,Mitch C69,C70
Ryles,John Wesley M78

S
Saad,Sue P18
Sad Cafe P39,S67
Sadista Sisters T16
Sadistic Mika Band T16
Saffan,Mark P18

Saga H45
Sager,Carole Bayer A24
Sagittarius B18,U2
SAHB (WA) B12,P32
Sahm,Doug C40,H27,M1,M35,W13
Sail G60
Sailcat C10
Sailor B18,G66,J21,L33
Salsoul Orchestra M88
Sammy R48
Sam The Band M55
Sam The Sham K19
Samson P23,W33
Samudio,Sam D46
Sanborn,David C66,R3,S32
Sancious,David O6
Sand M31
Sanders,Ed S4
Sanders,Pharoah and Norman
Connors C76
Sandpipers H62
Sands,Evie S69
Sanford Townshend Band B22,H1,W23
Sang,Samantha B50,D18,K24
Santana B22,C19,L7,O10,R44,R50
   S79,W23
Sanatana,Jorge B50,C38,Q1,T27
Sargeant,Bob M18,R38,S7
Sarstedt,Clive N4,S34
Sarstedt,Peter D31,S34
Sassafras G1
Saunders,Merl A33,F16,K1
Savage Grace H1
Savage Rose M67
Savalas,Telly G12
Savoy Brown L12,V5,W48
Sawyer,Ray H2
Saxon,Sky T31
Saxon B17,G31,T18
Sayer,Leo B6,C67,F2,M35,N6,P18,T6
Sayers,Pete C54
Scaggs,Boz B70,G61,H5,J18,S10,W19,W50,
Scandal P27
Scars B37
Schaeffer,Leonard J5
Schaffer,Janne B52
Schenker,Michael B32,G35,N9
Schlitz,Don A31
Schnieder,Helen S58
Schreiber,Avery R44
Schwartz,Stephen Michael K17
Scooters W2
Scorpions D35
Scott,Freddie B29
Scott,Terry M55
Scott,Tim G52

Scott,Tony S48
Scott-Heron,Gil C19
Scrambled Feet s/t W49
Screen Idols M18
Scritti Politti K20
Scruggs,Earl B40,J20,M76,S15,W29
Scullion M43
Sea Level L36,W28
Seals,England Dan L27,S25
Seals,Troy B67
Seals & Crofts S25,S32
Seanor & Koss T3
Searchers H26,M82
Sea Train M40
Seawind L45
Sebastian,John B9,J5,R42
Secret Affair T7,T21
Section A21
Second Image W42
Section 25 H15
Sector 27 L43
Sedaka,Neil A21,B97,G39,H22,M40
Seeds F22,T31
Seeger,Pete P15
Seemon and Marijke N5
Seger,Bob B22,I5,P38,R21
Selecter L52,R40
Sembello,Michael R3
Sensational Alex Harvey
Band B8,W1
Sessions,Ronnie Y2
Sesto,Camilo M44
Sete,Bola D19
Seventy-Sevens S44
Sex Pistols P34,T16
Seymour,Phil P25
Sgt.Pepper s/t M40
Shades Of Joy M83
Shakers P24
Shakin' Pyramids A18,B19
Shakin' Stevens C54,E4,H71,N6
Shakin' Street P15
Sham 69 W38
Shandi C24
Shanghai F1,G58
Shango B9
Shangri-La's L28,M85
Shankar,Ananda H24
Shankar,L. Z3
Shankar,Ravi B44,H20
Shankar Family H20
Sha Na Na B10,D44,I1,K34,R24
Shannon L42
Shannon,Del B5,E4,O9,P20
Sharkey's Machine s/t G12
Sharks J15

Sharpe,Rocky V5
Shaver,Billy Joe A5,A7,J20
Shaw,Graham E6
Shaw,Marlena B50
Shaw,Woody C76
Shear,Jules R46,
Shearston,Gary M93
Sheena & The Rockets C1
Sheila O10
Shiela & B.Devotion R35
Shelley,Pete R48
Shelton,Louie B56
Sheppard, T.G. N17
Sheriff,Jamie S13
Shine,Johnny R44
Ship,The U2
Shipley,Ellen S28,T22
Shirts P3,T20
Shoes D6,S71
Shooting Star D49,E11,M18
Shorrock,Glenn B60
Shot In The Dark S66
Shotgun L56
Showaddywaddy H71
Shrapnel C63,K29
Shurtleff,Jerry P42
Sidewinders K10
Sidran,Ben B52,M22
Siebel,Paul S30,Z1
Siegel,Janis D41
Siegel-Schwall M89
Sierra P6
Silencers C38
Silk S79
Sill,Judee L41
Silver S18
Silver,Horace C76
Silverado J11
Silverbird L29
Silver Condor F12
Silverstein,Shel H2,M59
Simmons,Gene D22
Simmons,Jeff H72,Z3
Simmons,Patrick R50,T12
Simms Brothers Band S71
Simon,Carly M22,M35,P18,T12
Simon,Joe S22
Simon,John S32
Simon,Lucy D41,P13
Simon,Paul B22,H5,R3,T24,W11
Simon & Garfunkel H5,J20,R3
Simple Minds H42,L24,L43,W5
Sinatra,Frank G18
Sinceros D49,W50
Sinclair,Stephen B97,F3
Single Bullet Theory F30

Sinnamon,Shandi G12
Siouxsie & The Banshees G55,L43,S76
Sir Douglas L31,M35,M54
Siren A10
Sister Sledge D20,R35
Skellern,Peter H23
Skid Row D10
Skids B12,G32,N7
Skin Alley F41,N16
Skrewdriver A23
Skyhooks L32
Skyking C70,F19
Skyliners D11
Slade C23,P39
Slater,Nelson R9
Slaughter G63
Slaughter & The Dogs T7
Slick,Earl M44
Slick,Grace F26,N9
Slits B53
Sloan P.F. A13,D46
Slow Children H3
Small Talk F3
Small Wonder W50
Smith,Clay F24
Smith G.E. C39
Smith,Gordon V5
Smith,Lonnie Liston D20
Smith,Margo W37
Smith,Mike K32
Smith,Patti C4,D44,I5,R46
Smith,Rex C6,C30,N9
Smith,Russell B22
Smith, T.V. G64
Smith,Perkins,Smith H55
Smithereens B31
Smithers,Chris C76,F26
Smiths P28
Smoke F22,L48
Smokey & The Bandit 2 s/t G12
Smokie C24,C26,
Smotherman,Michael H59
Snafu P31,R43,S43
Snail B39
Sneaker B15
Sneakers B31
Sneaky Pete (Kleinow) M80
Sniff 'n' The Tears H64
Snips L43
Snow,Phoebe B22,L2,R3,R44
Snow,Tom J2,J11,P7
Snuff G22
Soft Boys C49
Soft Cell T20
Soft Machine T20
Softies J24

Sokolow,Fred D27
Solid Senders B12
Song B18,O10
Son House H13
Sonics D26
Sonny And Cher G12
Sons Of Champlin B49,O10
Sons Of Heroes W59
Sopwith Camel J5
Sorrows L60,T3
Soul,David M46,M53
Sound J24
Soup For One s/t R35
Souther,John David A27,C19
Souther Hillman Furay D46,P25
Southern Comfort G54,K1
Southern Death Cult H28
Southside Johnny B22,G3,M66,R34
Southwind L45,T11
Spacek,Sissy C73
Spandau Ballet B91,S77
Spanky & Our Gang K37,Y2
Spann,Otis C29
Spanos,Danny A8,J17
Sparks H53,M16,M84,R46,V8,W46
Spear Of Destiny L17,T7
Specials C65,J29
Specimen P39,T7
Spector,Ronnie R6
Spedding,Chris M87,T16
Speedway Blvd K6
Spellbound H10
Spencer,John & his Louts R22
Spheeris,Jimmie C21,L29,L41
Spicher,Buddy M59
Spider C24,C47,S19,T30
Spinozza,David M22
Spirit A4,B67,S9
Spitballs K9,L4
Splinter H20,P42
Split Enz E12,P1,T22
Spoelstra,Mark C40,R42,S30
Spooky Tooth B34,M67
Sports S45
Spreadeagle T3
Spriguns R30
Springfield,Dusty B3,B9,D46, L7, M35,
    W23,W53
Springfield,Rick O10,W13
Springsteen,Bruce A20,L9,M66,P24
Spys K16
Squeeze B19,C4,M7,W54
Squier,Billy M16,O6
S.S.Fools P25
St.James,William C15
St.John,Bridget L62

St.Marie,Buffy L41,P42,S46
Stackridge A29,F41,M40
Stackwaddy P16
Stafford,Jim G22
Stainton,Chris K21
Stamey,Chris E1
Stamp,Terry C57
Stampede T7
Stampley,Joe S26
Standells C42
Stanky Brown F26,M55
Stanley,James Lee F5
Stanley,Michael B39,C38,K34, L12, M44,S79
Stanley,Paul G31
Stanshall,Vivian B61
Staples B22,W23
Staples,Mavis B22,W23
Starcastle B3,L33
Starjets B12,D9,W33
Starland Vocal Band B22
Starling,John A31,G20
Starr,Charlie M63
Starr,Ringo D48,H20,M2,M35,M40,M93,
    P18, P27,W4
Starr,Ruby C8
Starry Eyed & Laughing L51
Starwood B52
Starz D44,R21
States B49,R50
Staton Brothers S32
Status Quo E3,W33
Staying Alive s/t R20
Stealers Wheel L28,W32
Steding,Walter S59
Steel Breeze F22
Steeleye Span B13,D49,R30
Steely Dan K5
Steinman,Jim R46
Steppenwolf M57,P25
Sterling K17
Stevens,Cat H71,K17,S3
Stevens,Jon L19
Stevenson B.W. K17,L45,M78
Steven T. F22
Stewart,Al A19,P10
Stewart,Didi G3
Stewart,Gary M76
Stewart,John A27,C11,G24,S69, V3,W32
Stewart,Rod D46,J17,R11
Stewart,Wayne D23
Stiff Little Fingers B26,T7,T19
Stills,Stephen A6,G19,H10,K30
Stills Young Band D46,G19
Stillwater D88
Stingers K15
Stitt,Sonny M35

Stokes,Simon B67,L48,R13
Stompers C63,K22,K29
Stone,Sly L36,L60
Stone Country J11
Stoneground D39,E9,G18,S17
Stoneman,Scotty D23
Stone Mountain Boys B28
Stone Poneys V3
Stooges C4,G5
Stories K15,K34,W48
Stormin' Norman & Suzy R21
St.Paradise F12
Straight Eight H64,R48
Straight Lines L33
Straker,Peter B3,F37,M16
Strandlund,Robb M31
Strange Advance F1
Stranglers C32,R48,V8,W43
Strapps G35,K18
Strawbs A10,D49,H53,L33,V8
Stray B32,M93,S36
Stray Cats E4
Streetband J9
Streets K16
Streetwalkers P36
Streisand H53,K24,L33,P18, R3,R20
Stride,Pete M82
Striker M44
Stringcheese F5
String Driven Thing J17,T3
Strong, C.K. M69
Stuff C70
Style Council W38
Styvers,Laurie M93
Styx R50
Suburban Lawns M52
Suicide L312,O2
Suicide Romeo S1
Sullivan,Ira D46,W23
Sullivan,Rocky C46
Sulton,Kasim F1
Summer,Donna B24,M84,O12
Summers/Fripp F39
Sumner N15
Sunday Funnies O9
Sundholm Roy G55
Sunnyland Slim V5
Sunrise J21,M63
Sunshine Company S6
Supa,Richard H10,S74
Supercharge L12
Superman III s/t M84
Supertramp H33,S13
Supremes W14
Surprise Sisters V8
Surrender B84

Sutherland Brothers A6,S53,W18,W46
Sutton,Gregg B49
Swallow B88
Swampwater M31,M95
Swan,Billy J23,Y2
Swarbrick,David W54
Sweat Band C41,C53
Sweet C26,W2
Sweet,Rachel R48,S45,S62,W43
Sweet Inspirations M77
Sweet Lightnin' S48
Sweet Salvation M68
Sweet Sensation H26
Sweet Thursday M93
Swift,Jonathan R48
Swing P18
Sykes,Roosevelt E5
Sylvain,Sylvain B50,Q1
Sylvers M84
Sylvian,David N19

T
Taff,Russ S10
Taggett H40
Taj Mahal G59,R44,W31
Talbert,Wayne M54
Talbot Brothers H10
Talking Heads B50,E13,Q1
Talk Talk F37,T21
Talley,James B78
Tank C35,G55
Tanner,Marc M75,S53
Tantrum R50
Taos S16
Target H57,R50
Tarney/Spencer K17,M17
Tate,Eric Quincy H57
Tate,Howard R1
Tate,Snuky S59
Tattoo R45
Taupin,Bernie D49
Tavares C55,F21,L7
Taxi Girl B93
Taylor,Alex S5
Taylor,Chip P3,T9
Taylor,James A27,S52,T24,W11,
Taylor,Johnnie D11,S22
Taylor,Kate B22,H4
Taylor,Livingston B15,B60,D18,L9
Taylor,Rod P24
Tazmanian Devils J5
Tchaikovsky,Bram G16,K14
T-Connection C55,S1
Teardrop Explodes H64,L13,L14
Tears S74
Tears For Fears H68

Teaze B35,G48
Teddy Bears S51
Tee,Richard J6
Teeley,Tom K16
Teenage Cruisers s/t W17
Telephone E21,R48
Television J10,J17
Tempchin,Jack C10
Temperance Seven M40
Tempest B73
Temptations B9,L6
Tenille,Toni W15
Tenpole Tudor A18,W43
Ten Years After D49,V5
Terry,Dewey S79
Terry & The Pirates S61
That Was The Week That Was M40
Marty Thau Presents 2 x 5 D29
Theatre Of Hate J25
Them R44,S14
They Called It An Accident s/t B34
Thin Lizzy A8,N9,T7,T30,V8,W56
Third World B34,S1,W47
Thirty Days Out M38
Thomas B,J, D48,M76,M78
Thomas,Joe Q1
Thomas,Guthrie V3
Thomas,Mickey B39,S79
Thompson,Ali K13
Thompson,Richard B59,W54
Thompson,Richard & Linda B59,W54
Thompson Twins B53,H64,L43,S1
Thorinshield D45
Thorpe,Billy P37
Thorogood,George N2
THP 2 L60
Threadgill C76
Three Degrees M84
Three Dog Night I1,M57,M77,P25
Three's A Crowd B9
Thunder L27
Thunders,Johnny M67
Thunderclap Newman T28
Tight Fit F37
Tillis,Mel B54
Tillison,Roger D12
Timber L41
Timberline H62
Time P22
Tin Huey W24
Tiny Tim P18
Tippetts,Julie C31,G45
Tir Na Nog F9
Titus,Libby R3
TKO F12
Toby Beau D22,M80,P33

Tolliver,Joan L28
Tomlin,Lily T23
Tomlinson,Malcolm A19,R21
Tompall & The Glaser Brothers B54
Tom Tom Club S56
Toni (Brown) & Terry
   (Garthwaite) M86,S69
Tonio K. C13,F25
Toots & The Maytals B34,B59,S1
Topaz D30
Top Secret C23
Torme,Bernie T7
Tornader R21
Toronto B84,H32,S42
Torrance,Richard C13,H1,S12
Tosh,Peter K21
Toto K28,W57
Tourists A10,P22
Toussaint,Alan G60,T27,W23
Tower Of Power C70
Townley,John A21
Townshend,Pete J18,T16
Townshend,Simon T28
Toyah L43,T7
Traffic B34,M67,W47
Translator K2
Transmitters S7
Trapeze M67,S36,S42
Travel Agency G12
Traveler L56
Travers,Mary P27
Travers,Pat A10,L33,M18,M89
Travolta,John B10
Traylor,Jack & Steelwind S9
Treasure C21
T.Rex V8
Trickster R48
Trillion B60,L61
Troggs C74,P2
Troiano,Domenic B84,O10
Tropea,John G3
Trower,Robin D11,E12,F9
Troy,Bill S15
Truckaway,William J5
Trust P23
TSOL W40
Tubb,Ernest D48
Tubes A19,F21,H33,K30,R46,S13
Tucker,Tanya C24,G12,G44,M25
Tucky Buzzard W59
Tufano-Giammarese A4,R21
Tuff Darts B50,Q1
Turner,Ike & Tina S51
Turner,Sammy L28
Turner,Tina M77,P37
Turtles D7,D43,H62,W50

Tutone,Tommy P24,T14,W57,TV21 B77
Twice,Richard H24
Twice As Much O9
Tune,Tommy & Twiggy E16
Twilight Zone s/t B52
Twilley,Dwight P24,S23,W57
Two Friends W39
Two Guns H57
Tycoon L12,P27
Tygers Of Pan Tang C51,M18,T30
Tyla Gang B95,K9,L4
Tyler,Bonnie C1,M17,M93,S60
Tzuke,Judy M90,P39

U
U-Boat B73
UFO G32,L61,L62,M40,N9
Uggams,Leslie L28
UK Players G50
Ullman,Tracey C51
Ultimate Spinach L53
Ultravox E13,L43,M40,P22
Uncle Dog P31
Uncle Jim's Music B60
Under Fire s/t B52
Underground All Stars F22
Undertones B19
Unknowns S62
Upchurch,Phil E5,T15
Upp B20
Up The Creek s/t P37
Urban Verbs G31,L43,T20
Uriah Heep B73,H61
Utopia R46

V
Valdy R42
Valente,Dino J20
Valentine,Hilton B68
Valli,Frankie C69,G18,M55
Vampires From Outer Space F22
Vance 32 D41
Van Der Graaf Generator A19
Van Duren T25
Van Eaton,Lon and Derek P18,S10,V9
Van Halen T12
Van Hoy,Rafe G9
Vanilla Fudge P37,M85
Vannelli,Gino E12
Van Ronk,Dave B78,G62
Vanwarmer,Randy K17,N10
Van Zandt,Johnny E11,K30
Van Zandt,Townes C39,E7,F26,M76
Vapors S43,T22
Vapour Trails C9
Vaughan,Stevie Ray H13

Vee,Bobby G12,S37
Vega,Alan O2
Velez,Martha G3,G52,L31,V5
Velvet Underground H23,W10,W39
Ventures G27,S6
Venus & The Razorblades F22
Vergat,Vic D35
Vibrators C49,M21
Victims C74
Victoria R44
Vigrass And Osbourne W13
Villa De Ville W3
Vincent,Gene W17
Vincent,Holly Beth T20
Violinski M16
Visage U1
Vitale,Joe A6,S79
Vivabeat L33
Volunteers G13,M46
Von Schmidt,Eric C29,C76
Voudouris,Roger C6,O12
Voyager D49

W
Wackers A2,U2
Wagner,Richard E21
Wagoner,Porter G12
Wailers (not Marley's) D37
Wailers B34
Wainwright III,Loudon J20,
    K11,L46,W54
Wate,John G21
Waitresses B98,P1
Waits,Tom H62,Y1
Walden,Narada Michael C38,D46
Waldman,Wendy F12,K34,P24,V3
Waldorf & Travers C67
Wales,Howard D42
Wales O'Regan B12
Walk Don't Run s/t J27
Walker,Bobbi L56
Walker,Jerry Jeff B22,B78,B99,D46, L55,M53
Walker,Sammy V3,O3
Walker,Scott N10,W5
Walker,T-Bone L28
Wall W38
Wallace,Eugene A19,C1
Wall Of Voodoo M52
Walsh,Joe S74,S79,W4
Wammack,Travis H6
Wanderers G32
Wang Chung H68
War G44
Ward,Clifford T.
Warman,Johnny S43

Warner,Florence M17
Warner,Steve W37
Warnes,Jennifer C4,F25,N17,P35
Waroff,Paul L38
War Of The Worlds W13
Warren,Paul & Explorer C47
Warriors s/t V1
Warsaw Pakt P39
Warwick,Dionne R1,R20
Washington,Geno B18
Was(Not Was)T4
Waterman,Dennis N6
Waters,Muddy M45
Waters,Roger K3
Watson,Doc C39,C43,L55
Watson,Doc & Merle C39,E7,G62
Watts,John M33
Wavelength N6
Waylon & Jessi A7
Waylon & Willie M58
Wayne,Carl P12
Wayne County B32,C75
Waysted G32
Weaver,Patty B9
Webb,Jim C1,L34,M3,M40,M75
Webb,Marti H36
Webb,Susan W14
Webster,Max B84,R21
Weider,John M7
Weinstein & Strodl M76
Weir,Bob L61,O10
Weirdos W24
Weisberg H66,S5
Welch,Bob B15,C13,V4
Weller,Freddy C16
Wells,Cory A15
Wells,Junior D46,W59
Wendroff,Michael M63
Wendy & The Rockets M90
Werewolves O9
Werner,David C38
Werth,Howard B11,B33
Wesley,Fred C41,C53
West,Dottie B99,G12
West,Leslie D40
West,Shelly G12
Wet Willie D46,H57,L61
West,Tommy C15
West,Bruce & Laing D40,J17
West Coast Pop Art Band B54,M37
Wetton,John P39
Wha-Koo A1,C2,H5
Wheeler,Billy Ed L28
Whirlwind S38
Whitcomb,Ian C62,D26,P26
White,Buck W29

White,Chris T3
White,Frank R30
White,Keiran C28
White,Snowy N11
White,Tony Joe A27,D46,M35,S78
White Face B22
White Lightnin' G51
White Mansions J18
Whitesnake B32,G35
White Witch A6
Whitford/St.Nicholas A10
Whitlock,Bobby B63,H10,H57,J17, M67,Z2
Whitman,Slim M78
Who A30,J18,L8,S79,T3
Widowmaker K21
Wier,Rusty M46,S53
Wijnkamp,Leo G65
Wilde,Kim W30
Wilder,Mathew B89
Wilderness Road R21
Wildlife H45,R2
Wild Horses W56
Wild Thing S30
Wild Turkey B1
Wilhelm,Michael O11
Wilk,Scott O12
Williams,Andy P18
Williams,Deniece F21
Williams,Jnr. Hank A7,B54,G22,G27,R44
Williams,Jerry B67,O1,K21
Williams,Jerry (soul version) K18
Williams,Mason G27,P30
Williams,Mentor W32
Williams,Paul J2,W32
(the songwriting Paul Williams)
Williams,Paul (ex-Juicy Lucy) T18
Williams,Robin A24,G2
Williams,Tony B52
Willoughby,Larry C73
Wilson,Carl B15,G66
Wilson,Dennis William B54
Wilson,Gerald (& Orchestra) B44
Wilson,Hank (aka Leon Russell) A31
Wilson,Joey D29
Wilson,Mari M32
Wilson,Nancy A33
Wilson,Tony A6
Wilson Brothers L27
Winchester,Jesse A5,M73,P42,R31,R46
Wind In The Willows K32
Winds Of Change W13
Wingfield,Pete W42
Wings M2,T16
Winkies S64
Winski,Colin B86
Winter,Edgar M80

Winter Brothers Band W28
Winter,Paul M40
Winwood,Steve B34,M92,W47
Wire T20
Wire Train K2
Wishbone Ash A10,D46,G55,H61, L18,S79
Withers,Bill J23
Witherspoon,Jimmy A33,G44,V5
Wiz s/t J27
Womack & Womack L36
Womack,Bobby B22,D11,O9,R44
WOMAD L54
Wombles B13
Wondergap A19
Wood,Lauren B89,J2,T12
Wood,Ron B3,J17,J18
Woods,Gay & Terry R30
Woolley,Bruce H71
Wopat,Tom P30
Workman,Nanette B35
World (UK) I3
World (US) B3,F20
Worrell,Bernie A15,C41
Wray,Bill R50,T14
Wray,Link G52,P5,V7
Wreckless Eric B16,L57,S45
Wright,Betty A6
Wright,Gary J17
Wright,Lorna L38
Wright, O.V. M73
Wright,Steve V2
Wright Brothers K24
Wyatt,Robert M47
Wyman,Bill K21
Wynette,Tammy S26
Wynne,Philippe C41

X
X M34
XTC L24,L43,N19,P1,S7

Y
Yachts G52,R48
Yamashta,Stomu M12
Yancey,Jimmy & Mama E16
Y&T (aka Yesterday and Today) N18,T30
Yankees R33
Yanovsky,Zalman Y1
Yardbirds G45,M87,N4,S3
Yellow Dog Y4
Yellowjackets L45
Yes C56,H56,O6
Yipes J10
York,Steve S43
You Are What You Eat s/t S32
Young,Jesse Colin J2,L1,P6
Young,John Paul V2
Young,Kenny A21,Y4
Young,Lester H13
Young,Neil B67,H16,L41,M53, M91, N15,S9
Young,Paul L16
Young,Steve T5
Young And Moody G35
Youngbloods D2,P6,
Young Rascals D46
Your Gang P13
Youth Brigade W40

Z
Zachariah s/t S79
Zak,Lenny P10
Zappa,Frank Z3
Zebra D44
Zelkowitz,Goldie L19,M57
Zephyr H10
Zeet Band D16
Zevon,Warren B85,L2
Ziggurat O6
Zones F37
Zoss,Joel S28
Z.Z.Top H11